I0882136

Multidisciplinary Approaches to Organizational Governance During Health Crises

Carla Sofia Vicente Negrão
CeBER, University of Coimbra, Portugal

Isabel Guerreiro Pimentel Maia
Centre for Business and Economics Research, University of Coimbra, Portugal

João António Furtado Brito
University of Cape Verde, Cape Verde

A volume in the Advances in Logistics, Operations, and Management Science (ALOMS) Book Series

IGI Global
PUBLISHER of TIMELY KNOWLEDGE

Published in the United States of America by
IGI Global
Business Science Reference (an imprint of IGI Global)
701 E. Chocolate Avenue
Hershey PA, USA 17033
Tel: 717-533-8845
Fax: 717-533-8661
E-mail: cust@igi-global.com
Web site: http://www.igi-global.com

Library of Congress Cataloging-in-Publication Data

Names: Negrão, Carla Sofia Vicente, 1978- editor. | Maia, Isabel Cristina Guerreiro, 1966- editor. | Brito, João António Furtado, 1978- editor.
Title: Multidisciplinary approaches to organizational governance during health crises / edited by Carla Negrão, Isabel Cristina Guerreiro Maia, João Antonio Brito.
Description: Hershey, PA : Business Science Reference, [2022] | Includes bibliographical references and index. | Summary: "The general objectives of this book are: Explore trends in governance models; Present the current state of governance; Explore / examine governance issues, challenges, and opportunities; Explore post-Covid-19 governance responses; Publish recent studies in the various disciplinary areas of governance; Contribute to new lines of research emerging from governance"-- Provided by publisher.
Identifiers: LCCN 2022050788 (print) | LCCN 2022050789 (ebook) | ISBN 9781799892137 (hardcover) | ISBN 9781799892144 (paperback) | ISBN 9781799892151 (ebook)
Subjects: LCSH: Organizational resilience. | Crisis management. | Organizational change. | COVID-19 Pandemic, 2020-
Classification: LCC HD58.9 .M858 2023 (print) | LCC HD58.9 (ebook) | DDC 658.4/062--dc23/eng/20221212
LC record available at https://lccn.loc.gov/2022050788
LC ebook record available at https://lccn.loc.gov/2022050789

This book is published in the IGI Global book series Advances in Logistics, Operations, and Management Science (ALOMS) (ISSN: 2327-350X; eISSN: 2327-3518)

British Cataloguing in Publication Data
A Cataloguing in Publication record for this book is available from the British Library.
All work contributed to this book is new, previously-unpublished material.

For electronic access to this publication, please contact: eresources@igi-global.com.

Advances in Logistics, Operations, and Management Science (ALOMS) Book Series

ISSN:2327-350X
EISSN:2327-3518

Editor-in-Chief: John Wang, Montclair State University, USA

MISSION

Operations research and management science continue to influence business processes, administration, and management information systems, particularly in covering the application methods for decision-making processes. New case studies and applications on management science, operations management, social sciences, and other behavioral sciences have been incorporated into business and organizations real-world objectives.

The **Advances in Logistics, Operations, and Management Science** (ALOMS) Book Series provides a collection of reference publications on the current trends, applications, theories, and practices in the management science field. Providing relevant and current research, this series and its individual publications would be useful for academics, researchers, scholars, and practitioners interested in improving decision making models and business functions.

COVERAGE

- Political Science
- Organizational Behavior
- Finance
- Decision analysis and decision support
- Information Management
- Operations Management
- Computing and information technologies
- Production Management
- Marketing engineering
- Networks

IGI Global is currently accepting manuscripts for publication within this series. To submit a proposal for a volume in this series, please contact our Acquisition Editors at Acquisitions@igi-global.com or visit: http://www.igi-global.com/publish/.

The Advances in Logistics, Operations, and Management Science (ALOMS) Book Series (ISSN 2327-350X) is published by IGI Global, 701 E. Chocolate Avenue, Hershey, PA 17033-1240, USA, www.igi-global.com. This series is composed of titles available for purchase individually; each title is edited to be contextually exclusive from any other title within the series. For pricing and ordering information please visit http://www.igi-global.com/book-series/advances-logistics-operations-management-science/37170. Postmaster: Send all address changes to above address.

Titles in this Series

For a list of additional titles in this series, please visit:
http://www.igi-global.com/book-series/advances-logistics-operations-management-science/37170

New Perspectives and Possibilities in Strategic Management in the 21st Century Between Tradition and Modernity
Javier Martínez-Falcó (University of Alicante, Spain & Stellenbosch University, South Africa) Bartolomé Marco-Lajara (University of Alicante, Spain) Eduardo Sánchez-García (University of Alicante, Spain) and Luis A. Millan-Tudela (University of Alicante, Spain)
Business Science Reference • © 2023 • 514pp • H/C (ISBN: 9781668492611) • US $315.00

Government Impact on Sustainable and Responsible Supply Chain Management
Atour Taghipour (Normandy University, France)
Information Science Reference • © 2023 • 354pp • H/C (ISBN: 9781668490624) • US $240.00

Transport and Logistics Planning and Optimization
Jaouad Boukachour (University of Le Havre, France) and Abdelhamid Benaini (University of Le Havre, France)
Business Science Reference • © 2023 • 317pp • H/C (ISBN: 9781668484746) • US $250.00

Black Women's Formal and Informal Ways of Leadership Actualizing the Vision of a More Equitable Workplace
Audrey D. Bowser (Arkansas State University, USA) Kimberley M. Davis (University of Arkansas at Pine Bluff, USA) and Natalie Ann-Marie Johnson-Leslie (Arkansas State University, USA)
Information Science Reference • © 2023 • 300pp • H/C (ISBN: 9781668438275) • US $215.00

Considerations and Characteristics of the Millennial Leader in Today's Global Society
Tymon M. Graham (TMGraham Consulting, LLC, USA)
Business Science Reference • © 2023 • 300pp • H/C (ISBN: 9781668447116) • US $240.00

For an entire list of titles in this series, please visit:
http://www.igi-global.com/book-series/advances-logistics-operations-management-science/37170

IGI Global
PUBLISHER of TIMELY KNOWLEDGE

701 East Chocolate Avenue, Hershey, PA 17033, USA
Tel: 717-533-8845 x100 • Fax: 717-533-8661
E-Mail: cust@igi-global.com • www.igi-global.com

Table of Contents

Detailed Table of Contents

In this chapter, the utilization of digital tools in the higher education system in India has been illustrated. Communication, education, work culture, information access, and health crisis time are all being transformed by digital technology. The digital components, dimensions, significance, and inclusion in higher education have been discussed. The various elements, extensive activities, and initiatives of implementing digital education in India. The implementation and utilization of life skills in digitalization and in the arts, engineering, and technical education have been discussed to extract the scope for future developments.

Chapter 2

Lydia Andoh-Quainoo, Pentecost University, Ghana
Paul Adjei Onyina, Pentecost University, Ghana

The Covid-19 global pandemic affected various dimensions, including social, cultural, behavioral, financial, and economic. Although various studies have focused on the effects of the pandemic on the economy, not many have been done on the economic outcomes from consumers' perspectives. The purpose of this chapter is to examine the economic effects of Covid-19 on the economy and its implications for consumers. The chapter seeks to contribute to ongoing discussions on economic shifts associated with Covid-19 with emphasis on the consumer perspective. Questionnaire was provided on social media platform for participants to respond using the same medium. Responses have been analyzed and found that people have been affected significantly by the pandemic. Their coping strategies in dealing with the pandemic have also been presented and implications for the government and employers provided in the tail end of the chapter.

Chapter 3

Hamida Mosharraf Moniea, North South University, Bangladesh
Mohammad Khasro Miah, North South University, Bangladesh
Tasnim Tarannum, North South University, Bangladesh
Carlos M. Osegueda, Independent Researcher, Bangladesh

The novel coronavirus, Covid-19, made its initial appearance in Wuhan, China, in December 2019. Since then, the virus has spread quickly over the globe and has been regarded as one of the deadliest pandemics. This study establishes a framework developed to identify and understand the role of specific central determinants of the psychological effects that the response to Covid-19 has had on Bangladeshi faculty members. An in-depth interview of 20 faculty members of Bangladeshi public and private universities provides acumen and guidance into the motives, strategic opportunities, and constraints of this research. The current study provides future implications of the vital distinctive facets of different contingent and contextual variables' influence on mental well-being, revealing a new avenue for developing a ground-breaking theory.

This study is divided into two phases: translation and the testing of NoMAD. Researchers adopted a four-step approach: forward and backward translation, expert reviews for the test, and improvement of content validity. The translated version was then adopted for understanding the implementation of social distancing in the context of Covid-19 in Pakistan. To analyze the scale validity of U-NoMAD, researchers calculated the Cronbach alpha value through the Confirmatory Factor Analysis approach and analyzed the U-NoMAD strength through a step-wise evaluation process – convergent validity and individual item validity, discriminant validity, and model significance. The initial factor analysis model showed a good fit for coherence and cognitive participation and an unsatisfactory fit for collective action and reflexive monitoring. The results confirmed the NoMAD structure in the Pakistani healthcare settings to acceptable standards. So, the U-NoMAD instrument is valuable in evaluating complex and innovative healthcare interventions.

In consideration of the importance and scope of epidemiology on SARS-CoV-2 (COVID-19), essential aspects are conveyed regarding how to improve vaccine confidence through awareness and education. Further, from a natural history context, the outbreak of the 2019 novel coronavirus diseases (COVID-19) occurred in Wuhan, Hubei Province, China and spread throughout the world. As a result, governments and organizations experienced challenges managing the pandemic. Explained are characteristics of the COVID-19 epidemiological approach. For example, the utilization of epidemiological studies is performed to obtain rates and probability of occurrence. Reviewed are the use of epidemiology in determining COVID-19 causality, the health status of the population, delivery of services, program planning, and social policy.

The handling of genetic residues, biohazardous waste, and other non-shrinkable materials such as e-waste is essential for the preservation of Mother Nature and human wellbeing. This chapter will bring forth different methods of managing biomedical wastes, inspecting the roots of the spread of the hazardous virus, and protecting the front-line warriors. To properly react to this disaster, each administration must create a backup strategy based on regional circumstances and the seriousness of the coronavirus's spread. Technology is being used to reduce the need for in-person medical appointments and save on the cost of treatment, which is a boon for human civilization in the context of the pandemic. The Central Pollution Control Board's existing rules provide a framework for managing healthcare waste with respect for the safety of the public. Bio-waste management strategies using IoT and IoMT techniques are illustrated in this chapter.

The impact of epidemics on urban restructuring is one of the most critical planning issues. This chapter presents a twin-track approach to intervention in the informal housing areas in Syria after investigating the ability to face the impact of Covid-19 epidemic. The informal housing "al-Radar" area in Tartous City was adopted as a case study. Both qualitative and quantitative methods were used for a multi-dimensional analysis of gathered data and site planning aspects. The goals are to achieve participatory decision-making to guide area restructuring aligned with national urban development laws. In addition, laying down the foundation of an area plan for future on-site redevelopment considers community cohesion and land-use improvements. Results illustrated the poor traditional planning criteria efficiency in achieving urban resilience/immunity required for a "new normal" and the need for good governance in land administration utilizing 15-minute city principles and a street-led citywide approach for the full integration into the city system as a tool to promote sustainable development.

The main focus of this study is on the topic of the global epidemic of Covid-19 and international peace and security. The practice of the council indicates the expansion of its competencies and its extension from military to civilian threats. The council has twice before adopted resolutions on AIDS and Ebola, which have deemed the situation a threat to international peace and security. If the council wishes to apply the same logic to the description and assessment of the Covid-19, it will, as in the previous two cases, declare it a threat to international peace and security, given the extent of the spread of the disease. However, the Security Council became passive in the wind, and more than three months after the announcement of Covid-19 as a global epidemic by the World Health Organization, with the passage of UNSCR 2532 dated 1 July 2020, it considered international peace and security.

This chapter examines the economic factors influencing working capital management and investment decisions in the automobile industry. It explores both macroeconomic and microeconomic elements that impact the industry's financial dynamics. The study also investigates future trends and prospects, including the shift towards electric and autonomous vehicles, sustainability practices, and digitalization. Based on the analysis, the chapter provides practical recommendations for improving working capital management practices, enhancing investment decision-making, and policy implications for industry stakeholders. The findings aim to assist automobile companies in adapting to the evolving market and achieving sustainable growth.

This case study examines employees' resilience at the Chamera power plant in Himachal Pradesh, India, during the COVID-19 pandemic. It investigates the impact of e-Training initiatives as catalysts for organizational change. The study utilizes a focus group interview method with nine participants, including executives and non-executives who actively engaged in e-Training. Findings reveal that the implementation of e-Training programs resulted in attributes such as time management, goal focus, self-driven orientation, collaboration, capacity building, positive mindset, and improved self-efficacy. These attributes contributed to employee resilience. The study highlights the importance of e-Training interventions and technology adoption in fostering employee resilience and bridging gaps in understanding organizational resilience.

In light of the COVID-19 pandemic, this chapter explores how Chinese leadership has changed since then. It provides an in-depth analysis of the profound societal and economic shifts that resulted from the pandemic and the novel responses that were necessary. Focusing on the importance of e-governance and AI technology, the chapter examines how the health crisis has affected Chinese politics, corporations, and health governance. New forms of governance that have emerged in reaction to the breakdown of established educational institutions are also explored. In addition, it investigates potential economic avenues for revival in the wake of the pandemic. Future directions for governance are discussed, with connections drawn to sustainability, entrepreneurship, and innovation. It is a great resource for learning more about how the world might change after COVID-19 due to new governance paradigms.

Preface

In the wake of the unprecedented COVID-19 pandemic, the world witnessed an upheaval of staggering proportions, shaking the very foundations of our societies and institutions. The shockwaves of this global crisis forced us to confront unforeseen challenges, both immediate and far-reaching, and compelled us to reevaluate and adapt our approaches to governance across various sectors. The pandemic's profound impact on our lives, economies, and health systems necessitated swift and innovative responses, propelling us into uncharted territories of organizational governance.

As editors, we found ourselves compelled by the urgency of the situation to embark on a quest to understand, analyze, and synthesize the multifaceted dimensions of governance during health crises. The result is "Multidisciplinary Approaches to Organizational Governance During Health Crises," a reference book that encapsulates the collective insights and wisdom of esteemed scholars, practitioners, and thinkers from diverse disciplines.

In these pages, we have curated a collection of chapters that span the spectrum of governance, from economics and management to law, sociology, psychology, education, and communication. Our aim is to offer a comprehensive exploration of governance models, both emerging and established, in the context of a world forever transformed by the events of 2020. This book serves as a testament to the power of multidisciplinary collaboration in unraveling complex challenges and shaping effective governance strategies for the future.

The chapters within this volume are not mere academic exercises; they are blueprints for resilience, adaptability, and renewal. Each chapter delves into a specific facet of governance, dissecting the effects of the pandemic and illuminating pathways toward enhanced and innovative governance approaches. From the intricacies of corporate governance and education to the intricate interplay between political structures and health crises, this book spans the gamut of crucial topics that have come to define our times.

We extend our gratitude to the esteemed contributors who have poured their expertise and insights into this volume, enriching its content with a diversity of perspectives and methodologies. Their collective efforts have resulted in a tapestry of knowledge that we hope will inform and inspire, not only scholars and researchers but also policymakers, practitioners, educators, and leaders who grapple with the challenges of governance in a rapidly evolving landscape.

ORGANIZATION OF BOOK

Chapter 1

This chapter delves into the sweeping transformation brought about by digital tools within India's higher education system. The contours of communication, education, work culture, information access, and health crisis response have all undergone profound change due to digital technology. The discussion extends to the various dimensions and significance of digital components in higher education, examining the implementation and utilization of life skills in digitalization. By exploring the implementation of digital education in various disciplines, from arts to engineering, the chapter uncovers a promising scope for future developments that can redefine the landscape of education in India.

Chapter 2

While economic repercussions of the global pandemic have been extensively studied, this chapter introduces a fresh perspective—consumer viewpoints. It meticulously explores the economic consequences of COVID-19 through the lens of individuals. By engaging participants through social media questionnaires, the study unearths the significant impact of the pandemic on people's lives. Coping strategies employed by individuals are unveiled, providing insights into government and employer implications. This chapter is a valuable addition to ongoing economic discourse, shedding light on the multifaceted dimensions of COVID-19's economic aftermath.

Chapter 3

Focusing on the psychological toll of the pandemic, this chapter presents an in-depth investigation into the experiences of Bangladeshi faculty members. Through interviews, the study identifies central determinants influencing their mental well-being during the pandemic. The analysis offers an intricate exploration of motivations, opportunities, and constraints faced by faculty members. By unraveling the interplay of contingent and contextual variables, this chapter provides a foundation for groundbreaking theories in the realm of psychological effects during health crises.

Chapter 4

This chapter introduces the innovative utilization of the NoMAD instrument to evaluate complex healthcare interventions in Pakistan's fight against COVID-19. Through a comprehensive translation and testing process, the chapter establishes the validity of the U-NoMAD scale. The study showcases the instrument's effectiveness in assessing healthcare interventions and offers valuable insights into the implementation of social distancing measures. By providing a structured approach to evaluating healthcare initiatives, this chapter contributes to the arsenal of tools for combating health crises.

Chapter 5

This chapter is a comprehensive exploration of the epidemiological aspects of COVID-19, emphasizing the importance of awareness and education in building vaccine confidence. The outbreak's origins and global spread are dissected, showcasing the role of epidemiology in understanding the disease's impact. The chapter also highlights the use of epidemiology in shaping healthcare policies and services, underscoring its significance in managing the pandemic and future health crises.

Chapter 6

This chapter addresses the critical issue of managing biomedical waste during health crises, highlighting the role of technology in safeguarding both the environment and frontline workers. The utilization of technology to mitigate the spread of hazardous viruses is explored, presenting strategies for efficient bio-waste management. The chapter underscores the importance of aligning technology and regulations to create a resilient healthcare waste management system.

Chapter 7

By focusing on the informal housing areas of Syria, this chapter offers a twin-track approach to urban restructuring during the pandemic. Through a multi-dimensional analysis, the chapter advocates for participatory decision-making and community-driven redevelopment. The study underscores the need for good governance and sustainable urban planning principles, presenting a roadmap for achieving urban resilience and sustainable development.

Chapter 8

Centered on international peace and security, this chapter examines the response of the global community, particularly the United Nations Security Council, to the COVID-19 pandemic. By tracing past resolutions and considering the implications of UNSCR 2532, the chapter offers insights into the evolving role of the Security Council in addressing global health crises. It sheds light on the delicate balance between international peace and the challenges posed by pandemics.

Chapter 9

In this chapter, a comprehensive analysis of economic factors influencing working capital management in the automobile industry is presented. The study delves into macroeconomic and microeconomic elements that impact the industry's financial dynamics. By exploring emerging trends such as electric and autonomous vehicles, sustainability practices, and digitalization, the chapter offers practical recommendations for improving working capital management and investment decisions in the sector.

Chapter 10

This chapter offers a case study of the Chamera power plant in India, investigating the role of e-Training in fostering employee resilience during the pandemic. Through focus group interviews, the study reveals the transformative impact of e-Training on attributes such as self-efficacy, collaboration, and positive mindset. By highlighting the interplay between technology adoption and organizational resilience, the chapter provides insights for bridging gaps in understanding and preparing for future challenges.

Chapter 11

This chapter takes a deep dive into the changes in Chinese leadership and governance following the COVID-19 pandemic. It examines the societal and economic shifts triggered by the crisis and the subsequent responses that reshaped Chinese politics, corporations, and health governance. The chapter emphasizes the significance of e-governance and AI technology in this evolution, while also exploring potential economic revival strategies. It serves as a roadmap for understanding the post-pandemic governance landscape in China.

Chapter 12

This chapter delves into the evolution of governance models within the education sector, characterized by their dynamic and intricate nature on a global scale. Focusing specifically on non-superior public education institutions in Portugal, the study analyzes the implementation of a new governance model that emphasizes the school's integration with society. Through a qualitative multiple case study approach and grounded theory principles, the chapter scrutinizes the components of the General Council, particularly examining their participation and impact. By examining four distinct school groups encompassing various academic and socioeconomic profiles, the research gathers data from interviews, document analysis, and unmarked observation.

As we navigate the complex aftermath of COVID-19, we find ourselves at an inflection point, presented with both challenges and opportunities. This book is an invitation to embark on a journey of discovery, exploration, and innovation—a journey that we hope will yield new insights, catalyze transformation, and ultimately contribute to the advancement of governance models that are agile, sustainable, and responsive to the needs of our interconnected world.

Carla Negrão
CeBER, Portugal

Isabel Cristina Guerreiro Maia
University of Coimbra, Portugal

João Antonio Brito
University of Cape Verde, Cape Verde

Chapter 1
Utilization of Digital Tools in the Indian Higher Education System During Health Crises

M. Durairaj
https://orcid.org/0000-0002-7930-380X
Department of English, Panimalar Engineering College, India

S. Jayakumar
Sri Sairam College of Engineering, India

Monika
Department of Education, B.P.S. Women University, India

V. S. Karpagavalli
PSGR Krishnammal College for Women, India

B. Uma Maheswari
https://orcid.org/0000-0001-9707-285X
Department of Computer Science and Engineering, St. Joseph's College of Engineering, India

Sampath Boopathi
https://orcid.org/0000-0002-2065-6539
Muthayammal Engineering College, India

ABSTRACT

In this chapter, the utilization of digital tools in the higher education system in India has been illustrated. Communication, education, work culture, information access, and health crisis time are all being transformed by digital technology. The digital components, dimensions, significance, and inclusion in higher education have been discussed. The various elements, extensive activities, and initiatives of implementing digital education in India. The implementation and utilization of life skills in digitalization and in the arts, engineering, and technical education have been discussed to extract the scope for future developments.

DOI: 10.4018/978-1-7998-9213-7.ch001

INTRODUCTION

This chapter introduces the study's history, motivation, and scope, as well as its structure. Globalization, the knowledge explosion, the communication revolution, and digital technology have all changed our lives, with digital communication, the internet, and e-learning replacing conventional means. AI, automation, Big Data, Cloud Computing, Virtual and Augmented reality are the most recent advancements in digital technology. Our lives have been altered by the digital revolution. The Information Age began with the digital revolution, which resulted in the global adoption of the Internet, cell phones, and digital communication technologies, transforming it into a powerful instrument for communication and information sharing. Information and technology co-create a technological ecology in which we live. The digital revolution has changed the way we live, the process of contact and communication, sharing, learning, work-culture, and leisure, and it has directly or indirectly influenced users' ideas, attitudes, behaviour, and ideologies. India has 462 million active internet users, with 430.3 million of them accessing the internet via mobile phones. The digital revolution has had a huge influence on our lives, enabling us to quickly access information from anywhere in the globe. This has resulted in the current civilization being a knowledge society(Aziz et al., 2020; Logemann et al., 2022; Zina & Ahlem, 2021).

The digital revolution is vital in developing nations because it allows liberalization, privatization, globalization, and simple access, resulting in knowledge explosion and freely available information. Digital technology have transformed education by delivering cost-effective and time-saving solutions to fulfil rising educational demands. India's goal is to become a developed country by 2020. The integration of ICT and associated technologies into the higher education system can empower governing bodies to manage educational and managerial goals and changes, offering better service to all stakeholders. In order to work and communicate in a digitalized environment, it is necessary to acquire technical abilities, which is leading to a paradigm change in education from teacher-cantered to learner-cantered instruction. Higher education is being transformed by digitalization by giving novel teaching tools, access to information, global cooperation chances, and alternative approaches to professional growth, all of which contribute to greater educational development. Technology has facilitated the creation of creative teaching methodologies in higher education, opening up a world of possibilities for teachers. Individual variances may be catered for using digital technology to customise learning experiences. Learning with digital technology allows students who are unable to attend conventional classrooms to participate and enables lifetime learning(Barone et al., 2021; Rani et al., 2021; Salem et al., 2020).

E-learning, blended learning, MOOCs, virtual universities, OERs, blogs, online platforms for sharing knowledge and resources, discussion forums, interactive boards, videoconferencing, webinars, smart classrooms, cloud computing, online research tools, and Web Based Learning are all examples of how technology has changed education (WBL). To stay up with quickly changing technology, it is critical to integrate technology into the educational system.

CONCEPTUAL FRAMEWORK

Digital Competence

Communication, education, work culture, information access, and leisure time are all being transformed by digital technology. However, not everyone possesses the necessary knowledge, abilities, and attitudes to use them in a critical, collaborative, and creative manner. In recent years, terms such as 21st century skills, ICT skills, technology skills, information technology skills, media literacy, digital literacy, and digital skills have been used to characterize the abilities and competence necessary for the use of digital technologies. It is necessary to describe the synonyms and associated ideas in order to encompass the entity of digital competency(Kivunja, 2014; Muthmainnah et al., 2022a; Park Yuhyun, 2016).

Computer literacy/ ICT literacy: Computer literacy is a skill-based pragmatic approach to utilizing computers and related applications. It includes an introduction to the abilities needed to run a number of computer software packages as well as general IT skills like transferring disks and printing physical copies. This fundamental idea and information is widespread.

Internet skills: The term "internet skills" is divided into four categories: Operational knowledge of internet browsers and search engines, Formal internet abilities are required to navigate the internet. Internet information abilities for locating, selecting, and evaluating information, as well as strategic information skills for performing successful goal-oriented tasks.

Information literacy: Information literacy is a critical component of today's necessary competences, and it is closely tied to ICT. People can be information literate without access to information or the ability to use ICT, but access to information and the ability to use ICT are required for people to utilize IL in a knowledge society.

Media literacy: Media literacy is a necessary ability for establishing and maintaining autonomous and productive engagement in digital media. It highlights the characteristics of various media genres as well as message production and interpretation strategies.

Digital literacy: The term "digital literacy" was coined to refer to "literacy for the digital age," with an emphasis on critical thinking and information technology skills. It has evolved throughout time as a result of the fast advancement of digital technology.

- Individuals may develop themselves in the information society by combining technical, intellectual, and responsible competencies.
- Background Information Digital literacy is a larger notion than ICT literacy, and it refers to the ability to access, use, and disseminate information in a digital environment. It is described as the abilities necessary to acquire digital competence, which is supported by basic computer and Internet technical knowledge. Digital Competence is the most current notion used to define technological knowledge and abilities.
- Competence is a new notion that has replaced skills in recent publications to represent the requirement for a broader and deeper understanding of digital technology. It entails being able to fulfil complicated demands by drawing on and mobilizing psychological resources, functional elements, interpersonal characteristics, and ethical beliefs. Digital competence encompasses a wide range of skills and abilities in technology, computers, literacy, media, information, and communication.
- The confident and critical use of Information Society Technology (IST) for business, recreation, and communication is referred to as digital competence. It is supported by fundamental ICT abilities such as using computers to obtain, analyse, save, generate, present, and exchange information, as well as interact and engage in collaborative networks. The Digital Agenda for Europe 2020 highlights the need of teaching Europeans how to use ICT and digital media, making it a necessary life skill for all.
- Digital Competence is the collection of knowledge, abilities, and attitudes required to accomplish activities, solve issues, communicate, manage information, collaborate, produce and share material, and develop knowledge using ICT and digital media.
- Digital competence is a multifaceted notion that encompasses technical, cognitive, and digital abilities, as well as metacognitive processes, social, emotional, and ethical awareness. It refers to the confident, critical, and creative use of digital technology for accessing, storing, retrieving, creating, sharing, and evaluating information in order to facilitate successful communication, problem solving, critical thinking, and creative thinking. Reading, numeracy, logical, inferential, problem solving, cooperation, decision making, and metacognitive skills are all interrelated and interdependent.

- Digital competence is a cross-cutting key competency that enables users to gain other key competencies such as communication, language skills, mathematics and science, cultural awareness, and learning to learn. It is required for active involvement in the knowledge and information society, as well as in the global economy.

Figure 1. Digital competence: Components

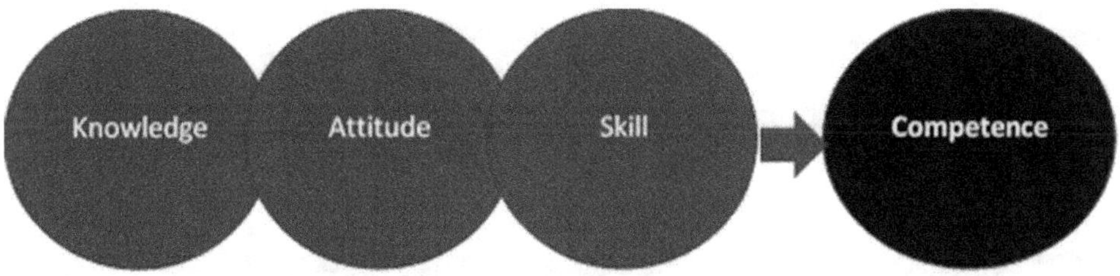

DIGITAL COMPETENCE: COMPONENTS

The report of the European Parliament and Council describes the essential competency components required for digital competence. Digital Competence: Components in Digital Education System is Shown in Figure 1.

Knowledge: Knowledge of computer operations, risk, creativity and invention, authenticity and trustworthiness of online information, ethics and etiquettes connected to collaborative technologies, and legal elements of ICT all contribute to digital competence.

Skills: Digital competence is based on understanding of computer operations, risk, creativity and innovation, the authenticity and dependability of online information, ethics and etiquettes connected to collaboration technologies, and legal elements of ICT.

Attitudes: Attitude is vital for sustained competent performance because it fosters critical and reflective thinking, engages individuals in online communities, drives them to become responsible users, provides autonomy, and encourages them to adhere to ethics and values.

Competence: Competence is described as a mix of context-specific knowledge, abilities, and attitudes. It is the most sophisticated component of the European Qualifications Framework, allowing users to apply knowledge and skills with a contextually relevant attitude.

Figure 2. Digital dimensions for digital education system

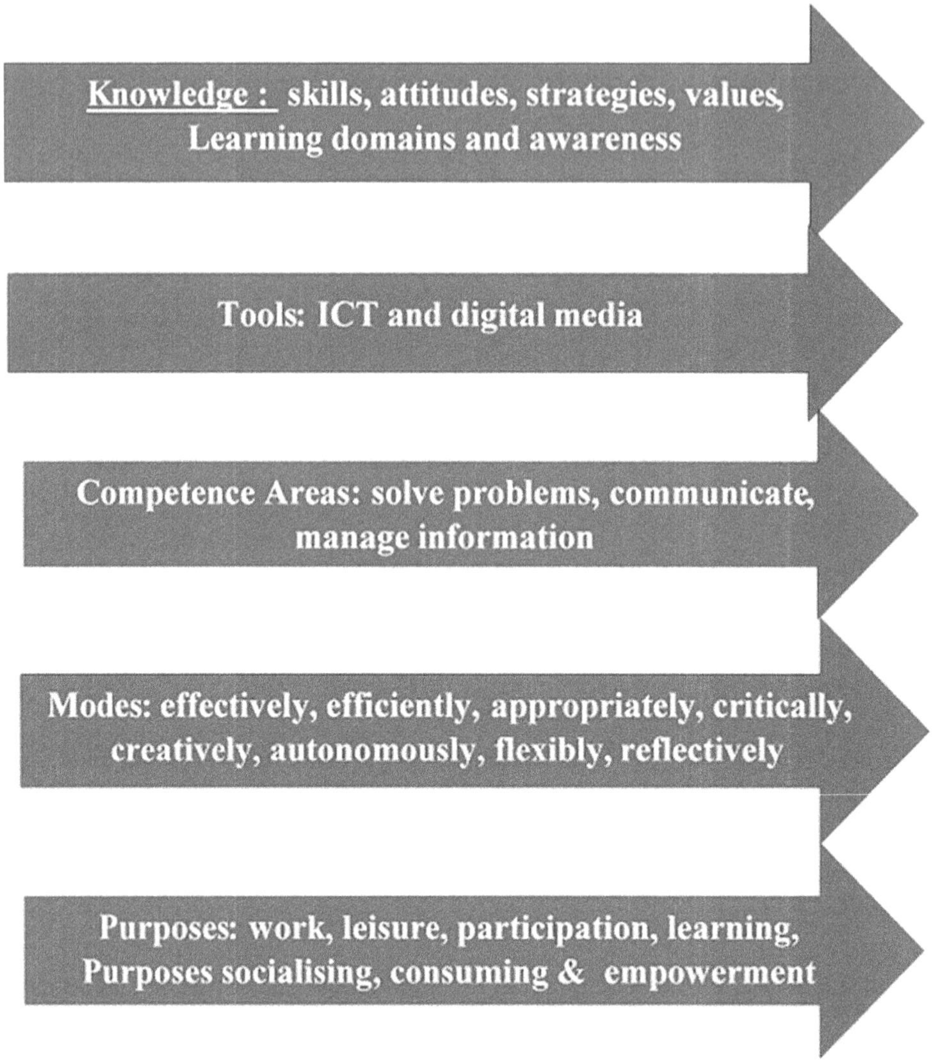

DIGITAL COMPETENCE: DIMENSIONS

Digital Dimensions for Digital Education System is illustrated in Figure 2.

Technological/ Instrumental Operation: Digital competence is defined as the knowledge, skills, attitude, and aptitude to operate technical components of digital tools. It entails being aware of relevant technologies, comprehending their usage and features, and being able to recognize and solve fundamental technological difficulties on one's own. It also involves the capacity to appraise one's own demands and stay up with current technological breakthroughs(Botha & Ford, 2008; Muthmainnah et al., 2022b).

Information Processing and Management: Because the digital world is a huge ocean of information, information processing and management are critical aspects of becoming digitally competent. This encompasses the knowledge, abilities, and attitudes needed to define information demands, as well as access, identify, search, manage, retrieve, store, critically appraise, integrate, and organize information for personal and professional use.

Cognitive, Pedagogic and Knowledge Construction: This dimension of digital tools and technology includes the awareness and understanding of the use of digital tools in the process of teaching and learning, the ability to express and communicate effectively, the expression of creativity and knowledge construction through digital tools, technology, and media, the ability to find online learning opportunities, participate in forums and online communities of interest, collaborate online with others, share and exchange id Intellectual Property Rights, Plagiarism, Open Educational Resources, Web 2.0 Tools, and Online Research Tools.

Digital Citizenship: The final factor of digital competence is the knowledge, attitude, and abilities required to use online technologies responsibly while keeping privacy, safety, and netiquette in mind. It also involves the understanding, abilities, and attitude to act ethically, respect socially accepted rules of good behavior, and address the environmental and ergonomic dangers of digital tools and technology.

DIGITAL COMPETENCE: SIGNIFICANCE IN EDUCATION

Digital competence has become an essential component of digitally mediated contexts, giving education the Midas touch. Web 2.0 tools, social networking platforms, e-books, MOOCs, online learning platforms, e-libraries, webinars, OERs, and virtual universities have all been introduced via technology. The incorporation of digital technology has altered the educational system, improving digital competency knowledge, abilities, and attitudes. Digital competence is a cross-curricular responsibility that focuses on the development of digital skills, attitudes, and abilities that may be applied to a variety of topics and contexts. It should be included into classroom activities, homework, teamwork, projects, and problem-solving skills. In 2011, UNESCO developed a framework for teachers' ICT competencies to describe a set of ICT competency abilities for instructors to incorporate technology in the teaching and learning process. The UNESCO ICT-CFT framework is divided into three levels, the highest of which is Knowledge Creation, which aims to generate new knowledge for more peaceful, satisfying, and affluent communities(Murphy, 2011; Nielsen et al., 2012; Singh & Guo, 2010).

Digital Generations

Today's pupils are not the people our educational system was created to teach. Digital technology has created a new world in which people may be classified based on their behavior and attitudes. This has resulted in a generation gap, resulting in separate digital generations.

Digital Immigrants: A digital immigrant is someone who was born before the digital age and is unfamiliar with the digital world. They are slower to embrace, adapt, and learn new technologies than digital natives, and prefer to edit papers by hand rather than onscreen. This generation finds it challenging to integrate into the digital world.

Digital Settlers: Individuals born before the introduction of technology but nevertheless rely primarily on traditional means of connection are referred to as digital immigrants. Digital settlers are familiar with the complicated digital environment, but their level of reliance and commitment to it differs. For example, they may talk with their pals online via a web-based service, but they prefer to meet over tea or on a morning stroll.

Digital Natives: Individuals born after 1980 who have been exposed to technology since childhood are considered digital natives. They share a worldwide culture that is defined by specific characteristics and experiences connected to how they engage with information technology, information itself, one another, and other people and organizations, rather than by age. This has resulted in a shift in how young people think and absorb information.

Figure 1.7 - Digital Generations Continuum

The division of digital generations into digital natives and digital immigrants is debatable. It is suggested that early exposure to technology leads to a fundamentally different approach to learning and utilizing technology, and that global adoption of digital technology did not occur at the same time. Prensky's notion of digital natives and digital immigrants was followed by the researcher.

DIGITALIZATION OF HIGHER EDUCATION SYSTEM IN INDIA

Digital Inclusion (E-Governance) in Administration of Higher Education System

The use of digital technology to improve the efficiency, effectiveness, transparency, and accountability of service (information) exchange between higher education institutions and their stakeholders is known as digital inclusion. It entails usability, empowerment, involvement, awareness, affordability, accessibility, and digital technology adoption. One of the most astonishing advances in the cyber world is e-governance.

Digitalization of Teaching Learning Process in Higher Education System

Digital technology have expanded the reach of educational programs outside of the classroom, giving individuals who are unable to attend regular sessions an alternative. Digital learning is high-tech, content-driven, and facilitates individual learning. Networked learners move themselves through a rich and sophisticated online information environment. Eminent educators from throughout the country and abroad might be requested to teach at their leisure using mobile and seamless communication technology. Through education, these online learning programs hope to motivate, encourage, and empower people.

Virtual learning, web-based learning, and e-learning are online programs that provide millions of students with access to a world of information via the internet. They are content-focused, deliverable-driven, personalized, and interactive. Blended Learning is a program that mixes conventional learning methods with e-learning. It combines the convenience, speed, and low cost of e-learning with the personalized touch of conventional learning. In traditional classroom instruction, time spent on input and output is minimized and used for the process, leaving more time for student engagement, involvement in activities, discussion, cooperation with others, and brain storming.

To develop a mixed learning environment, a teacher must integrate online materials, build Web pages, and use social networking sites and forums. Open educational resources (OERs) are being created and distributed through the Internet, most frequently in the form of e-books, lecture notes, courseware, syllabi, assignments, exams, audio, streaming videos, learning objects, animations, or software. Universities are also encouraging the global interchange of virtual courses and programs to meet learners' educational and professional development goals.

Virtual classrooms provide the satisfaction and enjoyment of traditional classroom teaching and learning by fostering interactive learning environments for presentations, assignments, seminars, conferences, and panel discussions. MOOCs are free web-based learning programs designed to accommodate a large number of learners from different locations. They provide the opportunity to enroll in a course without any obligation to attend, while also increasing participants' abilities, fostering active communication, and promoting lifelong learning. MOOCs also foster participatory communities and forums, making information available to anybody who wants it(Bakator & Radosav, 2020; Buchanan, 2011; Nielsen et al., 2015).

Digitalization of Evaluation Process in Higher Education System

Evaluation is the process of determining the result, efficiency, or effectiveness of an educational process. Online registration, digital exam scheduling, distributed authoring of question papers, secure delivery of question papers, software to scan, assess, and evaluate answer sheets, uploading of marks and preparing results, and printing of mark sheets and certificates are all examples of how digital technology can help with this process.

The intelliEXAMS program is an examination automation system that uses cutting-edge technologies. It offers effective examination administration and control, centralized and secure data management, examination fee and candidate attendance management, an e-communication system, automatic validation and layered document verification, and a tamper-proof admission card with a photograph. It also includes a Distributed Authoring System to eliminate question duplication, infallible examination, foolproof digital assessment, tamper-proof mark sheets and certifications, and seamless integration of old data and applications.

Digitalization of Research in Higher Education System

Research is an essential aspect of higher education, and digital tools are available to assist researchers at each level of the research process.

Digital Libraries: To Search for Data: Digital libraries are electronic collections of literature and information that provide electronic access to works. ACM, IEEE Xplore, PubMed, DBLP, ISIWOK, CiteSeerX, Scopus, Google Scholar Academia, Research gate, Eric, Inflibnet, Shodhganga, and other web-based tools employ URIs to identify and access resources linked to a publication and its author. Web 2.0 applications, such as Educlipper, Scoop.it, Biblio, Evernote, Dropbox, Google Drive, and Mendeley, enable producers to incorporate personal metadata, notes, remarks, comments, and keywords.

Digital Tools for Online Collection of Data: Online surveys are quickly becoming a key research tool in a wide range of subjects, accounting for 20% of global data-collection spending. Some of the most recent user-friendly tools for creating survey forms, storing recurring questions in a library, and sharing them with colleagues and respondents include KoBoToolbox, DiRT, Blog Analysis Toolkit, Edit Grid, Survey Gizmo, Survey Monkey, Zoomerang, and Google forms. They let you to develop numerous sorts of questions and gather data quickly and reliably on Android, iOS, and other devices. Web technologies enable data collection in novel ways that are not limited by time or place. However, it is critical to ensure quality, completeness, response rate, timeliness, secrecy and security, technological challenges, and survey sample selection.

Writing and Communicating Research Work Digitally: Academic writing differs from other types of writing, and there are several resources that may assist scholars. These websites offer both online and physical outlets for writing, recommendations, and corrections that may be shared through email or online drive. After finishing the essay, the researcher might submit it to online journals and webinars for publication.

Digital tools for Citation: To assist researchers in writing references, online programs such as RefWorks, EasyBib, Citelighter, Bibme, Citefast, and Citation Machine are available. These tools make reference authoring straightforward, with the opportunity to save citations for later use. Mendeley and Google Scholar both give the citation with the searched paper, which may be copied and pasted into the relevant location. Webinars are internet-based seminars in which lectures are broadcast and discussed. The existence of interactive components, which allow players to participate and discuss in real time, is the most distinguishing aspect. The presenter can exchange audio, papers, and other associated apps with the attendees using webinar software.

Figure 3. Various elements of digital higher education

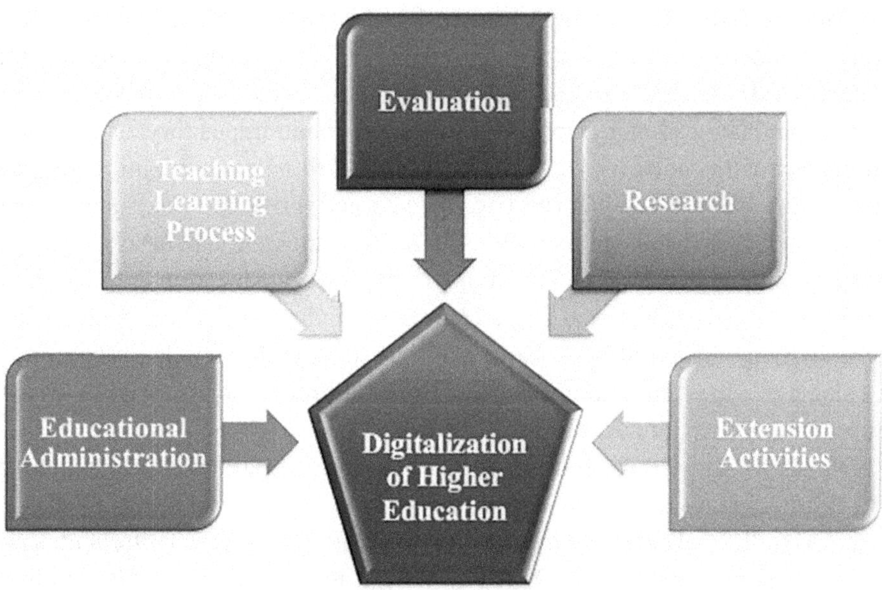

DIGITALIZATION OF EXTENSION ACTIVITIES IN HIGHER EDUCATION SYSTEM

University extension activities include dialogues, folk media, leisure activities, interactive and participatory programs, group working, and group debate. Electronic newsletters, blogs, teleconferences, self-made movies, and publishing them to social networking sites have all been utilized to improve extension initiatives. To assist people, families, and communities live successful lives in a constantly changing world, digital resources must be founded on fundamental human principles. Gender sensitization, women education, Swachh Bharat Abhiyan, open-learning system, and women empowerment should be promoted through extension initiatives. The various elements of digital higher education are shown in Figure 3.

DIGITAL EDUCATION INITIATIVES TAKEN BY GOVERNMENT OF INDIA

The Indian government has initiated a number of digital projects to promote fairness, increase access to excellent education, improve learning opportunities, expedite outreach, and improve access to quality educational resources. SWAYAM is an indigenously developed massive open online course (MOOC) that was launched in July 2017 to bridge the digital gap for students who have been unable to participate in the knowledge economy's mainstream. SWAYAM Prabha is a digital education program founded in 2017 to supply learners with high-quality educational information using satellite technology. It is broadcast on 32 DTH television channels in order to promote consistency to educational standards in rural and distant places.

The National Academic Depository (NAD) is an online repository for all academic honors awarded by universities, colleges, and school districts. Academic Institutions/ Boards/ Eligibility Assessment bodies, students, and verification users such as banks can register, post, view, and verify awards. It ensures the database's legitimacy, integrity, and confidentiality for employment, further education, and loans. The MHRD launched the National Digital Library of India (NDL India) in 2015, and it became live in 2016. It offers a search and browse capability for elearning materials in a single window, integrating e Content from multiple universities, and registering users from participating institutions.

INFLIBNET is a UGC project to create a high-speed nationwide communication network for Indian universities. Its goal is to modernize university libraries and enhance intellectual contact via electronic mail, file transfer, computer/audio/video conferencing, and other means. Dr. A.P.J. Abdul Kalam founded the UGC-INFONET digital library collaboration in 2003, which provides access to 15,000 core and peer-reviewed publications as well as 10 bibliographic databases. The Ministry of Human Resource Development of India has united three consortia to establish e-shodhsindhu, which includes 91 government supported technical institutes, 178 universities, 3000 colleges, 10000 e-journals, 3135000 e-books, 20 resources, and 4 databases.

INFLIBNET is a UGC effort to establish a high-speed nationwide communication network for Indian universities. It intends to modernize university libraries and enhance intellectual contact through electronic mail, file transfer, computer/audio/video conferencing, and other means. UGC-INFONET is a digital library collaboration founded in 2003 by Dr. A.P.J. Abdul Kalam that provides access to 15,000 core and peer-reviewed publications as well as 10 bibliographic databases. The MHRD of India has united three consortia to establish e-shodhsindhu, which includes 91 government supported technical institutes, 178 universities, 3000 colleges, 10000 e-journals, 3135000 e-books, 20 resources, and 4 databases.

LIFE SKILLS

Education is the process of humanizing people and building a civilized existence. It has been a feature of Indian society since the Vedic period and the Gurukul system, when individuals were taught self-awareness and empathy by performing'sewa' for the elderly and the underprivileged. Most educated youngsters were sent to Gurukuls to learn, allowing them to become independent and self-sufficient(Botha & Ford, 2008; Kivunja, 2014; Muthmainnah et al., 2022a, 2022b; Park Yuhyun, 2016). Various Skills in the Digital Higher Education system is illustrated in Figure 4.

Basic Categories of Life Skills

The World Health Organization has defined 10 basic life skills for the development of healthy individuals, which span cognitive, social, and affective elements of life. These abilities are necessary for leading a stress-free and psychosocially healthy existence.

Cognitive or Thinking Skills: Personal mental processing is linked to the four basic life skills of Critical Thinking, Creative Thinking, Decision Making, and Problem Solving. These abilities cover a key area of a person's life because most of their actions need thinking or cognitive abilities.

Social or Interpersonal Skills: Social skills are necessary for sustaining strong social relationships, which are fundamental in one's life. According to Aristotle, humans are "social creatures," and these abilities aid in the maintenance of good relationships.

Affective or Emotional Skills: Assertiveness and negotiating require adjustment and management abilities such as Coping with Emotions and Coping with Stress. These abilities aid in the expression of emotions and the management of stress. When applying these talents, it is critical to consider social elements of life and make sensible judgments.

Figure 4. Various skills in the digital higher education system

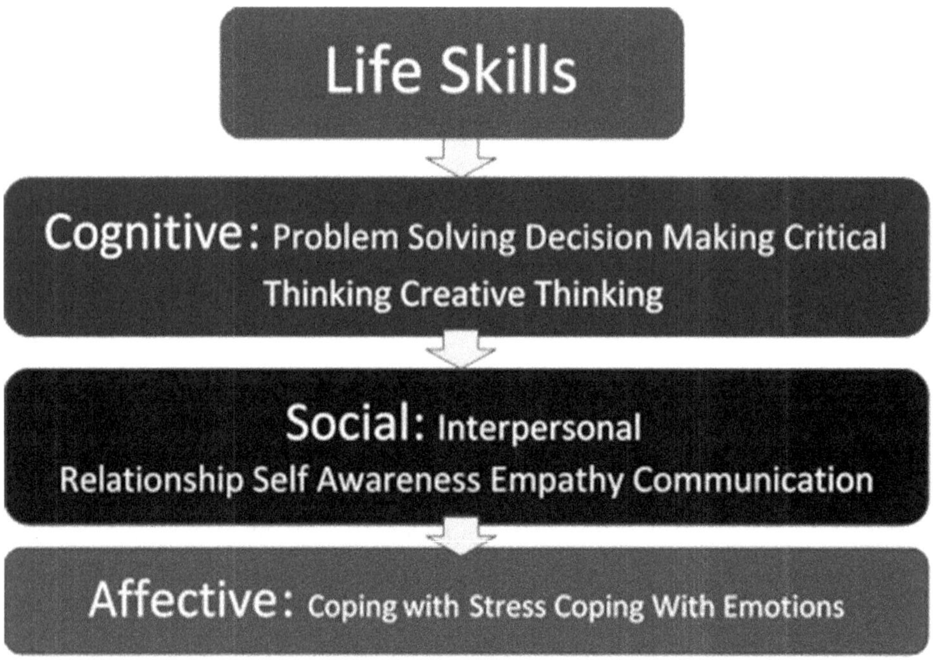

Core Life Skills

In schools, the World Health Organization recognized 10 basic life skills for children and adolescents.

Self-Awareness Skill: Understanding oneself, coping with stress, emotions, social interpersonal interactions, self-awareness, empathy, communication, problem solving, decision making, critical thinking, and creative thinking are all examples of self-awareness skills. Knowing oneself facilitates awareness of one's own physical, cognitive, behavioral, and social functioning, allowing for efficient communication, relationships, and empathy.

Empathy Skill: Empathy is the ability to comprehend and accept others, which improves social relationships and bonding. It is the practice of being respectful and thoughtful about another person's subjective experience while retaining an observing position. It can aid in the development of a caring attitude and tolerance for others.

Interpersonal Relationship Skill: The capacity to sustain healthy, effective, and good social interactions with others is referred to as interpersonal relationship skill. It allows a person to grasp their tasks and obligations and cope with them successfully. It is also possible to end relationships constructively, without bitterness or wrath.

Effective Communication Skill: The capacity to express and receive information in a meaningful, respectful, and aggressive manner is defined as effective communication skill. It also encompasses the capacity to communicate oneself plainly, clearly, and successfully in both verbal and nonverbal communication. It is the capacity to provide meaningful engagement and communication between two or more people.

Critical Thinking Skill: Critical thinking is a cognitive process that assists people in assessing and estimating the good and negative elements of any issue that may impact their attitude and behavior.

Creative Thinking Skill: The ability to think differently and see beyond the presence of objects is referred to as creative thinking. It possesses four qualities: fluidity, flexibility, uniqueness, and elaboration. It is a type of divergent thinking that is used to produce new ideas from current knowledge or thoughts.

Decision Making Skill: Decision Making Skill is a mental activity that assists people in making acceptable decisions. It involves logical thinking, problem solving, communication, interpersonal relationships, critical thinking, memory, reasoning, analysis, idea formulation, and other cognitive processes. It helps people to be more proactive in making decisions.

Problem Solving Skill: The capacity to detect, comprehend, and solve an issue is referred to as problem solving ability. It is a cognitive process that entails integrating prior experiences and following certain processes. It is a necessary ability in today's world, as unresolved conflicts can cause emotional and physical stress.

Coping with Emotions Skill: Managing Emotions The capacity to perceive and express one's own emotions, as well as understand the emotions of others, is referred to as skill. It helps a person to respond correctly to their own emotions while also being aware of the impact of emotions on behavior. If not managed properly, intense emotions can have a severe impact on a person's physical and mental health.

Coping with Stress Skill: Managing Stress A skill is the capacity to detect and cope with stress successfully. WHO has identified 10 fundamental life skills that are interconnected and difficult to separate? Adopting and practicing these abilities leads to increased self-esteem, sociability, decision-making, tolerance, and confidence.

Life Skills Selected for Study

Teachers' roles in the twenty-first century have evolved from that of an instructor to that of a constructor, facilitator, and developer of learning environments. This has prompted the introduction of 21st century abilities into instructors' and pedagogical practices. According to DIGICOMP, four life skills established by WHO researchers are important for study and equally important for higher education professors.

Effective Communication Skill: Communication is a necessary ability in both personal and professional life. It entails the interchange of words, symbols, or nonverbal clues, the ability to interpret the message analytically and synthetically, active listening, and feedback. Educational communication is the process through which teachers and students engage to improve knowledge and attain learning objectives. Educational communication can occur directly, such as in the classroom, or indirectly, such as through online education. It can happen in higher education through paper presentations, extended courses, and research activity. Individuals can now communicate using a variety of digital tools and technology, such as e-mails, podcasts, voice phone calls, audio, video, and text conferencing, blogs, wikis, online discussion forums, Facebook pages, Twitter, WhatsApp, You Tube, recorded video clips, lectures capture, shared whiteboards, eportfolios, blackboard collaborate, and collaborative browsing, in the digital era. Asynchronous technologies enable players to choose the time and location of their participation, whereas synchronous technologies compel all participants to participate at the same time.

Collaboration Skills: Collaboration is a soft talent that enables people to maintain positive professional and social connections. It contains subskills such as the capacity to work well with varied teams, to be flexible, to make concessions, to take shared responsibility, to appreciate individual contributions, and to communicate effectively with others. Academic cooperation is a joint effort by two or more academic faculty members to pursue a mutually beneficial and engaging project. It assists professors and students in learning new teaching strategies and implementing new pedagogical tools, increasing their chances of success and issue resolution. Collaboration entails online conversation, link sharing, collaborative work on Google Docs, and the use of online venues for publishing work. Users may create, collaborate, and share material online using Web 2.0 technologies such as Banyan, Google Drive, Etherpad, Mediawiki, VideoAnt, Eido, Diigo, and Padlet.

Critical Thinking Skill

A knowledge-based society requires critical thinking, problem-solving, and creative thinking. Critical thinking is a crucial talent that allows people to make sound judgments. It entails separating important from irrelevant information, establishing the factual correctness, reliability, and strengths of a statement or argument, and making educated judgments after seeking the truth and evaluating facts. For web searches, statistics, news, and information, critical thinking abilities are required. They allow consumers to find the most relevant information, evaluate its relevance, bias, and accuracy, and stay secure in the digital age. They also make people think about how they portray and shape their digital identity, discriminating between information that is restricted and content that is not, and safeguarding people from online fraud and cybercrime.

Creative Thinking Skills

Exploring ideas, developing possibilities, and producing something new, interesting, or uncommon are all examples of creative thinking. Teaching is viewed as a creative endeavour in which instructors are given creative freedom to educate. Brainstorming, Idea Pooling, Mind Mapping, Lateral Thinking, and Directed Creativity are all tools and strategies for promoting creativity. The recent advancement of digital tools and technology has provided a number of online activities that encourage diverse thinking, such as creative writing, graphics, colour, animation, and effects, the construction and administration of a personal website, and creative writing using a word processor. Students' best friends are cartoons and comics, and free and simple tools may be utilized to boost their creativity. Brainstorming, mind mapping, infographics, audio and video clips, and Web 2.0 technologies enable people to create, share, and interact. Teachers may use these tools and approaches to keep students' attention and promote creative thinking abilities in their students(Kumara et al., 2023; Sampath et al., 2022; Vanitha et al., 2023; Vennila et al., 2023).

RATIONALE OF THE STUDY

Digital technology has had a significant impact on our lives, and it has become critical to be technologically literate in our fast-paced technology-driven culture. Digital competence is a notion that refers to the technical skills and abilities required to use digital tools and technology effectively for study, work, communication, and enjoyment. It also involves the ability to evaluate digital technology and web-based information critically. The core notion of digital competency of professionals in the knowledge domain is expressed in the 21st century educational environment, and instructors must be regularly taught and updated to adopt the newest technology-based abilities.

Digital technology has had a significant impact on our lives, and it has become critical to be technologically literate in our fast-paced technology-driven culture.

Digital competence is a notion that refers to the technical skills and abilities required to use digital tools and technology effectively for study, work, communication, and enjoyment. It also involves the ability to evaluate digital technology and web-based information critically. The core notion of digital competency of professionals in the knowledge domain is expressed in the 21st century educational environment, and instructors must be regularly taught and updated to adopt the newest technology-based abilities.

Teachers' roles have evolved from that of an instructor to that of a constructor, facilitator, and developer of learning environments. To do so, students must be able to think critically and creatively, be digitally savvy, understand and manage emotions, impact social values, enhance interpersonal connections, and work together. Life skills assist individuals to develop healthy interpersonal skills, effective communication skills, self-awareness, and critical thinking and problem-solving ability. A teacher with digital mastery can cultivate critical thinking, creativity, and scientific temper in children, transforming them into life-long learners and innovators. They must appreciate lifelong learning as well as lifelong learning and lifelong learning(Babu et al., 2023; Boopathi et al., 2023; Jeevanantham et al., 2023).

The research is needed to analyse the degree of Digital Competence and Life Abilities necessary for higher education instructors in order to discover the elements that contribute to the development of these skills in this technological era. Teachers must be trained and retrained in order to fulfil their roles more meaningfully and successfully. A review of the research papers found that there were few studies that assessed or analysed teachers' digital competence in a broader sense of the phrase. The researcher conducted this study to analyze the degree of Digital Competence and Life Abilities necessary for higher education instructors, as well as to discover the factors associated with the development of these skills in this technological era.

FUTURE EXTENSION OF RESEARCH DEVELOPMENT

- Higher education is divided into four dimensions: technological, information processing and management, pedagogic/knowledge construction, and digital citizenship.
- Dimensions of higher education include technological, information processing and management, pedagogic/knowledge construction, and digital citizenship.
- Dimensions of higher education (technological, information processing, pedagogical, and digital citizenship).
- The most significant concept is to investigate higher education instructors' Life Skills in terms of successful communication, teamwork, creative thinking, and critical thinking.

- The main idea is to investigate higher education teachers' Life Skills in relation to Digital Generations, such as effective communication, collaboration, creative thinking, and critical thinking.
- Creating MOOCs to improve life skills among higher education instructors using DIGICOMP.

SUMMARY

The use of digital technologies in India's higher education system has been demonstrated in this chapter. Digital technology is transforming communication, education, work culture, information access, and health crisis response. The dimensions, relevance, and incorporation of digital components in higher education have been explored. Various components, intensive operations, and endeavours for introducing digital education in India throughout the epidemic. The implementation and application of life skills in digitalization, as well as in the arts, engineering, and technical education, have been explored in order to determine the potential for future advances.

REFERENCES

Aziz, A., Islam, M. M., & Zakaria, M. (2020). COVID-19 exposes digital divide, social stigma, and information crisis in Bangladesh. *Media Asia*, *47*(3–4), 144–151. doi:10.1080/01296612.2020.1843219

Babu, B. S., Kamalakannan, J., Meenatchi, N., M, S. K. S., S, K., & Boopathi, S. (2023). Economic impacts and reliability evaluation of battery by adopting Electric Vehicle. *IEEE Explore*, 1–6. IEEE. doi:10.1109/ICPECTS56089.2022.10046786

Bakator, M., & Radosav, D. (2020). Analyzing the Digital Education Revolution. *International Conference on Information Technology and Development of Education-ITRO*. IEEE.

Barone, M. T. U., Ngongo, B., Harnik, S. B., de Oliveira, L. X., Végh, D., de Luca, P. V., Pedrosa, H. C., Giraudo, F., Cardona-Hernandez, R., Chaudhury, N., & Menna-Barreto, L. (2021). COVID-19 associated with diabetes and other noncommunicable diseases led to a global health crisis. *Diabetes Research and Clinical Practice*, *171*, 108587. doi:10.1016/j.diabres.2020.108587 PMID:33307134

Ben Salem, S., Mansour, N., & Haddad, M. (2020). Health Crisis (Covid-19) and the French Economy. *Journal of the International Academy for Case Studies*, *26*(5), 1–10.

Boopathi, S., Arigela, S. H., Raman, R., Indhumathi, C., Kavitha, V., & Bhatt, B. C. (2023). Prominent Rule Control-based Internet of Things: Poultry Farm Management System. *IEEE Explore*, 1–6. IEEE. doi:10.1109/ICPECTS56089.2022.10047039

Botha, A., & Ford, M. (2008). "Digital Life Skills" for the young and mobile "Digital Citizens." *Policy*, 1–7. http://researchspace.csir.co.za/dspace/handle/10204/2513

Buchanan, R. (2011). Paradox, promise and public pedagogy: Implications of the federal government's digital education revolution. *The Australian Journal of Teacher Education*, *36*(2), 67–78. doi:10.14221/ajte.2011v36n2.6

Jeevanantham, Y. A., A, S., V, V., J, S. I., Boopathi, S., & Kumar, D. P. (2023). Implementation of Internet-of Things (IoT) in Soil Irrigation System. *IEEE Explore*, 1–5. doi:10.1109/ICPECTS56089.2022.10047185

Kivunja, C. (2014). Teaching Students to Learn and to Work Well with 21st Century Skills: Unpacking the Career and Life Skills Domain of the New Learning Paradigm. *International Journal of Higher Education*, *4*(1), 1–11. doi:10.5430/ijhe.v4n1p1

Kumara, V., Mohanaprakash, T. A., Fairooz, S., Jamal, K., Babu, T., & B., S. (2023). Experimental Study on a Reliable Smart Hydroponics System. In *Human Agro-Energy Optimization for Business and Industry* (pp. 27–45). IGI Global. doi:10.4018/978-1-6684-4118-3.ch002

Logemann, M., Aritz, J., Cardon, P., Swartz, S., Elhaddaoui, T., Getchell, K., Fleischmann, C., Helens-Hart, R., Li, X., Palmer-Silveira, J. C., Ruiz-Garrido, M., Springer, S., & Stapp, J. (2022). Standing strong amid a pandemic: How a global online team project stands up to the public health crisis. *British Journal of Educational Technology*, *53*(3), 577–592. doi:10.1111/bjet.13189 PMID:35600422

Murphy, I. (2011). Educational reform and the enacted curriculum in English - a narrative from the field of the digital education revolution. *Engineers Australia*, *46*(1), 62–72.

Muthmainnah, M., Al Yakin, A., Massyat, M., Lulaj, E., & Bayram, G. E. (2022a). Developing Students' Life Skills Through Edupreneurship in the Digital Era. In Contemporary Studies in Economic and Financial Analysis (Vol. 109A, pp. 169–190). Emerald Publishing Limited. doi:10.1108/S1569-37592022000109A011

Muthmainnah, M., Al Yakin, A., Massyat, M., Lulaj, E., & Bayram, G. E. (2022b). Developing Students' Life Skills Through Edupreneurship in the Digital Era. *Contemporary Studies in Economic and Financial Analysis*, *109A*, 169–190. doi:10.1108/S1569-37592022000109A011

Nielsen, W., Miller, A., & Hoban, G. F. (2012). *The digital education revolution : New South Wales science teachers ' response to laptop ubiquity.*

Nielsen, W., Miller, K. A., & Hoban, G. (2015). Science Teachers' Response to the Digital Education Revolution. *Journal of Science Education and Technology, 24*(4), 417–431. doi:10.100710956-014-9527-3

Park, Y. (2016). *8 Digital Life Skills All Children Need – and a Plan for Teaching Them.* In World Economic Forum.

Rani, R., Kumar, R., Mishra, R., & Sharma, S. (2021). Digital health: A panacea in COVID-19 crisis. *Journal of Family Medicine and Primary Care, 10*(1), 62. doi:10.4103/jfmpc.jfmpc_1494_20 PMID:34017704

Sampath, B. C. S., & Myilsamy, S. (2022). Application of TOPSIS Optimization Technique in the Micro-Machining Process. In Trends, Paradigms, and Advances in Mechatronics Engineering (pp. 162–187). IGI Global. doi:10.4018/978-1-6684-5887-7.ch009

Singh, M., & Guo, W. (2010). The digital education revolution and languages: Insights from Sassen on transforming a Chinese academic into a trans-national researcher. *Global Student Mobility in the Asia Pacific: Mobility, Migration, Security and Wellbeing of International Students*, 117–140.

Vanitha, S. K. R., & Boopathi, S. (2023). Artificial Intelligence Techniques in Water Purification and Utilization. In *Human Agro-Energy Optimization for Business and Industry* (pp. 202–218). IGI Global., doi:10.4018/978-1-6684-4118-3.ch010

Vennila, T., Karuna, M. S., Srivastava, B. K., Venugopal, J., Surakasi, R., & B., S. (2023). New Strategies in Treatment and Enzymatic Processes. In *Human Agro-Energy Optimization for Business and Industry* (pp. 219–240). IGI Global. doi:10.4018/978-1-6684-4118-3.ch011

Zina, A., & Ahlem, S. (2021). Perception of E-learning during the health crisis of COVID-19: Case of algerian university teachers. *Journal of Information Technology Management, 13*(2), 154–172. doi:10.22059/jitm.2021.80360

Chapter 2
The Post-COVID-19 Pandemic Economy of Ghana From the Consumer Perspective

Lydia Andoh-Quainoo
https://orcid.org/0000-0002-0674-7602
Pentecost University, Ghana

Paul Adjei Onyina
Pentecost University, Ghana

ABSTRACT

The Covid-19 global pandemic affected various dimensions, including social, cultural, behavioral, financial, and economic. Although various studies have focused on the effects of the pandemic on the economy, not many have been done on the economic outcomes from consumers' perspectives. The purpose of this chapter is to examine the economic effects of Covid-19 on the economy and its implications for consumers. The chapter seeks to contribute to ongoing discussions on economic shifts associated with Covid-19 with emphasis on the consumer perspective. Questionnaire was provided on social media platform for participants to respond using the same medium. Responses have been analyzed and found that people have been affected significantly by the pandemic. Their coping strategies in dealing with the pandemic have also been presented and implications for the government and employers provided in the tail end of the chapter.

DOI: 10.4018/978-1-7998-9213-7.ch002

INTRODUCTION

Wuhan is a city in China where the virus SARs-CoV-2 was initially reported; the city authority subsequently informed the World Health Organization local office early December 2019 (Onyina, 2021 and Gössling, Scott, Hall, 2020). This virus SARs-CoV-2 become popularly known as COVID-19, and has disrupted the socio-economic system globally (Khoo, 2020; Vinod & Sharma, 2021). In March 2022, the COVID-19 was professed by the WHO as a pandemic; hence it became an emergent global public health issue which required immediate attention (Aduhene and Osei-Assibey, 2021). Its devastating effects on the health of affected individuals have been tragic and unprecedented. Not only has it affected health, but also had a significant influence on a number of economic and business trends in the global economy. The pandemic has profoundly overwhelmed the global business arena with wide and fast changes on economies, firms and people with several effects (Pricy, Cuce & Sadhakar, 2021; Zahra, 2021).

Globally, it has been observed that the outbreak of the COVID-19 pandemic totally disrupted economic activities, and has different effects on countries. The pandemic has affected both the formal and informal sectors (Aduhene and Osei-Assibey, 2021). It disrupted the flow of goods and services as well as government reserves, income levels and borrowing. There are a number of proposals for new economic models and social policies to manage the world's economy to restore and grow it particularly in developing countries such as Africa and Ghana. The effects of the pandemic on the African economy have been distressing. Most economies on the continent have suffered significantly from job losses, closure of businesses. ILO (2020) reports that about 1.6 million jobs have been lost due to the pandemic and this development has slowed down economic and business operations in general.

Consequently, governments instituted control measures and policies to curb the spread of the pandemic. These measures include enhanced hygiene protocols such as frequent hand washing and sanitizing, social distancing, wearing of nose mask and restrictions on movements involving about 2.7 billion people (Aduhene and Osei-Assibey, 2021). Although the measures reduced the spread of the virus to some extent, it contributed significantly to the slowdown of financial markets, general economic and business activities (Baber, 2021; Zahra, 2021). There have also been greater cross border restrictions which affected trade in the AU/ECOWAS sub-regions. The restrictions on the flow of goods and services affected businesses and consumers harshly. The pandemic also had a lot of unintended consequences and distorted daily economic activities from groceries to travel, work to events and many others. These unintended outcomes have both positive and negative impacts resulting in economic recession.

In Ghana, the pandemic was recorded in March 2020. Since then, the cases increased astronomically and the country's healthcare system could not contain it. However, the country's daily cases have reduced in recent times through the stringent measures introduced by the government and health sector as well as the introduction of vaccines. Aduhene and Osei-Assibey (2021) stated that the lockdown introduced by an executive instrument on restrictions in the two main cities-Accra and Kumasi- brought trauma, panic, societal humiliation, rise in the level of sadness and uneasiness among the people.

The Ghanaian economy which is mainly import driven and dominated by the informal sector and SMEs rely heavily on imports, however as a result of the pandemic, trading reduced drastically, but inflation and exchange rates are on the rise (Adu Amoah, 2020; Aduhene & Osei Asigbey 2021; Khoo 2020). According to Jo, Shim & Kim (2020), the outbreak of the pandemic aside the economic outcomes also brought several interruptions in consumer behaviour including job losses, daily routines. Major sectors of the economy have been hit strongly and the effects are seen mainly on the workforce who are also consumers. Consumers have suffered from high unemployment, high inflation, foreign exchange rates and rising cost of living. However, many post covid economic studies have focused on the socio-economic effects without much emphasis on the consumer effects of COVID-19, leaving a major gap which needs to be filled. Hence the focus of this chapter is to describe the impact on the Ghanaian economy in post covid era from the perspective of consumers and the coping strategies adopted.

LITERATURE REVIEW

COVID-19 was predicted to significantly impact on the world's economy (Bridgewater Advisors, 2020). Indeed, it affected the world to the extent that as at August 24, 2022, death due to COVID-19 was 6,476,509 across the globe (Worldometer, 2022). Other sectors were not spared either. According to Oum, Kates and Wexlex (2022), the economic impact of COVID-19 caused most countries economy to shrink; for example, Nicaragua's economy experienced -0.04% GDP growth and that of Angola was – 30.9%. Estimates provided by the IMF indicate that the global GDP fell by 3.9% in 2020 compared to 2019 figures. The United Nations Framework Report (2020) listed the COVID-19 as the major severe pandemic that has plunged global economy into recession since WW II. Probably, COVID-19 pandemic is second to the 1930s Great Depression in its devastating effects on the world economy. The group of workers (consumers) who were seriously affected by the outbreak of the COVID-19 includes people who earn wages on daily bases, businesses owners, migratory employees and those in exiles throughout the world; other affected workers are those in the tourism, aviation and the hotel industry (Aduhene and Osei-Assibey, 2021).

As opined by Shang, Li and Zhang (2021), existing literature show that pandemics (such as COVID-19) leave three main impacts - heatlh, economic and social- on a country. They contend that earlier studies used the partial equilibrium approach since they only look at the health effects and overlook other sectors that may be affected by the pandemic. Further, they argued that, the general equilibrium technique is to broadly examine all the effects of pandemics. Nonetheless, the main impact of pandemics is the increase in the number of deaths. Among others, the economic impacts include a fall in tax revenues, increases in health-related facilities like isolation centres, human resources requirement with their implications for government expenditure to increase (Bridgewater Advisors, 2020, and Shang et. al 2021). The pandemic brought huge fiscal constraints to governments as a result of providing social protection for the vulnerable coupled with drastic fall in tax mobilization (Kentikelenis, Gabor, Ortiz, Stubbs, McKee, and Stuckler, 2020).

In the Ghanaian economy, there was a huge government over spending (GoG, 2021). There was also reduction in labour supply due to illness, interruption in commuting people to and from work, and general restrictions on movements of human beings as well as goods and services (Onyina, 2021). All these have both negative and positive consequences on consumers. Additionally, there were socio-political impacts, demographic shifts, movement of population, a rise in social pressure and discrimination, and political unrest in countries with fragile institutions (Shang et. al 2021).

Though, Thelen (2010) uses the liberal market economies and coordinated market economies framework to argue that market tensions will in the end efficiently converge, However, Shang et. al (2021) claimed that the allies and non-allies of the aforementioned framework don't agree on its role, and that the help from government is necessary for firms to succeed in the globalized economy directly or indirectly. All these have the consumer at the center of activities. It has been argued by Anner (2020) that in addition to health implications; COVID-19 produced significant social and economic consequences on mankind, and that over the last three decades, the world has never being affected both at agricultural and industrial fronts to this extent.

During the COVID-19 pandemic at the global level, increased nationalism and protection for manufacturing independence in countries, allowed them to suspend exports; as a result, scarcity of general health suppliers emerged including medicines and personal protective equipment (PPE kits) (Shang et al. 2021). This was at the time when these products were mostly needed by producers and consumers alike. Thus, the supply chain processes that end with the consumer were seriously affected (Onyina, 2021).

A probable important positive impact from the COVID-19 pandemic is the rise in the use of electronic transactions and virtual meetings by the business world as well as consumers. In order to prevent infection, digitalization became the order of the day, paying of transaction via on-line purchases. Thus, the pandemic brought a form of popularity to digital activities, working from home, virtual meetings, and digital payment among others (Shang et. al, 2021, Huang, Sunn and Sui 2020, BoG, 2020 and 2022). In Ghana, available data show that the total value of transactions using mobile money interoperability was GHC1,640 billion compared to GHC13.6 billion value of cheques cleared at the banks in March 2020; the corresponding figures for March 2022 for mobile money interoperability was GHC2,796.9 billion compared to GHC21.8 billion cheques cleared at the banks (BoG 2020 and 2022). This became an opportunity for the software developers to come out with a lot of applications to meet the "new" demand for businesses and consumers.

The Economy of Ghana

The population of Ghana as reported by the Ghana Statistical Service (GSS) after the 2021 population and housing census stood at 30.8 million (GSS, 2021). The Ghanaian economy is dominated by the informal sector. GSS (2019) reported that the private formal and private informal sector employs 92.8% of the labour force. The trend (GSS 2013, and 2019) show that the private formal may at most employ less than 10% of the 92.8%; thus, the informal sector dominates the economy as reported by Onyina (2021).

The macroeconomic indicators in Ghana before the COVID-19 pandemic years were very remarkable as publicized by international organizations. For example, between 2000 and 2009 Ghana's average GDP growth was 5.4 percent, and was 6.8 percent between 2010 and 2019; Ghana was constantly rated among the first ten fastest-growing markets in Africa south of the Sahara (CSJ, 2022). Despite these impressive indicators, the economy depends heavily on imports (Adu Amoah, 2020; Aduhene & Osei Asigbey 2021).

The pandemic took the world by surprise and impacted on the world economy in diverse ways.

Available literature indicates various impacts on the Ghanaian economy. For example, Aduhene & Osei Asigbey (2021); GoG (2020); Ofori-Atta (2020); Deloitte (2020); Bamfo et. al 2020; GSS, (2020); and Laing (2020) all reported on the state of the Ghanaian economy. The following tables depict some of the effects of COVID-19 pandemic on the economy.

Table 1. Shortfalls in Revenue and increases in expenditure on selected variables for Ghana

Description of the variable	2020 budget (GHC billion)	Revised budget 2020 (GHC billion)	Remarks
Tax revenue (non-oil)	44.9	40.7	Fall in revenue
Non tax revenue (non-oil)	8.4	4.5	Fall in revenue
Oil revenue	6.9	3.8	Fall in revenue
Government expenditure	86.0	97.7	Increase in expenditure
Interest payment	21.7	26.3	Increase in expenditure
Other expenditure	3.0	14.1	Increase in expenditure

Source: GoG (2020)

Table 2. Shortfalls in revenues and subsidies provided by government

Description of the variable	Shortfall due to COVID-19
GDP	From 6.8% to 1,5%
Annual budget funding	3.5 billion
Stabilization fund	1.1 billion
Fiscal deficit	To increase to 30.0 billion
	Increases due to COVID-19
Syndicated support for industries	GHC3 billion
Basic utilizes bill	Up to 50% absorption by government
Frontline health workers	Allowance of 50% basic salary a month
Frontline health workers	Insurance package GHC350.000
Vulnerable people during lockdown	Provision of food items for over 400,000

Source: Bridgewater Advisers (2020)

As shown in Table 1, whereas non-oil for both tax revenue and non-tax revenue fell during the COVID era, government expenditure, interest payments on loans and other expenditure by government increased. Table 2 depicts items where Ghana experienced shortfalls in revenue, and those that the government has to increase funds allocation.

In all these, it must be noted that in providing support of various forms, consumers were not excluded. For example, government provided support business of various categories such that by December 2020, about GHC413 million has being provided as support to businesses, this helped to ensure that over 65,000 jobs were secured

(GoG, 2021). Furthermore, pharmaceutical manufacturers experienced demand for their products such as personal health care items, hand sanitizers among others; others were provided with the needed help to expand the industry. The general public also benefited from free water and electricity bills as the government paid these bills for a period; to the building of hospitals in districts without designated district government hospital popular known as "Agenda 111", and other health facilities across the country. For details of how the government supported all sectors of the economy during the pandemic, see Akuffo-Addo (2020 various updates on the measures taken against spread of COVID-19), and GoG, (2021) for details.

METHODOLOGY

To present a very realistic view of the economy from the consumer perspective, this chapter adopted qualitative methodology. The study was carried out in September 2022. It was carried out among a cross section of formal employees in Ghana who are expected to have better understanding of economic issues. Participants answered the questionnaire using online platforms. Respondents were mostly from the formal sectors of the economy including banking, teaching, accounting, healthcare and other sectors. In all about 82 respondents from all over the country participated.

Data collection involved extensive questions on how the pandemic has affected their job, finances, shopping behavior and general state of wellbeing. The narratives from the questions have been used for the analysis to present insight into their livelihood practical economy issues facing consumers in the former sector following the COVID-19 Pandemic.

Table 3. Demographic profile of respondent

Variable	Responses (Frequency)	Responses (%)
Gender: Male Female **Total**	51 30 **81**	63.0 37.0 **100**
Diploma/training colleges/tech/voc First degree Masters Phd **Total**	10 37 28 5 **80**	12.5 46.3 35.0 6.2 **100**
Age; Between 20 to 29 years Between 30 to 39 years Between 40 to 49 years Between 50 to 59 years Over 59 years **Total**	19 40 6 13 3 **81**	23.5 49.4 7.4 16.0 3.7 **100**
Employment status: Yes No **Total**	72 10 **82**	87.8 12.2 **100**
Marital Status: Married Single **Total**	49 33 **82**	59.8 40.2 **100**
Monthly Income Levels Below 1000 Between 1000 to 1999 Between 2000 to 2999 Between 3000 to 3999 Between 4000 to 4999 Over 5000 **Total**	12 16 22 4 9 19 **82**	14.6 19.5 26.8 4.9 11.0 23.2 **100**

The descriptive analysis in Table 3 above represents the demographic and other personal details relevant to the nature of the population in the study. In most economic studies, a critical aspect useful in the analysis is the demographic characteristics such as age, gender, occupation and others. The gender side shows that the male respondents were 67.0%t, thus more than their female counterparts of 37.0%. This shows a possibility of male dominance in the formal sector in Ghana, it could also be that male participants were more willing than females to participate. It is further possible that male who are the breadwinners of their families may have more economic responsibilities and may therefore have more challenges in the economic crises than women.

Age has also consistently been a significant demographic factor influencing a number of economic issues and moderating a number of behaviours. Data from the table shows most respondents (49.4%) are at their sandwiched ages 30-49 years where they are well established in the jobs. They are also likely to have children and other family responsibilities. This finding means that if their economic states are bad or worse it will be difficult to switch to a new job(s) or career due the stage of life, they find themselves. Hence any economic crises would mean a big challenge to make ends meet particularly if they have more dependents.

On the educational levels, quiet a number of respondents (58.8%) have up to first degree. With the economic crises, what it means is that even if they have plans to continue their education, they might not be able to do that now due to the current economic situation especially if they are funding their children's education. It is possible that those with higher educational levels will earn more and will have a better economic condition than those with relatively lower qualification. The findings further show that a lot of respondents are couples and have family responsibilities since close to 60% are married; and their economic hardships affects other people. It is possible that the few who have lost their jobs are family people whose children are feeling the impact of the economic crises far more than those who are single.

Table 4. Employment sectors of respondents

Sector	Frequency	Percent
Education Sector	22	27.2
Manufacturing Sector	3	3.7
Health Sector	7	8.6
Financial Sector	14	17.3
Engineering	8	9.8
Information Technology	3	3.7
Media	2	2.5
Others Sectors	22	27.2
Total	81	100

Again, 87.8% of the respondents are employed showing that not many people have lost their jobs, even though; job losses appear to be one of the major flops of the economic impact of the COVID-19 pandemic. The findings from this report suggest that job loss is relatively minimal. This is a lot hope for the few who have lost jobs that there might soon find jobs. The last demographic issue is the earning per month which has become a major issue in the Ghanaian economy. The findings show that 46.3% earn between 1000-2999 Ghana Cedis with a few higher and lower earnings. This shows that before the pandemic a lot of these employees were able to manage their economic situations better. However, with the advent of the pandemic, their earnings have become static without salary increment and the depreciation of the local currency against major convertible currencies. Also, with price instability as a result of galloping inflation, consumers have doubled their expenditure with same earnings and that is challenging for a lot of people especially employees who earn below 3000 Ghana Cedis. It is more likely to be challenging for a lot of formal sector employee to make ends meet by meeting their basic needs.

Depending on the sector where a respondent is employed, economic conditions can be better managed or worse.

From Table 4, respondents from the education sector were 27.2, though other sectors was also 27.2%, it is fragmented including administrators, revenue officers, accountants, local council workers among others. However, it must be noted that health workers were supported in diverse ways during the pandemic and are not expected to be affected like the rest of the sectors. During the pandemic, government provided several incentives to health workers as contained in the Presidential Updates (See Nana Addo, 2020). The next section discuses areas respondents indicated that the COVID-19 pandemic have impacted in their lives.

THE AREAS THE COVID-19 PANDEMIC HAS AFFECTED CONSUMERS

The chapter uses responses from participants to portray areas they have been affected by the pandemic. The table below portrays areas respondents indicated have impacted in their lives based on the themes.

Table 5. Description of current economic situation of respondents

Themes	Sample Responses/ Narratives	Findings
Bad/worse	1. Absolutely in a mess, 2. Not good at all 3. Not good, below average 4. It is getting worse every day. 5. My standard of living has fallen	Majority of respondents were of the view that their personal economic state is bad or worse since the pandemic came
Static/ tough	1. Everything is static, nothing is working. 2. Things are tough 3. Its not easy for me at all	It is hard and challenging for them to cope
High cost of living	1.Cost of living is very high now. 2. Prices are increasing everyday	Living conditions are so high that it is becoming unbearable for consumer
Normal	1. Normal, 2. Manageable,	A few are also staying in their normal zone on life, the economic hardship has not had significant impact on them.

The themes have been grouped into four namely bad/worse, static/tough, high cost of living, and normal. Per the responses, most employees were of the view that their current situations are bad or have been worsened by the economic issues arising from the pandemic. Some responded their lives had become static, challenging for them. As indicated above, what some of the respondents said about worse economic condition include, "*their economic situation is absolutely in a mess, not good at all,* and *it is getting worse every day*". This can be concluded that the pandemic has impacted negatively on their economic situation. Thus, the finding suggests that even though government and employer are doing their best for growth and sustainability, consumers are feeling the direct effects of the economic crises and are thinking about how they can be supported. The result is an indication that consumers are really feeling the impact of the pandemic in all facets of their lives.

The second theme is economic situation is static. Some of the statements of respondents who were of the view that economic situation is static are "*everything is static, nothing is working, things are tough* and *it is not easy for me at all*". This suggests that they are neither enjoying nor suffering. For those who have experience a static and tough is still within something or they are still managing. Such situations however, may have social and psychological implications such as anxiety, depression and other. It is a situation that people who have seen steady progress may not be able to bear over a long period of time. The next cohort theme is those who said there is high cost of living. Some of the things they said were "*cost of living is very high now"* and "*prices are increasing everyday*". Such consumers see the rising cost of living but there is nothing they can do; they are filling the effects of the rising cost. Those who see their lives as normal may have something supporting their lives or they are earning enough to support their livelihood. It could also be that they have saved enough or have relatively smaller financial responsibility so the "economic heat" to them is manageable. Such people can still manage to improve on their lives or do something for themselves.

The worst situation is those whose current economic situation has become bad or worse due to the pandemic. Some of have a messy economic state because they have lost money or job and are living below average or their standard of living has fallen. This condition presents a serious and devastating economic state which has significant social and psychological impacts such as lack of basic needs, adjustment to new lower living standards and the burden of thinking about their needs and how these can be met. The post pandemic environment may appear normal as if everyone is going about their normal duties, but such environment includes people who are really suffering and battling with serious economic and financial situations which they need to adjust and manage to survive. These issues may present themselves as economic, but suggest possible psychological and social issues. The next question is how the consumers manage these economic situations; this is addressed in the next section.

Table 6. Coping strategies used by respondents to manage the economic crises

Theme	Sample Narratives/responses	Findings
Managing expenditure	Cut down on expenses such as food I live within my means and buy only things which are urgent, I have cut down on expenses (2) I priortise my expenditure, drinking sachet water instead of bottle water I use economy of scale to manage I cut off most of my expenses I have packed my car and I take public transport I buy in bulk	In economic crises consumers apply existing knowledge to manage existing resources
Financial planning	I live with in my means. I spend on only essential items. Staying within my means and not window shopping I am managing the number of days I go to work	Consumers plan to manage their finance better because the money is not enough
Managing by extra job/business	I have started farming I am selling other things to support my life	Still some consumers are finding ways of generating additional income

Based on the economic states many consumers in the formal sectors are working out various personal strategies to cope better with their current circumstances. The first strategy adopted by a lot of the consumers is to contain their expenditure. The findings suggest that people are using cost cutting, scale of preference and bulk purchasing to manage the little economic resources they have available. Others also strategize by planning their finances in different ways such as buying lower priced products, buying only essential items and managing to stay within their means. Others have started additional business by selling or going into farming so they can earn extra income to supplement their budgets.

All these responses on economic coping strategies show that consumers are rational so when there are changes in their environment they plan and manage to survive. It also shows that consumers are adaptable change to adapt to new situations in their economic. Although consumers are all trying to manage their economic situations, these strategies do not take away the negative effects particularly to social and psychological effects from the economic down turn arising from the pandemic.

IMPLICATIONS

Consumers are the heart of business decisions and activities because every business exists to provide the needs of consumers. Understanding how consumers behave in daily purchasing and consumption is crucial in the planning and management of business and marketing decisions. Consumers and consumption practices play critical roles in marketing and corporate strategy by ensuring customer acquisition, retention, growth and general sustainability of the business. With the current economic hardship businesses will suffer from low purchasing power; hence low profitability. Businesses should work hard to get consumers to patronize their products and services.

The current economic situation requires strong organizational leaders who take strong and innovative decisions to rebuild their organizations so the employees can enjoy conditions of service that will support them to rebuild their economic live. Organizations should rethink strategic direction for sustainability and growth to enable business turnarounds that will improve employee livelihood.

Governments must strengthen economic policies to rebuild the economy so that the economy will bounce back for consumers to restore the economic state and improve their livelihoods. There should be strong economic decisions to support the vulnerable employees to maintain basic needs.

Individual consumers must strengthen themselves and develop resilience to cope better with current economic conditions and manage psychosocial the impact on them

CONCLUSION

This chapter attempted to present a portrait of the Ghanaian economic and impact of the COVID-19 pandemic and how it is affecting consumers in the formal sectors of the economy. Some of the measures that the government took to prevent the spread of the pandemic were also discussed. Here, the chapter shows that whereas there were decreases in revenue to be received by the government, there were increases in government expenditure on health-related activities to help prevent the spread of the pandemic. Also, the government paid utility bills for the population during the heat of the pandemic. Notwithstanding these, people have been affected by the pandemic in different ways.

Questionnaire was administered to respondents using social media platforms, and respondents willing to answer the questions responded. People from different sphere of life participated and were found in different parts of the country. It must be stated that, a bigger number of respondents was expected, but this was not the case. The responses not withstanding this shortfall were analyzed and thematic areas have been discussed in this chapter

It was observed that although the pandemic may be global but every economy may have a unique experience and perspective in the way in which consumers describe their current economic state and experience. Whereas some were of the view that, the current economic situation is bad or worse, others said it is normal. In between the two are those who said things are static or tough and those who said there is an increasing cost of living. In view of these experiences, it is not surprising that they have adopted some strategies so that they can manage of cope with the situation. Thus, the study identified the current state and the coping strategies being adopted by the consumers to minimize the effects on “economic” lifestyle. Implications for both the government and employers have also been provided to help reduce the effects inflicted by the COVID-19 pandemic.

REFERENCES

Aduhene, D. T., & Osei-Assibey, E. (2021). Socio-economic impact of COVID-19 on Ghana’s economy: Challenges and prospects. *International Journal of Social Economics*, *48*(4), 543–556. doi:10.1108/IJSE-08-2020-0582

Akuffo-Addo. (2020). *Updates on how Measures taken against spread of the COVID-19*. Akuffo-Addo.

Anner, M. (2020) *Abandoned? The Impact of Covid-19 on Workers and Businesses at the Bottom of Global Garment Supply Chains.*

Bamfo, I., Sarfo, J. O., Ansah, E. W., & Amoah, S. K. (2020). The impact of health on economic development: Ghana's COVID-19 management so far. *European Journal of Economic Studies*, *9*(1), 3–10.

BoG. (2020). *Summary of Economic and Financial Data*. Bank of Ghana, Accra. https://www.bog.gov.gh/wp-content/uploads/2020/08/Summary-of-Economic-and-Financial-Data-July-2020

BoG. (2022). *Summary of Economic and Financial Data. Bank of Ghana, Accra.* BoG. https://www.bog.gov.gh/wp-content/uploads/2022/08/Summary-of-Economic-and-Financial-Data-July-2022

Bridgewater Advisors. (2020). *Economic Impact of COVID-19: A summary of economic implications*. Bridgewater Advisors Limited.

CSJ. (2022). *A 20-Year Review of Ghana's Public Debt: Trends*. Drivers and Implications.

Deloitte. (2020). *Economic impact of COVID-19 Pandemic on the economy of Ghana: summary of fiscal measures and Deloitte views*. Deloitte.

Ghana Statistical Service. (2020). Mobility Analysis to support the Government of Ghana in responding to the COVID-19 outbreak. *Stats Ghana*. https://statsghana.gov.gh/gsspublications.php?category=MTkwMDE4MjI2Ny4xMDg=/webstats/90r897632o (accessed August 2020).

GoG. (2020). *Mid-Year Review of the Biudget Statement of Economic Policy of Government of Ghana and Supplementary Estimates for the Financial Year*. Ministry of Financial and Economic Planning.

GoG. (2021). *The Budget Statement and Economic Policy of the Government of Ghana for the Year 2022*. Ministry of Finance.

Gössling, S., Scott, D., & Hall, C. M. (2020). Pandemics, tourism and global change: A rapid assessment of COVID-19. *Journal of Sustainable Tourism*, 1–20.

GSS. (2013). *2010 population and housing census: National analytical report*. Ghana Statistical Service.

GSS. (2019). *Ghana living standard survey (GLSS7). Main report*. Ghana Statistical Service Accra.

GSS. (2021). *2021 Population and Housing Census: Press Release on provisional results*. Ghana Statistical Service, Accra.

Huang, Y., Sun, M., & Sui, Y. (2020). How digital contact tracing slowed Covid-19 in East Asia. *Harvard Business Review*. https:// hbr.org/2020/04/how-digital-contact-tracing-slowed-covid-19-in-east-asia

Kentikelenis, A., Gabor, D., Ortiz, I., Stubbs, T., McKee, M., & Stuckler, D. (2020). Softening the blow of the pandemic: Will International Monetary Fund and World Bank make things worse? *The Lancet. Global Health*, *8*(6), e758–e759. doi:10.1016/S2214-109X(20)30135-2 PMID:32278363

Laing, T. (2020, April). The economic impact of the Coronavirus 2019 (Covid-2019): Implications for the mining industry. *The Extractive Industries and Society*, *7*(2), 580–582. doi:10.1016/j.exis.2020.04.003 PMID:32300537

Ofori-Atta. (2020). *Economic impact of COVID-19 pandemic on the economy of Ghana. Ministry of Finance statement to parliament on 30th March 2020*. Ministry of Finance.

Onyina, P. A. (2021). A Literature Review of the Consequences of a Lockdown Ghanaian Economy Dominated by the Informal Sector during the COVID-19 Pandemic Era. *Pentvars Business Journal*, *13*(1), 89–98.

Oum, S., Kates, J., & Wexlex, A. (2022). *Econiomic Impact of COVID-19 on PEPFAR Countries*. KKF Foundation.

Shang, Y., Li, H., & Zhang, R. (2021). Effects of Pandemic Outbreak on Economies: Evidence From Business History Context. *Frontiers in Public Health*, *9*, 632043. doi:10.3389/fpubh.2021.632043 PMID:33777885

Thelen, K. (2010). Varieties of capitalism and business history. *Business History Review*, *84*, 646–648. doi:10.2307/27917300 6

United Nations. (2020). *A UN framework for the immediate socio-economic response to COVID-19*. UN. https://www.un.org/sites/un2.un.org/files/un_framework_report_on_covid-19.pdf

Worldometer. (2022). *COVID-19 Coronavirus Pandemic Reported Cases and Deaths by Country or Territory*. WorldoMeter. www.worldometer.info [accessed on 24 Aug 2022, 7.53 am]

Chapter 3
A Conceptual Model Development of COVID-19's Impact on Bangladeshi Faculty Member's Psychological Wellbeing

Hamida Mosharraf Moniea
North South University, Bangladesh

Tasnim Tarannum
North South University, Bangladesh

Mohammad Khasro Miah
North South University, Bangladesh

Carlos M. Osegueda
Independent Researcher, Bangladesh

ABSTRACT

The novel coronavirus, Covid-19, made its initial appearance in Wuhan, China, in December 2019. Since then, the virus has spread quickly over the globe and has been regarded as one of the deadliest pandemics. This study establishes a framework developed to identify and understand the role of specific central determinants of the psychological effects that the response to Covid-19 has had on Bangladeshi faculty members. An in-depth interview of 20 faculty members of Bangladeshi public and private universities provides acumen and guidance into the motives, strategic opportunities, and constraints of this research. The current study provides future implications of the vital distinctive facets of different contingent and contextual variables' influence on mental well-being, revealing a new avenue for developing a ground-breaking theory.

DOI: 10.4018/978-1-7998-9213-7.ch003

INTRODUCTION

In December 2019, the first appearance of the novel coronavirus, COVID-19, was identified in Wuhan, China, and the virus spread rapidly across the world. The World Health Organization labeled it a global pandemic as the situation worsened. Mass confinement started across the globe through strict restrictions on outdoor activities and the closure of educational institutions, public spaces, and public congregations (WHO, 2020). As a safety measure, all educational institutions and private and official offices in Bangladesh were temporarily closed from March 16, 2020. As researchers studied the adverse impact of the COVID-19 pandemic on physical health, it was observed that this virus significantly influences individuals' psychological status and well-being (Huang & Zhao, 2020; Ahorsu et al., 2020). Several studies were conducted to assess the general population's psychological health and conditions and identify the various factors that can be catalysts for mental health disorders. Research by Wang et al. (2020) revealed moderate to severe psychosomatic impact, anxiety, depression, and stress among the Chinese population during the pandemic. The level of impact intensified among respondents' particular criteria, especially among females, students, and others with specific health problems.

Similarly, a study conducted by Huang and Zhao (2020) in China exhibits that, due to COVID-19, the younger generation is more likely to suffer from generalized anxiety disorder and depressive symptoms than the older generation. Constant exposure to negative information regarding COVID-19 made the participants suffer from fear, anxiety, and depression (Ahorsu et al., 2020). Ahorsu et al. (2020) reported that the distress surrounding COVID-19 had caused psychological trauma, such as widespread concern, fear, and anxiety among Iranian participants. Another study by Satici et al. (2020) on Turkey's general population to explore the relationships between fear of the infectious virus, mental distress, and life satisfaction showed that psychological trauma was positively correlated with the fear of COVID-19. Zhang et al. (2020) identified severe depressive symptoms and anxiety among the public and patients who already suffered from coronavirus infection; depression was high, mostly among patients infected with COVID-19.

Furthermore, individuals who contracted COVID-19 were shown to have a depressed mood and other symptoms such as anxiety and constant irritation. Many healthcare employees suffer from stress, anxiety, and depression (Spoorthy et al., 2020). Additionally, 24.9 percent of college students experienced anxiety due to the epidemic (Cao et al., 2020). Further research indicated that anxiety levels among college students varied depending on various circumstances, including where they lived, their parents' income source, and whom they lived with (e.g., their parents, a relative, or someone who was COVID-19 positive.

Spoorthy et al.'s (2020)study showed thatanxiety symptoms concerning COVID-19 were also linked to concerns about the virus's economic impact, academic delays, and impact on daily life. Additionally, 24.9 percent of college students experienced anxiety due to the epidemic (Cao et al., 2020). Akdeniz et al. (2020) observedthat Turkish university students were more fearful of their relatives being infected by the virus than themselves being infected by it. University faculty members underwent a similar situation, as they were also facing constant psychological pressure and fear of job loss, reduced salary, a tech-dependent education system, an altered lifecycle, and being infected with the virus (Imran & Ahmed, 2020; Talidong&Toquero, 2020; Ammar et al., 2020).

THE RATIONALE OF THE PROPOSED STUDY AND RESEARCH GAP

Since the outbreak of COVID-19, several studies have been conducted to assess the impact of the epidemic on various groups' psychological health, such as the public, healthcare workers, and students. However, to the best of the researchers' knowledge, no previous theoretical research has yet to be conducted to build and propose a conceptual framework to understand the impact of the COVID-19 pandemic on the psychological health of Bangladesh's academic personnel. Thus, this study will identify various potential factors responsible for psychosocial complications among private and public university faculty members. This framework can serve several purposes:

- It can be used to understand better the specific determinants and their effects on faculty members' mental health.
- The framework can provide valuable insights to the university and its faculty members as they prepare for, respond to, and recover from the pandemic's impact.
- This paper can create a pathway for researchers to conduct further studies examining and assessing the impact of the pandemic on academicians' psychological conditions.

METHODOLOGY

In-depth interview was conducted for this study, according to Saunders (2012). The purpose of the in-depth interviews was to obtain a deeper understanding of the effect of the COVID-19 outbreak on the psychological health of Bangladesh's faculty members. During the in-depth interview, participants were encouraged and prompted to speak at length on the subject matter that was being investigated. As a result of the limited number of participants, a more thorough analysis of the interviews was possible, making in-depth interviews an excellent choice for this study. 20 professors from four public universities and four private universities were asked about their experiences and their knowledgeable opinions on the topic. The researchers used this approach to gather data, preparing a detailed set of targeted questions. The researchers made sure to keep in mind the many domains and particular subject matters that were going to be discussed throughout the interview. This specific framework, which includes both internal and external contextual elements, has been designed based on the information acquired from interviews with university faculty members. During the COVID-19 outbreak, these factors have been discovered as having substantial detrimental effects on the psychological health of university faculty members in Bangladesh.

The Psychological Impact of COVID-19 on Faculty Members

TheCOVID-19 pandemic has had several adverse effects on Bangladesh's economic and social well-being. These include a decrease in economic activity, a substantial loss of employment, export reduction, and a rise in the prevalence of poverty (Bar, 2021). Several socio-cultural and demographic factors are essential to a person's psychological well-being during an epidemic outbreak. Faculty age, gender, marital status, academic position, kind of employment contract, type of institution, and a family's average annual income were all catalysts for causing stress and mental pressure among university faculty members (Liu et al., 2020; González-Sanguino, 2020; Malsich et al., 2020). Faculty members endure severe-moderate stress as they manage several teaching, research, administrative, and family responsibilities (Meng &Wang, 2018). Younger professors, particularly females and those in lower academic positions are at a higher risk of suffering mental distress as they are anxious about preserving their financial stability throughout the epidemic. COVID-19 triggered a severe economic downturn, resulting in significant scale reductions in production, supply, government spending, and long-term unemployment. People were worried about job loss, reduced income, debts, access to essential goods and commodities, unhealthy living conditions, and an uncertain future (Godinic et al., 2020). People face increasing difficulty procuring food, accessing healthcare facilities, and using daily utility services such as water, gas, and electricity during the lockdown (Odii et al., 2020). Food production and supply might emerge as one of the biggest COVID-19-related challenges, as 135 million people were already facing food shortages in developing countries, and the number was predicted to rise in 2020 as employment, GDP, and disposable income deteriorated due to the global crisis (WFP, 2020). The economic consequences of this pandemic have been profound for the academic community (Watermeyer et al., 2020; Imran & Ahmed, 2020; Li et al., 2020).

The growth of Bangladesh's GDP fell dramatically to 3.5% in fiscal year (FY) 2020 from 8.2% in fiscal year (FY) 2019. The estimated growth rate forFY 2021 was 5.5%. In light of this decline in growth, the International Labor Organization projected in November 2021 that Bangladesh lost 5 million full-time employments in FY 2021. Moreover, according to the Bangladesh Bureau of Statistics, the virus's spread in the second half of 2020 caused the unemployment rate to peak at 22.4%. As a result, the incidence of poverty was anticipated to rise above the pre-pandemic national average of 20.5%. With the significant expenditures on health, social security, and relief and recovery measures, the budget deficit was anticipated to exceed the government's objective of 5% until at least FY 2023 (Bar, 2021).

As COVID-19 spread, employees worldwide were compelled to adjust to working from home throughflexible working arrangements. University faculty members were in a similar predicament as they adjusted to online distance learning, a platform with which most students and professors needed to familiarize themselves. Teachers were immediately confronted with many of obstacles and issues resulting from online education. As distance learning is based entirely on online modes such as videos, exercises, images, and audio (Rapanta et al., 2020), preparing and uploading such content for timely learning was laborious. Moorhouse (2020) found that the main challenges in such cases were synchronizing activities and keeping students engaged in discussions. As a result, the classes became teacher-oriented, where the teacher kept repeating the contents, and most of the students remained silent. The students rarely talked and instead sent chat messages for communication.

As students kept their cameras off, non-verbal communication became limited, making it more difficult to involve students or ensure participation. As different universities adopted numerous online assessments for the mid-term and final examinations during the pandemic, checking these exam scripts online has been inordinately exhausting, painful, and tiresome for teachers. On the one hand, technical issues such as poor connectivity and low audio quality were the primary reasons for the students' absence from online classes. On the other hand, unstable internet connections, a lack of equipment, a large workload, and work-related anxiety were the primary reasons teachers remained absent from online classes (Zeeshan et al., 2020). Along with these factors, higher stress levels and the fear of adapting to complicated technological mechanisms negatively affected teachers' performance and productivity during the pandemic (Quezada, 2020; Christian et al., 2020).

Additionally, restrictions on local and international travel, a prohibition on large gatherings, and the closure of institutions were prevalent worldwide due to the COVID-19 outbreak (Khatatbeh, 2020). International travelers were urged to self-quarantine, and all domestic flights and public transportation were halted in

Bangladesh (Mahmud & Buckee, 2020). The public adopted various defensive measures, such as avoiding public gatherings, maintaining social distancing, wearing face masks, and frequent hand sanitizing (WHO, 2020). Several researchers have found negative psychological impactsfrom isolation, including irritability, anger, frustration, depression, loneliness, and even suicide (Jaiswal & Arun, 2020; Brooks et al., 2020). Post-traumatic stress disorder (PTSD) is positively related to quarantine length, and post-quarantine psychological effects can cause further significant psychological symptoms. Such a situation is also prevalent among academic personnel, as studies have shown that educators and researchers feel severe anxiety and stress during the pandemic due to restrictions on movement (Talidong&Toquero, 2020; Ammar et al., 2020).

Along with healthcare workers and medical academicians, university professors were also concerned with getting infected with COVID-19, economic uncertainty, adaptation to online teaching, and social isolation. According to Mowbray (2020), the fear of transmitting the virus or getting infected heightened the anxiety of healthy people and those with previous psychological disorders. In addition, mental health further deteriorated in families that maintained isolation at home due to a fear of contaminating each other or relatives. Concurrently, researchers showed in their studies that academic personnel experienced significant stress as a result of the fear and tension of spreading the virus among close family members (Ammar et al., 2020; Harper et al., 2020; Dryhurst et al., 2020).

Furthermore, Narayanan et al. (2020) have observed tremendous changes in the daily habits of the public, such as awareness about the disease, preventive measures followed, and changes in media and technology usage. Due to mass confinement worldwide, people's lifestyles have suddenly changed, changing their leisure activities, daily habits, and sleep quality. Such alternations have generated stress, anxiety, and worries about health, jobs, financial problems, and uncertainty regarding the future, leading to long-term psychological problems and mental health disorders (Morin et al., 2020). Teachers have also been affected by such sudden changes in lifestyle patterns. Those with children struggle to combine work with other family responsibilities, such as teaching their children, caring for older or sick family members, handling household chores, and managing their mental health. According to Ammar et al. (2020), changes in teaching, the closure of workplaces, and the termination or postponement of several research projects have created stress among university faculty members.

Conceptual Framework

This study establishes a framework developed to identify and understand the role of specific central determinants of the psychological effects that the response to

COVID-19 has had on faculty members, which are interconnected on theoretical grounds. These are the Conservation of Resources Theory, Maslow's Hierarchy, the Theory of Abnormality, and Circadian Rhythm. These contributing factors have been divided mainly into outer contextual contributors (factors beyond our control) and inner contextual contributors (within our control). The contingent variable in this research is the faculty members' mental well-being during the pandemic. The effect of economic volatility on faculty members' mental health can be linked with the Conservation of Resources Theory by Hobfoll (1989). During this COVID-19-linked economic instability, an individual faculty member could experience psychological stress on three occasions: when they risk losing resources, the loss resources, or are unsuccessful in obtaining resources (Debus & Unger, 2017; Halbesleben et al., 2014; Hobfoll, 1989). Connecting to the current crisis, the downsizing due to COVID-19-related economic uncertainty caused numerous people to lose competence, autonomy, and relatedness, negatively impactingtheir mental health (Godinic et al., 2020).

The impact of migrating to online learning platforms can be explained by the composition of abnormality (Feldman, 2014). Concerning this research, educators' actions and activities might be regarded as non-standard or atypical if they are rarely performed; such non-standard behavior produces personal distress and anxiety. In other words, using a virtual setting to perform essential tasks, such as giving exams to ensure students are learning well at university, can negatively affect faculty member's mental health.

The social need component of Maslow's hierarchy of needs theory can be linked toCOVID-19 combating measures. Jaiswal & Arun (2020) note that the combat measures have primarily threatened the fundamental need for a sense of belongingness and social connection, negatively affecting psychological well-being. As faculty members employ the virtual platform exclusively for work and not socializing, the self-containment tactics may harm their psychological impacts. Dubey et al. (2020) reported such a psychological impact on other professionals. According to the researchers, isolation has been reported to have psychological repercussions ranging from moderate irritability, anger, and frustration to extremes such as violence and suicide.

The outbreak has caused concern about human safety, directly affecting Maslow's safety needs component. This component becomes an active mobilizer of the organism's resources during awar, natural catastrophes, and illnesses (Wisner & Adams, 2002; Maslow, 1943). A fundamental characteristic of humanity has been the urge to be shielded from anything unknown that risks survival (Maslow, 1943). As a result, the fear of infection among faculty members is likely to grow if a close family member tests positive from the virus, thus endangering their safety.

This constrained but technologically gadget-dependent lifestyle significantly influences workers' circadian rhythms (Salgado-Delgado et al., 2011). According to Altena et al. (2020) and Feldman (2013), the circadian rhythm is important in controlling faculty members' biological clocks and sleep-wake cycles. The widespread use of technology gadgets encourages employees, particularly faculty members, to stay awake for extended periods at night, disturbing the circadian cycle. The circadian rhythm, which is governed by different elements such as daylight (Feldman, 2013), mealtimes and physical activities (Altena et al., 2020), and social and modern life activities, has a complicated psychological impact on faculty members and their families (Salgado-Delgado et al., 2011). Faculty members feel despair, stress, and anxiety due to the circadian rhythm disturbance during the COVID-19 crisis (Altena et al., 2020).

Figure 1. Factors determining psychological wellbeing of university faculty members

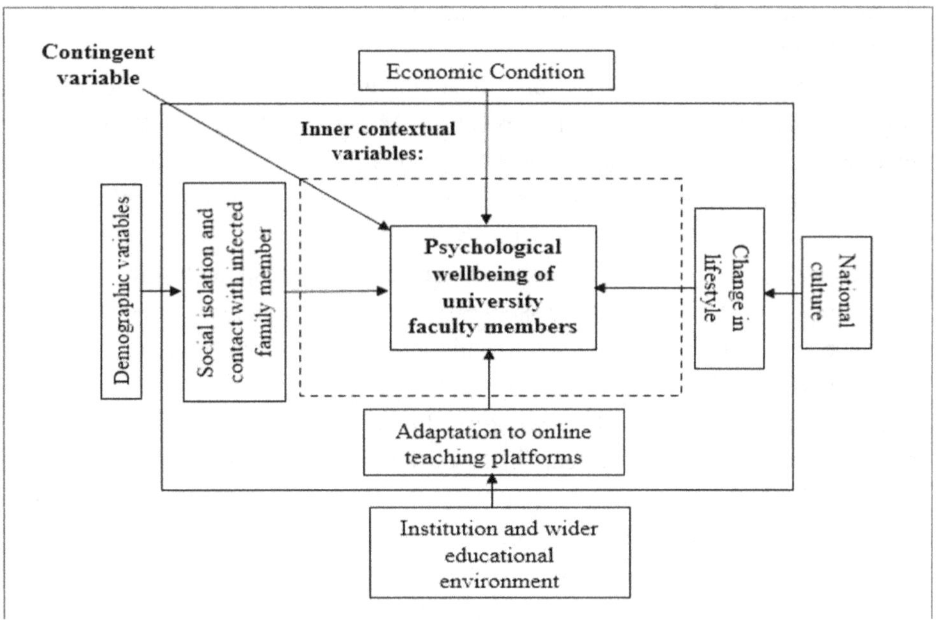

Factors that are beyond the control of a human being have been placed as external contextual contributing factors. These include national cultural elements such as social norms, rituals, and other regulations that govern social connections and relationships among people in a particular culture. For example, Bangladesh is a majority Muslim nation where participation in the Jum'ah prayer is a significant social norm. Jum'ah is the Friday noon prayer period when Muslims congregate for congregational devotion. Imams deliver a sermon (khutbah) after the prayer. In response to the coronavirus outbreak, Bangladesh's Prime Minister, Sheikh

Hasina, urged Muslims to do Friday prayers at home instead of at the mosque (Kamruzzaman, 2020). To prevent the spread of the virus, she recommended that residents avoid crowded locations and remain at home. However, the safety measures were negatively received by the majority-Muslim nation as the people responded in anger and frustration. People celebrated the Bengali New Year virtually under a nationwide lockdown (Mondira, 2021). Online celebrations were organized by cultural institutions and event venues. Chhayanaut organized virtual programs with Bangladesh Television (BTV) to celebrate PohelaBoishakh in lieu of its usual meeting at the capital's RamnaBatamul to usher in the Bengali 1428 calendar year. Mangal Shobhajatra is an annual procession organized by the Faculty of Fine Art at Dhaka University, also known as Charukola. This procession has been postponed two years in a row, and Charukola has responded by turning to the virtual media. Since they had never been in such a circumstance before, the professors and students of Charukola found the constraints brought on by the epidemic to be both shocking and challenging.

Demographic variables have also been included here, such as age, gender, religion,maritalstatus and academic position. Meng and Wang (2018) found that personal characteristics such as age, professional ranking, andemploymentlength significantly impact faculty members' stress levels. Younger faculty members below 40 were more stressed in their profession than older ones since they struggled more to maintain financial stability and combine work and family responsibilities. Assistant professors' stress was higher than associate professors and tenured professors due to the uncertainties of being promoted to a higher position. According to the findings of Mosleh et al. (2022), the number of years spent teaching was directly correlated to the amount of stress felt by the individual. In the study, participants who had 7–10 years of experience in online teaching reported higher levels of stress compared to those who had 4–6 years of experience in online teaching. Also, the research found, married academics with school-age children were more likely to experience personal exhaustion.

Horesh et al. (2020) conducted a preliminary study on 204 Israelis during the initial stage of COVID-19. They observed that most young participants perceive a moderate-high stress level, indicating that younger people, mostly with chronic illnesses, are more likely to perceive distress during this period. According to Huang et al. (2020), gender inequality in academia has become noticeable over the last few decades, and the pandemic has exacerbated these inequalities for women. During this pandemic, domestic chores, child nurturing, and elder care created additional burdens on female academicians in their most comfortable zones. Moreover, the burden has become heavier on women due to other unfavorable factors such as race, ethnicity, age, economic class, and dependent status.

Based on the above information, we present the first proposition of the study:

Proposition 1:National culture and socio-demographic variables psychologically impact university faculty members during the COVID-19 pandemic.

The country's wider educational environment and economic condition have been considered external contextual factors since these broadly vary from one country to another and often lie beyond the control or choice of individuals. Anderson et al. (2020) reveal that the private sector is most affected by the coronavirus in Denmark. Job insecurity has been higher in private sector jobs than in public sector jobs, as private business sector employees are losing jobs more frequently than in the public sector. The faculties of public universities failed to adapt efficiently to online teaching because they were overloaded with credit hours by the university authority and had little experience using audio-visual teaching aids (Zeeshan et al., 2020). As economic turmoil has worsened since the outbreak, innumerable people have lost their jobs. For this, many people are in deep fear of losing their job, reduced income, increased debts, and a lack of access to satisfactory essential services and resources that can significantly deteriorate their living standards (Hamouche, 2020; Shigemura et al., 2020; Godinic et al., 2020). Godinic et al. (2020) note that the downsizing due to COVID-19 is causing numerous people to lose their jobs and suffer financially, negatively impacting their mental health. The economic impact of this pandemic has been profound on the academic community. Watermeyer et al. (2020) surveyed educators working in different universities in the UK and showed that several respondents, whose job nature is contractual, are in deep uncertainty regarding contract renewal and are uncertain about their income source.

Along with other countries, Bangladesh has experienced a severe economic downturn due to the spread of the COVID-19 virus. Since mid-March 2020, the outbreak of COVID-19 has devastated the startup enterprises of Bangladesh. About 24% of enterprises stated that they were forced to cease operations, and 50% reported a decline in income, jeopardizing 1.5 million jobs, with a projected yearly loss of $53 million by 2020. In addition, the Economist Intelligence Unit (EIU) predicted that the graduate unemployment rate would rise from 47% to 58% in 2020 because of the economic crisis caused by COVID-19. The rise in unemployment diminished national and worldwide demand for commodities and RMG products. Three million graduates out of 25 million paid workers were expected to lose their jobs (Neazy, 2019).

Furthermore, Li et al. (2020) discovered that anxiety affects 13.67 percent of 88,611 Chinese teachers. A large percentage of respondents between the ages of 60 and 100 suffered from a high level of anxiety related to the anticipated risk of insufficient income to cover excessive spending on medical treatments. Imran and Ahmed (2020) found that employees in the education sector with a higher uncertainty of losing their jobs have severe stress levels compared to those who are not at the same risk. Most employees were not content with their salaries during the crisis period and felt they deserved extra care from the institution. Debus & Unger (2017) also showed that a life partner's job insecurity could be an additional threat that can negatively affect overall mental health.

Proposition 2: The institutional and wider educational environments, and economic conditions, have had a psychological impact on university faculty members during the COVID-19 pandemic.

Thisstudy identifies four internal contextual contributing factors that play a significant role in mental and psychological well-being. These are changes in lifestyle, a change in the teaching platform mode, social isolation as a preventive measure, and the fear of getting infected with the virus. In addition, other factors have been identified as "inner variables" since these are mainly under the control of individuals and can vary from person to person living in the same country.

The first internal contextual contributor is a lifestyle change. To prevent the virus's spread, the Bangladesh government decided on March 16, 2020, to shut all educational institutions, from elementary to tertiary, until March 31, 2020. This decision was extended until the end of September 2021. People's daily lives were significantly altered during the lockdown imposed due to the outbreak of the COVID-19 pandemic. Bangladeshi children awoke in the morning to attend their online lessons (Reza, 2021; Zarif, 2021). Preparing for school changed. Parents were not required to prepare them or make tiffin, but simply to ensure that the wi-fi was operational and the laptop's battery was well charged. Like rest of the world, people in Bangladesh had grown weary of staying indoors for a longtime. Thus, they experimented with different culinary preparations, paintings and shared them on social media to relieve the routine.The pandemic also caused a shift in the way people took care of their health in Bangladesh. People began wearing face masks, washing their hands and using hand sanitizer, inhaling vapor, drinking hot water, and taking medications and vitamin C. These practices became the new standard after the outbreak (Reza, 2021; Zarif, 2021). Research conducted in India by Narayanan et al. (2020) observed that people from all professional backgrounds exhibited changes in several life habits. The changes in life habits, such as preventive measures adopted, media/technology usage, and the growth of new hobbies or interests, had a noticeable impact on their mental health. A significant proportion of this study's respondents were involved in teaching, and it was found that their lifestyle patterns significantly changed during this period. According to Talidong and Toquero (2020), Philippine teachers coped by working out, consuming vitamins, and following government-provided safety measures to combat anxiety during COVID-19. During the period of the quarantine, these teachers engaged in the following activities in the following proportions: 25.6 percent watching television; 23.8 percent cooking; 11.9 percent working out; 8.7 percent sleeping; 5.9 percent playing games on electronic devices;

5.9 percent gardening; 4.1 percent writing; 3.6 percent making use of the internet; 3.2 percent cleaning the home; 2.3 percent reading; and 1.4 percent praying.

The second internal contributing factor is a change in the teaching platform. Switching to an online teaching platform created an additional burden on faculties. In July-2020, Dhaka University and several other institutions and colleges started offering online courses in Bangladesh (Hossain, 2020). Most campus activities before the changes were based on face-to-face sessions, such as delivering lectures, conducting interactive sessions, and conducting laboratory experiments. For online courses, teachers relied primarily on online content such as videos, exercises, images, and audio (Rapanta et al., 2020). The transition was difficult for most teachers, as online learning had several challenges. Mahmud et al. (2021) highlighted various concerns and challenges of instructors in Bangladeshi online education, including unfamiliarity with technology and difficulties in adapting to the new teaching platform. Another difficulty faced by teachers was the need for more communication. According to Moorhouse (2020), engaging students in online discussions is challenging. They rarely talked and preferred text chatting for communication, and the tutor reiterated the texts from the PowerPoint slides without further elaboration. Teachers lost touch with students during online courses because pupils were unresponsive to their teachings. When the pupils switched off their cameras, their professors could not establish eye contact or interpret their body language. Poorly presented class lectures caused students to disengage from a lesson; hence, they opted to stay silent rather than ask questions. When students turn off their cameras and hardly reply to lectures, instructors feel uneasy while lecturing, thus forcing them to exert more effort to capture students' attention in online classrooms. As students kept their cameras off due to privacy concerns, non-verbal communication was impossible, making it harder for the tutors to make sessions engaging and interesting. University teachers were also anxious about the increased possibility of cheating among students during online examinations and the requirement of more time and effort to prepare for and evaluate online reviews and evaluations (Akour et al., 2020).

As teachers attempted to adjust and adapt to sophisticated technology, work productivity fell due to technostress and techno-complexity (Christian et al., 2020; Zeeshan et al., 2020). According to Zeeshan et al. (2020), faculties face difficulties adapting to online teaching systems mainly because of their fear of technology and the lack of facilities such as electronic devices, poor camera and voice quality, and a loss of internet connection. Poor internet connection, lack of hardware, work stress, depression, and work-related anxiety are the primary reasons teachers remain absent from online classes. Experts, faculty members, and students also expressed concern over the accessibility of online classrooms for many students in Bangladesh. Poorer students, especially in rural areas, don't have the necessary hardware and internet connections to participate in their lessons (Jasim, 2020). The Daily Star (2020) argued that online courses would exacerbate the educational gap in Bangladesh by causing the most disadvantaged students, who often attend public colleges on scholarships, to lag behind their classmates owing to a lack of accessibility.

Proposition 3: Alteration in lifestyle and teaching platforms psychologically impact university faculty members during the COVID-19 pandemic.

COVID-19 safety measures, such as self-isolation and other quarantine strategies, may have had adverse psychological effects on faculty members as their fundamental duties mainly depend on face-to-face interaction, discussion, and consultation (Dubey et al., 2020). Due to the contagious nature of the disease, people feared spreading it to their close family members and getting infected with the virus. When any close family member is tested positive for this contagious disease, it creates a fear of getting infected, ultimately damaging their psychological condition. Mowbray (2020) found that the fear of getting infected and contaminating other family members can elevate anxiety in healthy personalities and those with existing mental health problems. A survey by Ammar et al. (2020) on dental academics found that the coronavirus was an essential source of stress. One of the primary sources of stress was restricted movement due to the lockdown and several protective measures, such as avoiding public places and mass gatherings and cleaning hands frequently. Talidong&Toquero (2020) note that Philippine teachers prefer social distancing, wearing a face mask to avoid public places as a precautionary measure, and are quite afraid to be a part of a large gathering. According to Ammar et al. (2020), the protective behaviors adopted by dental academics changed with other factors, such as fear of close ones getting infected and a lack of connection with family members, friends, or colleagues. Such fears and tensions induce severe stress among the respondents, as it was observed that fear of infection had a vital and direct relationship with stress levels (Harper et al., 2020; Dryhurst et al., 2020). As a result of these findings, self-isolation was identified as the third contextual contributing factor that affected mental and psychological well-being.

Self-isolation can result in several mental health disorders, such as irritation, anger, sleeping disorders, and insomnia, leading to violence and suicide. In addition, anyone remaining isolated due to suspected cases may have suffered from anxiety and developed obsessive-compulsive symptoms (Liu et al., 2020). Post-traumatic stress disorder (PTSD) was also positively related to the length of quarantine, and post-quarantine psychological effects caused significant psychological problems (Brooks et al., 2020). In a nation as densely populated as Bangladesh, it appeared unlikely that its citizens would be able to follow WHO and government recommendations about social distancing during the recent COVID-19 epidemic. Nevertheless, despite the challenges, distancing was one of the most critical and vital precautions that Bangladeshis took during the COVID-19 outbreak. These recommendations also led to several situations in Bangladesh where police officers used force to maintain order and social distancing (Sajid, 2020). Additionally, improperly maintaining social distancing measures created a fear of contracting COVID-19 and infecting other family members, friends, and acquaintances (Mahmud, 2020).

Our last proposition of the study draws from academicians' stress generated from fear of spreading the disease among close friends and relatives and maintaining isolation as a form of preventive measure:

Proposition 4: Social isolation and contact with infected family members psychologically impact university faculty members during the COVID-19 pandemic.

CONCLUSION

This study's significance lies in understanding the pandemic's acute and long-term psychological impact on Bangladesh's public and private university faculty members. Academic personnel have a significant role in expediting knowledge and building the backbone of a nation. Thus, understanding their mental health condition during the pandemic can positively contribute to their long-term development.

The literature, methodologies, models, and concepts we applied to build a conceptual framework managed a more significant phenomenon. The researchers constructed a conceptual framework that outlined the essential contributing factors and delineated their impact on mental health faculty members. For example, suppose the relationships between possible risk factors and other psychiatric distress (such as depression, fear, stress, and anxiety) can be established. In that case, the conceptual framework will help faculty members avoid unsafe factors and follow precautionary measures. The study will also help university authorities understand how a teacher's performance is affected during a pandemic. Since a teacher's performance has a crucial impact on the university, the administration can formulate effective measures to overcome it.

Furthermore, improving faculty members' psychological health will positively impact other related areas, such as teaching, research, innovation, and productivity, as they are among the main contributors to growth in those sectors. Finally, this framework can enable researchers to conduct additional studies examining and assessing academicians' psychological conditions during the global pandemic, advancing the discipline and practice of embedded research. Therefore, further studies are suggested with a larger population to refine and test the framework, which will help further explore and assess the psychological impact of the COVID-19 pandemic on university faculty members.

ACKNOWLEDGMENTS

This study was funded by a grant from the Conference Travel and Research Grants Committee 2020-2021, North South University. Nevertheless, the interpretations, conclusions, and recommendations are those of the writers and do not essentially represent the views of the Conference Travel and Research Grants Committee.

REFERENCES

Ahorsu, D. K., Lin, C.-Y., Imani, V., Saffari, M., Griffiths, M. D., & Pakpour, A. H. (2022). The Fear of COVID-19 Scale: Development and Initial Validation. *International Journal of Mental Health and Addiction*, *20*(3), 1537–1545. doi:10.100711469-020-00270-8 PMID:32226353

Akdeniz, G., Kavakci, M., Gozugok, M., Yalcinkaya, S., Kucukay, A., & Sahutogullari, B. (2020). A Survey of Attitudes, Anxiety Status, and Protective Behaviors of the University Students During the COVID-19 Outbreak in Turkey. *Frontiers in Psychiatry*, *11*(695), 1–9. doi:10.3389/fpsyt.2020.00695 PMID:32760303

Akour, A., Al-Tammemi, A. B., Barakat, M., Kanj, R., Fakhouri, H. N., Malkawi, A., & Musleh, G. (2020). The Impact of the COVID-19 Pandemic and Emergency Distance Teaching on the Psychological Status of University Teachers: A Cross-Sectional Study in Jordan. *The American Journal of Tropical Medicine and Hygiene*, *103*(6), 2391–2399. doi:10.4269/ajtmh.20-0877 PMID:33124547

Altena, E., Baglioni, C., Espie, C. A., Ellis, J., Gavriloff, D., Holzinger, B., Schlarb, A., Frase, L., Jernelöv, S., & Riemann, D. (2020). Dealing with sleep problems during home confinement due to the COVID-19 outbreak: Practical recommendations from a task force of the European CBT-I Academy. *Journal of Sleep Research*, *29*(4), 1–7. doi:10.1111/jsr.13052 PMID:32246787

Ammar, N., Aly, N. M., Folayan, M. O., Khader, Y., Virtanen, J. I., Al-Batayneh, O. B., Mohebbi, S. Z., Attia, S., Howaldt, H.-P., Boettger, S., Maharani, D. A., Rahardjo, A., Khan, I., Madi, M., Rashwan, M., Pavlic, V., Cicmil, S., Choi, Y.-H., Joury, E., & El Tantawi, M. (2020). Behavior change due to COVID-19 among dental academics—The theory of planned behavior: Stresses, worries, training, and pandemic severity. *PLoS One*, *15*(9), e0239961. doi:10.1371/journal.pone.0239961 PMID:32991611

Bar, G. (2021). ADB Helps Bangladesh on Road to Recovery from COVID-19. *Asian Development Bank*.https://www.adb.org/results/adb-helps-bangladesh-road-recovery-covid-19

Brooks, S. K., Webster, R. K., Smith, L. E., Woodland, L., Wessely, S., Greenberg, N., & Rubin, G. J. (2020). The Psychological Impact of Quarantine and How to Reduce it: Rapid Review of the Evidence. SSRN *Electronic Journal*, 1-20. doi:10.2139/ssrn.3532534

Cao, W., Fang, Z., Hou, G., Han, M., Xu, X., Dong, J., & Zheng, J. (2020). The psychological impact of the COVID-19 epidemic on college students in China. *Psychiatry Research*, *287*, 1–5. doi:10.1016/j.psychres.2020.112934 PMID:32229390

Debus, M. E., & Unger, D. (2017). The interactive effects of dual-earner couples' job insecurity: Linking conservation of resources theory with crossover research. *Journal of Occupational and Organizational Psychology*, *90*(2), 225–247. doi:10.1111/joop.12169

Dryhurst, S., Schneider, C. R., Kerr, J., Freeman, A. L. J., Recchia, G., van der Bles, A. M., Spiegelhalter, D., & van der Linden, S. (2020). Risk Perceptions of COVID-19 Around The World. *Journal of Risk Research*, *23*(7–8), 994–1006. doi:10.1080/13669877.2020.1758193

Dubey, D. (2020). Psychological Impact Of COVID-19. In S. Baker, R. R. Nadikattu, S. M. Mohammad, & S. Satish (Eds.), *COVID-19 Pandemic Update 2020* (pp. 165–175). Royal Book Publishing. doi:10.26524/royal.37.15

Feldman, R. S. (2019). *Essentials of Understanding Psychology*. McGraw-Hill.

Godinic, D., Obrenovic, B., & Khudaykulov, A. (2020). Effects of Economic Uncertainty on Mental Health in the COVID-19 Pandemic Context: Social Identity Disturbance, Job Uncertainty, and Psychological Well-Being Model. *International Journal of Innovation and Economic Development*, *6*(1), 61–74. doi:10.18775/ijied.1849-7551-7020.2015.61.2005

González-Sanguino, C., Ausín, B., Castellanos, M. Á., Saiz, J., López-Gómez, A., Ugidos, C., & Muñoz, M. (2020). Mental health consequences during the initial stage of the 2020 Coronavirus pandemic (COVID-19) in Spain. *Brain, Behavior, and Immunity*, *87*, 172–176. doi:10.1016/j.bbi.2020.05.040 PMID:32405150

Halbesleben, J. R. B., Neveu, J.-P., Paustian-Underdahl, S. C., & Westman, M. (2014). Getting to the "COR": Understanding the Role of Resources in Conservation of Resources Theory. *Journal of Management*, *40*(5), 1334–1364. doi:10.1177/0149206314527130

Hamouche, S. (2020). COVID-19 and employees' mental health: Stressors, moderators and agenda for organizational actions. *Emerald Open Research*, *2*, 1–15. doi:10.35241/emeraldopenres.13550.1

Harper, C. A., Satchell, L., Fido, D., & Latzman, R. D. (2020). Functional fear predicts public health compliance in the COVID-19 pandemic. doi:10.31234/osf.io/jkfu3osf.io/jkfu3

Hobfoll, S. E. (1989). Conservation of resources: A new attempt at conceptualizing stress. *The American Psychologist*, *44*(3), 513–524. doi:10.1037/0003-066X.44.3.513 PMID:2648906

Horesh, D., Lev-Ari, R. K., & Hasson-Ohayon, I. (2020). Risk factors for psychological distress during the COVID-19 pandemic in Israel: Loneliness, age, gender, and health status play an important role. *British Journal of Health Psychology*, *25*(4), 925–933. doi:10.1111/bjhp.12455 PMID:32656926

Huang, J., Gates, A. J., Sinatra, R., & Barabási, A.-L. (2020). Historical comparison of gender inequality in scientific careers across countries and disciplines. *Proceedings of the National Academy of Sciences of the United States of America*, *117*(9), 4609–4616. doi:10.1073/pnas.1914221117 PMID:32071248

Huang, Y., & Zhao, N. (2020). Generalized anxiety disorder, depressive symptoms and sleep quality during COVID-19 outbreak in China: A web-based cross-sectional survey. *Psychiatry Research*, *288*, 1–6. doi:10.1016/j.psychres.2020.112954 PMID:32325383

Imran, M. A., & Ahmed, I. (2020). Job Insecurity in Private Education Sector Considering COVID-19 Pandemic: Bangladesh Panorama. *American International Journal of Business and Management Studies*, *2*(2), 41–51. doi:10.46545/aijbms.v2i2.245

Jaiswal, A., & Arun, C. J. (2020). Unlocking the COVID-19 Lockdown: Work from Home and Its Impact on Employees.Research Square, 1-27. doi:10.21203/rs.3.rs-34556/v1

Jasim, M. M. (2020). Poor, rural DU students still missing out on online classes. *The Business Standard*. https://www.tbsnews.net/bangladesh/education/poor-rural-du-students-still-missing-out-online-classes-102625

Kamruzzaman, M. (2020). COVID-19: Bangladesh mulls suspending Friday prayers. *Anadolu Agency*. https://www.aa.com.tr/en/asia-pacific/covid-19-bangladesh-mulls-suspending-friday-prayers/1780251

Khatatbeh, M. (2020). Efficacy of Nationwide Curfew to Encounter Spread of COVID-19: A Case From Jordan. *Frontiers in Public Health*, *8*, 1–3. doi:10.3389/fpubh.2020.00394 PMID:32984234

Li, Q., Miao, Y., Zeng, X., Tarimo, C. S., Wu, C., & Wu, J. (2020). Prevalence and factors for anxiety during the coronavirus disease 2019 (COVID-19) epidemic among the teachers in China. *Journal of Affective Disorders*, *277*, 153–158. doi:10.1016/j.jad.2020.08.017 PMID:32828002

Liu, N., Zhang, F., Wei, C., Jia, Y., Shang, Z., Sun, L., Wu, L., Sun, Z., Zhou, Y., Wang, Y., & Liu, W. (2020). Prevalence and predictors of PTSS during COVID-19 outbreak in China hardest-hit areas: Gender differences matter. *Psychiatry Research*, *287*, 112921. doi:10.1016/j.psychres.2020.112921 PMID:32240896

Mahmud, A., & Buckee, C. (2020). Bangladesh must enact widespread surveillance and social distancing measures. *The Daily Star*. https://www.thedailystar.net/opinion/news/bangladesh-must-enact-widespread-surveillance-and-social-distancing-measures-1886344

Mahmud, A., Dasgupta, A., Gupta, A. D., Hasan, M. K., & Kabir, K. R. (2021). Current status about COVID-19 impacts on online education system: A review in Bangladesh. SSRN *Electronic Journal*.https://doi.org/ doi:10.2139/ssrn.3785713

Mahmud, F. (2020). Coronavirus: In dense Bangladesh, social distancing a tough task. *Aljazeera*. https://www.aljazeera.com/news/2020/3/20/coronavirus-in-dense-bangladesh-social-distancing-a-tough-task

Malisch, J. L., Harris, B. N., Sherrer, S. M., Lewis, K. A., Shepherd, S. L., McCarthy, P. C., Spott, J. L., Karam, E. P., Moustaid-Moussa, N., Calarco, J. M. C., Ramalingam, L., Talley, A. E., Cañas-Carrell, J. E., Ardon-Dryer, K., Weiser, D. A., Bernal, X. E., & Deitloff, J. (2020). Opinion: In the wake of COVID-19, academia needs new solutions to ensure gender equity. *Proceedings of the National Academy of Sciences of the United States of America*, *117*(27), 15378–15381. doi:10.1073/pnas.2010636117 PMID:32554503

Maslow, A. H. (1943). A theory of human motivation. *Psychological Review*, *50*(4), 370–396. doi:10.1037/h0054346

Meng, Q., & Wang, G. (2018). A research on sources of university faculty occupational stress: A Chinese case study. *Psychology Research and Behavior Management*, *11*, 597–605. doi:10.2147/PRBM.S187295 PMID:30573995

Mondira, R. T. (2021). PohelaBoishakh celebrations go virtual for the second year in a row. *The Daily Star.* https://www.thedailystar.net/arts-entertainment/news/pohela-boishakh-celebrations-go-virtual-the-second-year-row-2077605

Moorhouse, B. L. (2020). Adaptations to a face-to-face initial teacher education course 'forced' online due to the COVID-19 pandemic. *Journal of Education for Teaching*, *46*(4), 609–611. doi:10.1080/02607476.2020.1755205

Morin, C. M., Carrier, J., Bastien, C., & Godbout, R. (2020). Sleep and circadian rhythm in response to the COVID-19 pandemic. *Canadian Journal of Public Health*, *111*(5), 654–657. doi:10.1726941997-020-00382-7 PMID:32700231

Mosleh, S. M., Kasasbeha, M. A., Aljawarneh, Y. M., Alrimawi, I., & Saifan, A. R. (2022). The impact of online teaching on stress and burnout of academics during the transition to remote teaching from home. *BMC Medical Education*, *22*(1), 1–10. doi:10.118612909-022-03496-3 PMID:35725450

Mowbray, H. (2020). In Beijing, coronavirus 2019-nCoV has created a siege mentality. *BMJ (Clinical Research Ed.)*, *368*, m516. doi:10.1136/bmj.m516 PMID:32033967

Narayanan, L., Pandit, M., Basu, S., Karmakar, A., Bidhan, V., Kumar, H., & Brar, K. (2020). Impact of lockdown due to COVID-19 outbreak: lifestyle changes and public health concerns in India.Preprints,2020060129. https://www.preprints.org/manuscript/202006.0129/v1

Neazy, S. N. (2019). Rise of the educated unemployed. *Dhaka Tribune*. https://www.dhakatribune.com/opinion/op-ed/2019/06/28/rise-of-the-educated-unemployed

Odii, A., Odinakachukwu M. N., Aniakor,M. C.,Owelle, I. C., Aniagboso, M. C., &Uzuanwu,O. W. (n.d.). Effect of COVID-19 lockdown on poor urban households in Nigeria: Where do we go from here? *Ianna Journal of Interdisciplinary Studies, 2*(1).

Phillips, R. (2005). Challenging The Primacy Of Lectures: The Dissonance Between Theory And Practice In University Teaching. *Journal of University Teaching & Learning Practice*, *2*(1), 4–15. doi:10.53761/1.2.1.2

Rapanta, C., Botturi, L., Goodyear, P., Guàrdia, L., & Koole, M. (2020). Online university teaching during and after the Covid-19 crisis: Refocusing teacher presence and learning activity. *PostdigitalScience and Education*, *2*(3), 923–945. doi:10.100742438-020-00155-y

Raza, W. A. (Ed.). (2021). *Corona Tale*. Anyaprokash.

Sajid, E. (2020). Police enforce social distancing through humiliation, harassment. *The Business Standard*. .https://www.tbsnews.net/coronavirus-chronicle/coronavirus-bangladesh/police-enforce-social-distancing-through-humiliation

Salgado-Delgado, R., Osorio, A. T., Saderi, N., & Escobar, C. (2011). Disruption of Circadian Rhythms: A Crucial Factor in the Etiology of Depression. *Depression Research and Treatment, 2011*, 1–9. doi:10.1155/2011/839743 PMID:21845223

Satici, B., Gocet-Tekin, E., Deniz, M. E., & Satici, S. A. (2020). Adaptation of the Fear of COVID-19 Scale: Its association with psychological distress and life satisfaction in Turkey. *International Journal of Mental Health and Addiction*, 1–9. doi:10.100711469-020-00294-0 PMID:32395095

Saunders, M., Lewis, P., & Thornhill, A. (2012). *Research Methods for Business Students* (6th ed.). Pearson Education.

Shigemura, J., Ursano, R. J., Morganstein, J. C., Kurosawa, M., & Benedek, D. M. (2020). Public responses to the novel 2019 coronavirus (2019-nCoV) in Japan: Mental health consequences and target populations. *Psychiatry and Clinical Neurosciences*, *74*(4), 281–282. doi:10.1111/pcn.12988 PMID:32034840

Shovon, F. R. (2020). DU to start online classes in July. *Dhaka Tribune*.https://archive.dhakatribune.com/bangladesh/2020/06/26/du-to-start-online-classes-from-the-first-week-of-july

Spoorthy, M. S., Pratapa, S. K., & Mahant, S. (2020). Mental health problems faced by healthcare workers due to the COVID-19 pandemic–A review. *Asian Journal of Psychiatry*, *51*, 102119. doi:10.1016/j.ajp.2020.102119 PMID:32339895

Talidong, K. J. B., & Toquero, C. M. D. (2020). Philippine teachers' practices to deal with anxiety amid COVID-19. *Journal of Loss and Trauma*, *25*(6-7), 573–579. doi:10.1080/15325024.2020.1759225

The Daily Star. (2020). Online classes: Increasing the education divide. *The Daily Star.* https://www.thedailystar.net/opinion/news/online-classes-increasing-the-education-divide-1931409

Wang, C., Pan, R., Wan, X., Tan, Y., Xu, L., McIntyre, R. S., Choo, F. N., Tran, B., Ho, R., Sharma, V. K., & Ho, C. (2020). A longitudinal study on the mental health of general population during the COVID-19 epidemic in China. *Brain, Behavior, and Immunity*, *87*, 40–48. doi:10.1016/j.bbi.2020.04.028 PMID:32298802

Wang, M. Q. A. (2018). A research on sources of university faculty occupational stress: A Chinese case study. *Psychology Research and Behavior Management, 11*, 597–605. https://www.researchgate.net/publication/329458606_A_research_on_sources_of_university_faculty_occupational_stress_A_Chinese_case_study. doi:10.2147/PRBM.S187295 PMID:30573995

Watermeyer, R., Crick, T., Knight, C., & Goodall, J. (2021). COVID-19 and digital disruption in UK universities: Afflictions and affordances of emergency online migration. *Higher Education, 81*(3), 623–641. doi:10.100710734-020-00561-y PMID:32836334

Wisner, B., Adams, J., & World Health Organization. (2002). *Environmental health in emergencies and disasters: a practical guide.* World Health Organization. https://apps.who.int/iris/handle/10665/42561

World Food Programme. (2020). *Global Report on Food Crises.* United Nations World Food Programme (WFP).https://www.wfp.org/publications/2020-global-report-food-crises

World Health Organization. (2020). *Advice for the Public: Coronavirus disease (COVID-19).* World Health Organization. https://www.who.int/emergencies/diseases/novel-coronavirus-2019/advice-for-public

Zarif, M. M. (2021). Dhaka's online food business. *The Daily Star.* https://www.thedailystar.net/supplements/30th-anniversary-supplements/golden-jubilee-beginnings/news/dhakas-online-food-business-2046349?amp

Chapter 4
Developing a South Asian Version of an Implementation Instrument for Understanding the Policy Implementation:
Case of COVID-19 in Pakistan

Muhammad Fayyaz Nazir
Gent University, Belgium

Ellen Wayenberg
https://orcid.org/0000-0003-3357-1291
Ghent University, Belgium

Shahzadah Fahed Qureshi
Bahauddin Zakariya University, Multan, Pakistan

ABSTRACT

This study is divided into two phases: translation and the testing of NoMAD. Researchers adopted a four-step approach: forward and backward translation, expert reviews for the test, and improvement of content validity. The translated version was then adopted for understanding the implementation of social distancing in the context of Covid-19 in Pakistan. To analyze the scale validity of U-NoMAD, researchers calculated the Cronbach alpha value through the Confirmatory Factor Analysis approach and analyzed the U-NoMAD strength through a step-wise

DOI: 10.4018/978-1-7998-9213-7.ch004

evaluation process – convergent validity and individual item validity, discriminant validity, and model significance. The initial factor analysis model showed a good fit for coherence and cognitive participation and an unsatisfactory fit for collective action and reflexive monitoring. The results confirmed the NoMAD structure in the Pakistani healthcare settings to acceptable standards. So, the U-NoMAD instrument is valuable in evaluating complex and innovative healthcare interventions.

1. INTRODUCTION

Normalization MeAsure Development (NoMAD) survey tool is a British instrument (Finch et al., 2018) of the Normalization Process Theory (NPT) that is already translated into Swedish (Aberg et al., 2018), Dutch (Vis et al., 2019), and Brazilian Portuguese (Loch et al., 2020). However, no such translation has been done for more than two hundred and thirty million people in the world who are either native or second-language speakers of the Urdu language (Eberhard et al., 2022). We observed that the implementation literature continuously calls for the application, testing, and validation of the existing instruments to search for a sound implementation theory. For this, we conducted a scientific inquiry first to translate and then evaluate the newly translated U-NoMAD version of the instrument to assess its applicability in complex and novel healthcare interventions, such as in the implementation of Social Distancing (SD) in the context of the COVID-19 pandemic in Pakistan. So, this study provides a translation of the NoMAD instrument and tests the newly translated instrument in a novel situation. We observed in the literature that no study had been conducted using a newly translated instrument in search of a degree of applicability of the instruments while studying the SD. This gave us literature-supportive and demanding research questions: Is NoMAD a promising instrument for evaluating the implementation of social distancing in the Pakistani context? To answer this question, we adopted a translation and validation approach. So, we apply a systematic four-step approach for translation and confirmatory factor analysis in partial least squares by using Smart-PLS software for validation. The current study offers translation and pilot testing of NoMAD to South Asia version of the instrument, which we have named the Urdu-Normalization MeAsure Development (U-NoMAD) survey tool, considering the wider acceptability of the Urdu Language in South Asia. So, the study's objectives were to translate the NoMAD into Urdu Language and to undertake initial psychometric testing of the newly translated U-NoMAD across a sample of healthcare providers involved in implementing SD. The proposition that a South Asian version of U-NoMAD can satisfactorily assess the NPT constructs is tested. This study contributes to the implementation literature by extending the understanding of the policy implementation of healthcare intervention and testing the U-NoMAD instrument. The results of U-NoMAD validation show a good model fit; however, developing a highly reliable and valid instrument is an iterative process, requiring translations in more languages and validation in various settings. So, the U-NoMAD scale can also help in understanding the implementation of other policies in Pakistan.

2. IMPLEMENTATION LITERATURE

Implementation is a multi-actor (Mirnezami et al., 2019) interaction process (Ownes, 2008) and is a diversified phenomenon (Nevile et al., 2018). Its complexity can be assessed with the understanding of current research trends (La-Barbera, & Lombardo, 2019), such as theoretical integrations (Kennedy et al., 2014:: Band et al., 2017: Farr et al., 2018) and process normalisation. Normalization Process Theory (NPT) explains the implementation process and contains the capacity to explore complex healthcare interventions (May & Finch, 2009). NPT satisfies the mixed-method and quantitative study protocols (Farr et al., 2018). NPT supports understanding the implementation and analysis (Rostami et al., 2018) and assists in data collection (Lionis et al., 2016: Reeve et al., 2018).

The increasing interest in policy implementation research also develops. It validates instruments for analyzing the implementation context and its progress through various theoretical aspects (Finch et al., 2016). However, to comprehend the implementation context, it is pertinent to understand the implementation dilemmas, such as the implementation of disease prevention and control policy, in the context of the COVID-19 pandemic. Literature regarding healthcare interventions specifies the degree of their importance. Hasan (2020): Alimohamadi et al. (2020): and Battiston & Gamba (2021) present their findings about the implementation of SD as a healthcare intervention in the COVID-19 pandemic. The calls for a systematic implementation framework by Howlett (2019) and more theoretically sound research on implementation by Mavrot (2019) elaborated the need for experiments in the implementation research. It is worth mentioning that Elf et al. (2018) highlighted the need to test the NoMAD instrument in various settings and populations.

Although the literature presents the SD as a current implementation dilemma, a vital element to be practised and explored in managing the pandemic and understanding the core of implementation, however, no study has been conducted to validate and pilot test the existing tools, considering the implementation of SD as a case. So, the study satisfies the calls of implementation scholars about mix-methods study design, validating and pilot testing the already existing tools in the search for a sound implementation theory, with the addition of translating a widely utilised NoMAD instrument into Urdu language and creating an Urdu version of the instrument.

3. RESEARCH METHODOLOGY

Methods

The mix-methods study is divided into three phases. The first phase is based on the translation of NoMAD into Urdu, and the second phase is based on identifying the scale reliability of U-NoMAD. The third part of the study is based on pilot testing of U-NoMAD. The first part of the study adopted a systematic approach under a four-step process, including the forward and backward translation, expert reviews for the test, and improvement of content validity of the U-NoMAD at each stage of development. In the second part of the study, researchers analysed the scale reliability of the newly translated instrument through Cronbach's alpha. Final U-NoMAD was then adapted for a pilot study aimed at the implementation of SD. The results were analysed for internal construct validity and internal consistency by following the patterns of analysing the psychometric properties in the original NoMAD. We tested the U-NoMAD for the values of convergent validity & individual item validity (through the values of rho_A), discriminant validity (through Fornell-Larcker Criterion), and structural model significance (through *P*-Values).

Data were collected from the healthcare workers, including the healthcare managers, medical doctors, and allied healthcare professionals in three Pakistani hospitals in Pakistan at the peak time of the COVID-19 pandemic.

Description of Original Development of NoMAD

The NoMAD survey instrument was constructed under an iterative process by following the mixed methods study design. The interactive instrument development process consists of theoretical elaboration, item generation, and reduction, item appraisal and cognitive testing, theory validation, and pilot instrument testing. The initial version of the instrument adopted in the validation study consisted of forty-three items. The authors conducted online and paper-based surveys targeting the healthcare professionals implementing six healthcare interventions. Redundancy was removed through descriptive analysis and consensus methods, reducing the tool to twenty-three items.

Structure of Scoring of the Original NoMAD Instrument

The instrument is divided into three parts. Section A represents two questions about the respondents, section B has three general questions about the intervention, and finally, section C enquires twenty questions regarding the intervention under the four theoretical constructs. The theoretical construct Coherence (CO) and Cognitive

Participation (CP) have four items/questions, Collective Action (CA) has seven items/questions, and five more items/questions cover Reflexive Monitoring (RM).

Data Collection

We conducted semi-structured interviews with fifteen healthcare professionals, with open-ended questions designed to obtain the professional's reflections on the suitability of the South Asian version of the instrument for its utilization.

The survey was conducted face-to-face with healthcare providers involved in managing the pandemic in COVID-19 designated units within the hospitals, in all three study sites, in all three working shifts (Morning, Evening, and Night), with 288 participants. Participants were informed about the research objectives under the informed consent protocols and included in the data collection as per their willingness to participate.

4. DATA ANALYSIS AND RESULTS

The Translation and Adaption Process

We obtained the necessary permission from the developers to translate into the Urdu language, creating the Urdu version. We adopted the Polit and Beck (2008) approach to augment the conceptual and semantic equivalence between the original and the translated instrument. The approach consists of forward and backward translations and expert reviews. We identify the acceptability and content validity of the U-NoMAD through forward and backward translation, the first test of content validity of the translated tool, the final test of content validity of the revised instrument, and the adaptation of the finalized instrument.

Forward and Backward Translation

Two authors (with the Urdu language as their first language) autonomously translated the NoMAD into the Urdu language to protect the sense of every item/question. Before accomplishing unanimity on the furthermost suitable wording, the translations were reviewed, discussed, and argued. The South-Asian version of the instrument was then translated back into English. At this stage, the meaning of the back-translated and original items/questions were compared and discussed to achieve sufficient similarity.

Test of Content Validity of U-NoMAD

Fifteen healthcare professionals with healthcare intervention experience were engaged through purposive sampling in the validation study. The healthcare professionals include managers, medical experts, and allied healthcare professionals. They were requested to rate the items of relevance per the content validity index (Polit and Beck 2006) and their responses for qualitative analysis. However, the participants were encouraged to explain the items/questions, expressions, legibility, and layout.

Researchers adopted the Content Validity Index method to enhance the item's construct validity. It measures whether the particular items suitably represent the construct and whether items/questions in the subject tool are relevant. The items are assessed on a 4-point scale ranging from not relevant to highly relevant, with an additional response option, 'do not understand the item.' Items content validity and scale content validity were calculated based on the expert ratings. We calculated I-CVI for each item by adding the highly relevant respondents rating the item/ questions divided by the total number of respondents rating the items/questions. Moreover, we calculated the II-CVI by summating the average values and dividing them by the total number of items.

Content analysis on a manifest level was used to analyze the interviews. The items required to revise were identified, such as those with CVI less than 0.78, according to Policy and Beck (2012). The expert's comments also resulted in modifications to the translated version of NoMAD.

Test of the Content on the Final Adopted Instrument

A few experts (n=2) once again assessed the content validity of the translated and adapted NoMAD using the CVI, resulting in the instrument's final version.

Adoption of the Finalized Instrument

Finally, the translated version was recorded digitally. The adaptation of the finalized U-NoMAD version of the instrument to a digital version needs minor editing revisions.

Table 1. Original and South Asian U-noMAD final version

Original and South Asian U-NoMAD Final Version		
Original Questionnaire		**Urdu-NoMAD**
Part-A		
Characterization of the Participant	How many years have you worked for this organization?	آپ نے اس تنظیم کے لیے کتنے سال کام کیا ہے؟
	How would you describe your professional job category?	آپ اپنی پیشہ ورانہ ملازمت کے زمرے کی وضاحت کیسے کریں گے؟
Part-B		
General Questions about the intervention	When you use the intervention (social distancing), how familiar does it feel?	جب آپ سماجی دوری کا استعمال کرتے ہیں، تو یہ کتنا مانوس محسوس ہوتا ہے؟
	Do you feel intervention (social distancing) is currently a normal part of your work?	کیا آپ محسوس کرتے ہیں کہ سماجی دوری فی الحال آپ کے کام کا ایک عام حصہ ہے؟
	Do you feel intervention (social distancing) will become a normal part of your work?	کیا آپ کو لگتا ہے کہ سماجی دوری آپ کے کام کا ایک عام حصہ بن جائے گی؟
Part-C		
Coherence	I can see how intervention (social distancing) differs from usual ways of working?	میں دیکھ سکتا ہوں کہ سماجی دوری کام کرنے کے معمول کے طریقوں سے کس طرح مختلف ہے؟
	Staff in this organization has a shared understanding of the purpose of intervention (social distancing)?	اس تنظیم کے عملے کو سماجی دوری کے مقصد کی مشترکہ سمجھ ہے؟
	I understand how intervention (social distancing) affects the nature of my own work?	میں سمجھتا ہوں کہ سماجی دوری میرے اپنے کام کی نوعیت کو کیسے متاثر کرتی ہے؟
	I can see the potential value of intervention (social distancing) for my work?	میں اپنے کام کے لیے سماجی دوری کی ممکنہ قدر دیکھ سکتا ہوں؟
Cognitive Participation	There are key people who drive this implementation forward and get others involved?	اس عمل کو آگے بڑھانے اور دوسروں کو شامل کرنے والے اہم لوگ ہیں؟
	I believe that participating in implementing intervention (social distancing) is a legitimate part of my role?	مجھے یقین ہے کہ سماجی دوری کو نافذ کرنے میں حصہ لینا میرے کردار کا ایک جائز حصہ ہے؟
	I am open to working with colleagues in new ways to use the intervention (social distancing)?	میں سماجی دوری کو استعمال کرنے کے لیے ساتھیوں کے ساتھ نئے طریقوں سے کام کرنے کے لیے تیار ہوں؟
	I will continue to support implementation of intervention (social distancing)?	میں سماجی دوری کے نفاذ کی حمایت جاری رکھوں گا؟

Continued on following page

Table 1. Continued

Original and South Asian U-NoMAD Final Version		
	Original Questionnaire	**Urdu-NoMAD**
Collective Action	I can easily integrate the intervention (social distancing) into my existing work?	میں اپنے موجودہ کام میں سماجی دوری کو آسانی سے ضم کر سکتا ہوں؟
	Intervention (social distancing) disrupts working relationships?	سماجی دوری کام کرنے والے تعلقات کو متاثر کرتی ہے؟
	I have confidence in other people ability to use intervention (social distancing)?	مجھے دوسرے لوگوں کی سماجی دوری کو استعمال کرنے کی صلاحیت پر اعتماد ہے؟
	Work is assigned to those with skills appropriate to the intervention (social distancing) implementation?	سماجی دوری کے نفاذ کے لیے مناسب مہارت رکھنے والوں کو کام تفویض کیا جاتا ہے؟
	Sufficient training is provided to enable to support intervention (social distancing)?	سماجی دوری کو سہارا دینے کے لیے کافی تربیت فراہم کی گئی ہے؟
	Sufficient resources are available to support implementation of intervention (social distancing)?	سماجی دوری کے نفاذ میں مدد کے لیے کافی وسائل دستیاب ہیں؟
	Management adequately supports the implementation?	انتظامیہ مناسب طریقے سے نفاذ کی حمایت کرتا ہے؟
Reflexive Monitoring	I am aware of reports about the effects of the intervention (social distancing)?	میں سماجی دوری کے اثرات کے بارے میں رپورٹس سے واقف ہوں؟
	The staff agree that the intervention (social distancing) is worthwhile?	عملہ متفق ہے کہ سماجی دوری قابل قدر ہے؟
	I value the effects that intervention (social distancing) has had on my work?	میں ان اثرات کی قدر کرتا ہوں جو سماجی دوری نے میرے کام پر پڑی ہے؟
	Feedback about the intervention (social distancing) can be used to improve it in the future?	سماجی دوری کے بارے میں تاثرات مستقبل میں اسے بہتر بنانے کے لیے استعمال کیے جا سکتے ہیں؟
	I can modify how I work with the intervention (social distancing)?	میں ترمیم کر سکتا ہوں کہ میں سماجی دوری کے ساتھ کیسے کام کرتا ہوں؟
Table 1.		

Scale Reliability

To identify the reliability of U-NoMAD, the values of Cronbach Alpha are higher than the threshold value of 0.7, representing the scale's validity (Gliem, 2003). The results in Table-2 and the graphical illustration in Figure-1 & 2 confirm the reliability of U-NoMAD.

Table 2. Values of Cronbach alpha

Values of Cronbach Alpha		
Variable	**Value**	
	First Iteration	**Second Iteration**
Normalization	0.766	0.764
Coherence	0.716	0.716
Cognitive Participation	0.731	0.731
Collective Action	0.602	0.814
Reflexive Monitoring	0.672	0.738
Table-2		

Figure 1. Values in first iteration

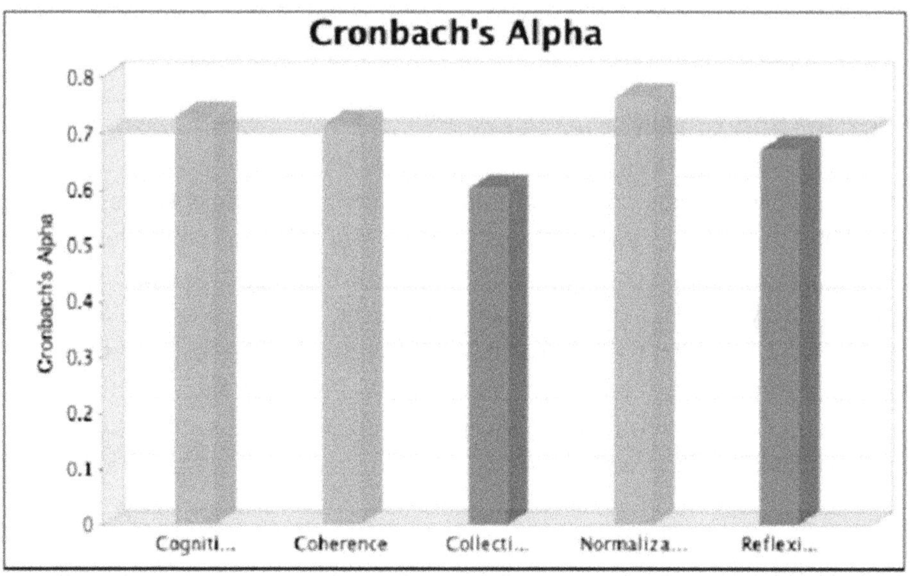

Figure 2. Values in second iteration

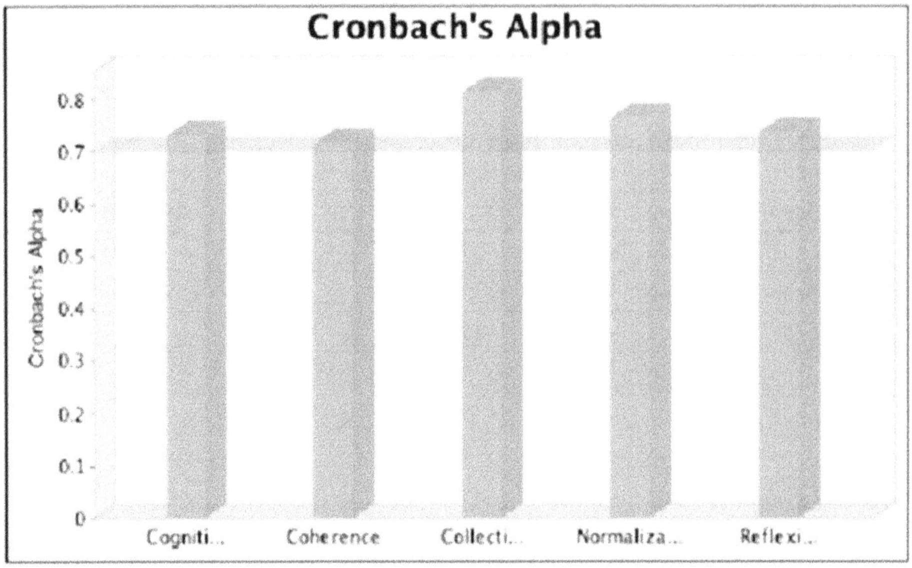

Pilot Testing of U-NoMAD

After analysing the scale validity, the translated version of U-NoMAD was utilized in the pilot testing to understand the implementation of SD in the professional lives of healthcare workers in Pakistan. We tested the U-NoMAD for psychometric properties as followed by developing the original instrument. We tested the U-NoMAD for rho_A, Fornell-Larcker Criterion, and P-Values values. In the first step, the validity was tested through the values of rho_A. The results given in Table 3 and illustrated in Figure 3 confirm the validity in confirmatory factor analysis under the structural equation modelling approach.

Table 3. Values of rho_A in first iteration

Values of rho_A		
Constructs	**Values**	**Comment**
Normalization	0.839	Acceptable
CO	0.915	Acceptable
CP	0.788	Acceptable
CA	0.837	Acceptable
RM	0.776	Acceptable
Table 3		

Figure 3. Graphical illustration of rho_A values

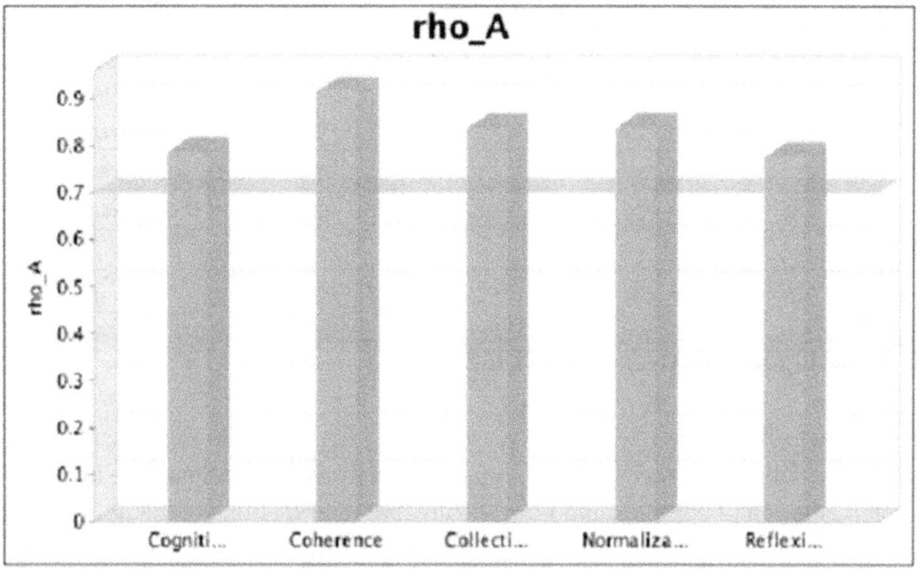

In the second step, after evaluating the scale validity, the discriminant validity of the latent variables was analyzed through the Fornell-Larcker Criterion, which specifies the degree to which a specific construct is unique among all others (Liu, 2012). The results given in Table-4 confirm the discriminant validity of the U-NoMAD.

Table 4. Analysis of discriminant validity through Fornell-Larcker criterion

Constructs	Cognitive Participation	Coherence	Collective Action	Normalization of SD	Reflexive Monitoring
CP	**0.747**				
CO	0.687	**0.725**			
CA	0.801	0.658	**0.806**		
Normalization	0.811	0.750	0.818	**0.824**	
RM	0.817	0.667	0.801	0.813	**0.822**
			Table 4		

The U-NoMAD model significance was analyzed using the p-values in Table 5, confirming the instrument's significance.

Table 5. Significance

Structural Model Significance		
Constructs	***P*-Values**	**Result**
CO	0.000	Significant
CP	0.001	Significant
CA	0.001	Significant
RM	0.000	Significant
Table 5		

5. DISCUSSION AND CONCLUSION

The study provides the U-NoMAD version of the implementation assessment tool of the normalization process theory. It provides a tested questionnaire to assess the implementation of complex and novel healthcare interventions in the South Asian context. The methodology was chosen rigorously to ensure reliable results. Literature supports the forward and backward translation and pilot testing in the context of cross-cultural adaptation of the survey instruments. Moreover, the study followed the same methodology of testing the scale validity before pilot testing, making it a three-phase study.

There was consistency between the original version and the back-word translation. Most of the adjustments concerned language precision. It is pertinent to mention that a few items in the original version of the instrument were found difficult to translate into Urdu. For example, in the backward translation, the word "understand" was adopted in replacement of the word "see" and "relevant" in replacement of the word "legitimate," and its impact on the instrument validity and reliability was considered a vital element and discussed with the other experts, resulted in satisfactory adoption.

The results of testing U-NoMAD represent good scale validity. The values of Cronbach's alpha (for normalization 0.764, Coherence 0.716, Cognitive Participation 0.731, Collective Action 0.814, and Reflexive Monitoring 0.738) in the second iteration are higher than the benchmark value of 0.7, which confirms the scale validity.

The confirmatory factor analysis under the structural modeling approach allowed to conduct of the rho_A test, and the values confirm the validity of the pilot testing of the U-NoMAD. The discriminant validity of the instrument was analyzed through Fornell-Larcker Criterion, and the resultant values (for Coherence 0.725, Cognitive Participation 0.747, Collective Action 0.806, and Reflexive Monitoring 0.822) were relatively higher among all other constructs and confirmed the discriminant validity of the U-NoMAD version. The *P*-Values confirm the significance of the South Asian version of U-NoMAD.

The study resulted in a South Asian version of an instrument/questionnaire that could analyze participants' involvement, perception, collective actions, and assessment in implementing complex or novel healthcare interventions. Translating the instrument would help the policy actors better understand the implementation of a policy. The mixed-methods study results represent that the South Asian version of U-NoMAD is a promising instrument for evaluating the implementation of SD in Pakistan and would be adoptable in complex and novel healthcare interventions in South Asian countries.

REFERENCES

Åberg, A. C., Elf, M., Nordmark, S., Lyhagen, J., Lindberg, I., & Finch, T. (2018). 66 *The swedish version of the normalisation process theory measurement s-nomad: translation, adaptation, and pilot testing*. Biomed Central.

Alimohamadi, Y., Holakouie-Naieni, K., Sepandi, M., & Taghdir, M. (2020). Effect of social distancing on COVID-19 incidence and mortality in Iran since February 20 to May 13, 2020: An interrupted time series analysis. *Risk Management and Healthcare Policy*, *13*, 1695–1700. doi:10.2147/RMHP.S265079 PMID:33061703

Band, R., Bradbury, K., Morton, K., May, C., Michie, S., Mair, F. S., Murray, E., McManus, R. J., Little, P., & Yardley, L. (2017). Intervention planning for a digital intervention for self-management of hypertension: A theory, evidence-and person-based approach. *Implementation Science : IS*, *12*(1), 1–13. doi:10.118613012-017-0553-4 PMID:28231840

Battiston, P., & Gamba, S. (2021). COVID-19: R0 is lower where outbreak is larger. *Health Policy (Amsterdam)*, *125*(2), 141–147. doi:10.1016/j.healthpol.2020.10.017 PMID:33309293

Eberhard, D. M., Simons, G. F., & Fennig, C. D. (Eds.). (2022). *Ethnologue: Languages of the World*. Twenty-fifth edition. Dallas, Texas: SIL International. http://www.ethnologue.com

Elf, M., Nordmark, S., Lyhagen, J., Lindberg, I., Finch, T., & Åberg, A. C. (2018). The Swedish version of the Normalization Process Theory Measure S-NoMAD: Translation, adaptation, and pilot testing. *Implementation Science : IS*, *13*(1), 1–12. doi:10.118613012-018-0835-5 PMID:30509289

Farr, M., Banks, J., Edwards, H. B., Northstone, K., Bernard, E., Salisbury, C., & Horwood, J. (2018). Implementing online consultations in primary care: A mixed-method evaluation extending normalization process theory through service co-production. *BMJ Open*, *8*(3), e019966. doi:10.1136/bmjopen-2017-019966 PMID:29555817

Finch, T., Girling, M., May, C., Mair, F., Murray, E., & Treweek, S. (2016). Can we measure implementation progress using Normalization Process Theory? Development and validation of the NoMAD survey tool. *48th Congress of the international Society of Paediatric oncology*. National Institutes of Health.

Finch, T. L., Girling, M., May, C. R., Mair, F. S., Murray, E., Treweek, S., McColl, E., Steen, I. N., Cook, C., Vernazza, C. R., Mackintosh, N., Sharma, S., Barbery, G., Steele, J., & Rapley, T. (2018). Improving the normalization of complex interventions: Part 2 - validation of the NoMAD instrument for assessing implementation work based on normalization process theory (NPT). *BMC Medical Research Methodology*, *18*(1), 135. doi:10.118612874-018-0591-x PMID:30442094

Gliem, J. A., & Gliem, R. R. (2003). *Calculating, interpreting, and reporting Cronbach's alpha reliability coefficient for Likert-type scales*. Midwest Research-to-Practice Conference in Adult, Continuing, and Community Education.

Hasan, H. F. (2021). Legal and health response to COVID-19 in the Arab countries. *Risk Management and Healthcare Policy*, *14*, 1141–1154. doi:10.2147/RMHP.S297565 PMID:33758566

Howlett, M. (2019). Moving policy implementation theory forward: A multiple streams/critical juncture approach. *Public Policy and Administration*, *34*(4), 405–430. doi:10.1177/0952076718775791

Kennedy, A., Rogers, A., Chew-Graham, C., Blakeman, T., Bowen, R., Gardner, C., Lee, V., Morris, R., & Protheroe, J. (2014). Implementation of a self-management support approach (WISE) across a health system: A process evaluation explaining what did and did not work for organizations, clinicians and patients. *Implementation Science : IS*, *9*(1), 129. doi:10.118613012-014-0129-5 PMID:25331942

La Barbera, M., & Lombardo, E. (2019). "The Long and Winding Road": A Comparative Policy Analysis of Multilevel Judicial Implementation of Work–Life Balance in Spain. *Journal of Comparative Policy Analysis*, *21*(1), 9–24. doi:10.1080/13876988.2017.1363949

Lionis, C., Papadakaki, M., Saridaki, A., Dowrick, C., O'Donnell, C. A., Mair, F. S., van den Muijsenbergh, M., Burns, N., de Brún, T., O'Reilly de Brún, M., van Weel-Baumgarten, E., Spiegel, W., & MacFarlane, A. (2016). Engaging migrants and other stakeholders to improve communication in cross-cultural consultation in primary care: A theoretically informed participatory study. *BMJ Open*, *6*(7), e010822. doi:10.1136/bmjopen-2015-010822 PMID:27449890

Loch, A. P., Finch, T., Fonsi, M., & Soárez, P. C. D. (2020). Cross-cultural adaptation of the NoMAD questionnaire to Brazilian Portuguese. *Revista da Associação Médica Brasileira*, *66*(10), 1383–1390. doi:10.1590/1806-9282.66.10.1383 PMID:33174931

Mavrot, C., Hadorn, S., & Sager, F. (2019). Mapping the mix: Linking instruments, settings and target groups in the study of policy mixes. *Research Policy*, *48*(10), 103614. doi:10.1016/j.respol.2018.06.012

May, C., & Finch, T. (2009). Implementing, embedding, and integrating practices: an outline of normalization process theory. *Sociology, 43*(3), 535-554. Doi.org/10.1177/0038038509103208

Mirnezami, S. J., de Boer, C., & Bagheri, A. (2019). Groundwater governance and implementing the conservation policy: The case study of Rafsanjan Plain in Iran. *Environment, Development and Sustainability*, 1–28.

Nevile, A., Kay, A., & Carey, G. (2018). Value choices in a mixed economy of care: How politics shapes the implementation of complex social policies. *Social Policy and Administration*, *52*(7), 1290–1302. doi:10.1111pol.12391

Polit, D. F., & Beck, C. T. (2006). The content validity index: Are you sure you know what's being reported? Critique and recommendations. *Research in Nursing & Health*, *29*(5), 489–497. doi:10.1002/nur.20147 PMID:16977646

Polit, D. F., & Beck, C. T. (2008). *Nursing research: Generating and assessing evidence for nursing practice*. Lippincott Williams & Wilkins.

Polit, D. F., & Beck, C. T. (2012). Nursing research: generating and assessing evidence for nursing practice. 9th ed. Baltiomore: Wolters Kluwer Health/Lippincott Williams & Wilkins.

Reeve, J., Britten, N., Byng, R., Fleming, J., Heaton, J., & Krska, J. (2018). Identifying enablers and barriers to individually tailored prescribing: A survey of healthcare professionals in the UK. *BMC Family Practice*, *19*(1), 17. doi:10.118612875-017-0705-2 PMID:29334913

Rostami, P., Ashcroft, D. M., & Tully, M. P. (2018). A formative evaluation of the implementation of a medication safety data collection tool in English healthcare settings: A qualitative interview study using normalization process theory. *PLoS One*, *13*(2), e0192224. doi:10.1371/journal.pone.0192224 PMID:29489842

Vis, C., Ruwaard, J., Finck, T., Rapley, T., Beurs, D. D., Stel, H. V., & Smit, J. (2019). *Towards an objective assessment of implementation processes for innovations in healthcare: a psychometric evaluation of the NoMAD questionnaire among mental healthcare professionals.* NIH.

Chapter 5
The Impact of Epidemiology on COVID-19 Vaccine Confidence

Abeni El-Amin
https://orcid.org/0000-0001-7506-1658
University of Kentucky, USA

ABSTRACT

In consideration of the importance and scope of epidemiology on SARS-CoV-2 (COVID-19), essential aspects are conveyed regarding how to improve vaccine confidence through awareness and education. Further, from a natural history context, the outbreak of the 2019 novel coronavirus diseases (COVID-19) occurred in Wuhan, Hubei Province, China and spread throughout the world. As a result, governments and organizations experienced challenges managing the pandemic. Explained are characteristics of the COVID-19 epidemiological approach. For example, the utilization of epidemiological studies is performed to obtain rates and probability of occurrence. Reviewed are the use of epidemiology in determining COVID-19 causality, the health status of the population, delivery of services, program planning, and social policy.

INTRODUCTION

The global COVID-19 initiative was developed to improve population health status and to proactively eliminate the disease. COVID-19 mitigation strategies and programs have been implemented to mitigate disease transmission by utilizing quarantining, isolation, social distancing, and improved sanitation measures (Liu et

DOI: 10.4018/978-1-7998-9213-7.ch005

al., 2020; El-Amin, 2022). Anecdotal evidence suggests that many people still do not understand the harmful effects of COVID-19 and subsequent variants. Nevertheless, governments have used their authority to contain COVID-19 and reduce transmission incidence since December 2019. Organizations and governments use public health to educate healthcare workers, policymakers, and the government. Additionally, to reduce COVID-19 virulency, public health must improve vaccine confidence through awareness and education.

BACKGROUND

Epidemiology

The study of disease transmission or epidemiology is a term that provides an understanding of its importance. The study of disease transmission originates from the Greek words epi (upon) + demos (individuals) + logy (investigation of) (Friis & Dealers, 2014). The study of disease transmission is concerned with the incidence, conveyance, and determinants of healthcare-related instances. Epidemiologic investigations are applied to contain medical issues in populations (Friis & Dealers, 2014). The central aspects of the epidemiological definition are determinants, distribution, population, and health care delivery.

The study of disease transmission examines disease among population groups rather than individuals (Jin et al., 2020). Thus, epidemiology is the study of disease transmission as an interdisciplinary field; the study of disease transmission draws from biostatistics, the social and behavioral sciences, and natural history just as from the therapeutically related fields, for example, toxicology, pathology, virology, hereditary qualities, microbiology, and clinical medicine (Friis & Venders, 2014; Kakodkar et al., 2020).

Issues, Controversies, Problems

Workplace Stress During the COVID-19 Epidemic and Post COVID-19

Workplace stress arises when an individual is overworked or has poor management experience, whereas they need to understand the needs and time constraints under division of work practice. COVID-19 has made simple tasks more stressful than not, which may impact a company's performance (El-Amin, 2022). For instance, an example of workplace stress arises when a report is expected for a quarterly meeting. Still, the requested ad hoc report needs at least 6 hours of completion time and needs inputs from other team members, but it still needs to be completed on time. As a result, reports take longer than necessary. Undoubtfully, the entire process of making timely reports in times of crises increases stress levels. Regardless, corrective action determines the capabilities and workflow of employees. Likewise, workforce stress takes energy away from an individual. Often placing a person in a position to decide whether to stay with that company or to move into a less stressful environment (Grant & Palmer, 2015).

Indeed, Berger and Czakert (2022) defined workplace stress and discussed it concerning workplace experiences. Workplace stress is a harmful physical and emotional response that happens when there is a conflict between job demands and the amount of control an employee has in meeting these demands. Based on this definition, workplace demands provide constant stress due to COVID-19 protocols. The ever-shifting demands during COVID-19 contribute to workplace stress, including that of Post-COVID-19. One of the workplace stresses endured was completing projects within established deadline periods with an optimized standard of work quality. However, breaking down the work into small milestone and working on each milestone as per schedule may reduce stress, and incorporating online stress medication apps are helpful (Wolever et al., 2022). This practice helps in reducing workplace stress and achieves work performance objectives.

Prevalence of COVID-19

Identified is the incidence and prevalence of the public health issue comparing the national, state, and local level rates of COVID-19. The outbreak of severe acute respiratory syndrome coronavirus 2 (SARS-CoV-2) disease (COVID-19) became a global pandemic declared by the World Health Organization (WHO) on March 11, 2020 (Jin et al., 2020). Regardless of the specific therapeutics and vaccines available for disease control, the epidemic of COVID-19 will continue to pose a significant threat to global public health (Riggioni et al., 2020; Qiu et al., 2020; Xu et al., 2020). To provide a comprehensive summary of public health methodologies and understand how COVID-19 development measures evolve.

Population Rates

Deliberated are population undercurrents and health with deference to the phases of the demographic conversion and trends in populations (Zhang & Shaw, 2020). Categorized are measures of mortality and morbidity (proportions, rates, ratios, and adjusted rates) of COVID-19. Included are rates among specific age, race, or gender groups. From a descriptive epidemiological perspective, the prevalence and distribution of COVID-19 occurred by person, place, and time. To provide context, an outbreak of the 2019 novel coronavirus disease (COVID-19) in Wuhan, Hubei Province, China, occurred and spread globally (Surveillances, 2020).

Stress Factors

The main COVID-19 risk factors and determinants for the epidemiological problem occurred because populations traveled from one region to another (Wu et al., 2020; Arslan & Allen, 2022). Additionally, migrant workers exacerbated the issue as well. For example, Shanghai experienced increased transmission when travelers of the COVID-19 infection entered the city because of the mass population of transient workers. However, disease transmission did not spike (Qiu et al., 2020). This directly results from Shanghai's well-developed healthcare system (Qiu et al., 2020).

Prevention Strategies

Prevention strategies include screening programs for the detection of COVID-19 based on criteria such as sensitivity, specificity, and predictive value (Zhang et al., 2020). Developed and authenticated are e-learning models constructed on clinical structures for severity risk assessment and triage for COVID-19 patients at hospital admission (Wu et al., 2020). Further, the e-learning model, nomogram, and online calculator may be practical to access the onset of severe and life-threatening illnesses among COVID-19 patients and triage at hospital admittance (Wu et al., 2020).

For instance, present research information regarding primary, secondary, and tertiary prevention strategies and treatment indicated that the COVID-19 pandemic is because of infection transmitted by the novel SARS-CoV-2 infection that impacts the lower respiratory region. Uddin et al. (2020) determined that the range of side effects ranges from asymptomatic infections to moderate respiratory side effects linked to the deadly form of COVID-19, which is related to severe pneumonia, intense respiratory degradation, and casualty. To address this worldwide emergency, trends, and evidence on viral genomics and transcriptomics (pharma) are pivotal for comprehension of the origins and global dispersion of the infection, providing insights into viral pathogenicity, transmission, and the study of disease transmission, and enabling procedures for therapeutic interventions, inoculations, and vaccine advancement (Uddin et al., 2020; Zhang & Shaw, 2020). Therefore, the study of disease transmission, genomic etiology, and findings from ongoing transcriptomic global positioning systems (GPS) investigation is vital. Likewise, viral-human protein interactions, sub-atomic diagnostics, vaccine status, and novel therapeutic intervention advancement are needed to combat the virus.

Trends and Technologies

The latest trends and technologies are identified to mitigate COVID-19 transmission (Zhang & Shaw, 2020). Undoubtedly, the COVID-19 pandemic has influenced the world. Lives and the economy have been altered, and the disease has affected healthcare policies by encouraging innovation through expedited vaccine development (Qiu et al., 2020). Noteworthy innovations in the field of virology and the study of disease transmission have scaled. Similar patterns were seen after the Severe Acute Respiratory Syndrome coronavirus (SARS-CoV) and the Middle East Respiratory Syndrome Coronavirus (MERS-CoV) (Jin et al., 2020). Critical advancement is needed in virology, the study of disease transmission, and infectious illnesses. As a result, improving vaccine confidence through awareness and education is a strategy to alleviate the prevalence of COVID-19 transmission.

Notwithstanding, research links health, public health management, innovation with risk management, and communication strategy concerning the containment of COVID-19. As a result, there are information gaps. Although the World Health Organization (WHO) has distinguished emendations for multi, cross, and transdisciplinary solutions identified to improve healthcare, COVID-19 and its variants continue to spread globally (Sagulkoo et al., 2022).

SOLUTIONS AND RECOMMENDATIONS

Future State of the Issue

The epidemiologic triangle (an external agent, a susceptible host, and an environment that brings the host and agent together) seeks to mitigate the occurrence of viruses (for example, variations in the severity of illness, components of the infectious disease process, mechanisms of disease transmission, and common source versus contagious disease outbreaks) (CDC, 2012). An epidemic is characterized as a bourgeoning disease, injury, or other well-being than anticipated in a given region or among a particular gathering of people during a specific period (Friis & Sellers, 2014). Further, the epidemiologic triangle is vital to understand how illness spreads and determining how to contain it. The epidemiologic triangle comprises three aspects: agent, host, and environment. The agent delineates the microorganism that causes the ailment. An agent is a microscopic organism, infection, growth, or parasite. A host is where the agent taints the host, which is the microbe that delivers the sickness. A host does not necessarily become outwardly ill. Hosts act as transporters for an agent without showing any outward side effects of the illness. A Host becomes ill because their physiology is agreeable to the agent. The environmental aspect comprises external components which can influence an epidemiologic instance. The environment incorporates any elements that influence the spread of the infection yet are not necessarily part of the agent.

Regarding the future status of COVID-19, epidemiologic research will improve COVID-19-19 immunizations and potent medications to treat COVID-19-19 (Zhai et al., 2020). These pharmaceuticals will decrease severe illness and death transmission rates among COVID-19-infected patients (Haque & Pant, 2022). Also, super-spreaders account for earlier GPS technology applications (Sun et al., 2020). With the advancement of symptomatic innovation, potential super-spreaders might be found soon than later. In counteraction to the spread, thereby social policy solutions for decreasing the incidence and prevalence rates of COVID-19-19, asymptomatic spreaders are urged to wear masks, increase sanitary behavior, social distancing, remote working measures, school closings, and quarantine when possible (Sun et al., 2020).

Organizational Application

Delineated are the epidemiologic aspects of COVID-19 (multifactorial nature of etiology, long latency period, indefinite onset, the differential effect of factors on incidence and prevalence of disease) (Lythgoe & Middleton, 2020). Presently, specific antibodies do not exist to alleviate COVID-19. Moreover, healthcare-related transmission, illness, and worker death are significant issues. As a result, healthcare workers utilize personal protective equipment (PPE) and execute standard, contact tracing, and airborne safety measures, including visual protection (Del Rio & Malani, 2020). To prevent disease transmission, healthcare delivery workers should always wear a gown, gloves, an N95 respirator, a face shield or goggles, or a powered respirator. There are numerous difficulties in the epidemiology field, including atypical introductions and restricted respiratory protocols. The rapid advancement that science and healthcare delivery has made in combating the COVID-19 outbreak is unparalleled. However, there is a need to accelerate testing that informs epidemiologists of exposure, effective antiviral treatments, and, eventually, a protected and immunogenic antibody.

Health Promotion in Action

Health promotion is necessary to reduce the social determinates of health (SDOH). When developing a health promotion program, professionals must determine the geographic area(s) in which their organization plans to deliver the proposed activities outlined in a plan. For instance, public health professions must also define their targeted population. Some examples include underrepresented ethnic and racial minority groups. Notwithstanding, these individuals may represent intersectionality in the following ways: People living in rural areas, people with substance use disorders (SUD), people identifying as LGBTQ+, people age 65+, people living in congregate settings, people experiencing homelessness, people who are incarcerated or are in transitional housing as a result of prior incarceration, people who have been displaced or are in transitional housing due to other mitigating circumstances, people with disabilities, non-U.S. born persons, people of a religious minority, and communities that have experienced disproportionately high rates of COVID-19 infection and severe COVID-19 disease or death.

Public health professionals must determine a method or process to capture client engagement and feedback to evaluate and address the unmet needs of the defined population. To address the social determinants of health (SDOH) the plan should identify the conditions in the environment where people are born, live, learn, work, play, worship, and age that affect a wide range of health, functioning, and quality-of-life outcomes and risks with regards to economic stability, education, social and community context, health and health care, neighborhood and built environment. Notwithstanding, public health entities must provide COVID-19 and public health awareness and education through a "boots on the ground" approach by training, coaching, and developing a community health media campaign to encompass the target population.

Of the supported SDOH activities and services related to COVID-19 vaccine administration, information, and support, public health entities must focus on awareness, education, and media outreach to fulfill program goals. Therefore, the plan may be to increase vaccine confidence through community engagement and dissemination of factual information. Public health entities must address the SDOH and provide these services where individuals where live, work, learn, play, and worship, to impact their health and health outcomes. Community partners may include: faith communities, school districts, government, health providers, social and nonprofit organizations. Further, measurable outcomes are critical to ensure effective programming.

According to the County Health Rankings (2022), the COVID-19 pandemic is the worst public health crisis in more than a century and has disproportionately burdened certain communities and population groups across the U.S., particularly women, people of color, seniors, and people with low incomes. During the first full year of the pandemic, the U.S. saw the largest single-year decline in life expectancy since World War II (1.8 years, down from 78.8 years in 2019) and the largest single-year increase in the death rate on record (up 17% from 2019 to 835 deaths per 100,000 people). Provisional data for 2021 show a national death rate that remains well above the pre-pandemic level. From the beginning of 2020 through 2021, COVID-19 officially claimed more than 800,000 U.S. lives, and experts speculate the actual number could be much higher. Overall, the novel coronavirus was the third leading cause of death in 2020 and 2021 (provisional), and it was the leading cause of death in the U.S. at multiple times during those two years.

The purpose of health promotion services (education and media campaign) is to address the COVID-19 vaccine confidence pre-defined goals. The objective is to implement evidence based and best practices in the delivery of activities and services which address the inequities that are widening the health disparities in underserved communities by prompting COVID-19 awareness and education through capacity building, partnering, promoting COVID-19 messaging in accordance with global and governmental organizations such as the World Health Organization and the Centers For Disease Control (CDC).

COVID-19 Awareness and Education Programming

Identify the tools and techniques that will be used to identify and characterize uncertainties at the beginning of the COVID-19 Awareness and Education and during COVID-19 Awareness and Education execution. This could involve a formal risk assessment workshop, brainstorming sessions, and/or interviews at the beginning of each timeline milestone phase. COVID-19 Awareness and Education project risks are attained by implementing a comprehensive public health strategy that incorporates evidence-based administrative practices and a communication plan. Weekly meetings keep all stakeholders informed. This involves a weekly formal risk strategic planning session with periodic updates in strategic planning sessions. It is important for the COVID-19 Awareness and Education project manager to monitor and ensure that stakeholders convene in order to establish a plan to mitigate future risks and resolve issues and challenges that will arise within public health by tracking and monitoring the COVID-19 Awareness and Education plan to ensure consultants focus on building capacity through building partnerships. Most importantly, communication in project planning is paramount to minimizing COVID-19 outbreaks. Risk mitigation plans are continually re-evaluated based on the probability of occurrences leading to project risks. Additionally, programs must provide evidence of readiness to implement and provide feasible sustainability plan.

COVID-19 Vaccine Confidence Program Implementation and Feasibility Sustainability Plan

Public health must promote the understanding of the root causes of health disparities and promote health equity among racial, ethnic, rural, and low-income populations. Health equity is achieved when all individuals can attain their full health potential, have access to health information, receive quality healthcare that values inclusivity and cultural and social norms. Public health supports activities and evidence-based strategies that address health disparities and health inequities to achieve and sustain optimal community health through education and health promotion. Public health equity activities support activities that address health disparities through key partnerships with government, health departments, universities, nonprofit organizations, and faith-based organizations. Public health must amplify stakeholder engagement to operationalize equity, reduce COVID-19 infections, disease severity, hospitalization, morbidity, and mortality.

Roles and Responsibilities

A COVID-19 Vaccine Confidence program is best managed by organizations that are public health focused because they are:

- Community based.
- Dedicated to improving the health and wellness of the communities served and have knowledgeable and qualified staff to lead the program.
- To improve program outcomes, leadership has assigned four consultants to collaborate and oversee the implementation of the program (Project Manager/Media Campaign, Training and Education, Community Outreach, and Evaluation/Reporting).

COVID-19 Project Management Risk Mitigation Strategic Plan

- The COVID-19 Awareness team will meet weekly to determine program activities.
- Develop trainings.
- Set schedule and budgets.
- Collaborate with Internal and External Stakeholders.
- Identify person(s) responsible for implementation activities.
- Report to leadership/evaluation team member a progress report at weekly internal COVID-19 Awareness meetings.

COVID-19 Risk Mitigation Strategic Marketing Plan

- A media campaign is developed to provide awareness about preventive measures to mitigate COVID-19 contraction.
- The media campaign is ongoing throughout the grant cycle.
- Partner organizations are encouraged to participate and assist in dissemination of health promotion materials and information.
- Media promotion will be posted on partner social media sites (Facebook and Twitter) *monthly*.

Barriers Implications and Remedies

- Barriers that may affect change management are constraints such as how leaders and consultants work through operational changes.
- This barrier is overcome by scheduling weekly progress meetings to ensure alignment.
- A lack of flexibility is a barrier for how teams can execute program implementation.
- This barrier is reduced as project members work on the implementation of the COVID-19 Awareness project plan.
- Further, managing processes provides advantage and flexibility, but must be developed in context to the business environment, organizational standards, budgetary, and time constraints.
- These barriers are reduced when management allots consultant time, fees, and support to the project.
- Barriers to fiscal constraints are reduced with appropriate grant funding.

Community Outreach/Engagement Plan

- Lead: Demonstrate leadership principles that facilitate strategic and fiscal resources in order to administer a COVID-19 Awareness Health Education/ Promotion program.
- Research: Research, develop, and select appropriate health information and resource materials to promote health literacy.

- Analyze: Analyze best practices to assess needs, resources, and capacity for COVID-19 Awareness Health Education/Promotion in the community.
- Develop: Develop a plan for COVID-19 Awareness Health Education/Promotion that uses problem-solving to develop innovative strategies and interventions for priority populations, partners, and/or stakeholders.
- Implement: Implement and monitor a COVID-19 Awareness Health Education/Promotion plan and activities operating with professional standards.
- Evaluate: Manage a systematic evaluation plan to draw conclusions and to disseminate findings to stakeholders.
- Integrate: Integrate messages of COVID-19 Awareness Health Education/Promotion in media campaign, community outreach, and presentations.
- Engage: Engage community volunteers in COVID-19 Awareness Health Education/Promotion programming for individuals, schools, communities, and stakeholders.

FUTURE RESEARCH DIRECTIONS

Scientific Methods

Differentiated among the types of research designs used in the etiologic investigation of COVID-19, such as retrospective (case-control), prospective (cohort), historical perspective, cross-sectional, and experimental (prophylactic and therapeutic trials) (Friis & Sellers, 2014). Case control is selected for the research design methodology for this study because it is non-interventional. Case-control observational studies analyze subjects with no trial intervention by the epidemiologist. Observational investigations can be either surveys, e.g., utilizing a current clinical, regulatory, or informed base to characterize study participants or characterize the group before the study, selection, and convenience sampling (Kakodkar et al., 2020). Case-control observational studies are commonly far less expensive, more straightforward, and less morally complex than clinical trials.

CONCLUSION

The pandemic capability of human CoVs remains an incredible danger to global general health and well-being (Jin et al., 2020). Be that as it may, epidemiologists need to gain more understanding of past diseases such as SARS and MERS. After the outbreak of COVID-19 in China, SARS-CoV-2 has garnered responsiveness as a significant microorganism and respiratory infectious disease. Millions of confirmed global COVID-19 cases (WHO, 2020b). To contain the spread of COVID-19, governments comprise containment as a crisis response and improvement of vaccine confidence through awareness and education. Even so, considering the current information, the virus's capacity to spread is beyond the current assessment. To provide a synopsis, general healthcare specialists and epidemiologists worldwide now have a greater understanding of COVID-19 and implement innovations for care. Although COVID-19 vaccinations have not proven effective in completely eradicating COVID-19, public health awareness and education are strategies to curtail disease transmission.

REFERENCES

Arslan, G., & Allen, K. A. (2022). Exploring the association between coronavirus stress, meaning in life, psychological flexibility, and subjective well-being. *Psychology Health and Medicine*, *27*(4), 803–814. doi:10.1080/13548506.2021.1876892 PMID:33487048

Berger, R., & Czakert, J. P. (2022). Stress Management and Resilience Building. In *Organisational Excellence and Resilience* (pp. 63–88). Springer., doi:10.1007/978-3-030-85120-0_2

Center for Disease Control (CDC). (2018). Lesson 1: Introduction to epidemiology. CDC. [REMOVED HYPERLINK FIELD]

County Health Rankings. (2022). *2022 County Health Rankings National Findings Report*. County Health Rankings. https://www.countyhealthrankings.org/reports/2022-county-health-rankings-national-findings-report

Del Rio, C., & Malani, P. N. (2020). COVID-19—New insights on a rapidly changing epidemic. *Journal of the American Medical Association*, *323*(14), 1339–1340. doi:10.1001/jama.2020.3072 PMID:32108857

El-Amin, A. (2022). The benefits and impact of COVID-19 lockdown on the environment. *Environmental Sciences and Ecology: Current Research (ESECR)*, *3*(1).

Friis, R., & Sellers, T. (2014). *Epidemiology for public health practice* (5th ed.). Jones & Bartlett Learning.

Haque, A., & Pant, A. B. (2022). Mitigating COVID-19 in the face of emerging virus variants, breakthrough infections, and vaccine hesitancy. *Journal of Autoimmunity*, *127*, 102792. doi:10.1016/j.jaut.2021.102792 PMID:34995958

Jin, Y., Yang, H., Ji, W., Wu, W., Chen, S., Zhang, W., & Duan, G. (2020). Virology, epidemiology, pathogenesis, and control of COVID-19. *Viruses, 12*(4), 372. https://www.mdpi.com/1999-4915/12/4/372/htm. doi:10.3390/v12040372 PMID:32230900

Kakodkar, P., Kaka, N., & Baig, M. N. (2020). A comprehensive literature review on the clinical presentation and management of the pandemic coronavirus disease 2019 (COVID-19). *Cureus, 12*(4). doi:10.7759/cureus.7560 PMID:32269893

Liu, J., Zhou, J., Yao, J., Zhang, X., Li, L., Xu, X., & Yan, J. (2020). Impact of meteorological factors on the COVID-19 transmission: A multi-city study in China. *The Science of the Total Environment, 726*, 138513. doi:10.1016/j.scitotenv.2020.138513 PMID:32304942

Lythgoe, M. P., & Middleton, P. (2020). Ongoing clinical trials for the management of the COVID-19 pandemic. *Trends in Pharmacological Sciences, 41*(6), 363–382. doi:10.1016/j.tips.2020.03.006 PMID:32291112

Qiu, J., Shen, B., Zhao, M., Wang, Z., Xie, B., & Xu, Y. (2020). A nationwide survey of psychological distress among Chinese people in the COVID-19 epidemic: Implications and policy recommendations. *General Psychiatry, 33*(2), e100213. doi:10.1136/gpsych-2020-100213 PMID:32215365

Riggioni, C., Comberiati, P., Giovannini, M., Agache, I., Akdis, M., Alves-Correia, M., & Beken, B. (2020). A compendium answering 150 questions on COVID-19 and SARS-CoV-2. *Allergy, 75*(10), 10–1111. https://www.researchgate.net/profile/Rodrigo_Jimenez-Saiz2/publication/342165769_A_compendium_answering_150_questions_on_COVID-19_and_SARS-CoV-2/links/5f168b824585151299ad5a51/A-compendium-answering-150-questions-on-COVID-19-and-SARS-CoV-2.pdf. doi:10.1111/all.14449 PMID:32535955

Sagulkoo, P., Plaimas, K., & Suratanee, A., & Maes, M. (2022). Immunopathogenesis and immunogenetic variants in COVID-19. Current Pharmaceutical Design.

Sun, P., Lu, X., Xu, C., Sun, W., & Pan, B. (2020). Understanding of COVID-19-19 based on current evidence. *Journal of Medical Virology, 92*(6), 548–551. doi:10.1002/jmv.25722 PMID:32096567

Surveillances, V. (2020). The epidemiological characteristics of an outbreak of 2019 novel coronavirus diseases (COVID-19)—China, 2020. *China CDC Weekly, 2*(8), 113–122. doi:10.46234/ccdcw2020.032 PMID:34594836

Uddin, M., Mustafa, F., Rizvi, T. A., Loney, T., Suwaidi, H. A., Al-Marzouqi, A. H. H., & Nowotny, N. (2020). SARS-CoV-2/COVID-19: Viral genomics, epidemiology, vaccines, and therapeutic interventions. *Viruses, 12*(5), 526. doi:10.3390/v12050526 PMID:32397688

Wolever, R. Q., Finn, M. T., & Shields, D. (2022). The relative contributions of live and recorded online mindfulness training programs to lower stress in the workplace: Longitudinal observational study. *Journal of Medical Internet Research, 24*(1), e31935. doi:10.2196/31935 PMID:35060911

World Health Organization (WHO). (2020a). *WHO Coronavirus Disease (COVID-19) Dashboard – China.* WHO. https://COVID-1919.who.int/region/wpro/country/cn

World Health Organization (WHO). (2020b). *WHO Coronavirus Disease (COVID-19) Dashboard – International.* WHO. https://COVID-1919.who.int

Wu, G., Yang, P., Xie, Y., Woodruff, H. C., Rao, X., Guiot, J., & Li, J. (2020). Development of a clinical decision support system for severity risk prediction and triage of COVID-19 patients at hospital admission: An international multicenter study. *The European Respiratory Journal*, 2001104. doi:10.1183/13993003.01104-2020

Xu, C., Dong, Y., Yu, X., Wang, H., Tsamlag, L., Zhang, S., & Wang, Y. (2020). Estimation of reproduction numbers of COVID-19 in typical countries and epidemic trends under different prevention and control scenarios. *Frontiers of Medicine, 14*(5), 1–10. doi:10.100711684-020-0787-4 PMID:32468343

Zhai, P., Ding, Y., Wu, X., Long, J., Zhong, Y., & Li, Y. (2020). The epidemiology, diagnosis, and treatment of COVID-19. *International Journal of Antimicrobial Agents, 55*(5), 105955. doi:10.1016/j.ijantimicag.2020.105955 PMID:32234468

Zhang, H., & Shaw, R. (2020). Identifying research trends and gaps in the context of COVID-19. *International Journal of Environmental Research and Public Health, 17*(10), 3370. doi:10.3390/ijerph17103370 PMID:32408679

Zhang, S., Wang, Z., Chang, R., Wang, H., Xu, C., Yu, X., & Cai, Y. (2020). COVID-19 containment: China provides important lessons for a global response. *Frontiers of Medicine, 14*(2), 1–5. doi:10.100711684-020-0766-9 PMID:32212059

ADDITIONAL READING

Chaney, D., & Lee, M. S. (2022). COVID-19-19 vaccines and anti-consumption: Understanding anti-vaxxers hesitancy. *Psychology and Marketing*, *39*(4), 741–754. doi:10.1002/mar.21617 PMID:35465079

Liao, Q., Cowling, B. J., Xiao, J., Yuan, J., Dong, M., Ni, M. Y., Fielding, R., & Lam, W. W. T. (2022). Priming with social benefit information of vaccination to increase acceptance of COVID-19 vaccines. *Vaccine*, *40*(8), 1074–1081. doi:10.1016/j.vaccine.2022.01.031 PMID:35090777

Pertwee, E., Simas, C., & Larson, H. J. (2022). An epidemic of uncertainty: Rumors, conspiracy theories, and vaccine hesitancy. *Nature Medicine*, *28*(3), 456–459. doi:10.103841591-022-01728-z PMID:35273403

Siani, A., & Tranter, A. (2022). Is vaccine confidence an unexpected victim of the COVID-19 pandemic? *Vaccine*, *40*(50), 7262–7269. doi:10.1016/j.vaccine.2022.10.061 PMID:36333226

KEY TERMS AND DEFINITIONS

COVID-19 (SARS-CoV-2): The outbreak of severe acute respiratory syndrome coronavirus 2 (SARS-CoV-2) disease (COVID-19) became a global pandemic declared by the World Health Organization (WHO) on March 11, 2020 (Jin et al., 2020).

Epidemiology: The study of disease in population with regards to epidemiologic investigations are applied to the containment of medical issues in populations (Friis & Dealers, 2014).

Vaccine Confidence: Heightening COVID-19 prevention strategies to include screening programs for the detection of COVID-19 based on criteria such as sensitivity, specificity, and predictive value (Zhang et al., 2020).

Virology: Virology is the scientific discipline that studies the biology of viruses and viral diseases, including spreading, biochemistry, physiology, molecular biology, ecology, evolution, and clinical aspects of viruses (Jin et al., 2020).

Chapter 6
Bio-Medical Wastes Handling Strategies During the COVID-19 Pandemic

M. Aaschita Reddy
Sreenidhi Institute of Science and Technology, India

A. Gaurav
Sreenidhi Institute of Science and Technology, India

S. Ushasukhanya
SRM Institute of Science and Technology, India

V. Chandra Shekhar Rao
Kakatiya Institute of Technology and Science, India

Sumanta Bhattacharya
https://orcid.org/0000-0003-2563-2787
MAKAUT, India

Sampath Boopathi
https://orcid.org/0000-0002-2065-6539
Muthayammal Engineering College, India

ABSTRACT

The handling of genetic residues, biohazardous waste, and other non-shrinkable materials such as e-waste is essential for the preservation of Mother Nature and human wellbeing. This chapter will bring forth different methods of managing biomedical wastes, inspecting the roots of the spread of the hazardous virus, and protecting the front-line warriors. To properly react to this disaster, each administration must create a backup strategy based on regional circumstances and the seriousness of the coronavirus's spread. Technology is being used to reduce the need for in-person

DOI: 10.4018/978-1-7998-9213-7.ch006

medical appointments and save on the cost of treatment, which is a boon for human civilization in the context of the pandemic. The Central Pollution Control Board's existing rules provide a framework for managing healthcare waste with respect for the safety of the public. Bio-waste management strategies using IoT and IoMT techniques are illustrated in this chapter.

INTRODUCTION

The bewilderment of the coronavirus in late 2019 created threats to individual health, affected our societies and economy with no uniform intensity, and transposed the general strata of perception of safety, health, and livelihood by the masses. In 2020, WHO declared COVID-19 an outbreak. What the planet did not foresee was the number of lives that would be lost. In respect to the above statement, the healthcare sector has then gained prominence over other services by saving lives, spreading awareness,, training their staff, and expecting a steadfast result from the battle of saving thousands of people against COVID 19. The Indian subcontinent has an unprecedented menace at hand: the rising pile of bio-medical waste. However, the jeopardy it has pushed upon the earth due to the mammoth sized amounts of increase in the biomedical waste that is being produced by hospitals that are treating COVID-infected patients is a fact that cannot be overlooked. However, it is not a revelation to assert that effectively managing medically contaminated trash contains the answer to controlling the coronavirus cycle. Hospitals guard human life, but, hazardous, COVID-led clinical waste created, particularly in the current pandemic crisis, continues to do irreparable harm. Mismanagement of health care waste increases the number of airborne pathogenic infectious organisms, implying a growing hazard to the immediate environment of numerous pharmaceutical centres, research facilities, and public areas. While some of the top brains are contemplating finding a cure for the ongoing Corona virus, medical garbage contaminated with hazardous communicable pathogens has now turned into a distress for healthcare facilities as they can ramp up the curve of the affected cases. This book chapter focuses on the covivirus-infected trash handling system in the midst of the coronavirus pandemic. We systematically unravel the strata of knowledge between the surface of the panic caused by the recent coronavirus and the profundity of the dire need for the urgent management of biomedical waste, and everything in between. This book chapter has its objective to throw light on many topics that are of profound importance in the nightmare that this situation is turning into at the moment,, like the amendments made for treating the genomic misuse pre- and post-coronavirus upsurge, how the Internet of Medical Things is perceived as a boon to managing the healthcare sector, and the aggravating amounts of its subsequent trash(Glasser et al., 1991). We move forward with special emphasis on the risks and repercussions of poor management of COVID-infected waste on scavengers and rag pickers,, and the front line warriors in particular in the medical field. We lay out some of the suggestions that might ameliorate the ongoing trepidation that the pandemic has pushed us towards(Reddy et al., 2023; S. et al., 2022).

The goal of this chapter is to manage current HWM procedures in the midst of the epidemic and identify the best strategy to control biomedical waste practises that are simple to implement using practical ways. For health care waste management and how to modify it, COVID-19 says waste management may necessitate particular measures, equipment, provision, operations, and administration during emergency scenarios.

BIOMEDICAL WASTE MANAGEMENT

A crystal-clear scenario is, with the growth of civilization, a larger population now has access to health care than ever before. Increased accessibility to healthcare facilities has not only enhanced the population's quality of life, but it has also put the community's health at risk due to the massive volume of biological waste produced. Because biomedical waste has both environmental and health dangers, it should be handled with care and properly disposed of. The regulation of biological waste is known as biomedical waste management. Multiple biological waste management failures have occurred in India, and the continuing covid-19 outbreak has made matters much more difficult(Ilyas et al., 2020).

As an outcome, the governments and management have noticed an increase in biological waste as a result of the sudden development of a virus. Furthermore, the issue was compounded by weak infrastructure and a paucity of supplies. Management and the government have created a variety of SOPs as well as altered prevalent points to properly address this issue.

Levels and Analysis of Biomedical Waste

According to the BMW rules of 2016, each waste category is sub partitioned into a colour code of red, yellow, blue, and white. The most common source of BMW is formed in the handling or immunisation of covid-19, which is infectious when exposed to the elements. As a result, waste management is necessary for controlling and implementing awareness campaigns(Behera, 2021) (Figure 1).

The procedures by which garbage is managed and kept safe are referred to as levels.

Location of Root: According to bio-medical waste management guidelines, garbage must be collected from sources such as hospitals, medical shops, and medical labs, and must be done under the supervision of a medical professional (in case of any misguide). Human or animal corpses should be eliminated of within 48 hours.

Classification: After the waste has been classified at the source level, it must be dispersed into different colour bags with correct labels, each with a specific capacity. Before coding, items like plastic, metals, and piercing objects must be removed.

Management and depository: After the colour bags have been coded, they must be precisely labelled with symbols, the date of entry, and the quantity, as well as the sender's and collector's information. Bags containing hazardous trash, such as radioactive and cytotoxic waste, that were dumped before 48 hours cannot be reused, and must not be stored after that time.

Transportation: According to BMWM,2018 rules, trucks or hospital facilities are employed to transport the tagged bags from adjacent hospitals that must be kept away from patients and visitors. The transport should be done on wheeled trolleys with no leaks or gas releases. The individual performing this procedure should be highly competent and aware of the risk of infection as well as the source of contamination in the event of a gas leak.

Treatment and scraping: The majority of the waste collected from medical facilities during COVID-19 is classified as general garbage. Those should be given to municipal employees, who will then separate them and dispose of them properly. Autoclaves, incineration, landfills, and deep burial are some of the treatment methods.

Figure 1. Levels of bio-medical waste

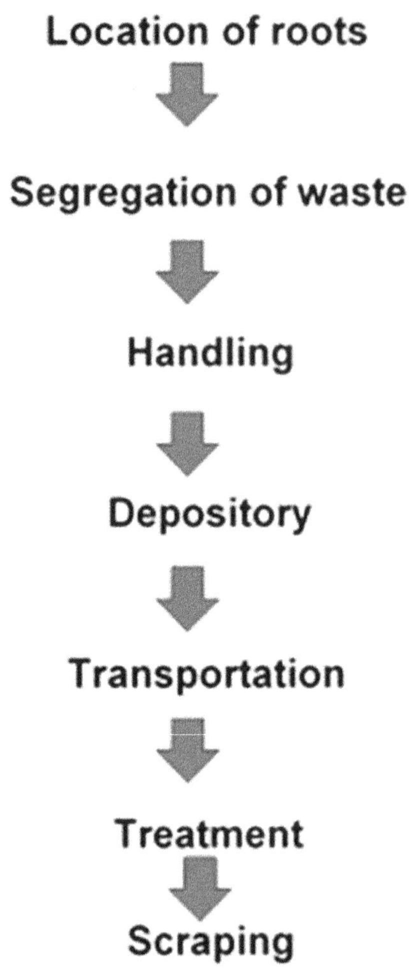

Some Effective Directives for Management of Biomedical Garbage

Many phases exist in the in the residual handling procedure that BMW management is fully reliant. Federal, sub-urban, and municipal governments will be able to draw a breath of healthcare/medical waste management policies(Ilyas et al., 2020). During this time of Covid-19, the waste policies in the municipal waste zone are beneficial to medical professionals. Those who did not have any kind of policy or strategy suffered a great deal during COVID-19. Municipalities or localities should include emergency preparation for unanticipated events, and ongoing pandemic COVID-19 waste management provocations can provide this knowledge (Figure 2).

The policy document should contour the logic for the legislation and national intentions. The main points needed for achievement of the policies.it may contain the following:

- Explanation of the health and safety issues that have arisen due to increased use of medical residue.
- The need for a safe environment for the introduction of HCWM at the outset of medical practise.

Following the approved disposal procedures

- The use of damaging practises, such as disposal of hazardous medical waste in municipal areas, is discouraged.
- Costs of health-care waste management are being assessed.
- The following policy procedures should be outlined in technical guidelines: minimization, detachment, identification, management, treatment, and final ejection of trash.
- It should be digitally recorded or documented/written on paper
- Prepare before entering into the field.
- Governing the rules for the workers' safety and health

Biomedical waste management is based on the above-mentioned waste handling stages. As a result, in compliance with the Annual Health Survey, the (DLHS) has been confirmed to obtain advice on BMW arrangements. During the Covid-19 outbreak, the DLHS conducted a biological waste study across the country, which includes 30 states and union territories. The survey system consists of protocols that have been followed by collecting waste in different colour bins labelled as yellow for toxic waste and red for biohazard symbol(Datta et al., 2018). The survey system consists of protocols that have been followed by collecting waste in different colour bins labelled as yellow for toxic waste and red for biohazard symbol. Plastic ware is blue, sharps are white, and organs are black. Different techniques of biological waste treatment, such as autoclaves, chemical disinfectants, shedders, incinerators, and deep burial pits are used to dispose them(Boopathi, 2022; Boopathi, Balasubramani, et al., 2023; Gowri et al., 2023; Janardhana et al., 2023; Kannan et al., 2022; Trojovský et al., 2023).

According to the facts provided above, many countries' problems include not just enforcing compliance but also formulating regulations and providing guidance.

In times of political decision-making or government mobilisation, a medical waste management policy is required, and resources must be available to assist in policy implementation.

- **Regulations** stating medical residual organization as well as many sectors' transportation, training qualifications.
- **Updating**: Check the facts, resources, and explain the options to the authorities for waste employees and actions.
- **A Red alert plan**: We can declare that we have an emergency strategy in place for unforeseen situations and to ensure that all HCWM services are available. In such cases, an alternative plan could include personal cars, disinfectant washing, and volunteer street cleaning services. If the environment is clear of diseases, one can feel safe.

Figure 2. Social order of regulatory and organizational structure

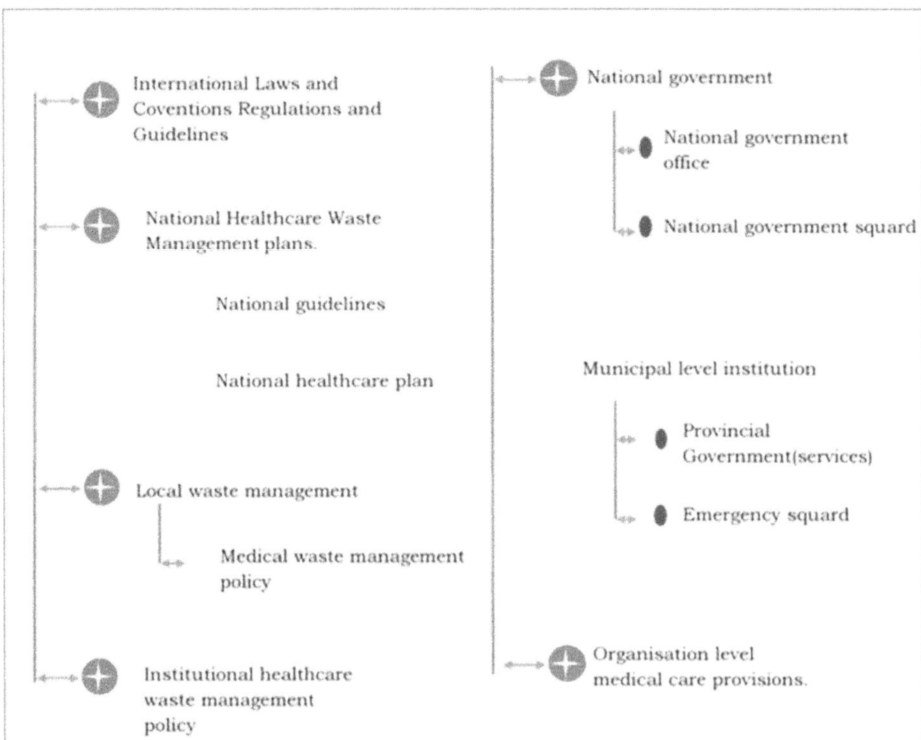

Bio medical waste management depends on various steps of handling waste as mentioned above. consequently, the DLHS has been documented to procure advice on BMW according to the AHS. A survey was conducted regarding BMW all over our country 21. This survey was done to accumulate inputs from medical hospitals, households., The survey system consists of protocols followed by collecting the waste in different colour bins labelled as yellow for toxic waste, red for bio hazard symbol, blue for plastic ware and white for sharps and black for organs etc. They are disposed by different methods.

BIO-WASTE SEGREGATION, STORAGE, AND TRANSPORTATION OF COVID-19 DISPOSALS

Treatment And Disposal Methods

The current focus is on creating rapid assessments, therapies, and immunizations, as well as persuading the public to adopt control steps. Identifying and reacting to potential pandemic spread via different kinds of associated debris has received insufficient focus. While the regulations are being amended, a sudden shift in the categorization of certain rules may result in improper handling(Capoor & Bhowmik, 2017).

The NDMC gathered 3,599 kgs of BMW and 11,438 kgs of NBMW from many isolation centres and residences of patients. For this reason, the NDMC has partnered with other organizations. The refuse gathered is moved to designated hospitals/ dispensaries for treatment and removal via a shared biological waste treatment centre.

Some low-income countries are still leading a gruelling struggle against the topic in light. A few nations have used modern technology to steam-sterilize or chemically cleanse their medical waste, but these are the exception.

When dangerous and benign materials are mixed, the total refuse becomes toxic. Typically, discarded medical supplies and other kinds of medical debris are disposed in a clean dump or burned as part of a waste-to-energy reclamation program. However, in many developing countries, hospital refuses are discarded in the open or in badly administered dumps, where rubbish collectors and animals are regularly seen.

Regarding the pandemic's retreat, changes to the BMWM standards require that some bio-hazardous material be divided into well-labeled receptacles or sacks at the point of production before being kept, moved, treated, and disposed of. Only a specific vehicle held by a responsible authority, as specified by the government, may transport unprocessed medical refuse. Untreated medical refuse should not be kept or held for longer than 48 hours. The municipality will continue to gather and convey non-medical solid refuse produced in hospitals and care homes, as well as correctly cleaned medical waste, to a city dumpsite. Every year, each agency is required to file a report to the appropriate authorities documenting the kinds and quantities of medical refuse managed the previous year.

In this upcoming discussion, we lay out some of the safety directives following which will shield all the personnel irrespective of their sector of employment against the spread of covid 19 via the covid infected clinical waste handling. Some of these regulations that we garnered via our research are

Disposal guidelines

- Follow national directives and WHO/WASH regulations.
- Separate coronavirus residues from other infectious trash at the source.
- Dangerous refuse should be discarded of in a colored foot-driven receptacle.
- Accumulation, transportation, and retention of the corona infected clinical waste should be carried out with extreme care.
- Utilize PPE and maintain hand cleanliness.
- Hybrid stream systems, microwaves, and ecological approachable handling techniques.
- Combined conductivity with sterilizer and radiation
- Use low-resource chlorine, an immersion sterilizer on the maximum level, sealing, and sterile interment for regular refuse receptacle decontamination and cleansing.
- The rag pickers or personnel associated to covid-led biomedical waste collection and handling, must fortify themselves against the risk of infection spread by wearing double layered, least penetration masks along with sturdy boots and gloves .
- The societies as a whole, must finance in waste disposal groundwork which will aid them in effectively managing the clinical or suspected biohazardous garbage.

Treatment Options

Due to the uncommon output of waste from both homes and clinics, there appears to be a garbage emergency due to the accumulation of gloves, robes, masks, and other protective apparel and equipment. Failure to correctly handle garbage produced by clinics may exacerbate the spread of the pandemic through secondary transmission. The potential rampant dumping, open combustion, and incineration could affect air quality and health outcomes due to toxin exposure. Here we present to you some of the most defined treatment options by which we can manage the healthcare waste:

- Hydrogen Peroxide (H2O2) >0.5% • Sustainable modifications with long-term improvements in system strengthening: steam-based treatment, autoclaving, or microwaving are chosen for waste treatment. Requirements.
- Improve tracking of the biomedical waste units which come out of the hospitals and reduce incineration.
- Waste may be sent for disposal after disinfection.
- Recycling should proceed as usual and dental should be held with care

Challenges in managing the Bio medical waste during coronavirus.

One of UNEP's main themes is to make full use of current waste management systems. "Disaster is the worst time for trading professional cards," as the saying goes in emergency management. It is also a bad time to build new medical WMS during an epidemic(Pasupathi et al., 2011). In today's date, Covid 19 pandemic has spawned many challenges and setbacks in various walks of our lives.Some of the challenges are explored below:

- At the moment, no appropriate drugs has been disclosed for addressing COVID-19; administration and companies are battling to discover operational medicines. The public are consuming medicines for curing themselves from the pandemic, which unnecessarily increases BMW.
- One of the most ignored aspects of health care in India is BMW regulation. Since the the administration made changes by providing simpler classifications for division of separate BMWs, an update in 2018 was passed with the objective of increasing regulation compliance. With a marginal growth rate, appropriate classification, management, and removal remained a critical issue.
- People admit themselves out of fear and add to the BMW generation.

The Usage of PPE Kit

According to preliminary reports, conditions may worsen amid the epidemic, with large PPE supplies in hospitals. Despite WHO and Government of India guidelines on personal protective equipment (PPE), health care settings are experiencing high PPE demand due to infection fear. Fear frequently leads to PPE misuse, worsening the situation by causing BMW, which are difficult to keep and transport.

Unusual Demand of Safety Apparels

Medical supplies are in higher demand. Even in the community, the haphazard use and dumping of disposable medical shields adds to the danger. They are commonly discarded with inert trash from homes and domestic situations where colored BMW receptacles are scarce. Facial coverings have accumulated along the territory's environment routes and coastlines as a result of erroneous disposal in rivers and lakes, disturbing the aquatic ecosystem. Aquatic life suffers as a result of aquatic ecosystems mistaking inert polymers from facial shields for sustenance.

Expertise of Some Countries to Handle COVID-Led Clinical Waste

Production soared, but most nations were not prepared to manage such massive volumes of Bio hazardous trash. Today, most nations, particularly developing nations, suffer the same problem as Wuhan did in the past: insufficient medical waste treatment facilities. Since the established BMW facilities in developing countries lack the ability to handle a rise in medical waste during a epidemic, existing facilities must be extended. New treatment centers must be built.

Building Cleansing Employees' Capacity to Safeguard Their Own Opposing Contamination Progression

Clean-up employees, such as medical professionals and nurses, are a similarly important set of players engaged in effective COVID-19 epidemic control.

One of the most serious problems is that people who are subjected to biological garbage at different levels are completely ignorant of the risk. Raising knowledge and instruction of human resources engaged in BMW gathering and dumping are the primary areas for keeping safety and averting dangers. Non-technical hospital employees and college medical students lack adequate understanding of BMW administration. The workers should be educated on infection control measures, hand cleanliness, breathing decorum, social space, and the use of PPE, according to guidelines for BMW management.

ALTERNATIVE TECHNOLOGIES THAT HELP BIO MEDICAL WASTE MANAGEMENT

IOT

In terms of technology, the importance of healthcare waste management cannot be overstated. The IoT has the ability to revolutionize waste management. At all refuse sites, connected sensing devices and an organized IoT-based environment can be implemented. Smart garbage bins may be used to develop intelligent ways by combining the system, networks, and technology suppliers with IoT-based devices. In the BMW, intelligent receptacles with sufficient classification and upkeep can be used.. In medical clinics, the traditional method of trash collection might expose personnel to harmful diseases and injuries(Selvaraj et al., 2022).

IoT sensors and devices can be used to transmit data related to significant variables involved in BMW. The implementation of IoT-based trash management also requires a comprehensive investigation of the problem from multiple perspectives. Implementing a solid refuse management framework helps to create a clean atmosphere as well as a safe community.

The following some topics are in practice of medical waste management which are majorly contributed by IOT:

- In garbage management, the Internet of Things is revolting.
- Medical waste management research based on resources
- In the field of healthcare waste management, wearable technologies are being developed.
- Possibilities for reducing healthcare waste
- Smart technology has made a significant contribution to hospital waste management.
- A sophisticated healthcare waste monitoring system.
- Infectious and hazardous waste management systems have taken on new approaches in recent years.
- In healthcare, IoT-based scrap management

IoMT

The IoMT is a medical innovation. Social distancing norms, which have prompted the development of modern devices with internet of things (IoMT), such as using Wifi or Bluetooth to connect with patients without touching or standing nearby patients and allowing aid to be delivered remotely, have increased the need in the health-care system (Figure 3). If every individual in a large population country gets infected (for example, the Covid-19 pandemic), this technology will come in handy so that competent doctors can manage high-risk patients.

This enables us to expand our networks while still safeguarding people and assuring business. The goal of this study was to look into places where we could use technological advances to significantly improve the client's treatment process despite increasing costs(Reddy et al., 2023; S. et al., 2022; Samikannu et al., 2023).

While IoMT and advances in medical treatment are wide subjects, this study concentrated on 9 particular applications and questioned ten physicians from the United States and India. One of the objectives of the initiative is to find applications that have a greater probability to be available for implementation at the moment rather than those that require greater hazards or additional time to develop.(Anitha et al., 2023; Jeevanantham et al., 2023; Subha et al., 2023)

Among the most common applications were drone transportation, patient video tracking, in-patient monitoring, hospital trash management, and condition monitoring.

Figure 3. IoMT Technology

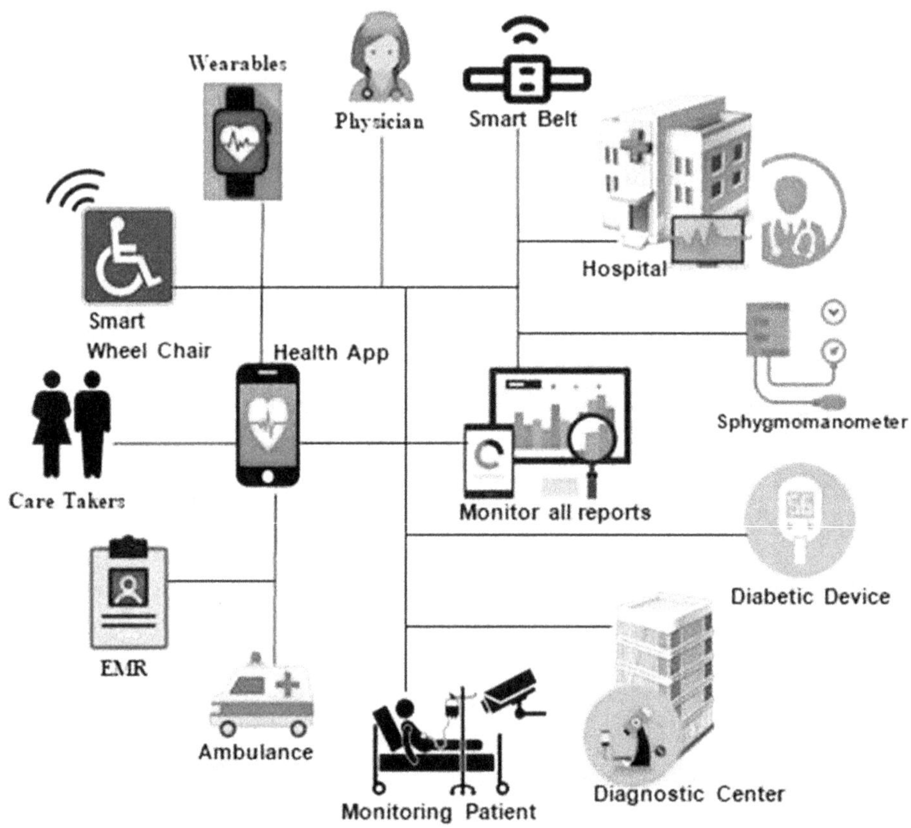

Waste Management Monitoring

Many hospitals' existing waste management systems entail inefficient rubbish collection since trash fluctuates over time. Trash administration tracking at medical facilities could notify healthcare facilities when containers achieve topping and avoiding redundant accumulations. Rubbish is currently collected on a schedule; for example, certain hospitals may only collect garbage once a week. This can lead to overflowing trash bins. Material administration observing should use detectors to alert healthcare facilities as inefficiency amounts grow above 75%, permitting the establishment to be more productive.

These innovations, corresponding to the medical professionals polled, are currently in use in many medical facilities, and the priority ought to be on employing recyclable materials, that could decrease both garbage and expenditure.

IOMT Helping in BMWM To Prevent the Spread of COVID-19

BMW arrangements comprise intelligent smart bins with correct waste material classification and maintenance. However, no one can handle the bins during the COVID-19 epidemic, therefore clever smart bins with automated lid opening come into play. Weight could be computed using IoMT, and signals sent to garbage collectors to pick up the rubbish could be sent automatically(Anitha et al., 2023; Subha et al., 2023)(Figure 4).

Smart pill technology is used to meet pharmaceutical needs, as well as to categorise pharmaceuticals into two groups: helpful and non-essential for human usage, which helps with waste management.

Figure 4. Advantages of IoMT

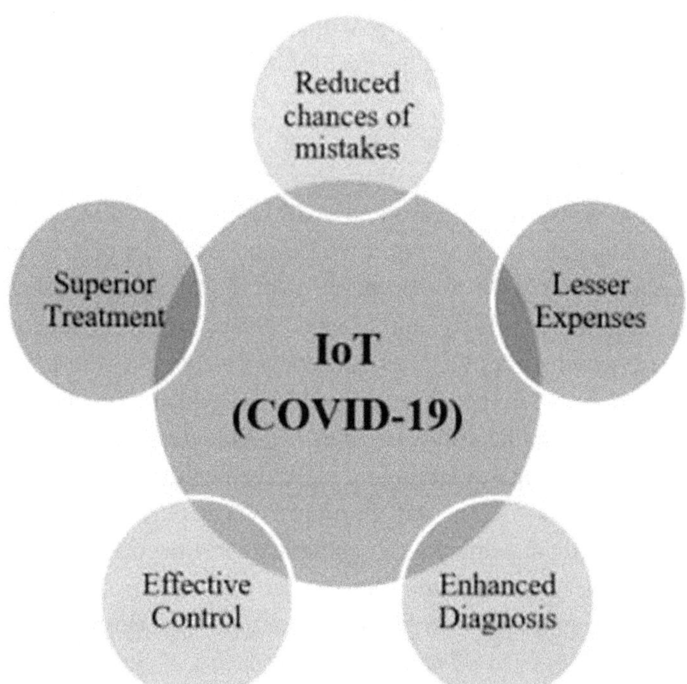

The projects mentioned below are only a few of the many that Health Care Without Harm and its partners are working on across the world. The following are some projects that are useful to medical therapy without creating harm:

The Bagamayo project: An imaginative preliminary investigation employing a sterilizer for disinfecting infectious garbage is currently underway at HCWH where workers are instructed about discrimination. A sterilizer and splitter in collaboration with native non-governmental organizations were used. A waste administration group was formed(Jeevanantham et al., 2023; Saha1 et al., 2022).

The GEF Project: The HCWH is working on a global ecological equipment-assisted undertaking with the WHO and the UNO. The project's title is "Demonstrating and Promoting Best Techniques and Practices for Reducing Health Care Waste to Avoid Dioxin and Mercury Environmental Releases." It was primarily established to help poor nations. By encouraging best practises for reducing and managing health-care waste, the project's ultimate objective is to reduce dioxin and mercury emissions into the environment.

Advantages (Pros) of Waste Management in Bio Medical Field

Compliance with state and federal rules is the most fundamental advantage of effective hospital waste disposal. The WHO, CDC, OSHA, and USEPA have enacted rules to implement the cleanliness and waste regulation of medical facilities. If garbage management is carried out in accordance with their guidelines, it will be an advantage for getting support from higher authorities for doing so.

- Biomedical waste management may lead to a cleaner environment as there are so many diseases due to improper waste management like virus and many diseases. Used medical goods will be maintained in one location due to waste management. Water and wildlife habitats can be contaminated due to inadequate HWM. If not properly disposed of, toxic hospital waste can endanger humans, animals, and plants. Medical waste is sometimes placed in sewage, which flows to lakes and contaminates the water, as well as the organisms that live in the water and animals(Reddy et al., 2023).
- Healthcare garbage handling is often implemented for accepted, but there are numerous benefits to having an effective healthcare garbage framework, like individuals as well as staff harmony of awareness and assurance. Poor hospital waste management exposes patients to infectious pathogens, needle sticks, and other harmful situations.
- Aids in the prevention of hospital-acquired illnesses by enhancing the preventive impact of good handwashing;

- Cuts infection cycles; and targets health-care personnel in a simple and cost-effective manner.
- When precise instructions and guidelines are followed at each step, waste management is extremely effective and efficient. The first stage should be to determine viable choices for BMWM based on the budget, technology, and preferences of the local community. When selecting the proper treatment technique for health care waste, several variables (such as volume, temperature, and composition) must be addressed. whether the waste is liquid or solid, hazardous or infectious).by determining these all we can be able to use precise technology and money to keep the hospitals labs clean
- One of the benefits of waste management is that it classifies garbage into distinct types of dry and wet trash, as well as different coloured trash. The hue development corresponds to a specific category of garbage and disposal alternatives. As a result, the procedure is simple.
- Many dangerous diseases have been halted as a result of biomedical waste management. This is due to the presence of hazardous miniature infectious agents like viruses, microbes, and bugs. If waste is not handled in a manner that destroys these infectious organisms, chemicals may penetrate the human system through cuts and other fluid layers in the oral cavity.

Limitations to Waste Management in Bio Medical Field

- Front line warriors have used many medical kits as well as surgical equipment. Yet, the problem comes after its usage which is a disadvantage. As public outcry grows in many nations, the US has seen an exponential surge in medical waste production. Every hour, 45 tonnes of garbage are created, necessitating biomedical waste management.
- Many components or goods, such as syringes, pills, ppe kits, vaccinations, and so on, are non-biodegradable trash that takes many years to degrade, resulting in contamination of the environment and land use.
- Because much of the globe was impacted by the covid 19 epidemic, many pharmacies raised their output by 40 to 50 percent, resulting in a loss in natural resources.
- The total garbage from covid 19 unaffected individuals, including food conceals thrown by them, is three times that of confined individuals. As a result of the waste, employees may be afflicted and may infect others without their knowledge. Some countries, such as Indonesia (the Java area), suffer from poor garbage management.

- Burning waste management is less attractive when there is less of an emergency or a need for temporary disposal.
- In the event of impacted situations, transportation would be problematic.
- As the number of cases grew, so did operational capacity.
- Medical waste handles are at high risk during this pandemic in case of high injury or infection, especially from sharp objects.
- Most of the garbage is radioactive, rag pickers must use caution.

Waste management itself doesn't have any faults .But the types of BMWM have some disadvantages also such as:

Incineration: There appears to be an environmental crisis due to the accumulation of coverings, dresses, respirators, and other PPE owing to the unprecedented volume of trash from each household and healthcare establishments (Metal. 2020). Inability to properly manage garbage generated by medical institutions as well as households could lead to supplementary COVID-19 transfer. In this sort of BMWM, the procedure is too costly. As a result of the process, various harmful gases are released, potentially polluting the air. The heavy metals that remain in the ash residue after the incineration are harmful. It's also a significant generator of dioxin and a colourless flammable poisonous liquid chemical(Boopathi, Khare, et al., 2023; S. et al., 2022; Senthil et al., 2023; Vanitha et al., 2023).

Autoclave: The trash should be processed first and foremost using a drying system to dry any wet components that may be present. In the case of insufficient air supply, odours might be a concern near autoclaves. The procedure is confined to particular types of wastes and is not suited for all sorts of trash. We need to use a shredder to minimise the volume of garbage, and processed garbage can be maintained due to its physical appearance which requires further processing of final ejection.

Microwave: Some chemicals, such as volatile and semivolatile organic mixtures, mercury, and other hazardous chemical wastes, are not handled by microwave treatment, necessitating a different ultimate disposal technique, and volume and weight reduction are limited.

RECOMMENDATIONS

Some Chinese regions bought portable rehabilitation automobiles as safeguards over the last ten years and acquired considerable expertise. As a backup plan for unforeseen circumstances, every nation and fundamental town should have some portable healthcare garbage implementation. amenities. While required, these establishments may help certain isolated regions and territories with the correct healthcare squander treatment(Boopathi, Arigela, et al., 2023; Jeevanantham et al., 2023).

- More abilities for portable amenities should be preserved, especially during epidemics, which can be critical for acquiring nations with limited healthcare garbage elimination facilities. Portable amenities are not only useful in a crisis, but they can also be used as a tactical protection ability for the nation in the years to come.
- Using societal mediums enhance belonging, worldwide, and worldwide consciousness.
- Choose the Basel convention regulations and have nations implement and tailor them to their specific circumstances.
- The societies as a whole, must finance in waste disposal groundwork and in the raising the cognizance in their residents by conducting online awareness sessions.

CONCLUSION

Because of the world's overpopulation, demand for healthcare is uncertain. Improving healthcare effectiveness is the only way to reduce biological waste. This book chapter was a laborious effort to gather information and review all parameters related to the management of general medical waste on one hand and medical waste specific to the pandemic on the other. This is because, clinical waste requires special treatment due to its ramifications on the environment and the human race.

Furthermore, a clean human existence and a green environment are only achievable if one has a healthier environment thanks to a better BMWM system. It gives off a positive feeling about reducing occurrences caused by infectious illnesses, regulating the transmission of viruses and germs during the process, reusing, recycling, and reducing needless waste, and generating income via effective management in BMW. To summarise, each individual may contribute to the total eradication of the pandemic scenario caused by Covid 19 by obeying the government's as well as BMWM's laws and regulations to safeguard the environment and health quality. Many laws and regulations, such as adequate waste generation and segregation, a hospital-based biomedical waste management plant, and better health-care member measures, are adopted as emergency requirements and practised by every member of medical units in order to protect public health. Many organisations have been successful in supporting or maintaining the awareness programme and effort to organise knowledge for both health care personnel and covid 19 patients.

Owing to the strides in IOMT, medical equipment and use cases will be able to communicate with the patient and the emergency system workplace in the future, and with further analysis, it will be able to predict disease outcomes and prepare medicines in the event of a new disease outbreak, such as smart hospital data collection (disease health insurances clinical trial data and medical data).

ACRONYMS

Associated Chambers Of Commerce And Industry Of India (ASSOCHAM)
Municipal Solid Waste (MSW)
Central Pollution Control Board (CPCB)
World Health Organization (WHO)
BMWM Biomedical Waste Management
Dental Waste (DW)
Personal Protective Equipment (PPE)
Indian Medical Association (IMA)
Syndrome Coronavirus 2 (SARS Cov2)
Healthcare Risk Waste (HCRW)
District Level Health Survey
Annual Health Survey
Sustainable Development Goals (Sdgs)
Single-Use Plastic (SUP)
North Delhi Municipal Corporation (NDMC
Internet of Medical Things (Iomt)

REFERENCES

Anitha, C., R, K. C., Vivekanand, C. V., Lalitha, S. D., Boopathi, S., & R, R. (2023, February). Artificial Intelligence driven security model for Internet of Medical Things ({IoMT}). *IEEE Explore*. IEEE. doi:10.1109/ICIPTM57143.2023.10117713

Behera, B. C. (2021). Challenges in handling COVID-19 waste and its management mechanism: A Review. *Environmental Nanotechnology, Monitoring \& Management, 15*, 100432.

Boopathi, S. (2022). Cryogenically treated and untreated stainless steel grade 317 in sustainable wire electrical discharge machining process: A comparative study. *Environmental Science and Pollution Research International*, 1–10. doi:10.100711356-022-22843-x PMID:36057706

Boopathi, S., Arigela, S. H., Raman, R., Indhumathi, C., Kavitha, V., & Bhatt, B. C. (2023). Prominent Rule Control-based Internet of Things: Poultry Farm Management System. *IEEE Explore*, (pp. 1–6). IEEE. doi:10.1109/ICPECTS56089.2022.10047039

Boopathi, S., Balasubramani, V., & Sanjeev Kumar, R. (2023). Influences of various natural fibers on the mechanical and drilling characteristics of coir-fiber-based hybrid epoxy composites. *Engineering Research Express*, *5*(1), 15002. doi:10.1088/2631-8695/acb132

Boopathi, S., Khare, R., Jaya Christiyan, K. G., Muni, T. V., & Khare, S. (2023). Additive manufacturing developments in the medical engineering field. In Development, Properties, and Industrial Applications of 3D Printed Polymer Composites (pp. 86–106). IGI Global. doi:10.4018/978-1-6684-6009-2.ch006

Capoor, M. R., & Bhowmik, K. T. (2017). Current perspectives on biomedical waste management: Rules, conventions and treatment technologies. *Indian Journal of Medical Microbiology*, *35*(2), 157–164. doi:10.4103/ijmm.IJMM_17_138 PMID:28681801

Datta, P., Mohi, G., & Chander, J. (2018). Biomedical waste management in India: Critical appraisal. *Journal of Laboratory Physicians*, *10*(01), 6–14. doi:10.4103/JLP.JLP_89_17 PMID:29403196

Glasser, H., Chang, D. P. Y., & Hickman, D. C. (1991). An analysis of biomedical waste incineration. *Journal of the Air \& Waste Management Association, 41*(9), 1180–1188.

Gowri, N. V., Dwivedi, J. N., Krishnaveni, K., Boopathi, S., Palaniappan, M., & Medikondu, N. R. (2023). Experimental investigation and multi-objective optimization of eco-friendly near-dry electrical discharge machining of shape memory alloy using Cu/SiC/Gr composite electrode. *Environmental Science and Pollution Research International*, 1–19. doi:10.100711356-023-26983-6 PMID:37126160

Ilyas, S., Srivastava, R. R., & Kim, H. (2020). Disinfection technology and strategies for COVID-19 hospital and bio-medical waste management. *The Science of the Total Environment*, *749*, 141652. doi:10.1016/j.scitotenv.2020.141652 PMID:32822917

Janardhana, K., Anushkannan, N. K., Dinakaran, K. P., Puse, R. K., & Boopathi, S. (2023). *Experimental Investigation on Microhardness, Surface Roughness, and White Layer Thickness of Dry EDM*. Engineering Research Express. doi:10.1088/2631-8695/acce8f

Jeevanantham, Y. A., A, S., V, V., J, S. I., Boopathi, S., & Kumar, D. P. (2023). Implementation of Internet-of Things (IoT) in Soil Irrigation System. *IEEE Explore*, 1–5. doi:10.1109/ICPECTS56089.2022.10047185

Kannan, E., Trabelsi, Y., Boopathi, S., & Alagesan, S. (2022). Influences of cryogenically treated work material on near-dry wire-cut electrical discharge machining process. *Surface Topography : Metrology and Properties*, *10*(1), 15027. doi:10.1088/2051-672X/ac53e1

Pasupathi, P., Sindhu, S., Ponnusha, B. S., & Ambika, A. (2011). Biomedical waste management for health care industry. *International Journal of Biological and Medical Research*, *2*(1), 472–486.

Reddy, M. A., Reddy, B. M., Mukund, C. S., Venneti, K., Preethi, D. M. D., & Boopathi, S. (2023). Social Health Protection During the COVID-Pandemic Using IoT. In *The COVID-19 Pandemic and the Digitalization of Diplomacy* (pp. 204–235). IGI Global. doi:10.4018/978-1-7998-8394-4.ch009

S., P. K., Sampath, B., R., S. K., Babu, B. H., & N., A. (2022). Hydroponics, Aeroponics, and Aquaponics Technologies in Modern Agricultural Cultivation. In *Trends, Paradigms, and Advances in Mechatronics Engineering* (pp. 223–241). IGI Global. doi:10.4018/978-1-6684-5887-7.ch012

Saha1, B. C., R, D., A, A., Thrinath, B. V. S., Boopathi, S., * J. R., & Sudhakar, M. (2022). *IOT Based Smart Energy Meter For Smart Grid*.

Samikannu, R., Koshariya, A. K., Poornima, E., Ramesh, S., Kumar, A., & Boopathi, S. (2023). Sustainable Development in Modern Aquaponics Cultivation Systems Using IoT Technologies. In *Human Agro-Energy Optimization for Business and Industry* (pp. 105–127). IGI Global. doi:10.4018/978-1-6684-4118-3.ch006

Selvaraj, S., Prasadh, S., Fuloria, S., Subramaniyan, V., Sekar, M., Ahmed, A. M., Bouallegue, B., Hari Kumar, D., Sharma, V. K., Maziz, M. N. H., Sathasivam, K. V., Meenakshi, D. U., & Fuloria, N. K. (2022). COVID-19 Biomedical Plastics Wastes—Challenges and Strategies for Curbing the Environmental Disaster. *Sustainability (Basel)*, *14*(11), 6466. doi:10.3390u14116466

Senthil, T. S. R. Ohmsakthi vel, Puviyarasan, M., Babu, S. R., Surakasi, R., & Sampath, B. (2023). Industrial Robot-Integrated Fused Deposition Modelling for the 3D Printing Process. In Development, Properties, and Industrial Applications of 3D Printed Polymer Composites (pp. 188–210). IGI Global. doi:10.4018/978-1-6684-6009-2.ch011

Subha, S., Inbamalar, T. M., R, K. C., Suresh, L. R., Boopathi, S., & Alaskar, K. (2023, February). A Remote Health Care Monitoring system using internet of medical things ({IoMT}). *IEEE Explore*. IEEE. doi:10.1109/ICIPTM57143.2023.10118103

Trojovský, P., Dhasarathan, V., & Boopathi, S. (2023). Experimental investigations on cryogenic friction-stir welding of similar ZE42 magnesium alloys. *Alexandria Engineering Journal*, *66*(1), 1–14. doi:10.1016/j.aej.2022.12.007

Vanitha, S. K. R., & Boopathi, S. (2023). Artificial Intelligence Techniques in Water Purification and Utilization. In Human Agro-Energy Optimization for Business and Industry (pp. 202–218). IGI Global. doi:10.4018/978-1-6684-4118-3.ch010

Chapter 7
A Twin-Track Approach for Informal Settlements Restructuring in Response to the Impact of COVID-19:
A Case Study

Tarek Fouad Rahmoun
https://orcid.org/0000-0001-5112-2487
Tishreen University, Syria

Maya Hassan
https://orcid.org/0000-0002-8350-6634
Tishreen University, Syria

Ali Naddeh
Syrian Virtual University, Syria

ABSTRACT

The impact of epidemics on urban restructuring is one of the most critical planning issues. This chapter presents a twin-track approach to intervention in the informal housing areas in Syria after investigating the ability to face the impact of Covid-19 epidemic. The informal housing "al-Radar" area in Tartous City was adopted as a case study. Both qualitative and quantitative methods were used for a multi-dimensional analysis of gathered data and site planning aspects. The goals are to achieve participatory decision-making to guide area restructuring aligned with national urban development laws. In addition, laying down the foundation of an area

DOI: 10.4018/978-1-7998-9213-7.ch007

plan for future on-site redevelopment considers community cohesion and land-use improvements. Results illustrated the poor traditional planning criteria efficiency in achieving urban resilience/immunity required for a "new normal" and the need for good governance in land administration utilizing 15-minute city principles and a street-led citywide approach for the full integration into the city system as a tool to promote sustainable development.

INTRODUCTION

Diseases shape cities (Das, Roy, Parvez, & Hasan, 2020). Epidemics such as the plague and the Spanish flu changed the cities' planning and conducted the shifts in building codes that are still in use today. Many cities, such as Paris, New York, and Rio de Janeiro, have been redesigned to include higher hygiene standards and to upgrade sewage facilities (UN-Habitat, 2020) . Urban planning and public health have been historically associated (Olszewska-Guizzo, Fogel, Benjumea, & Tahsin, 2022). The connection between these two terms in the calls of the early planning movement of the late nineteenth century helped reshape the urban form and influenced housing planning standards in rapidly developing European cities; to handle the concerns about public health and slum conditions (Scott, 2020). Consequently, city planning is critical for infectious disease management (AbouKorin, Han, & Mahran, 2021). Several urban planning innovations arose to respond to the health crises, such as the urban parks movement in the nineteenth century in the United States of America and the sewage system reform in Britain (Crompton, 2013; Bereitschaft & Scheller, 2020). While the pursuit of healthy and modern spaces was a major factor in the twentieth-century leap embodied in Howard's ideas of the Garden City and Le Corbusier's Social Housing, where cleanliness and moral health depend on the city planning, and the social unit becomes atrophied without them. The social unit "Neighborhood Unit" introduced by Clarence A. Perry illustrates the relationships between the residential components of the neighborhood and the various non-residential usages. The goal was to catch the daily services within a 5-minute walk as an integrated community based on self-sufficiency with open spaces and complete separation between vehicular and pedestrian traffic (Patricios, 2002; Mehaffy, Porta, & Romice, 2014). This theory provides a schematic guide to the space and facilities that can uphold routine life within spatial boundaries (Byun, Choi, & Choi, 2014). The neighborhood unit with the planning assets of the garden city formed the spatial patterns of the contemporary to generate the theory of new urbanism in an attempt to solve the problem of the garden city and modernity, which included new ways of thinking about the urban form (Jin, 2020). Hence, the decentralized city proposed establishing intimate settlements and distributing production, considering the negative impact of polluting industry on human health and creating a closer relationship between the city and the countryside. However, despite these good intentions, many of these spaces have not stood the test of time due to the gradual move away from health concerns and public health assets and the increasingly planning trend towards acting as a facilitator of market-led development. That is reflected in the increasing privatization of open and green spaces, poorly designed neighborhoods, low-quality housing, rapid planning with a rapidly increasing population, and urban sprawl (UN-Habitat, 2019; Okech & Nyadera, 2022). These issues are considered reasons that caused some urban developments since the 1960s in parallel with the increase in human activities and their effects on the environment to be effective in allowing the spread of epidemics, the latest but not least of which was Covid-19 (Scott, 2020; Pire & Boivin, 2020).

On the other hand, at the spatial dimension of the city, rapid urbanization exacerbated city public health problems. Slums are considered an integral part of urbanization (Ooi & Kai, 2007). Slums and informal housing areas constituted the nucleus of urban poverty associated with weak urban immunity to epidemics (Brotherhood, Cavalcanti, Da Mata, & Santos, 2022). According to the United Nations, about one billion people currently live in slums, and an additional 3 billion people will need adequate housing by 2050 (UN-Habitat, 2010). These slums are formed from informal or unplanned land use without prior official plans. In this context, informal slums, the most vulnerable neighborhoods, are critical as many urban slum dwellers lack access to basic services such as water, sanitation, housing, and health care and are in the transition zone (Izutsu & Tsutsumi, 2010). Such facts put this spatial sector at a double risk of infection due to the difficulty of adhering to the rules of social distancing based on its form, physical structure, and social aspects. However, master planning is one of the intervention policies for a holistic spatial reconstruction that assists slums to rapidly and sustainably transform towards solving the associated housing and health problems. In African countries, for example, new urban planning strategies were adopted, including the removal of slums and the improvement of urban infrastructure to counter the outbreak of cholera and plague (AbouKorin, Han, & Mahran, 2021). At the same time, informal societies are often a critical demographic lever for economic activities at the city level. Therefore, the wrong intervention in addressing them may have negative social and economic consequences that will likely extend beyond their borders. Therefore, a new planning conviction that the solution must start from within, meaning that the solution is based on the basis for community participation in identifying planning problems and challenges to propose sustainable planning alternatives (Ragheb & El-Ashmawy, 2021).

Slums in Syria fall under the name of "informal housing areas". Informal housing in Syria constitutes a major urban challenge facing major cities. 2011 witnessed an upsurge in informal housing due to the demographic displacement trends as the war results (GCSC & RPC, 2020). The impact of the problem of informal housing is not limited to the service and social suffering of the dwellers. Still, it goes beyond it to sag in the fabric of existing cities, a decline in the effectiveness of transportation networks, and a limitation in providing job opportunities. Informal housing areas in Syria are characterized by continuous gradual growth, high population density, and permanent construction structures, giving them a different character from slums in other countries (RPC-Syria, 2011). These areas formed a fertile ground for the spread of Covid-19 infection in several Syrian cities, which necessitated a move to develop a new planning vision for the confrontation as the most vulnerable areas in the city's structure. This chapter discusses a new approach to intervention in one of the informal areas in Syria located within the organizational plan of Tartous City called "Hayy Al-Radar- al-Radar area" taking into consideration the impact of covid-19 during the pandemic response period and beyond on the one hand, and the new national urban development laws on the other hand.

REVIEW OF LITERATURE

Restructuring the Current City Form Under the Impact of Covid-19

Covid-19 has attacked the concept of the city. The current urban structure of the city, with its physical, social, and environmental dimensions, suffers from many weaknesses that have emerged clearly in the face of this epidemic. Most researchers agree that emergent changes in behavior during the crisis will continue in the medium and long term. It is unlikely that the post-Covid-19 world will look the same as before (Das, Roy, Parvez, & Hasan, 2020). The outdated planning legislation and zoning "land use" laws were among the most critical problems, which is a prerequisite for achieving active mobility and improving public health (J Nieuwenhuijsen, 2020). Although the required changes in the field of urban planning are still in the process of being completed to achieve the required efficiency in the face of the Covid-19 epidemic and what is the worst in the future if human activities continue in their effects. Nevertheless, it is time to rethink urban renewal strategies (Bereitschaft & Scheller, 2020). The local authorities are supposed to work to leave spatial spaces within the urban structure to promote clean connectivity, improve air/water quality, and manage risks. Such transformative actions steer urban planning towards creating more sustainable, resilient cities and strengthen the urban immune system (Taşan-Kok, 2020; Megahed & Ghoneim, 2020). The tangible feeling of inertia that the "me" cannot live without the "you" can generate a real opportunity for more progressive development from urban planning. Thus, the disaster represented by Covid-19 can generate an opportunity for authorities and operators to reconfigure urban systems that provide real benefits so that recovery is rapid and life returns to the way it was before Covid-19 (Das, Roy, Parvez, & Hasan, 2020). Moreover, the involvement of both local authorities and citizens is required to develop urban and environmental protocols, as well as planning and design strategies, where their responses affect the livelihoods in their cities (Allam & S. Jones, 2020). Thus, new planning dimensions must be taken into consideration within the spatial dimensions of current and future cities. The goal is to achieve a flexible neighborhood that deals with the current density with a kind of "environmental friendliness" that does not condone or compete with the improvement of human conditions that can be measured through socio-economic impacts (Jon, 2020; Sharifi & Khavarian-Garmsir, 2020). Yet, the interest alliances of the stakeholders in the urban environment can achieve stronger points for positive change in an innovative and integrated way to lead in the face of epidemics toward sustainable development and the recovery of the local economy of urban communities (van den Berg, 2020; Barnwal, 2020), down to providing a flexible network of energy savings, transportation networks, and food production through a range of stages from preparation to relief response to reconstruction and resilience building for future development (Pelling, 2020; Singh, Ramesh Kumar, & Tiwari, 2021).

Density is an essential issue in urban environments, provided that it is achieved positively. It is not necessary to contain it in towers or residential buildings with large areas, but in the vital environment currently missing in the open public spaces of which the streets and parking lots occupy 70% of its area (Jon, 2020; Lak, Shakouri Asl, & Maher, 2020). The current pandemic challenges planning principles, which mistakenly confuses density and overcrowding or disruptions in connectivity as an accelerator of the spread of infection and the inability to reach the required health services in formal and informal settlements alike (UN-Habitat, 2020; Teller, 2021). Density should not become an urban curse; it is required for social connectivity, expanding access to key services, and economic growth. Moreover, no clear relationship between density and risk of transmission of the Coronavirus was proven in a study conducted by the World Bank on 284 Chinese cities, as well as Singapore and Seoul in South Korea (Mackres, 2020; Gold, 2020). Thus, the challenge for urban spatial planning stands in the transformation process in both physical and social functions to restructuring the urban living space towards an actual medium of social interaction within a flexible urban system achieving the harmony between density, required urban services and also being able to host smart urban systems (Kakderi, Oikonomaki, & Papadaki, 2021; Song, et al., 2021). The importance of the urban form in determining the spatial distribution of land uses, mobility options, agglomeration, and mass ratio to the area collectively affects the relationship between human concentration and accompanying economic activities and urban immunity, on the other hand (Khavarian-Garmsir & Sharifi, 2020; Oriewo, 2020). Such transformation action could be according to a new urban administrative approach that allows authorities and operators to significantly reshape urban systems by confronting the established legislation to bring life back, similar to the pre-Covid19 world. According to the "New Urbanism" approach, the social scope of the neighborhood concept is central to its renewal as it naturally helps to establish the vital center and boundaries of the required social relations and advocates the design of integrated mixed-use environmentally friendly projects (Grant, 2006; Lucka, 2018). Nevertheless, innovation in the transition towards sustainable, flexible systems can significantly change confrontation policies. As, transportation systems constitute the nucleus of the urban reconfiguration process, "framing" and "enabling" are two integrated actions that could be taken in light of epidemics and health crises. Firstly, "framing" refers to reallocating the urban space allocated to transportation components from infrastructure "roads, sidewalks, car parking spaces". Secondly, "enabling" in the sense of re-governing the system and reassessing investments in transportation infrastructure such as using clean transportation systems, encouraging mobility based on bicycles and electric cars, reducing cross-sectional crossing of neighborhoods as much as possible, and re-investing the spaces allocated for surface parking by multi-floor parking buildings (Das, Roy, Parvez, & Hasan, 2020).

In fact, the crisis has shown that current practices are not sustainable, and maybe the planning policy choices we make to face its impacts will shape the cities of tomorrow for decades to come. As a result, rational revisions of several planning concepts have begun, and the creation of other approaches in line with the "new normal" (UNESCO, 2020). Trends were calling for harmonizing the Superblock model as a concept has emerged intending to reshape urban space with more green spaces, fewer roads network, and cohesive social relations within giant square units 400 * 400 meters and a population of 5000-6000 people and a range of 5-minute walking (López, Ortega, & Pardo, 2020; Camerin & Fabris, 2021). Clarence Perry's neighborhood concept is a socio-economic unit that fulfills the daily functional needs of its residents within a time scale equivalent today of 15-20 minutes due to the change in transportation almost 100 years after the concept of neighborhood unit was born in 1923. Clarence Perry's neighborhood principles included dimensions, boundaries, open spaces, institutional places, local shops, and the internal road system. Such a concept makes references to creating a 15-min city containing the required urban density within a self-sufficient spatial space that is more like urban enclaves within cities. It works with an integrated, decentralized, participatory approach in services with multi-use land planning to develop a flexible social-functional space but ready to close and open inward to face a situation similar to the "new normal" (Pinto & Akhavan, 2022; Pozoukidou & Chatziyiannaki, 2021). 15-Minute City is a form of "post-traumatic urbanism" as a method of socio-economic recovery and organizing principle for urban development that will help bring about a safe and sustainable urban life in the aftermath of COVID-19 (Moreno, Allam, Chabaud, Gall, & Pratlong, 2021). Its basic principles are embodied in four focal points: easy and safe access for residents to essential urban goods and services, each neighborhood has a variety of housing of different sizes and spaces to accommodate many types of families, and enables residents to live near their work, providing green spaces and wide interactive spaces that provide health and environmental conditions Suitable for residents, reducing the use of cars for commuting within the neighborhood while rapid and frequent public transit links remain the most reliable way to connect parts of the city (C40 Cities Climate Leadership Group, 2020; Willberg, Fink, & Toivonen, 2023).

Multiple worldwide attempts have succeeded in implementing a 15-minute city to recover from Covid-19, foremost of which is the La villa du quart d'heure experiment in Paris by Professor Carlos Moreno from Sorbonne University (Capolongo, Buffoli, Brambilla, & Rebecchi, 2020). In the context of structuring the urban form, the "blank mechanism" strategy appeared for spatial protection of the urban environment that is implemented in two methods. The first is based on reserving urban spaces, "leaving a void" within the structural plan according to multiple planning levels. Such spaces intersect as defense units for the urban body during war or natural/ human disasters by providing emergency health services at specific and influential non-random points. The second has relied on the mixed and intensive use of land uses that combines the required urban services within specific spatial scales in times of war and peace (Jin, 2020).

Legislation and Laws Regulating Planning Intervention in Informal Housing Areas in Syria

Although the phenomenon of informal settlements in Syria dates back to the mid-twentieth century, the past three decades have grown significantly. The reasons could be attributed to 1- The demographic shifts in the Syrian population map due to rural push factors and urban pull factors. Plus, the displacement from the war since 2011 towards the safe areas was an influential cause. 2- The planning defect reflected in a dual case; First is related to the delay in approving the organizational plans for cities; such reason led to making the goal of these plans to address problems instead of being directive/regulation plans for urban growth. Second is the inability of the public housing sector to secure affordable housing according to a specific timetable to meet the needs of the growing demand (Al-Dairi, 2007). The result was the transformation of the informal character into a realistic element in the urban fabric of the Syrian cities, with its social and economic dimensions. On the other hand, a set of legislations kept pace with this phenomenon to curb its expansion. Whereas, since the year 2000, Syria has witnessed an upward governmental movement towards finding an integrated strategy to address the issue of random housing and liberalize urban planning procedures in an attempt to legalize the status of tenure and integrate informal housing areas within the urban fabric of the city without ignoring the social and economic dimensions of the fabric of these areas. It began with the issuance of Law No. 26 of 2000 to amend Law No. 60 of 1979 to define areas of urban expansion and introduce the land readjustment tool to address the issue of informal areas (UN-Habitat, February 2022). However, the length of the executive procedures and the varying levels of interaction of its application by administrative units made the positive repercussions of Law No. 26 within minimum limits. Later, Law No.1 of 2003 was issued as the building Violations Law, the removal of violating buildings, followed by resolution 16/M of 2007, a regulating decision to build new suburbs outside the administrative borders. However, The reflection of these directions and procedures on the situation of informal housing areas had no significant impact (Al-Dairi, 2007).

In 2008, Law No. 15 of the Real Estate Development and Investment Law was issued, with one of its objectives addressing informal settlements according to the concept of sustainable urban development and on-site redevelopment. The on-site redevelopment approach refers to a complete replacement of the physical fabric through gradual demolition and in-situ construction of alternative housing to release the added value of the land. It needs exceptional legislative and legal support to create alliances between the public and private capital for spatial restructuring. It respects residents' legal right to alternative housing and the dependence of their livelihood on staying in the same location of the city (Abdelhalim, 2010; Upadhya & Rao, 2022). The street-led slum upgrading strategy supports such an approach to the urban renewal of informal settlements for physically and spatially integrating with the host city; enhancing streets and pathways at the city level is dynamic for improving infrastructure provision and more accessibility. Moreover, it helps to lay down the basis for future land tenure regularization (Acioly, 2021). Under this umbrella, the goals were to provide an integrated urban environment, encourage the national private sector, and attract foreign investment in this field. Such goals could be achieved by converting random housing areas into real estate development areas according to administrative and legal procedures stipulated in detail by law. Moreover, Law No. 15 confirmed that the developer needs to provide alternative housing for the occupants of the dwellings inside or outside the real estate development area or cash allowance as compensation for housing based on the occupants' desire according to the social survey results process (Al-Ruwaili, 2017). Nevertheless, the permanent and non-permanent tenure of the occupants remained one of the most critical planning problems. Hence, Law 33 of 2008 was issued regarding the organization of informal areas and the granting of recognition to subdivisions of lands and their registration to obtain official title deeds (Syrian Law Journal, 2018). Due to the global economic recession and the war since 2011, Laws 15 and 33 could not achieve the desired goals despite their importance. Therefore, Law No. 2 of 2023 was issued to amend Investment Law No. 18 of 2021 and cancel Real Estate Development and Investment Law No. 15 of 2018. Law No. 2 expands the scope of Law No. 18 to include real estate development and investment projects stipulated by Law No. 15. This law aims to enhance the competitive investment environment to attract capital and contribute to the construction and urban development. Additionally, it is meant to simplify investment procedures for real estate development and stimulate investment via a handful of tax exemptions and administrative facilities for Syrian and foreign investors.

However, the destruction suffered by Syrian cities, including the informal settlement during the war, increased the complexity of the issue of tenure; moreover, in an effort to integrate the intervention mechanism in the informal housing areas with consolidating the aspects of community participatory on the one hand, the administrative decentralization, and participatory between the public and private sectors on the other hand, in formulating planning decisions to intervene in these areas. Law 23 of 2015, Urban Planning and Urbanisation Law, and Law 10 of 2018, The New Urban Renewal law, were issued to allow municipalities as “Local administrative authorities” to intervene according to the following:

1- Municipalities can use Law no. 23 /2015 to implement detailed plans alternative to the old masterplan either by rezoning the area using land pooling and readjustment as needed or by requesting landowners to subdivide their initiative. 2- Municipalities can implement Law no. 10 /2018 in designating the area for redevelopment, which would pool individual real estate and convert them to commercial shares in a new development scheme implemented by public-private partnership companies, with original rightsholders (UN-Habitat, February 2022). Both laws created the legal framework to ensure tenure security by finding alternative housing for the residents of the informal settlement subjected to redevelopment, pending the completion of the construction of new accommodations and allocated to be transferred to it. Therefore, in this chapter, under the umbrella of relevant laws and legislation Table 1, we will work through a community survey to contribute to developing the planning recommendations for intervention in the “Al-Radar area”, considering the “New Normal” situation due to Covid-19.

Table 1. New Syrian Laws might contribute to planning intervention in informal housing areas

Description	Classification	Law
On building violations and the removal of offending buildings	Informal settlements	Law 1/2003
On regularizing informal settlements	Urban maintenance	Law 33/ 2008
On the creation of urban development zones	Urban planning and urbanisation	Law 23/2015
On the creation of new organizational area/s within the organizational charts.	The New Urban Renewal	Law 10/2018
On the simplify investment procedures for real estate development	Amending the Investment Law 18/2021	Law 2/2023

Source: (Al-Ruwaili, 2017; Syrian Law Journal, 2018; UN-Habitat, February 2022)

RESEARCH GAB AND RESEARCH AIMS

For over 40 decades, the case of informal housing areas in Syria has been a growing urban problem. Until now, there have been no sustainable solutions. Meanwhile, many studies dealt with this issue from a theoretical perspective at the national/ local level before/after the war based on non-updated demographic statistics. Some other studies argued on the legal frameworks and urban planning legislation in this scope. However, the research on the impact of Covid-19 pandemic on urban restructuring intervention in these vulnerable areas didn't issue as research work before in Syria. Therefore, this research is considered the first research that combines the theoretical and legislative dimensions, quantitative and qualitative analysis, and field investigation in the study area under the specificity of its planning aspects and the influence of the "new normal" on urban planning. Moreover, this research sheds light on the ability of the new national laws issued on urban planning to adapt to the principles of sustainable urban planning required to achieve urban immunity and urban resilience.

In fact, for more than one year, this research transformed the targeted informal housing area into a large laboratory for examining the socio-demographic characteristics, assessing the impact of Covid-19, and evaluating reactions to the restructuring vision. Accordingly, the research aim was to build a new integrated approach to intervention that relied on the spatial, social, and legislative dimensions while attention to the sustainable development guiding principles to face a "new normal" in a twin track. The first track worked on ensuring a participatory approach in decision-making to solve the problem of informal areas. In contrast, the second track moved toward innovative global planning trends to confront the new normal situation. The final goal of this integrated approach was reflected by the foundation of an area plan for the future on-site redevelopment of the targeted area to become a neighborhood considering community cohesion and land-use improvements through good governance in land administration as a tool to promote sustainable development. Hence, to achieve the mentioned goals, the research dealt with answering a set of questions that can be summarized as follows: First, How can the functional and spatial urban environment be protected and enhanced in cases of the epidemic? Second, How can density be adapted to fragmentation that allows facing challenges in our urban life? Third, it relates to the second: Is it possible to restructure the most vulnerable urban areas towards resilient environments closely and aligned with national urban development-issued laws?.

Case-Study Area and Research Hypothesis

The Case-study location and boundaries meet the vision of a sustainable planning intervention of informal settlements within the concept of the 15-min city. The goal is to transform the most vulnerable areas into areas of immunity in the face of the current Covid-19 epidemic and the future epidemics expected to affect urban areas. Today, the area of the informal settlements covers 400 hectares south of Tartous city with approximately 50.000 inhabitants, as shown in Figure 1(b), is divided into three areas "Wadi Al-shater", "Ra's ash Shaghri", and "Al-Radar" as shown in Figure 1(c). However, based on 15-min city dimensions, the illustration zoning could be within two circles with 800 meters radius for each one, Figure 1(d).

Informal settlements' annual population growth rate is 1.62%, almost three times the coastal region's annual population growth. Nevertheless, building expansion didn't keep up with this population growth. The occupancy rate remained nearly constant at 60%, which means expansion took place vertically 2-3 layers for each building, even though 75% of the buildings' classification is "in bad physical status". Hence, the study-case area was determined within the intersection of two circles of the 15-min city, where "Al-radar area" location. It is the highest-density area with a net population density of almost 295 inhabitants/hectare within a built-up area of 85 Ha. and an occupancy rate of 68% of the informal housing areas. It is home to low-income residents with a good level of education. At the same time, the social fabric is characterized by youth but by approximately 27% of the unemployed.

The Case-study area is currently occupied by informal housing, it is considered one of the vital futuristic areas south of Tartous City. A distinguished sea view characterizes it due to its height of 55 meters sea level and a distance of no more than 1 km from the coastline. Within the spatial dimension, it is split up from the segments of tourism investment specified in the organizational plan by a regional linkage road between Tartous City and the Lebanese border, parallel with a railway linking Tartous City with Homs City. Moreover, part of it is allocated to expand the adjacent industrial area. In other words, the case-study hosts much more development dimensions for Tartous City than remaining an area for informal housing, and this constitutes a strong justification for intervention to redevelopment it, taking into account the current social fabric. Thus, the goal is to build a concept for new planning interventions based on a multi-dimensional analysis.

Figure 1. (a, b) Informal settlements in Tartous city, (c, d) 15-min city illustration zoning, and the case-study location

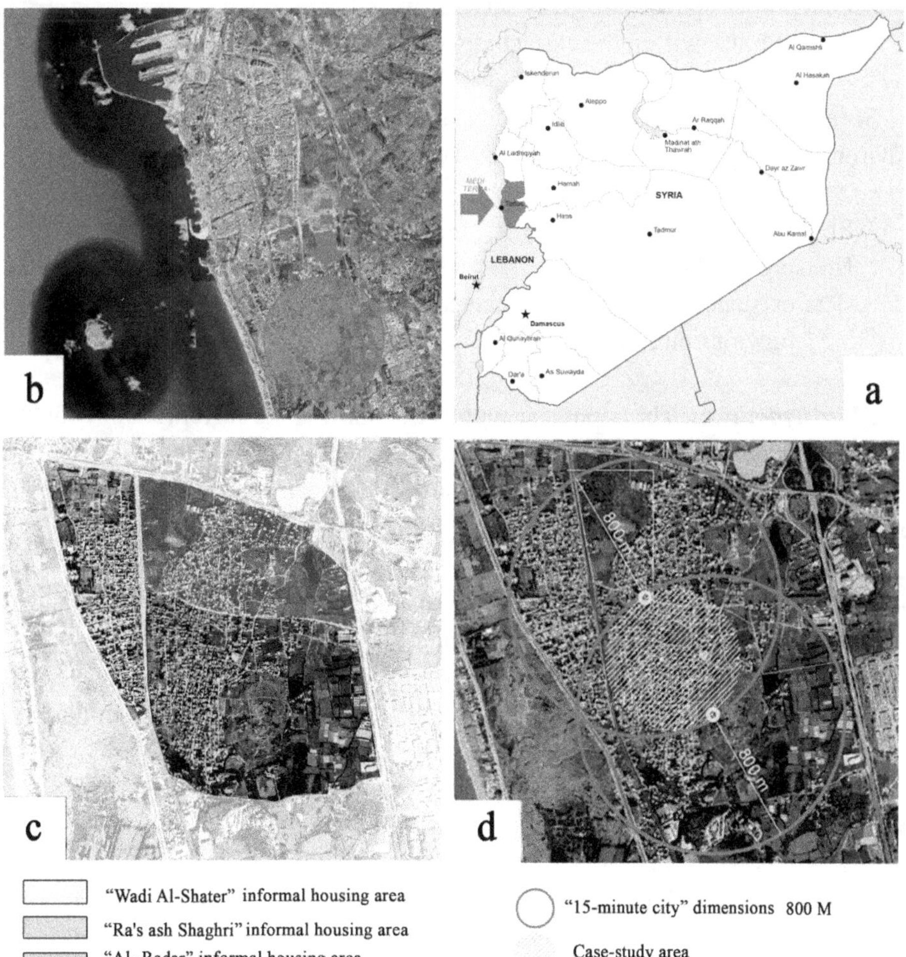

Research Hypothesis

The analysis deals with various points: the informal settlement planning situation, the current capacity to face epidemics and crises, and the future interventions to raise urban immunity. Each point was addressed on the principle of proving or disproving the hypothesis, which could be listed as follows:

First hypothesis. The urban and service environment did not address the urban needs of the residents. The hypothesis includes investigating:

- Public services and infrastructure
- Public/open spaces and green spaces
- Accessibility within the case study area and linkages with the city

Second hypothesis. The case study area residents suffer from unsatisfactory environmental and housing conditions. The hypothesis includes investigating:

- Environmental conditions
- Housing conditions
  -The existence of a special social fabric in the case study area, despite the previous circumstances

Third hypothesis. The popular acceptance to improve the current socio-economic situation under the laws and legislation in force, including on-site redevelopment.

Fourth hypothesis. There is a relationship between the quality of the spatial planning environment and the possibility of facing epidemics includes:

- There is a direct relationship between the lack of urban services and the absence of a defense system to counter the impact of epidemics.
- There is a direct relationship between the principles of sustainable development in establishing a system to reduce epidemics and increase urban immunity.

METHODS AND RESEARCH TOOLS

This research uses a mixed methodology to achieve the goals of a twin-track approach intervention. Both quantitative and qualitative techniques are used to analyze the available data and information within the study area. Thus, a questionnaire has been used as an instrument in data collection. The questionnaire was conducted with 350 families as a random sample " after lifting the lockdown in Syria in November 2020" to better understand the challenges and problems during the Covid-19 pandemic. Although 317 responses were received, with a 90.5% response rate, such a questionnaire was the first step under the umbrella of a participatory approach. At the same time, it helped to form a mini-perception of the local community's acceptance of conducting a comprehensive survey dealing with more in-depth investigations to build an accurate vision of the feasibility of intervention based on on-site redevelopment according to the new laws/legislations. The questionnaire was divided into three parts; the first part was to investigate human-environmental living in the case study area and their challenges in reaching services and economic activities during the quarantine using the checkboxes method. The second part adopted a Likert scale with three points: agree, neutral, and disagree, to rank respondents' agreement on approaches for changing the spatial structure of their living area. The third part was designed to know the respondents' satisfaction surveys with the services and hard/soft infrastructures before the pandemic; this part used a matrix/ rating scale with five points of importance from 1-5, where 5 is the highest rating.

After data collection, quantitative tools were used to analyze the gathered data. We used IBM/SPSS statistical with the following statistical treatments; standard deviation and arithmetic mean. The arithmetic means were converted to percentages, and the results were interpreted according to the criteria for approval as shown in Table 2. Three tests were used in analysing data as following:

Table 2. Percentages of criteria for approval to interpret the results

weighted average	scale	percentage
1-1.79	Poor	Less than 36%
1.8-2.59	Average	36%-51%
2.6-3.39	Good	52%-67%
3.4-4.19	Very good	68%-83%
4.2-5.0	Perfect	More than 84%

Chi-Square (X2) Test

We used the chi-square (X2) statistic as a quantitative measure of statistical significance based on nonparametric tests, given that the nature of data collected from the questionnaire was nominal. Chi-square follows five basic steps, which include: a) making assumptions "random sampling", b) stating the research and null hypotheses and selecting an alpha value, c) selecting the sampling distribution and specifying the test statistic, d) computing the test statistic and e) making a decision and interpreting the results (Sachan & Bhattacharya., 2012). The mathematical process involved is given in the formula:

$$\chi^2 = \sum \frac{(Oi - Ei)^2}{Ei}$$

Where χ^2 = chi-square, Oi = the observed value and Ei = the expected value

Moreover, our study used a goodness of fit test, then tested the variables' independence.

Test of Goodness of Fit

This test is used to determine whether there were significant differences between the observed frequencies of a categorical variable and match some expected frequencies. The aim of this test is to identify "what and how" the basic categorical variables pulled a sample of respondents. The research hypothesis (H1) (H1: $Oi \neq Ei$, i=1,2,….,k) while the null hypothesis (H0) (H0: Oi = Ei, i=1,2,….,k) states that The expected repetitions mean that there is no specific direction in opinion, therefore, the variables are statistically independent. The Degree of Freedom (DF) is determined as follows: DF = (k – 1), and k = the number of categories of the variable under study.

Test of Independence

It is used in many studies/situations, such as tests that study the independence or relationship between two variables or characteristics of a society (Onu, Surendran, & Price, 2014; Usman, Malik, & Alausa, 2015). In addition, the test tries to answer the question, is there a relationship between the independent and dependent variables in which society was investigated? It is also considered a test to study the independence of more than two samples drawn from the same statistical community. In this test, the research hypothesis (H1), the two variables are not independent, while in the null hypothesis (H0), the two variables are independent.

Where; DF= (m–1) *(n–1), m = the number of rows and n = the number of columns.

The p-value is the probability of obtaining a test statistic at least as extreme as the one that was actually observed, assuming the null hypothesis to be true. In this research, the significance level is $\alpha = 0.05$ (5%). If it gets the iterations of a note that are clearly different from theoretical or expected iterations, we reject null hypothesis and accept the research hypothesis. The rule of decision on the null hypothesis is:

The null hypothesis is rejected if: P-value £ α, $\chi^2(n-1,\alpha)$ £ χ^2, While the null hypothesis is accepted if: P-value > α, $\chi^2(n-1,\alpha) > \chi^2$.

On the other side, the second field survey was conducted in the al-Radar area "after the Covid-19 pandemic". It included 1,570 families currently living at a rate of more than 95% of the population. The case study area was divided into 11 spatial sectors, depending on the current routes and narrow streets. Workgroups of fifth academic year students of the Faculty of Architecture at Tartous University helped in the field investigation.

Like the first questionnaire, the second survey was designed in Arabic for local respondents. It was divided into two categories of directed questions: A first section is a group of closed questions according to four answers (yes / rather yes/ no / rather no). This section includes four directions of questions; the environmental aspect, the social aspect includes the ownership case, the economic aspect, and the infrastructure/ housing conditions. The second section includes four open questions: the spatial memory of the population, the preference/ no preference of the residents to stay in their location after the on-site redevelopment intervention, the futuristic urban morphology of the intervention, and planning services expected in the new neighborhood in the future. In this step, qualitative methodology was used to analyze the results. Thereby, the first track targets the participatory approach in planning decision-making. In contrast, the second track covers national urban development laws issued to form the intervention framework. Additionally, an analysis of the location's spatial dimensions by PESTLE analysis followed by deducting/subtracting the results to complete and deepen the analysis using SWOT analysis and a critical review of traditional planning criteria in the organizational plan, Figure 2.

Figure 2. Critical review

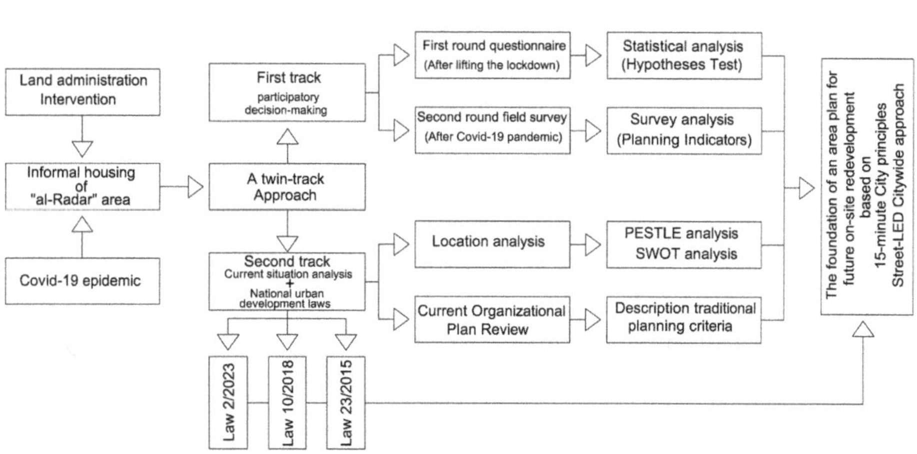

RESULTS AND DISCUSSION

The process of analyzing the results and the discussion forms a logical conceptual intervention framework that passes through four stages: the first stage analyzes the results of the random sample questionnaire. The second stage includes analyzing the comprehensive survey results. The third stage adopts PESTLE/SWOT analysis. The fourth stage: the analysis of the proposed intervention plan according to the organizational chart of the study area by the relevant authorities, which was approved before the issued Law No. 23/ 2015 and Law No.10/ 2018, as well as before the planning impact of Covid-19.

The First Stage: Questionnaire Results Analysis and Test the Hypotheses

The demographic study forms the starting point for any intervention in the informal settlement due to the unique spatial dimensions of the topological structure. Hence, this sector presents the results of respondents' background characteristics. The distribution of the variables discussed is shown in Table. 3. The major household characteristics considered were gender, age, work, household size, and educational attainment.

Table 3. The demographic status of the random sample

	variables	Number of respondents N=317	Percentage %
Gender	Male	169	53.3%
	Female	148	46.7%
Age	18-30	83	26.2%
	30-50	164	51.7%
	50 and more	70	22.1%
Work	Public sector	106	33.4%
	Special sector	114	36%
	Unemployed	97	30.6%
Family Members	1-3	76	24%
	4-6	200	63.1%
	7 and more	41	12.9%
Educational attainment	Primary education	98	30.9%
	Secondary education	106	33.4%
	University education	108	34.1%
	High education	5	1.6%

Chi-Square Analysis of The Social Fabric

To investigate the social fabric that characterizes the case study area. A group of questions targeted this part with a statistical result shown in Table. 4, emphasizes that a social relations network and social integration in the area with 61.8% of answers and significant at)138.366(. In addition, other analyses showed that the statistically significant result could be considered trustworthy where the critical table value from the Chi-square analysis is 5.99 at an alpha level of 0.05, with a degree of freedom (DF) of 2 when the significant value at (76.7, 54.17, and 196.644) respectively. Therefore, the hypothesis of this variable is accepted, which means that these variables have a significant impact and confirm that the case study area has a special social fabric characterized and should take into account with any futuristic intervention.

Table 4. The Chi-square analysis of the social fabric

Significant value	Chi-square value	No		Almost		Yes		Questions	
		%	F	%	F	%	F		
0.000	138.366	8.2%	26	30%	95	61.8%	196	Is there a social relations network and social integration?	1
0.000	76.7	55.5%	176	27.4%	87	28.1%	89	Do you want to leave your home and move to another one outside the current area?	2
0.000	54.17	20.2%	64	27.4%	87	52.4%	166	Do you feel that you have enough time to spend it with the neighbors	3
0.000	196.644	12.3%	39	17.4%	55	70.3%	223	Do you agree to participate in social events?	4
DF = (K- 1)= (3-1) = 2, Alpha level of 0.05, Table value is 5.99									

Test Fit of Goodness for Urban Services and Infrastructures

Chi-square analysis (test of fit of goodness), standard deviation, and arithmetic means of the results were performed to determine if the urban services and infrastructures did not address the residential needs. The statistical results show that commercial and educational services and sanitation networks are good with percent (54%, 55%, 55.2%) and significant at (134.000, 77.591, 65.098) in the order. In addition, the statistical results show that recreation and sports services, public health services, and soft and hard networks are average with percent of (37.6%, 45.6%,44.8%,46.4%) and significant at (223.873, 191.120, 137.621, 77.924) respectively. Moreover, the statistical results show that cultural and social services, religious services, and the availability of job opportunities are poor, as shown in Table. 5. Such analysis confirms that the statistically significant result can be considered trustworthy. The critical table value from the Chi-square analysis is 9.49 at an alpha level of 0.05, with a degree of freedom (DF) of 4. Therefore, the hypothesis of this variable is accepted, which means that these variables have a significant impact and confirm that urban services and infrastructures do not meet residential needs.

Test Fit of Goodness for Public and Open/Green Spaces

For determining if the public spaces, pedestrian paths, and roads did not fit into the planning criteria and the residential needs, the statistical results show that the availability of (green areas (parks, gardens), parking spaces, public transportation, and secondary roads) are average with percent of (36.4%, 38%, 43.6%, 38.4%), and significant at (247.338, 201.375, 129.633, 194.467) respectively. In addition, the statistical results show that the availability of (open areas and children's play areas, public squares, street furniture, and continuous pedestrian paths) is poor, with percent of (33.6%, 33.6%, 34.4%, 32.4%), as is shown in Table. 6. These confirm that the statistically significant result can be considered trustworthy, where the critical table value is 9.49 at an alpha level of 0.05, with a degree of freedom (DF) of 4. Therefore, the hypothesis of this variable is accepted, which means that these variables have a significant impact and confirm that the public spaces, pedestrian paths, and roads do not meet the residential needs.

Table 5. Test fit of goodness for urban services and infrastructures

Significant value	Chi-square value	%	Level	Mean	Std. deviation	Questions	
0.000	134.000	54%	Good	2.7	1.005	What is your assessment of the commercial services?	1
0.000	77.591	55%	Good	2.75	1.112	What is your assessment of the educational services?	2
0.000	223.873	37.6%	Average	1.88	1.099	What is your assessment of the recreation and sport services?	3
0.000	658.662	27.8%	Poor	1.39	0.863	What is your assessment of the cultural and social services?	4
0.000	395.319	32%	Poor	1.60	0.938	What is your assessment of the religious services?	5
0.000	191.120	45.6%	Average	2.28	0.947	What is your assessment of the public health services?	6
0.000	457.270	31%	Poor	1.55	0.917	What is your assessment of the availability of job opportunities?	7
0.000	137.621	44.8%	Average	2.24	0.991	What is your assessment of the electricity and water network?	8
0.000	77.924	46.4%	Average	2.32	1.188	What is your assessment of communications networks?	9
0.000	65.098	55.2%	Good	2.76	1.130	What is your assessment of the sanitation network?	10
0.000	139.987	43.2%	Average	2.16	1.262	What is your assessment of the solid waste management system?	11
DF = (K- 1) = (5-1) = 4, Alpha level of 0.05, Table value is 9.49							

Table 6. Test fit of goodness for public and open/green spaces

Significant value	Chi-square value	%	Level	Mean	Std. deviation	Questions	
0.000	247.338	36.4%	Average	1.82	1.056	What is your assessment of the availability of green areas (parks, gardens)?	1
0.000	360.019	33.6%	Poor	1.69	1.028	What is your assessment of the availability of open areas and children's play areas?	2
0.000	323.339	33.6%	Poor	1.69	0.958	What is your assessment of the availability of public spaces?	3
0.000	298	34.4%	Poor	1.72	0.974	What is your assessment of the availability of street furniture?	4
0.000	201.375	38%	Average	1.90	0.959	What is your assessment of the availability of parking spaces?	5
0.000	129.633	43.6%	Average	2.18	1.016	What is your assessment of the availability of public transportation?	6
0.000	358.473	32.4%	Poor	1.62	0.894	What is your assessment of the availability of safe and continuous pedestrian paths?	7
0.000	194.467	38.4%	Average	1.92	1.019	What is your assessment of the availability of service roads?	8
DF = (K- 1) = (5-1) = 4, Alpha level of 0.05, Table value is 9.49							

Chi-Square Analysis for The Environmental Aspect

The statistical results show that the area suffers from pollution, with a confirmation rate of 68.1%. It should be noted that study location pollution results from solid waste and noise pollution due to the railway. On the other side, the questionnaire results refer accepted rate of the respondents' sense of spatial isolation, with 44.8% and Chi-square value significant (59.666). As per the previous analysis, other questions are significant, with (29.798, 33.962, 141.849, 49.861, 82.852, and 108.953) as shown in Table. 7. Thus, this confirms that the statistically significant result can be considered trustworthy under Chi-square analysis, where the critical table value is 5.99 at an alpha level of 0.05, with a degree of freedom (DF) of 2. Therefore, such results mean that these variables have a significant impact and confirm that the environmental and physical dimensions are not satisfied. Thus, the hypothesis of this variable is accepted.

Table 7. Chi-square Analysis for the environmental aspect

Significant value	Chi-square value	No		Almost		YES		Questions	
		%	F	%	F	%	F		
0.000	181.558	9.1%	29	22.7%	72	68.1%	216	Does the area suffer from pollution (water, air, noise, etc.?)	1
0.000	59.666	12.9%	41	42.3%	134	44.8%	142	Do you feel the living area's physical environment (topology) is closed and not integrated with the city?	2
0.090	4.814	30%	95	30.9%	98	39.1%	124	Does the railway create noise pollution for the residents?	3
0.000	29.798	45.1%	143	34.7%	110	20.2%	64	Are there enough spaces available to host the population increase in the future?	4
0.000	33.962	37.9%	20	43.8%	139	18.3%	58	Are there designated places for daily solid waste collection?	5
0.000	141.849	62.8%	199	28.4%	90	8.8%	28	Does your house consider the environmental and health conditions ..ventilation, sanitation?	6
0.000	49.861	51.4%	163	28.4%	90	20.2%	64	Is your house in good physical condition?	7
0.000	82.852	57.1%	181	24.9%	79	18%	57	Is the area of the dwelling commensurate with the number of its members and suitable for living conditions?	8
0.000	108.953	60.9%	193	17.7%	56	21.5%	68	Are current housing patterns fit with the current social fabric?	9
DF = (K- 1)= (3-1) = 2, Alpha level of 0.05, Table value is 5.99									

Analyzing Quality of the Spatial Planning Environment and the Possibility of Facing Epidemics in the Case Study Area

During Covid-19 pandemic "al-Radar area" like other city parts, was exposed to the impact of the steady spread of infection. Nevertheless, the lack of urban services, including health services, the far between the residence place and job place, moreover the lack of public spaces and appropriate transportation systems have exacerbated the spread of infection and the imposition of home quarantine for a long period as an emergency response to the epidemic. The results were more social isolation and the deteriorating economic situation of the residents due to depending on daily work to earn. Based on the analysis of the questionnaire results related to the impact of the Covid-19 pandemic on the spatial planning structure and the willingness of the target social segment to accept the proposed planning interventions as long-term solutions to raise urban immunity in the face of health crises and confront epidemics. A set of intersections between the relevant variables of the questionnaire were conducted to prove hypotheses to arrive at planning indicators for spatial intervention as the following:

The Relationship Between the Absence of a System to Mitigate and Reduce the Impact of Epidemics and The Lack of Urban Services

This hypothesis has verified the role of the lack of urban services in the study area with the absence of a system to limit epidemics in cities and neighborhoods through Chi-square analysis (test of independence). Here the critical table value from the Chi-square analysis is 9.49 at an alpha level of 0.05, with a degree of freedom (DF) of 4. Therefore, the calculated values of the cross of the absence of a system to limit the impact of epidemics in cities and areas with a lack of urban services, which are (environmental and health conditions in houses, use of renewable sources, diversified commercial and economic activity, job opportunities, public spaces, and garden, accessibility, health services), were (11.085, 26.473, 10.584, 44.926, 10.862, 15.223, 11.874) in order. They show that the calculated values are greater than the critical table value, as shown in Table. 8. Since the calculated Chi-square values are greater than the critical table value, the previous hypothesis is accepted.

Table 8. The relationship between the lack of urban services and the poor defense system to face the impact of epidemics.

Is there a system to reduce and mitigate the effects of epidemics in the "al-Radar area"?				N
Remark	**Significant value**	**Chi-square value**		
significant relationship	0.026	11.085	Do you find your house considers environmental and health conditions?	1
significant relationship	0.000	26.473	Is there any use of renewable energy resources?	2
significant relationship	0.032	10.584	Do you see that the economic activities are diversified and well-distributed?	3
significant relationship	0.000	44.926	Are there good job opportunities in your location?	4
significant relationship	0.028	10.862	Did the public/open spaces suffice the residents' need to achieve social interaction during the Covid-19 pandemic?	5
significant relationship	0.004	15.223	Did pedestrian paths achieve good accessibility within the area and between it and the city during the pandemic time?	6
significant relationship	0.018	11.874	Did health services adequate and available in the area during the Covid-19 pandemic?	7
DF = (m- 1) (n-1) = (3-1) (3-1) = 2*2 = 4, Alpha level of 0.05, Table value is 9.49				

The Relationship Between Creating a System to Limit and Mitigate the Effect of Epidemics and Improving Urban Services in The Study Area

The purpose of this hypothesis, "through the test of independence" is to determine the role of sustainable development principles, including improving urban services for creating a system to limit and reduce the effect of epidemics and increase urban immunity.

Investigating the hypothesis led to testing the intersection between creating an urban sustainable defense system face of epidemics on the one hand and improving urban services on the other. Creating sustainable housing, using renewable energy, establishing a multi-economic activity within 15 minutes, hosting job opportunities, heightening public spaces and open spaces area, using sustainable transport, and enhancing health services, especially after covid-19, are all goals of the urban defense system. The table value from the Chi-square analysis is 9.49 at an alpha level of 0.05, with a degree of freedom (DF) of 4, while the calculated values were (40.861, 81.466, 53.602, 37. 926, 37. 856, 24.478, 13.317) in order as shown in Table. 9. The hypothesis is accepted since the calculated Chi-square values are greater than the critical table value.

Table 9. The relationship between creating a system to limit the effect of epidemics and improving urban services in the study area.

Do you agree with the need to establish a system to reduce and mitigate the effects of epidemics on cities and neighborhoods?				N
Remark	Significant value	Chi-square value		
significant relationship	0.000	40.861	Do you consider establishing eco-friendly, self-contained housing with suitable spaces for residents necessary, especially after Covid-19?	1
significant relationship	0.000	81.466	Do you consider it necessary to adopt renewable energy sources to supply the future neighborhood?	2
significant relationship	0.000	53.602	Do you agree with encouraging establishing of the necessary economic activities for the neighborhood to be within a local dimension not exceeding 15 minutes?	3
significant relationship	0.000	37. 926	Do you prefer creating job opportunities and developing investment projects in your neighborhood through future intervention?	4
significant relationship	0.000	37. 856	Do you agree with the necessity of increasing the public/ green spaces in the new neighborhood as interactive spaces?	5
significant relationship	0.000	24.478	Do you find that switching to sustainable modes of transportation (bicycles, electric buses) is critical to reducing traffic congestion and increasing accessibility?	6
significant relationship	0.010	13.317	Did you suffer from a lack of urban services during Covid-19?	7
DF = (m- 1) (n-1) = (3-1) (3-1) = 2*2 = 4, Alpha level of 0.05, Table value is 9.49				

The Second Stage: Survey Results Analysis

The survey results formed a solid information bank on the current situation in the study area, as it turned into an expanded laboratory to examine the planning problems and the aspirations of the residents upon the new planning intervention by the concerned authorities according to the relevant laws and legislation. The survey contributed to collecting possible data on each household's current ownership and relocation preferences to stay in the location or leave it in return for fair financial compensation. The results were correlated with the partial spatial sectors of the study location to assess the planning aspects of a particular spatial scale Figure. 3. At the same time, the other part of the results drew the planning indicators for intervention strategies at the comprehensive spatial level of the study area.

Figure 3.

The Survey Results Analysis and Planning Indicators

The study area constitutes an important demographic lever for the city of Tartous, where 72% of population are of the productive category, with ages ranging between (18-50) years. In contrast, approximately 73% of households include at least one employee working in the public or private sector or free professions. Such results mean that about 27% of families do not have a fixed income.

Accommodation and Ownership Case. The results showed that half of the respondents lived in the area for more than 31 years, and about 34% have lived for more than ten years. This means that the area includes two generations of families: The first generation: the families that moved from other cities or regions and established these settlements. The second generation: the new families that moved to this area or families born and raised within, Table 10. This factor is contributed to social relations and social intimacy or adapting to the current conditions during their stay. It is also reflected in the relocation preferences rate, where the survey showed about 74% of respondent's preferences not to leave the location after the redevelopment intervention, Table 11. In this social aspect, about 60% of those who prefer to stay were because of their sense of social integration; moreover, the results refer to 55% of respondents spending daily time with their neighbors and 65% participating in public social events. On the other hand, about 26% of the respondents looked forward to moving out of the area due to the lack of adaptation or difficulty securing urban services and/or hard accessibility to the city center. In addition, 66% said the area is unsafe as required. It should be noted that 77% of the respondents answered that they own their house/apartment, compared to 23% of the renters. In contrast, 85% said they do not own another house in the city, Table 11.

Table 10. Duration of stay classification in "al-Radar area"

How long have you lived in the area?			
Percent %	**Frequency**		
15.2	239	1-10	Valid
17.3	273	11-20	
16.3	257	21-30	
50.8	801	>31	
99.6	1570	Total	
0.4	6	System	Missing
100.0	1576	Total	

Table 11. Accommodation and ownership case

Would you like to stay in the location after the redevelopment intervention?		**Do you own another house/ apartment in the city?**		**Do you own the house/ apartment you live in?**			
Percent %	**Frequency**	**Percent %**	**Frequency**	**Percent %**	**Frequency**		
66.3	1045	13.9	217	76.4	1204	yes	Valid
7.4	117	0	0	0	0	rather yes	
25.5	402	85.5	1339	22.7	357	no	
0.4	6	0.6	10	0.5	9	rather no	
99.6	1570	99.4	1566	99.6	1570	Total	
0.4	6	0.6	10	0.4	6	System	Missing
100	1576	100	1576	100	1576	Total	

Services Infrastructure and Accessibility Case

The results showed that 70% feel difficulty moving within the study location, and 61% do not find the required urban services package within the living area. Poor availability of administrative services was the majority of responses received a percentage of 81%. In comparison, 52% answered that the area lacks medical services such as specialized clinics and an ambulatory hospital, where medical services are limited to a general clinic and one pharmacy. In addition, 53% indicated that the educational services are at a minimum, with one school for basic education and no other educational institutes. On the other side, 80% of the respondents said that access to urban services in the city to obtain the missing urban services is complex. Moreover, they referred to the problem of daily moving to the workplace, as 62% of the residents work outside the study area location. Moreover, the results showed that the study area does not constitute a child-friendly environment at all, where 79% answered that it does not provide the necessary spaces for children to play, and 86% of the answers expressed the lack of green spaces and the required open spaces Table 12.

Table 12. Case study area urban environment

Did you think your living area achieves a child-friendly environment?		**Did your living area offer public/ open or/and green spaces?**			
Percent %	**Frequency**	**Percent %**	**Frequency**		
7.4	116	4.7	74	yes	Valid
0	0	0	0	rather yes	
79.1	1247	86.3	1360	no	
13.1	2.6	8.6	136	rather no	
99.6	1569	99.6	1570	Total	
0.4	7	0.4	6	System	Missing
100	1576	100	1576	Total	

Regarding Housing Conditions

Most residents look to the house as a functional space for various daily activities and social gatherings. At the same time, 93% of the respondents refer to the scarcity of public social encounters areas like cafes or popular breaks. Despite this, the results showed that 66% do not find the required privacy due to disrespect the planning dimensions of the setbacks, 54% attain that their homes do not provide the necessary health conditions such as ventilation and insolation, and 62% admit that the structural safety is questionable. In comparison, 49% of the results showed satisfaction with the interior design, with an average area of 90-125 square meters. Table. 13,14.

Table 13. Housing conditions, part one

Did you think your dwelling/ apartment achieves safe construction requirements?		**Are you satisfied with the urban plot setbacks and the design of the façades in your residence area?**			
Percent %	**Frequency**	**Percent %**	**Frequency**		
23.2	366	13.8	218	yes	Valid
14.7	231	19.3	303	rather yes	
36.9	582	33.8	533	no	
24.7	389	32.7	515	rather no	
99.6	1570	99.6	1569	Total	
0.5	8	0.4	7	System	Missing
100	1575	100	1575	Total	

Table 14. Housing conditions, part two

Is the dwelling you live in suitable for a healthy/environmental aspect?		**Is the dwelling/apartment you live in suitable (space and use)?**			
Percent %	**Frequency**	**Percent %**	**Frequency**		
31.7	501	48.2	762	yes	Valid
14.2	224	6.8	107	rather yes	
46.9	738	19.8	311	no	
6.8	107	24.8	390	rather no	
99.6	1570	99.6	1570	Total	
0.4	6	0.4	6	System	Missing
100	1576	100	1576	Total	

Survey Results Analysis and the Planning Indicators Related to the Spatial Sectors

A group of open questions aimed to collect parts of the future image of the neighborhood residents in their different spatial slices (A, B, C......., J) Fig 3. Such an image could reflect essential sides of the new morphology of the neighborhood after its redevelopment, as well as could contribute in parallel to the results collected from the various stages of the previous analysis in determining the planning standards required in the expected intervention to raise the efficiency of the new neighborhood in facing urban challenges. The results came from the tendency of residents of sectors (F, G, H, I, and J) to live in high-rise buildings in the future, at a rate of about 65%, compared to 33% of the respondents who preferred to live in low-rise buildings. In contrast, the percentages were close in sectors A and D, while respondents in sectors B, C, and E clear desire to stay in low-rise residential buildings. For the services required in the new neighborhood, commercial services came among the priorities of the services demanded by the respondents in most sectors, with a rate of 52%, health services came second with approximately 46%, educational services with 42%, and recreational services with 32%. On the other hand, the respondents expressed the need to provide public/open spaces and green spaces for children's activities at a rate of 72%. Regarding spatial memory, school, clinic, railway, and the entrance to the current location constituted the most important points that the respondents referred to in their answer about the special place associated with their memory.

The Third Stage: Location PESTLE / SWOT Analysis

PESTLE analysis is used to determine the influence of the external factors (Political, Economic, Sociological, Technological, Legal, and Environmental) affecting the planning intervention process. PESTLE analysis is used in parallel with SWOT (Strengths, Weaknesses, Opportunities, Threats) analysis to understand the impact/risk factors that relate to the current and futuristic situation of the neighborhood. Based on data/information from the previous analysis and Field monitoring. Figure. 4,, Figure. 5; where:

- IMPACT: How large the effect of the SWOT item will be in the future. This is a positive impact for strengths & opportunities, and a negative impact for weaknesses & threats.
- RISK: Probability of a negative outcome.
- TBC: To Be Considered.

Figure 4. SWOT impact-risk map for the case-study area. based on the results of Re-planning al-Radar area workshop, 5th academic year, ATU 2022

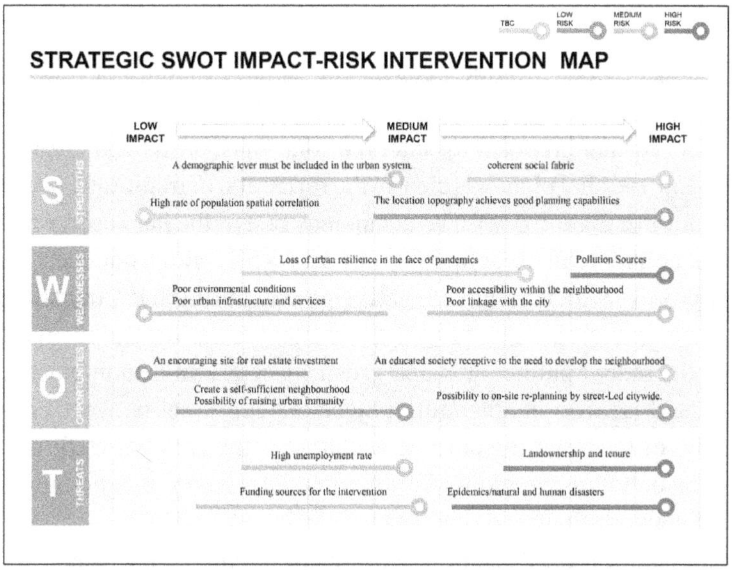

Figure 5. PESTLE impact map for the case-study area. based on the results of Re-planning al-Radar area workshop, 5th academic year, ATU 2022

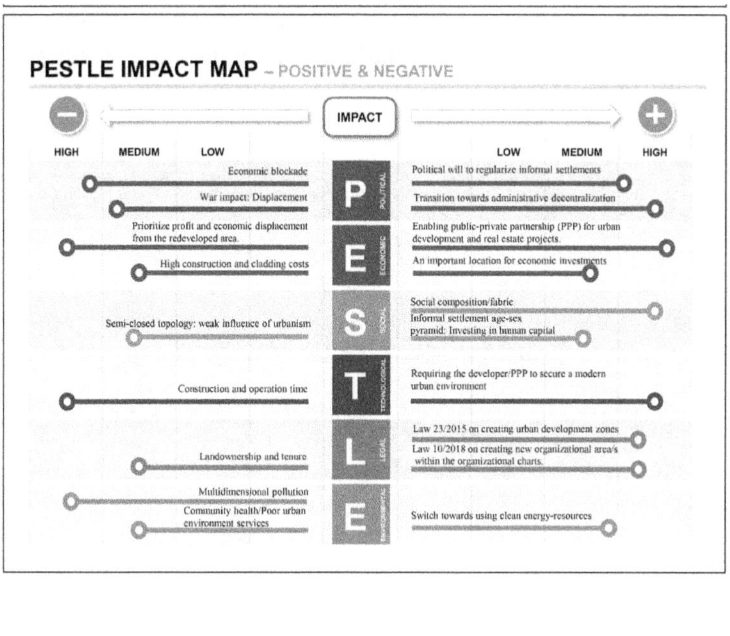

The Fourth Stage: The Current Organizational Plan Review

During 2006- 2008, an organizational plan was drawn up for the informal housing areas of Tartous city to solve its problems. Even this plan still needed to find its way to implementation. It did not clarify the future of tenure or even the kind of intervention (renewal, upgrade, redevelopment). However, until now, there has not been any other formal proposal for intervention. Thus, based on the analysis of the proposed organizational plan. It is clearly the reflection of traditional urban planning criteria in land-use Figure. 6 (a). The occupancy rate of the land use (residential use, services use, commercial use, others) is almost 60.5%, with a notable adopted focal services approach, which yielded negative results during the Covid-19 pandemic due to a problem of mobilizing at runtime in many cities around the world. On the other hand, the rate of public/open and green space is almost non-existent at 4.5%, fragmented and far from its planning objective. The street network covers a high rate of 21.5% of the area; in contrast, walkable paths are restricted to the narrow sidewalks surrounding streets and buildings, unclear, and not continuous because of the street network Figure. 6 (b,c,d,e).

While the plan ignored the source of noise pollution, the "Railway" by residential use along the line. An extra point on the previous analysis, the external effects indicators "Limitations and possibilities" at the city level, Figure. 7 (a), could be an added value in formulating logical recommendations to the relevant authorities and the developer "public-private partnership" alike in directing the intervention plan under the laws and legislation issued to find sustainable solutions for informal housing settlements. Therefore, the physical, social, and economic effects of the Covid-19 epidemic set these criteria and the proposed plan in front of a critical review to propose an alternative plan under the principles of sustainable planning.

Figure 6. Traditional urban planning criteria

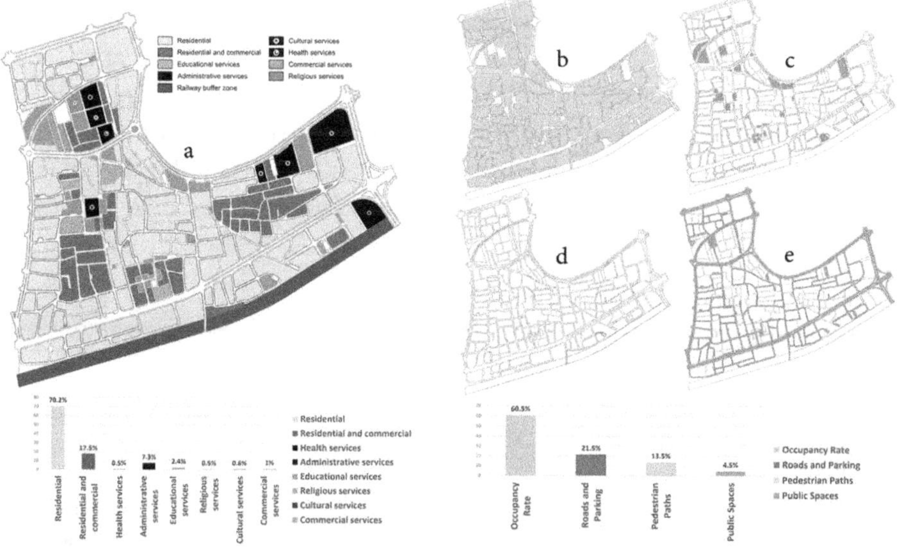

The Foundation of an Area Plan for Future On-Site Redevelopment

Based on the previous analysis results, we need a paradigm shift where new planning criteria should be consistent with the necessities imposed by the epidemic's effects in the various urban areas worldwide. The priorities are multiple and complex, but they could include securing a self-sufficient urban environment within a sustainable urban space. In addition, a settlement able to host the current and futuristic density in open spaces/green areas play an assigned planning role in social interactions to build a sense of belonging and safety and is covered by urban services to be an integrated habitat in times of crisis and epidemics. Such principles reflect the spirit of 15-minute city idea combined with Legislation/laws appropriate to intervention in the study location "Law No. 23 /2015 or Law No.10/2018" and Law No. 2/2023 on the simplify investment procedures for real estate development. These are helpful tools in the foundation of a plan for on-site redevelopment strategy to achieve transformation of the informal housing area to become a sustainable neighborhood. Hence, the intervention process should focus on investing in the socioeconomic fabric and spatial dimensions. The new "al-Radar" neighborhood plan work to upgrade the proposed organizational plan to align with the principles of sustainable development addressed in the previous discussion. Thus, the adoption street-Led citywide approach delivers serviced land that is intrinsically connected to the city plan, improves land regularisation, and increases community resilience. This resilience refers to the ability of society to quickly secure resources when facing natural or human disasters and the capability to adapt to emergency changes when switching to the response phase (Wang, Xu, & Lin, 2022). The modifications seek to achieve more spatial accessibility on a citywide level that would hold more efficient functional integration, Figure. 7 (b). Hence, new infrastructure constitutes an added value in changing the traditional planning criteria by shifting the pattern/type of land use and reducing the land occupancy rate but not at the expense of density.

Figure 7. Limitations and possibilities

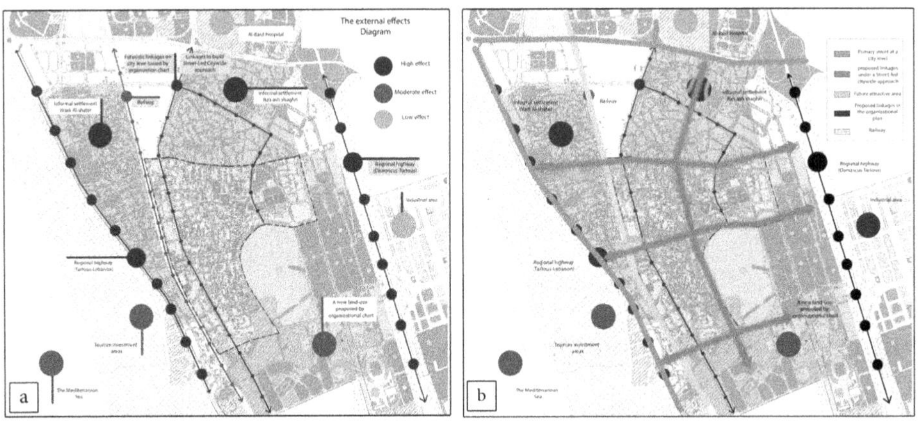

CONCLUSION

This chapter presents an analytical, logical approach to intervention in the most vulnerable areas within the urban fabric of the cities. In Tartous City, the informal settlement occupies a vital location for urban expansion under a scarcity of urban land in the city. Thus, land-use re-development is very valuable due to the spatial dimension's ability to attract various investments. However, avoiding socio-economic displacement and building sustainable, resilient urban spaces should be planning priorities. The research provides a literature review on restructuring the current city form and urban governance in the face of Covid-19 through the principles of a 15-minute city planning that corresponds to the standards of sustainable planning. At the same time, the research gives a brief review of the national urban planning laws, which constitute the legislative and lawful bases to interfere in the irregular housing areas in Syria as a development goal in the stage of reconstruction after the war. The research adopts the multi-dimensional spatial-social-environmental analysis method and utilizes quantitative and qualitative techniques to answer research questions and reduce the research gap. The results show the importance of the proposed twin-track approach in achieving the required urban governance for intervention to solve the current problem of the informal housing areas in Syria under the impact of the Covid-19 epidemic and what is worse in the future. Its strength is not only the ability to combine the participatory approach in decision-making with the national development laws but also its power to open doors for a new vision of on-site redevelopment by adopting sustainable development criteria of 15-minute city principles and a street-led citywide upgrading approach to take part in the official planning and urban management systems. Therefore, this approach could form a new framework to change the traditional urban planning criteria in land use that stood helpless in the face of the impact of health crises, especially since the world entered the epidemics and natural disasters era. In this context, the initial reviews of planners and decision-makers after the devastating earthquake that struck parts of Syria last February emphasized the need to reconsider the current planning and design criteria that did not provide urban safety/resilience when shifting to the response phase.

Hence, the research findings could provide a useful "road map" for policymakers interested in participatory redevelopment approaches to face urban challenges. In addition, it contributes to developing viable strategies for the intervention and negotiation of informal/illegal settlements in Syria in the same line with the current efforts to provide a national map of informal housing in preparation for long-term sustainable solutions. Such intervention strategies could transform targeted settlements to become sustainable neighborhoods with compact mixed-use structures and functional areas integrated spatially, legally, socially, and economically with the host cities. In sum, this measurable and reproducible research could be applied in similar environments by considering the different social peculiarities of informal housing areas to form rescue windows in health crises. Moreover, the results could sustainably solve the problem of informal housing based on increasing resilience and urban immunity. As well as build urban environments ready to provide the urban services required in exchange for the population density imposed by securing economic housing for the reconstruction phase in Syria.

ACKNOWLEDGEMENTS

The authors acknowledge immensely grateful to the students of the urban planning course of the fifth academic year (2022) of Tartous University for their efforts in the research survey.

REFERENCES

C40 Cities Climate Leadership Group. (2020, July). *How to Build Back Better with a 15-Minute City*. C40 Knowledge Hub. https://www.c40knowledgehub.org/s/article/How-to-build-back-better-with-a-15-minute-city?language=en_US

Abdelhalim, K. (2010). Participatory Upgrading of Informal Areas: A Decision-makers' Guide for Action. Cairo: Participatory Development Programme in Urban Areas (PDP) in Egypt.

AbouKorin, S. A., Han, H., & Mahran, M. G. (2021). Role of urban planning characteristics in forming pandemic resilient cities – Case study of Covid-19 impacts on European cities within England, Germany and Italy. *Cities (London, England)*, *118*, 103324. doi:10.1016/j.cities.2021.103324 PMID:34539022

Acioly, C. (2021). Street-Led Citywide Slum Upgrading: Connecting the Informal and the Formal City Through Area-Based Planning and Infrastructure Improvement. In O. García-Villalba, Resilient Urban Regeneration in Informal Settlements in the Tropics: Upgrading Strategies in Asia and Latin America (pp. 11-35). Singapore: Springer Nature Singapore. doi:10.1007/978-981-13-7307-7_2

Al-Dairi, A. (2007). *Informal housing areas in Syria and linking them with the characteristics of families and population (In arabic)*. Damascus. http://cbssyr.sy/studies/st24.pdf

Al-Ruwaili, A. K. (2017). *Real Estate Development and Investment Law (15) of 2008 AD and its amendments (In arabic)*. Damascus University.

Allam, Z., & Jones, S. (2020, September). Pandemic stricken cities on lockdown. Where are our planning and design professionals [now, then and into the future]. *Land Use Policy*, *97*, 104805. doi:10.1016/j.landusepol.2020.104805 PMID:32508374

Barnwal, A. (2020). *How can covid 19 steer city leadership sustainability?* Global Environment Facility. https://www.thegef.org/blog/how-covid-19-can-steer-city-leadership-sustainability

Bereitschaft, B., & Scheller, D. (2020). How Might the COVID-19 Pandemic Affect 21st Century Urban Design, Planning, and Development? *Urban Science (Basel, Switzerland)*, *4*(4), 56–78. doi:10.3390/urbansci4040056

Brotherhood, L., Cavalcanti, T., Da Mata, D., & Santos, C. (2022). Slums and pandemics. *Journal of Development Economics*, *157*, 102882. doi:10.1016/j.jdeveco.2022.102882 PMID:35463050

Byun, N., Choi, Y., & Choi, J. (2014). The Neighborhood Unit: Effective or Obsolete? *Journal of Asian Architecture and Building Engineering*, *13*(3), 617–624. doi:10.3130/jaabe.13.617

Camerin, F., & Fabris, L. (2021). Towards the Post-Pandemic (Healthy) City: Barcelona's Poblenou Superblock Challenges and Opportunities. *Housing and Home*, *2*, 65–74. doi:10.2307/j.ctv1rnpj94.12

Capolongo, S., Buffoli, M., Brambilla, A., & Rebecchi, A. (2020). Healthy urban planning and design strategies to improve urban quality and attractiveness of places. TECHNE-Journal of technology for architecture and environment, 271-279. doi:10.13128/techne-7837

Crompton, J. (2013). The health rationale for urban parks in the nineteenth century in the USA. [Retrieved from CGTN.]. *World Leisure Journal*, *55*(4), 333–346. doi:10.1080/04419057.2013.836557

Das, A., Roy, S., Parvez, M., & Hasan, M. M. (2020, September). Decentralized activity centers in rural Bangladesh: A step towards effective emergency situation management in the post-pandemic cities. *Journal of Urban Management, 10*(3), 242-254. doi:10.1016/j.jum.2021.07.002

GCSC & RPC. (2020). *Regional Planning Project for the coastal region.* Damascus.

Gold, K. (2020). *COVID-19 puts urban density to the test.* THE GLOBE AND MAIL. https://www.theglobeandmail.com/real-estate/article-covid-19-puts-urban-density-to-the-test/

Grant, J. (2006). Planning the good community: New urbanism in theory and practice. London: Routledge (Taylor and Francis).

Izutsu, T., & Tsutsumi, A. (2010). Quality of Life of Urban Slum Residents. In V. Preedy & R. Watson (Eds.), *Handbook of Disease Burdens and Quality of Life Measures* (pp. 3383–3396). Springer. doi:10.1007/978-0-387-78665-0_195

Jin, D. (2020). Rethinking of the Development of Urban Planning Disciplines in Response to COVID-19 Epidemic. *Journal of Human Settlements in west China,* (5), 1-6. doi:10.13791/j.cnki.hsfwest.20200501

Jon, I. (2020). A manifesto for planning after the coronavirus: Towards planning of care. *Planning Theory*, *19*(3), 329–345. doi:10.1177/1473095220931272

Kakderi, C., Oikonomaki, E., & Papadaki, I. (2021). Smart and Resilient Urban Futures for Sustainability in the Post COVID-19 Era: A Review of Policy Responses on Urban Mobility. *Sustainability (Basel)*, *13*(11), 6486. doi:10.3390u13116486

Khavarian-Garmsir, A., & Sharifi, A. (2020, September 18). The COVID-19 pandemic: Impacts on cities and major lessons for urban planning, design, and management. *The Science of the Total Environment*. PMID:33370924

Lak, A., Shakouri Asl, S., & Maher, A. (2020). Resilient urban form to pandemics: Lessons from COVID-19. *Medical Journal of the Islamic Republic of Iran*, *71*. Advance online publication. doi:10.47176/mjiri.34.71 PMID:33306051

López, I., Ortega, J., & Pardo, M. (2020, April). Mobility infrastructures in cities and climate change: An analysis through the superblocks in Barcelona. *Atmosphere (Basel)*, *11*(4), 410. doi:10.3390/atmos11040410

Lucka, D. (2018). How to build a community. New Urbanism and its critics. *Urban Development Issues*, 17-28. doi:10.2478/udi-2018-0025

Mackres, E. (2020). *Insights from Big Data on How COVID-19 Is Changing Society*. TheCityFix. https://thecityfix.com/blog/insights-big-data-covid-19-changing-society-eric-mackres/

Megahed, N., & Ghoneim, E. (2020). Antivirus-built environment: Lessons learned from Covid-19 pandemic. *Sustainable Cities and Society*, *61*, 102350. doi:10.1016/j.scs.2020.102350 PMID:32834930

Mehaffy, M., Porta, S., & Romice, O. (2014). The "neighborhood unit" on trial: A case study in the impacts of urban morphology. *Journal of Urbanism*, *8*(2), 1–19.

Moreno, C., Allam, Z., Chabaud, D., Gall, C., & Pratlong, F. (2021). Introducing the "15-Minute City": Sustainability, Resilience and Place Identity in Future Post-Pandemic Cities. *Smart Cities*, *4*(1), 93–111. doi:10.3390martcities4010006

Nieuwenhuijsen, J. M. (2020). *Post-COVID-19 Cities: New Urban Models to Make Cities Healthier*. IS Global. https://www.isglobal.org/en/healthisglobal/-/custom-blog-portlet/post-covid-19-cities-new-urban-models-to-make-cities-healthier/4735173/0

Okech, E., & Nyadera, I. (2022). Urban green spaces in the wake of Covid-19 pandemic: Reflections from Nairobi, Kenya. *GeoJournal*, *87*(6), 4931–4945. doi:10.100710708-021-10540-0 PMID:34776594

Olszewska-Guizzo, A., Fogel, A., Benjumea, D., & Tahsin, N. (2022, may 3). Sustainable Solutions in Urban Health: Transdisciplinary Directions in Urban Planning for Global Public Health. In W. V. Leal Filho, Sustainable Policies and Practices in Energy, Environment and Health Research. World Sustainability Series. (pp. 223-243). Springer, Cham.

Onu, B., Surendran, S. S., & Price, T. (2014). Impact of inadequate urban planning on municipal solid waste management in the Niger Delta Region of Nigeria. *Journal of Sustainable Development, 7*(6), 27–45. doi:10.5539/jsd.v7n6p27

Ooi, G., & Kai, H. (2007). Urbanization and Slum Formation. *Journal of Urban Health, 84*(S1), 27–34. doi:10.100711524-007-9167-5 PMID:17387618

Oriewo, O. (2020). *THE EFFECT OF LAND USE PLANNING ONECONOMIC VULNARABILITY TO DISASTERMANAGEMENTINLOW INCOME NEIGHBOURHOODS OFELDORET URBAN AREA, KENYA*. MMUST.

Patricios, N. (2002). The neighborhood concept: A retrospective of physical design and social interaction. *Journal of Architectural and Planning Research*, 70–90.

Pelling, M. (2020). *Tomorrow's Cities and Covid-19: A discussion document.* Tomorrow's Cities is the UK Research and Innvovation (UKRI) & Global Challenges Research Fund (GCRF). https://www.tomorrowscities.org/tomorrows-cities-and-covid-19-discussion

Pinto, F., & Akhavan, M. (2022). Scenarios for a Post-Pandemic City: Urban planning strategies and challenges of making "Milan 15-minutes city. *Transportation Research Procedia, 60*, 370–377. doi:10.1016/j.trpro.2021.12.048

Pire, J., & Boivin, G. (2020). Pandemics Throughout History. *Frontiers in Microbiology, 11*, 631736. doi:10.3389/fmicb.2020.631736 PMID:33584597

Pozoukidou, G., & Chatziyiannaki, Z. (2021). 15-Minute City: Decomposing the New Urban Planning Eutopia. *Sustainability (Basel), 13*(2), 928. doi:10.3390u13020928

Ragheb, A., & El-Ashmawy, R. (2021). Strategic actions of urban development to define the intervention policies of slums. *City. Territory and Architecture, 8*(1), 1–18. doi:10.118640410-021-00139-w

RPC-Syria. (2011). *National framework for regional planning, draft copy (in arabic)*. RPC.

Sachan, M., & Bhattacharya, A. (2012). Mining statistically significant substrings using the chi-square statistic. *Proceedings of the VLDB Endowment International Conference on Very Large Data Bases, 5*(10), 1052–1063. doi:10.14778/2336664.2336677

Scott, M. (2020). Covid-19, Place-making and Health. *Planning Theory & Practice, 21*(3), 343–348. doi:10.1080/14649357.2020.1781445

Sharifi, A., & Khavarian-Garmsir, A. (2020). The COVID-19 pandemic: Impacts on cities and major lessons for urban planning, design, and management. *The Science of the Total Environment*, *749*, 142391. doi:10.1016/j.scitotenv.2020.142391 PMID:33370924

Singh, S., Ramesh Kumar, R., & Tiwari, M. K. (2021). Impact of COVID-19 on logistics systems and disruptions in food supply chain. *International Journal of Production Research*, *59*(7), 1993–2008. doi:10.1080/00207543.2020.1792000

Song, X., Cao, M., Zhai, K., Gao, X., Wu, M., & Yang, T. (2021). The Effects of Spatial Planning, Well-Being, and Behavioural Changes During and After the COVID-19 Pandemic. *Frontiers in Sustainable Cities*, *3*, 686706. doi:10.3389/frsc.2021.686706

Syrian Law Journal. (2018). The New Urban Renewal Law in Syria. *Syrian Law Journal*. https://www.syria.law/index.php/new-urban-renewal-law-syria/

Taşan-Kok, T. (2020, july 16). *How to be Truly Open: Rethinking Public Spaces in the Post-Covid City*. Urbanet. https://www.urbanet.info/truly-open-rethinking-public-spaces-post-covid-city/

Teller, J. (2021). Urban density and Covid-19: Towards an adaptive approach. *Buildings & Cities*, *2*(1), 150–165. doi:10.5334/bc.89

UN-Habitat. (2010). *Sustainable urban development and agenda 2030: UN habitat's programme framework: Participatory slum upgrading programme transforming the lives of one billion slum dwellers*. Nairobi: UN-Habitat. https://www.mypsup.org/library_files/downloads/SDGs%20and%20PSUP.pdf

UN-Habitat. (2019). *City-wide public space strategies a compendium of inspiring practices*. Nairobi: UNON Publishing Services Section. https://unhabitat.org/city-wide-public-space-strategies-a-compendium-of-inspiring-practices

UN-Habitat. (2020). *spatial planning guidelines during covid-19*. Kenya: UN Habitat. https://unhabitat.org/sites/default/files/2020/11/covid19_spatialplanning_eng1.pdf

UN-Habitat. (February 2022). *Analysis of Syrian Urban Law, Legal Thematic Paper*. Egypt: UN-HABITAT Regional Office for Arab States.

UNESCO. (2020). *Urban Solutions: Learning from cities responses to COVID-19*. Online meeting report, Paris. m Rivista Siti. https://en.unesco.org/urban-solutions-Learning-from-cities-responses-to-COVID19

Upadhya, C., & Rao, D. (2022). Dispossession without displacement: Producing property through slum redevelopment in Bengaluru, India. *Environment and Planning A. Economy and Space, 1*(17). doi:10.1177/0308518X221073988

Usman, B. A., Malik, N. A., & Alausa, K. M. (2015). Factors determining the choice of residential location in Ilorin, Nigeria. *Zaria Geographer, 22*(1), 109–122.

van den Berg, R. (2020, april 10). *Will covid 19 affect urban planning?* TheCityFix. https://thecityfix.com/blog/will-covid-19-affect-urban-planning-rogier-van-den-berg/

Wang, C., Xu, H., & Lin, A. (2022). Informal settlements in the context of COVID-19: Pandemic restrictions and the building of community resilience. *Indoor and Built Environment, 0*(0), 1–9. doi:10.1177/1420326X221097821

Willberg, E., Fink, C., & Toivonen, T. (2023). The 15-minute city for all? – Measuring individual and temporal variations in walking accessibility. *Journal of Transport Geography, 103521*, 103521. doi:10.1016/j.jtrangeo.2022.103521

KEY TERMS AND DEFINITIONS

15-Minute City: A concept of urban planning that promotes the idea of creating self-sustaining neighborhoods where people can access all the services and amenities they need within a 15-minute. The goal is to create socially and environmentally sustainable urban communities based on a mixed-use development that combines residential areas with businesses, services, and interactive public spaces.

Informal Settlement: A residential area in or near urban areas where housing is constructed spontaneously on land that is not owned or legally controlled by the occupants, characterized by a special social fabric. It presents a challenging environment for urban planning efforts due to inadequate living conditions, lack of basic urban services/infrastructure, and lack of property rights.

A New Normal: The term "new normal" in the context of COVID-19 and urban planning refers to the adaptation and transformation of urban spaces, infrastructure, and services to be more resilient, inclusive, connected, and sustainable to reimagine and redesign the urban environment after the pandemic.

On-Site Redevelopment: A participatory redevelopment intervention policy to solve the problem of informal settlements avoiding socio-economic displacement to prepare sustainable neighborhoods with compact mixed-use structures and functional areas integrated spatially, legally, socially, and economically with the host cities.

Street-Led Citywide Approach: This refers to one of the slums/informal settlements redevelopment processes, which aims to create more vibrant urban environments that foster social interaction and community resilience based on the role of streets as lifelines for the full integration into the city system as a tool to promote sustainable development.

Chapter 8
Legal Studies Over the Impacts of the COVID-19 Pandemic on International Peace and Security

Nima Norouzi
https://orcid.org/0000-0002-2546-4288
Bournemouth University, UK

ABSTRACT

The main focus of this study is on the topic of the global epidemic of Covid-19 and international peace and security. The practice of the council indicates the expansion of its competencies and its extension from military to civilian threats. The council has twice before adopted resolutions on AIDS and Ebola, which have deemed the situation a threat to international peace and security. If the council wishes to apply the same logic to the description and assessment of the Covid-19, it will, as in the previous two cases, declare it a threat to international peace and security, given the extent of the spread of the disease. However, the Security Council became passive in the wind, and more than three months after the announcement of Covid-19 as a global epidemic by the World Health Organization, with the passage of UNSCR 2532 dated 1 July 2020, it considered international peace and security.

DOI: 10.4018/978-1-7998-9213-7.ch008

INTRODUCTION

The outbreak of Covid-19 in 2020 became a major problem for the international community, and unfortunately, starting in China, it quickly became a pandemic. An epidemic is currently affecting many countries, including Iran. The nature of this virus requires an international community to respond appropriately to its inherent nature. Weapons and weapons will have no place for Arabs in this campaign. But because of the importance of this issue to the international community, some statesmen describe the fight against the Covid-19virus and the situation in their country in the literature more or less as "war [for health] and battle with the invisible enemy."The Covid-19 virus attacks everyone regardless of gender, color, age, ethnicity, race, nationality, or religion. This invisible enemy will severely afflict the vulnerable. The spread of the Covid-19 virus has severely overshadowed various aspects of the social, economic, and cultural life of individuals and has caused great loss of life and property to individuals and legal entities around the world. The prevalence of contagious and contagious diseases is not new, and different lands have experienced it throughout history. Governments and international organizations have taken many steps to work together to prevent such diseases(Szymanski et al., 2020).

Apart from the dimensions of health and hygiene in the national arena, the World Health Organization (WHO) is its main trustee in the international arena. The preamble of the founding document of this organization specifically refers to the connection and connection of the two issues of health and hygiene with peace and security. On the other hand, international peace and security have been identified as one of the goals of the United Nations. The main task of maintaining international peace and security is with the Security Council. In achieving this goal, the council has the main task and not the exclusive one. The General Assembly and the Secretary-General of the United Nations may therefore take action following the provisions of the Charter; It seems that some measures have been taken in this regard. In the past, peace was meant to mean no war; today, this attitude has changed; many factors, such as poverty, climate change, terrorism, and the spread of infectious and contagious diseases worldwide, can jeopardize international peace and security. Due to the multifaceted nature of the Covid-19 outbreak, the international dimension can be analyzed from different angles. The legal aspects of the subject of the Covid-19 can be considered in various sections of international law, such as the law of international organizations, the settlement of disputes and international liability, and so on. The human and commercial dimensions of Covid-19 should not be overlooked(Siche, 2020).

Regarding the dimensions of human rights, the issue of individual rights and freedoms is raised; What is more, the implementation of collective quarantine will create restrictions on the movement and residence of individuals. In the field of trade, these three issues can be considered; Because the principle of trade liberalization is one of the important goals of the World Trade Organization on the one hand, and the imposition of restrictions and bans on imports and exports, on the other hand, can create problems. In general, various issues related to the trade of goods, services, and intellectual property of vaccine and drug companies in international trade law and the right of individuals to access vaccines, drugs, and disinfectants are necessary to prevent the spread of disease and disease. They incite humanity. Governments have long quarantined efforts to prevent the spread of infectious diseases such as cholera, plague, yellow fever, etc.

On the other hand, the states were faced with two necessities: protecting national security and protecting the freedom of exchange, which must somehow reconcile the two. In other words, guaranteeing a minimum of trade in exchange for ensuring maximum safety and health could be considered a way out of the current situation. The main topic of this research is the Covid-19 outbreak and international peace and security. This study seeks to answer whether the spread of Covid-19 is a threat to international peace and security. To answer this question, the international dimension of Covid-19 and its description as a civilian threat to international peace and security is examined, followed by the initial inaction of the Security Council and finally, the adoption of a recent resolution on this issue(Pooter, 2013).

COVID-19 GLOBAL EPIDEMIC AS A THREAT TO INTERNATIONAL SECURITY

Traditionally, military force and war have been considered the most important threat to peace and security. This approach continued until the end of the Cold War and was largely subject to a narrow interpretation of the concept of international peace and security. By changing the traditional approach and the broad interpretation of this concept, the acceptance of other factors threatening international peace and security was provided. It is no longer just a matter of war that threatens international peace and security, but another issue poses a civilian threat. For example, in Security Council Resolution 748 on the Lockerbie case, the Libyan government described the Libyan government's refusal to extradite two Libyan suspects in the Pan-American bombing to threaten international peace and security. In other words, in Resolution 917, the council considered the absence of Aristide, President-elect of the Haitian Legislature, a threat to peace and security. Reports from the UN Secretary-General indicate this. In his peace program, as well as in his lecture at The Hague Academy, entitled "International Law in the Pursuit of Its Values: Peace, Development, Democracy," Batrous Ghali addressed this issue. In his peace plan, the Secretary-General mentions cases, including infectious diseases, which are both the source of conflict and the cause of conflict, and reaffirms this in another report prepared at the request of Kofi Annan by a group of experts(Maurel, 2020).

The report lists some of the threats to international peace and security, poverty, infectious diseases, and environmental degradation are all economic and social threats that threaten peace and security. Many factors can directly or indirectly threaten international peace and security. For example, currently, two important factors of climate change in the environment and the spread of infectious diseases in health and hygiene are all threats to international peace and security. If we compare environmental factors with the Covid-19 virus, they have one thing in common, and that is that they are cross-border. Elements such as air, water, and animal species are not known; In other words, political boundaries make sense to human beings, and these elements move easily. The Covid-19 virus is also easily transmitted and is not subject to the will of international law enforcement. The virus is naturally transmitted through people and goods, and an epidemic can easily turn into a pandemic. The rapid spread of infectious and contagious diseases such as plague, cholera, Ebola, SARS, and Covid-19 will seriously threaten human health and health. Therefore the international community has taken measures to combat these diseases. Maintaining health has long been the exclusive domain of governments. Gradually, with the fundamental change in speech, these matters are considered matters of governance. Trade between governments and their interdependencies has shown that states can not take appropriate and prompt action against communicable diseases. Cooperation between governmental and non-governmental actors in the age of globalization in Covid-19 is inevitable, and all tools should be used in this field to overcome such diseases(Laborde et al., 2020).

CONTAGIOUS DISEASES AS A THREAT TO INTERNATIONAL SECURITY

Undoubtedly, the maintenance of international peace and security is the most important goal enshrined in the Charter of the United Nations. This serious task has been entrusted to the Security Council. Following its functions under the Charter, the council calls on the parties to the dispute to settle their disputes peacefully and act as a mediator. If it jeopardizes the friction and conflict of international peace and security, it acts as a regulator under Chapter VII of the Security Council Charter and can take decisions under this chapter to maintain international peace and security. Chapter 7 of the Charter identifies the concepts of threat to peace, breach of peace, and aggression. The Security Council will decide which of the above concepts is appropriate by describing the current and incidental situation. The threat to peace is a general concept and can cover a wide variety of situations(Lipscy, 2020). To this end, the Security Council shall consider the seriousness of the situation and the actual nature of the situation to establish a threat to peace. The practice of the Security Council indicates that in most cases, it refuses to declare its status under these headings and merely mentions and cites Chapter VII of the Charter. A mere reference to Chapter VII frees the council from entering into a description and conformity of the situation to the above concepts. Such a measure leaves the Security Council free to expand its competence in describing new situations. Describing the spread of contagious and contagious diseases as a threat to international peace and security is one of the good examples of this. Threats to health and well-being are, in principle, civilian threats. Many issues can be raised on this issue beyond the scope of this article and require separate research. Issues such as the use of the virus by one state against the territorial integrity or political independence of another state, biological aggression and aggression, the criminal responsibility of its perpetrators in the field of international criminal law, and its proof are all issues to consider. In any case, the Security Council can, within the framework of its responsibilities, act in cases where it is not intentional, but the situation has such a potential that it threatens international peace and security. We certainly need criteria to describe each situation with the help of assessing the fulfillment of that threshold. It is noteworthy that in addition to Article 2 of the Instruction, to apply the provisions of Article 6 itself, there are criteria (being serious, unusual, international health, unexpectedness, significant international expansion risk, and the risk of travel restrictions). In case of fulfillment of these criteria, information will be issued, in particular, with the existence of a content sharing of the criteria of the international health emergency. We are not here to explain the criteria set out in the World Health Organization (WHO) regarding the implementation of the obligations of member states. To describe the spread of contagious and contagious diseases as a threat to international peace and security, it is necessary to meet the thresholds for the council to be able to make decisions. It seems that the threshold of infectious and contagious diseases can be examined from both quantitative and qualitative perspectives, and the two can not be easily separated from each other. Considering a situation as an epidemic or a pandemic has quantitative and qualitative factors within it(Kandel et al., 2020). The spatial and geographical spread of the disease from one region to another (nationally and internationally), susceptibility to transmission (from human to human, animal to human) and the rate of spread of the virus, and the number of victims in all Is. The epidemic and pandemics of infectious and contagious diseases have been initiated several times in the agenda of the Security Council, beginning with the adoption of resolutions on AIDS, and ended with two. Recent decisions regarding Ebola have continued. On AIDS, Resolutions 1308 and 1983 were adopted in 2000 and 2011, respectively. In Security Council Resolution 1308, "the outbreak of AIDS is a threat to stability and security," In its second resolution, it emphasizes the need for a commitment by States to cooperate in the international arena. As with AIDS, the Security Council has taken decisions on Ebola. Despite many similarities between the two issues, in Security Council Resolution 2177 adopted in 2014 on Ebola, the Security Council used other literature to declare: "The Ebola outbreak in Africa is a threat to international peace and security." "The epidemic is causing internal unrest and social unrest and is exacerbating the political situation and exacerbating insecurity," he said, justifying his decision to indicate that the Ebola virus was a threat to international peace and security. With this action, the council seems to be trying to link the two issues of the spread of the Ebola virus with the turmoil and internal tensions in the Black Continent. The impact of the epidemic on the political, social, and security situation in the African countries of Liberia, Guinea, Sierra Leone, and Nigeria led the council to conclude that the current situation posed a threat to peace and security. The question now is, what action has the Security Council taken on the status of Covid-19? The short answer to this question indicates the inaction of the Security Council in this regard. A comparison of the two cases of Ebola and Covid-19 shows that Ebola covered only one continent, the continent of Africa and that of West Africa; Covid-19, on the other hand, has taken over the world, and the World Health Organization has described its health as a pandemic. However, the global Covid-19 situation is far more severe than that of Ebola, and the Security Council is expected to step out of its inactivity(Jacobsen, 2020).

SECURITY COUNCIL INACTIONS ON COVID-19 DISEASE

It is clear that the Security Council is political authority, and political factors are heavily involved in the decisions of this pillar. If we pay attention to the decisions made by the Council on AIDS and Ebola, it becomes clear that the council has linked the political and social situation with epidemics and, from this perspective, has posed a threat to peace. The task of the Security Council is not simply to maintain peace and security, But this pillar also participates in establishing and consolidating peace. In cases where civilian threats do not have a specific audience but relate to the international community as a whole, there is no room for doubt to prevent the situation from deteriorating through timely and timely decisions(Grange, 2014). In the case of Ebola, several African countries were the main addressees of the Security Council resolution. But other parts of the world have also been addressed in terms of financial aid, equipment, facilitating action, and cooperating with affected governments and humanitarian organizations. The situation was more or less the same with AIDS. The question now is, what is the difference between Ebola and Covid-19 to prevent the Security Council from making a quick decision? The political factor seems to have been too effective in preventing the Security Council from reacting quickly. The approach of Russia and China was different from that of the other permanent members of the Security Council, which led to the inaction of the Security Council on the Covid-19. One of the formal objections was raised by Russia during the Security Council meeting. Of course, this objection is not limited to holding a possible meeting on Covid-19. Russia initially believed that it was opposed, citing the provisions of the UN Charter on holding a Security Council meeting. Russia justifies its position by citing paragraph 3 of Article 28 of the Charter(Fierke, 2015).

Moreover, voting, as usual, although apparently, such an inference from paragraph 3 is correct because of 2 by raising the hand. However, it cannot be compiled at the same time as paragraph 1 of this article. On the other hand, the logic of legal logic does not support such an inference; How is it possible to perform permanent duties and activities on the one hand and the ban on holding virtual meetings in the Security Council on the other hand, given the prevalence and spread of the Covid-19 virus in the world. Given the current state of the Covid-19 virus, if physical presence is insistent, there is no choice but to hold meetings following health protocols and social distance, or new technology should be resorted to, and council meetings should be held virtually. However, with this interpretation of Article 28 of the Charter, Russia was able to make a brief break in the virtual meetings of the Security Council, which later held a virtual meeting and showed that such an understanding of the provisions of the Charter is inconsistent with the reality of today. The main reason for the inaction and non-decision of the Security Council in this regard was related to the disagreement between the permanent members. Where US President Trump directly blames another member of the Security Council for the spread of the Covid-19 virus and even calls the Covid-19 virus a Chinese virus, what can be expected from the Security Council? In other words, the United States was seeking a resolution explicitly stating the origin of the Covid-19 virus. This disagreement severely challenged the decision-making process in the council(De Pooter, 2019).

On the other hand, the US government is very dissatisfied with the performance of the World Health Organization (WHO) towards the Chinese government. This dissatisfaction stems from the fact that the US government believes that the International Atomic Energy Agency (IAEA) has not taken a hard line on the Chinese government. According to the United States, the Chinese government has failed to meet its obligations under the rules of this organization, and due to the lack of time and timely notification and information, it has caused the spread of Covid-19. The president of the United States has taken a hard line on the World Health Organization and ironically calls it the China Organization over which he has complete control. At present, the relationship between the United States and the World Health Organization (WHO) is not in good condition, and for this reason, this government has submitted a request to leave that organization.

In light of the Security Council's initial and significant silence on Covid-19, the Secretary-General and the General Assembly have taken action. The UN Secretary-General likens the Covid-19 virus to a common enemy and calls on all parties to the conflict to end the war and fight Covid-19 together. In the context of the global Covid-19 epidemic, the Secretary-General's emphasis is on immediate ceasefire. The General Assembly adopted two resolutions in April 2020. These resolutions relate to the global solidarity against the disease and the Covid-19 virus, and in general, terms emphasize the concern for the health, safety, and well-being of humanity as a result of the spread and spread of this disease. In this regard, the General Assembly resolutions point to the disruption of societies and economic exchanges and state that Covid-19 requires global action based on unity, solidarity, and multilateral cooperation. Normally, General Assembly resolutions do not have as much binding force as Security Council resolutions. The two Covid-19 resolutions adopted by the Assembly are no exception to this rule, and the literature used in both documents does not impose a strong commitment on governments. Eventually, the Security Council's initial inaction came to an end, with the Covid-19 epidemic seen as a threat to international peace and security. The council unanimously adopted Resolution 2532 on 1 July 2020 without explicit reference to Chapter 7 of the Charter. Negotiations on a draft resolution took a long time; its prolongation was also due to the sharp differences between the permanent members of the Security Council. In other words, the resolution was passed more than three months after the World Health Organization declared Covid-19 a global pandemic. The recent Security Council resolution is somewhat similar to previous resolutions on AIDS and Ebola; However, the Ebola resolution seems to be much stronger than the Covid-19 resolution. In terms of writing, the Ebola Resolution is a sign of certainty and certainty that it is considered a threat to international peace and security, whereas it is not the case with Covid-19(Dannreuther, 2014).

Resolution 2532 focuses on the interrelationship between violence and the instability of the ruling conflict and the intensification of the Covid-19 epidemic. To this end, paragraph 2 of the resolution emphasizes the need for a 90-day cessation of hostilities for humanitarian reasons to allow for the delivery of humanitarian aid. In other words, with this measure, the Security Council seeks to facilitate the necessary assistance to the warring parties and to take necessary measures to prevent the spread of Covid-19 by establishing a ceasefire for at least 90 days. Despite the emphasis on a quarterly ceasefire to send humanitarian aid safely and without hindrance, paragraph 3 of the resolution states that a total and immediate cessation of hostilities over the Islamic State of Iraq and the Levant (ISIL), al-Qaeda, etc., Groups, companies and other terrorist groups do not apply. Comparing paragraphs 2 and 3 of the resolution is remarkable; One emphasizes the immediate cessation of hostilities and the observance of humanitarian principles to send humanitarian aid.

The other emphasizes the non-imposition of this cessation on military operations directed against some terrorist groups. In other words, paragraph 3 somehow sets out the general rule in paragraph 2 of the resolution and limits its scope. The principle is to stop the conflict immediately so that humanitarian aid can be sent. However, this rule does not apply to terrorist groups listed in paragraph 3 and is excluded.

Another point is that paragraph 1 of the resolution considers the immediate cessation of hostilities raised in the Security Council and, as a result, does not include situations that have not yet been raised. The question is whether there is no precedence between health and the observance of humanitarian principles on the one hand and the fight against terrorism and terrorists on the other? In other words, are the principles set out in paragraph 2 of the resolution transferable and exceptional?

It seems that both principles are on the same level. In the field of human rights, this issue has been raised about the priority of freedom of information over privacy in connection with the screening of a film about professional murder murderers who are going through the last days of their captivity and will soon be released and absorbed into society. Time and place conditions are effective in determining priority. If the film had been made at the time of his imprisonment, the principle of freedom of information would have taken precedence there, but now that the offender has served his sentence and is about to be absorbed into society, the principle of privacy takes precedence over freedom of information. Concerning paragraph 3 of the resolution, it seems that this allocation can be justified based on more important expediency, and thus it is possible to prevent the creation of a possible opportunity to equip and strengthen the military of these groups(Cha, 2004). There is a consideration here, and that is the indisputable humanitarian principles of the International Committee of the Red Cross. The principle of non-discrimination between the warring parties undoubtedly has a high place in international humanitarian law. The discrimination in question here is not positive discrimination but negative discrimination that will have no place among the Arabs and is completely outlawed in international humanitarian law. The US approach to terrorism seems to have cast a heavy shadow over the resolution. The government believes that the rules of international humanitarian law do not cover the fight against terrorism, and that is why it has been talking about the concept of illegal combat since 9/11. Such a fighter's perception would change the concept of a prisoner of war and the rules governing their treatment(Couture Ménard & Pavot, 2016).

As noted earlier, another point of contention in the resolution was the United States' stubbornness and opposition to its inclusion and emphasis on the central role of the World Health Organization in dealing with Covid-19. However, in its recent resolution, the council emphasizes the provisions of the General Assembly resolution on "Global Solidarity in the Fight against Covid-19," adopted on 2 April 2020, which mentions the role of the World Health Organization.

DISCUSSION

Countering the Covid-19 virus requires the cooperation of all relevant governments and international organizations. In this campaign, the World Health Organization (WHO) plays a key role as the main trustee. The cooperation of governments with each other and with the responsible organization can effectively coordinate and facilitate actions. Undoubtedly, the inaction and inaction of the Security Council on Covid-19 could do much damage to multilateralism. Before adopting UN Security Council Resolution 2532, there were numerous proposals and speculations and the request for consultation of the International Court of Justice in academic circles. This request must be made in the form of a question or legal issue, whether by the World Health Organization or any other specialized body or directly by the General Assembly. The next point is the subject of this question and how it is formulated(Brown, 1993).

In other words, the main issue is the question or the ambiguity in the exercise of the powers and powers of the World Health Organization in the case of Covid-19 disease that the organization wants to seek the advice of the Court in this regard. Finally, the most important thing is to obtain permission from the UN General Assembly and submit it to the International Court of Justice. Given that the organization has already obtained the permission of the General Assembly to seek the advice of the Court, and the prevention and control of diseases that endanger global health, it is within the competence of the organization(Norouzi et al., 2021). However, in its Advisory Opinion of 25 February 2019 on the legal effects of the separation of the Chagos Archipelago from Mauritius in 1965, the International Court of Justice stated: is not. The jurisdiction of the Court does not require that authority to issue an advisory opinion. In addition to having jurisdiction over the advisory theory, the Court should recognize that the answer to the question raises the question of the authority and integrity of the Court's judicial function as a key judicial organ of the United Nations(Norouzi & Ataei, 2021). "The presentation of an advisory opinion is a manifestation of the Court's participation in the activities of the United Nations, and the Court should not, in principle, evade or refuse such participation, unless the reasons for the Court's decision refuse to issue an advisory opinion." Finally, with the passage of Resolution 2532, the above speculation faded. The delay in passing the resolution in the Security Council marked the culmination of sharp differences between the United States and China over the origin of the Covid-19 virus, on the one hand, and the United States' dissatisfaction with the World Health Organization's approach to China, on the other. This prompted the United States to call for a withdrawal from the upper house at a recent request. The Security Council described the Covid-19 epidemic as a threat to international peace and security(Buzan & Hansen, 2009; Norouzi, 2021). The arrival of the Security Council and the decision on Covid-19 could, in the context of Chapter Seven of the

Charter, in addition to the inherent necessity of these decisions, provide a reliable and credible guarantee for the implementation of the 2020 international health emergency. In other words, fill the gap left by the lack of guarantees for implementing the 2005 International Health Directive through the Security Council resolution. While the Security Council has a great deal of freedom in describing the situation within the framework of Article 39 of the Charter of the United Nations, it should be noted that the council describes the situation as a threat to peace by declaring a state of an international health emergency. It will be facilitated. The council's adoption of a strong resolution could pave the way for a discussion of collective health security action and, following Article 41 of the Charter, decide on the issue of civilian coercion as appropriate. The problems of the international community in solving the Covid-19 pandemic are not small. At present, beyond the differences between some of the permanent members of the Security Council over the origin of Covid-19, the lack of a vaccine is not in itself a small problem that can be easily overcome. In addition, there is a violation of the provisions of Article 14 of the 1944 Chicago Convention, according to which governments must take effective measures to prevent the transmission of infectious diseases by air. Most governments initially did not take action but intensified the spread of the virus as foreign flights continued between countries(Buzan et al., 2003; Norouzi & Movahedian, 2021).

CONCLUSION

Finally, it should be noted that improving the current situation and effectively countering Covid-19 in the world depends on the cooperation of governments and international organizations. The first step in this regard was taken within the framework of the Security Council's efforts to maintain international peace and security with the adoption of the resolution. Undoubtedly, its implementation requires the cooperation of all governments, especially the permanent members of the Security Council, to put aside their differences and give priority to the interests of the international community in this area. In addition, due diligence and a precautionary and preventive approach are required, States should take all necessary measures to prevent the spread of the virus and to exercise good neighborliness to exchange information on the disease and to fully monitor their border crossings. At the national level, governments can play their role in combating the Covid-19 household virus by enforcing health guidelines and monitoring compliance. The only way to overcome this invisible enemy is to finally find the Covid-19 vaccine, follow the health instructions and take preventive measures.

REFERENCES

Brown, M. E. (Ed.). (1993). *Ethnic conflict and international security*. Princeton University Press.

Buzan, B., Buzan, B. G., W'ver, O., Wæver, O., & Buzan, O. W. B. (2003). *Regions and powers: the structure of international security* (Vol. 91). Cambridge University Press. doi:10.1017/CBO9780511491252

Buzan, B., & Hansen, L. (2009). *The evolution of international security studies*. Cambridge University Press. doi:10.1017/CBO9780511817762

Cha, V. D. (2000). Globalization and the study of international security. *Journal of Peace Research*, *37*(3), 391–403. doi:10.1177/0022343300037003007

Couture Ménard, M. E., & Pavot, D. (2016). INTRODUCTION: LES PANDÉMIES ET LE DROIT: VERS UNE PLUS GRANDE SOLIDARITÉ?. *Revue de droit de l'Université de Sherbrooke*, *46*(2), 251-259.

Dannreuther, R. (2014). *International security: The contemporary agenda*. John Wiley & Sons.

De Pooter, H. (2019). Aperçu de la coopération internationale en matière de surveillance et de riposte aux épidémies et aux pandémies. In Santé et droit international, Actes du colloque de Rennes I de la SFDI (pp. 225-245).

Fierke, K. M. (2015). *Critical approaches to international security*. John Wiley & Sons.

Grange, M. (2014). Ebola: Le droit international au soutien de la lutte contre une épidémie transfrontière. *Annuaire Français de Droit International*, *60*(1), 685–706. doi:10.3406/afdi.2014.4770

Jacobsen, K. H. (2020). Will COVID-19 generate global preparedness? *Lancet*, *395*(10229), 1013–1014. doi:10.1016/S0140-6736(20)30559-6 PMID:32199074

Kandel, N., Chungong, S., Omaar, A., & Xing, J. (2020). Health security capacities in the context of COVID-19 outbreak: An analysis of International Health Regulations annual report data from 182 countries. *Lancet*, *395*(10229), 1047–1053. doi:10.1016/S0140-6736(20)30553-5 PMID:32199075

Laborde, D., Martin, W., Swinnen, J., & Vos, R. (2020). COVID-19 risks to global food security. *Science*, *369*(6503), 500–502. doi:10.1126cience.abc4765 PMID:32732407

Lipscy, P. Y. (2020). COVID-19 and the Politics of Crisis. *International Organization*, *74*(S1), E98–E127. doi:10.1017/S0020818320000375

Maurel, R. (2020). " L'(in) activité du Conseil de sécurité face au Covid-19: où est confinée la "communauté" internationale"?", Dossier. *[Colloque virtuel] Droit et Coronavirus. Le droit face aux circonstances sanitaires exceptionnelles.* RDLF Revue des droits et libertés fondamentaux. Revue des droits et libertés fondamentaux.

Norouzi, N. (2021). Post-COVID-19 and globalization of oil and natural gas trade: Challenges, opportunities, lessons, regulations, and strategies. *International Journal of Energy Research, 45*(10), 14338–14356. doi:10.1002/er.6762 PMID:34219899

Norouzi, N., & Ataei, E. (2021a). Covid-19 Crisis and Environmental law: Opportunities and challenges. *Hasanuddin Law Review, 7*(1), 46–60. doi:10.20956/halrev.v7i1.2772

Norouzi, N., & Ataei, E. (2021b). Environmental Protection Regulations in the Light of Public Law and Social Obligations. *Research Journal of Ecology and Environmental Sciences, 1*(1), 1–16.

Norouzi, N., Khanmohammadi, H. U., & Ataei, E. (2021). The Law in the Face of the COVID-19 Pandemic: Early Lessons from Uruguay. *Hasanuddin Law Review, 7*(2), 75–88. doi:10.20956/halrev.v7i2.2827

Norouzi, N., & Movahedian, H. (2021). Right to Education in Mother Language: In the Light of Judicial and Legal Structures. In Handbook of Research on Novel Practices and Current Successes in Achieving the Sustainable Development Goals (pp. 223-241). IGI Global.

Pooter, H. D. (2013). *Le droit international face aux pandémies: vers un système de sécurité sanitaire collective?* [Doctoral dissertation, University of Paris].

Siche, R. (2020). What is the impact of COVID-19 disease on agriculture? *Scientia Agropecuaria, 11*(1), 3–6. doi:10.17268ci.agropecu.2020.01.00

Szymanski, F. M., Smuniewski, C., & Platek, A. E. (2020). Will the COVID-19 pandemic change national security and healthcare in the spectrum of cardiovascular disease? *Current Problems in Cardiology, 45*(9), 100645. doi:10.1016/j.cpcardiol.2020.100645 PMID:32646545

ADDITIONAL READING

Brown, M. E. (Ed.). (1993). *Ethnic conflict and international security.* Princeton University Press.

Buzan, B., Buzan, B. G., W'ver, O., Wæver, O., & Buzan, O. W. B. (2003). *Regions and powers: the structure of international security* (Vol. 91). Cambridge University Press. doi:10.1017/CBO9780511491252

Buzan, B., & Hansen, L. (2009). *The evolution of international security studies*. Cambridge University Press. doi:10.1017/CBO9780511817762

De Wet, E. (2004). The Chapter VII Powers of the United Nations Security Council (Vol. 3). Hart Publishing.

Happold, M. (2003). Security Council resolution 1373 and the constitution of the United Nations. *Leiden Journal of International Law*, *16*(3), 593–610. doi:10.1017/S0922156503001304

Kuziemko, I., & Werker, E. (2006). How much is a seat on the Security Council worth? Foreign aid and bribery at the United Nations. *Journal of Political Economy*, *114*(5), 905–930. doi:10.1086/507155

Szasz, P. C. (2002). The security council starts legislating. *The American Journal of International Law*, *96*(4), 901–905. doi:10.2307/3070686

Talmon, S. (2005). The Security Council as world legislature. *The American Journal of International Law*, *99*(1), 175–193. doi:10.2307/3246097

KEY TERMS AND DEFINITIONS

Environmental Law: Environmental law is a collective term encompassing aspects of the law that protect the environment. A related but distinct set of regulatory regimes, now strongly influenced by environmental legal principles, focuses on managing specific natural resources, such as forests, minerals, or fisheries. Other areas, such as environmental impact assessment, may not fit neatly into either category but are nonetheless important components of environmental law. Previous research found that when environmental law reflects moral values for betterment, legal adoption is more likely to be successful, usually in well-developed regions. In less-developed states, changes in moral values are necessary for successful legal implementation when environmental law differs from moral values.

Equity: Defined by UNEP to include intergenerational equity - "the right of future generations to enjoy a fair level of the common patrimony" - and intragenerational equity - "the right of all people within the current generation to fair access to the current generation's entitlement to the Earth's natural resources" - environmental equity considers the present generation under an obligation to account for long-term impacts of activities and to act to sustain the global environment and resource base for future generations. Pollution control and resource management laws may be assessed against this principle.

Precautionary Principle: One of the most commonly encountered and controversial principles of environmental law, the Rio Declaration formulated the precautionary principle as follows, to protect the environment, States shall widely apply the precautionary approach according to their capabilities. Where there are threats of serious or irreversible damage, lack of full scientific certainty shall not be used as a reason for postponing cost-effective measures to prevent environmental degradation. The principle may play a role in any debate over the need for environmental regulation.

Prevention: The concept of prevention etc. can perhaps better be considered an overarching aim that gives rise to a multitude of legal mechanisms, including prior assessment of environmental harm, licensing, or authorization that set out the conditions for operation and the consequences for violation of the conditions, as well as the adoption of strategies and policies. Emission limits and other product or process standards, the use of best available techniques, and similar techniques can all be seen as applications of the concept of prevention.

The Polluter Pays Principle: The polluter pays principle stands for the idea that "the environmental costs of economic activities, including the cost of preventing potential harm, should be internalized rather than imposed upon society at large." All issues related to responsibility for cost for environmental remediation and compliance with pollution control regulations involve this principle.

Public Participation and Transparency: Identified as essential conditions for "accountable governments,... industrial concerns," and organizations generally, public participation and transparency are presented by UNEP as requiring "effective protection of the human right to hold and express opinions and to seek, receive and impart ideas, etc. a right of access to appropriate, comprehensible and timely information held by governments and industrial concerns on economic and social policies regarding the sustainable use of natural resources and the protection of the environment, without imposing undue financial burdens upon the applicants and with adequate protection of privacy and business confidentiality," and "effective judicial and administrative proceedings." These principles are present in environmental impact assessment, laws requiring publication and access to relevant environmental data, and administrative procedures.

Sustainable Development: Defined by the United Nations Environment Programme as "development that meets the needs of the present without compromising the ability of future generations to meet their own needs," sustainable development may be considered together with the concepts of "integration" (development cannot be considered in isolation from sustainability) and "interdependence" (social and economic development, and environmental protection, are interdependent). Laws mandating environmental impact assessment and requiring or encouraging development to minimize environmental impacts may be assessed against this principle. The modern concept of sustainable development was discussed at the 1972 United Nations Conference on the Human Environment (Stockholm Conference) and the driving force behind the 1983 World Commission on Environment and Development (WCED, or Bruntland Commission). In 1992, the first UN Earth Summit resulted in the Rio Declaration, Principle 3 of which reads: "The right to development must be fulfilled to equitably meet developmental and environmental needs of present and future generations." Sustainable development has been a core concept of international environmental discussion ever since, including at the World Summit on Sustainable Development (Earth Summit 2002) and the United Nations Conference on Sustainable Development (Earth Summit 2012, or Rio+20).

Transboundary Responsibility: Defined in the international law context as an obligation to protect one's environment. UNEP considers transboundary responsibility at the international level to prevent damage to neighboring environments at the international level as a potential limitation on the rights of the sovereign state. Laws that limit externalities imposed upon human health and the environment may be assessed against this principle.

Chapter 9
Economic Studies on Automobile Management:
Working Capital and Investment Analysis

A. Ravisankar
https://orcid.org/0000-0002-7679-7541
Erode Sengunthar Engineering College (Autonomous), India

B. Sampath
Mythayammal Engineering College (Autonomous), India

M. Mohammed Asif
Vignan's Lara Institute of Technology and Science, India

ABSTRACT

This chapter examines the economic factors influencing working capital management and investment decisions in the automobile industry. It explores both macroeconomic and microeconomic elements that impact the industry's financial dynamics. The study also investigates future trends and prospects, including the shift towards electric and autonomous vehicles, sustainability practices, and digitalization. Based on the analysis, the chapter provides practical recommendations for improving working capital management practices, enhancing investment decision-making, and policy implications for industry stakeholders. The findings aim to assist automobile companies in adapting to the evolving market and achieving sustainable growth.

DOI: 10.4018/978-1-7998-9213-7.ch009

INTRODUCTION

The automobile industry is crucial for global economic growth, employment, and technology advancement. It has evolved due to technological advancements, consumer preferences, and environmental concerns, making automobile management a complex and dynamic field. This chapter focuses on working capital and investment analysis, which impact automobile companies' operations and long-term growth. Working capital directly impacts short-term obligations and production cycles, while investment decisions determine long-term competitiveness and growth. Understanding these financial aspects is essential for effective automobile management(Jafari & Prabhakar Rao, 2015).

This chapter aims to provide a comprehensive overview of working capital management in the automobile sector, focusing on components, the working capital cycle, and factors influencing requirements. It also discusses strategies employed by companies to efficiently manage working capital and optimize cash flows. The chapter also analyzes investment decisions within the automobile industry, discussing various appraisal techniques, costs and benefits evaluation, and risk identification and mitigation. It also presents a comparative study of investment projects, highlighting decision-making processes and recommending best practices for effective capital allocation(Rao, 2015).

This chapter will analyze case studies of prominent automobile companies, focusing on their working capital management practices and investment decisions. It will highlight successful strategies employed by industry leaders and emphasize the importance of understanding economic factors in automobile management. Understanding the influence of macroeconomic and microeconomic trends is crucial for developing robust financial strategies and adapting to changing market conditions(Lind et al., 2012).

The automobile industry faces challenges and opportunities due to technological advancements, regulatory changes, global economic shifts, and changing consumer preferences. Effective working capital management and investment decisions are crucial for automobile companies' success and survival. Working capital management involves inventory management, accounts receivable and payable, and cash flow optimization. Efficient management ensures organizations meet short-term obligations, maintain production, and capitalize on growth opportunities. This chapter discusses how automobile companies can balance liquidity and profitability to achieve success in this dynamic landscape(Pirttilä et al., 2020; Viskari et al., 2012).

Investment decisions in the automobile industry require a thorough analysis of projects and their alignment with strategic objectives. Popular appraisal techniques like Net Present Value, IRR, and Payback Period evaluate financial viability, while non-financial factors like market demand, technological feasibility, and environmental impact are also considered.

Case studies of top automobile companies provide practical examples of concepts discussed in the chapter. These case studies reveal successful companies' management of working capital and investment choices, emphasizing strategic planning, risk management, and adaptability in The chapter explores the impact of economic factors on the automobile industry, including macroeconomic factors like interest rates, inflation, and exchange rates, as well as microeconomic factors like supply chain disruptions and consumer behavior. Understanding these drivers is crucial for developing robust financial strategies that can withstand market fluctuations. The chapter concludes with a future outlook, considering emerging trends, technological disruptions, and regulatory changes. It offers recommendations for improving working capital management practices and enhancing investment decision-making, equipping stakeholders with the knowledge and tools to thrive in an ever-evolving economic landscape(Pratap Singh & Kumar, 2014; Vazquez et al., 2016).

This chapter on Economic Studies on Automobile Management aims to bridge the gap between theoretical concepts and practical applications in the automobile industry. It provides readers with a comprehensive understanding of economic factors influencing decisions, empowering them to make informed choices for sustainable growth and success in the dynamic automotive sector(Lind et al., 2019). The automobile industry has been a significant driver of economic growth and industrial development for over a century. However, it has also presented new challenges in managing financial aspects of automobile businesses. Efficient working capital management and strategic investment decisions are crucial for success. The industry's capital-intensive nature, fluctuating market conditions, regulatory pressures, and competitive dynamics require a comprehensive understanding of financial management principles. This research chapter aims to explore the economic aspects of automobile management, focusing on working capital and investment analysis, to address these challenges and opportunities.

OBJECTIVES OF THE STUDY

The primary objectives of this research chapter are as follows:

- To provide a comprehensive overview of working capital management in the automobile industry: This includes understanding the concept of working capital, its importance, and the components that constitute it. The chapter will analyze the working capital cycle in the context of automobile management and explore the factors that influence the working capital requirements of automobile companies.

- To examine strategies for efficient working capital management: The chapter will delve into the various working capital management practices adopted by successful automobile companies. This includes inventory management techniques, accounts receivable and payable optimization, and cash flow forecasting methods.
- To conduct an in-depth analysis of investment decisions in the automobile sector: The chapter will explore the process of investment appraisal in the industry, highlighting the various techniques used for assessing the financial viability of projects. It will also consider non-financial factors that impact investment decisions, such as market demand, technological feasibility, and environmental considerations.
- To present case studies of leading automobile companies: The chapter will include case studies of prominent automobile manufacturers, analyzing their working capital management practices and investment decisions. These case studies will offer practical insights into successful strategies and lessons learned from industry leaders.
- To explore the impact of economic factors on automobile management decisions: Understanding the influence of macroeconomic and microeconomic factors on working capital and investment choices is crucial for developing effective financial strategies. The chapter will analyze how economic trends and fluctuations impact the automobile industry and its financial decisions.
- To offer recommendations and future outlook: Based on the research findings, the chapter will provide recommendations for improving working capital management practices and enhancing investment decision-making in the automobile industry. It will also present a future outlook for the industry, considering emerging trends and potential challenges.

Scope and Limitations

This research chapter explores economic studies on automobile management, focusing on working capital management and investment decisions. It focuses on areas such as working capital management and investment decisions.

Scope:

- Working Capital Management: The chapter offers an overview of working capital management in the automobile industry, focusing on components, the working capital cycle, and factors influencing requirements. It analyzes strategies for efficient management, including inventory management, accounts receivable and payable optimization, and cash flow forecasting.

- Investment Analysis: The chapter explores investment decisions in the automobile sector, using appraisal techniques like NPV, IRR, and Payback Period, while considering non-financial factors like market demand, technology feasibility, and environmental considerations.
- Case Studies: Chapter explores case studies of top automobile companies to illustrate working capital management practices and investment decisions.
- Economic Factors: Exploring macroeconomic and microeconomic factors' impact on automobile management decisions, examining economic trends' influence on working capital and investment choices.

Limitations:

The research focuses on the global automobile industry, but may not cover specific regional nuances due to its vastness and diversity. Data availability is crucial for accuracy and completeness, and proprietary information may be unavailable for case studies. The industry undergoes rapid changes, including technological advancements and regulatory shifts, and real-time information capture may be limited. The findings may not be universally applicable to all automobile companies due to variations in organizational size, business models, and market positioning.

This research chapter utilizes a mixed-method approach, combining qualitative and quantitative methodologies for objectives.

- A literature review will analyze academic journals, industry reports, books, and publications to develop a theoretical foundation for working capital management and investment analysis in the automobile industry.
- Case studies will analyze automobile companies' working capital management practices and investment decisions, selecting cases based on industry significance and representativeness.
- Data analysis involves collecting and analyzing quantitative data, including financial statements and industry statistics, to evaluate working capital performance and investment outcomes.
- Conduct surveys and interviews with industry experts, managers, and stakeholders to gather qualitative data on working capital management and investment practices.
- Comparative analysis of working capital management strategies and investment outcomes across automobile companies.

OVERVIEW OF THE AUTOMOBILE INDUSTRY

The automotive industry, a global giant, involves designing, developing, manufacturing, and selling motor vehicles. It has experienced significant growth and transformation due to technological innovations, consumer preferences, and economic shifts. This section provides an overview of the industry's history, key players, market share analysis, and prevailing trends and challenges(Demiraj et al., 2022).

Historical Development of the Automobile Industry

The automobile industry began in the late 19th century with the introduction of gasoline-powered vehicles by Karl Benz and Henry Ford. Rapid technological advancements, such as electric vehicles, fuel-efficient engines, safety features, and autonomous driving, revolutionized the industry. Ford's mass production techniques made cars more affordable and accessible. Global demand for automobiles soared, leading to the establishment of numerous manufacturing companies worldwide(Brandenburg, 2016).

Current State of the Automobile Industry

The automobile industry is a significant contributor to economic growth and employment in many countries. It is highly competitive, with established companies, emerging players, and startups competing for market share. The industry is shifting towards sustainable and electric mobility due to environmental concerns and government regulations. Automakers are adopting new technologies and business models, such as ride-sharing services and MaaS solutions. Digitalization and connectivity have enhanced vehicle capabilities, enabling advanced features like ADAS and smart infotainment(Huang et al., 2022).

Key Players and Market Share Analysis

The global automobile market comprises major companies like General Motors, Toyota, Volkswagen Group, Ford, Honda, BMW, and Tesla, competing in various segments and regions. Market share analysis examines automakers' positions based on sales volume, revenue, and geographical presence, identifying dominant players and assessing the competitive landscape(Jafari & Prabhakar Rao, 2015).

Trends and Challenges in the Automobile Sector

Automobile industry faces significant challenges and notable trends, including:

- Electrification: The shift towards electric vehicles (EVs) and the development of charging infrastructure to support their adoption.
- Autonomous Driving: Advancements in autonomous driving technology and its integration into vehicles for enhanced safety and convenience.
- Connectivity: Increasing connectivity features in vehicles, enabling seamless communication with other devices and networks.
- Shared Mobility: The rise of ride-sharing services and car-sharing platforms, altering consumer mobility preferences.
- Sustainability: Growing emphasis on sustainability and eco-friendly practices, encouraging companies to adopt greener manufacturing processes.
- Digitalization: Integration of digital technologies in vehicles, such as advanced infotainment systems and vehicle-to-vehicle communication.

Despite These Opportunities, the Automobile Industry Also Faces Various Challenges

Regulatory compliance involves adhering to global emission standards and safety regulations. Supply chain disruptions, technological complexity, and changing consumer preferences are crucial for success. Technological complexity involves integrating advanced technologies into vehicles, ensuring reliability and safety. Consumer preferences, including electric and autonomous vehicles, must be anticipated and responded to. Market competition includes established players, startups, and tech giants entering the automotive market.

WORKING CAPITAL MANAGEMENT IN THE AUTOMOBILE INDUSTRY

Efficient working capital management is essential for the financial health and operational stability of automobile companies. This section will explore the various aspects of working capital management in the automobile industry, including its definition, importance, components, cycle, factors affecting working capital requirements, and strategies employed by companies to optimize their working capital(Jafari & Prabhakar Rao, 2015; Lind et al., 2012; Rao, 2015).

Definition and Importance of Working Capital

Working capital is the difference between a company's current assets and liabilities, allowing funds to finance daily operations like inventory purchases, supplier payments, and meeting short-term obligations. Proper working capital management ensures sufficient liquidity for business activities without disruptions. In the automobile industry, it is crucial for smooth production and distribution, managing inventory levels, meeting supplier payments, and fulfilling customer demands. Effective working capital management prevents stockouts, manages cash flows, and maintains a competitive edge in the market.

Components of Working Capital in Automobile Management

Working capital in the automobile industry comprises various components, including:

- Inventory: Inventory represents the raw materials, work-in-progress, and finished goods stored by automobile companies. Optimizing inventory levels is essential to prevent excess carrying costs and minimize stockouts.
- Accounts Receivable: Accounts receivable includes the outstanding payments due from customers for vehicles sold on credit. Efficient management of accounts receivable ensures timely collection of receivables and reduces the risk of bad debts.
- Accounts Payable: Accounts payable refers to the payments owed by the company to its suppliers for raw materials, components, and services. Careful management of accounts payable helps improve cash flow and supplier relationships.
- Cash and Cash Equivalents: Cash and cash equivalents include cash on hand and short-term investments that are easily convertible into cash. Maintaining sufficient cash reserves is crucial for meeting immediate financial obligations.

Working Capital Cycle in the Automobile Industry

The working capital cycle in the automobile industry involves the process of converting cash into raw materials, finished goods, selling to customers, and collecting cash. A shorter cycle indicates efficient resource use and faster cash conversion. This cycle includes procurement, production, distribution, and sales stages. Optimizing this cycle is crucial to reduce cash outflows and inflows(Raman, 2021a).

Factors Affecting Working Capital Requirements

Several factors influence the working capital requirements of automobile companies, including:

- Seasonality: Seasonal variations in demand for automobiles can impact working capital needs, necessitating careful planning and inventory management.
- Production Cycle: The time required to manufacture and assemble vehicles affects the working capital tied up in work-in-progress inventory.
- Credit Terms: The credit terms offered to customers and received from suppliers influence the cash conversion cycle and working capital requirements.
- Technological Changes: Rapid technological changes in the industry can lead to fluctuations in inventory levels and working capital needs.
- Economic Conditions: Changes in economic conditions, such as inflation, interest rates, and consumer spending, can impact working capital requirements.

Strategies for Efficient Working Capital Management

Automobile companies employ several strategies to optimize their working capital, including(Jeong et al., 2009):

- Inventory Optimization: Implementing just-in-time (JIT) inventory systems and adopting lean manufacturing practices to reduce excess inventory and holding costs.
- Cash Flow Forecasting: Creating accurate cash flow forecasts to anticipate working capital needs and ensure sufficient liquidity.
- Credit Policies: Adopting prudent credit policies for customers and suppliers to strike a balance between sales growth and credit risk.
- Supply Chain Collaboration: Collaborating with suppliers and dealers to improve supply chain efficiency and reduce lead times.
- Working Capital Financing: Exploring working capital financing options, such as short-term loans and lines of credit, to meet temporary cash flow requirements.

Efficient working capital management enables automobile companies to improve financial performance, optimize resource utilization, and maintain a competitive edge in a dynamic market. It enables short-term obligations while investing in long-term growth and innovation, improving operational efficiency and financial health.

INVESTMENT ANALYSIS IN THE AUTOMOBILE SECTOR

Investment analysis is crucial in the automobile industry for capital-intensive projects, ensuring financial viability and alignment with strategic objectives. This section covers appraisal techniques, cost-benefit analysis, risk analysis, and long-term investment evaluation in the automobile sector(Lokhande & Rana, 2016; Raman, 2021b).

Investment Appraisal Techniques for Automobile Projects

Investment appraisal techniques help assess the profitability and potential risks associated with automobile projects. Some commonly used methods include:

- Net Present Value (NPV): NPV calculates the present value of future cash flows generated by an investment, considering the initial investment and the required rate of return. A positive NPV indicates that the project is financially viable.
- Internal Rate of Return (IRR): IRR represents the rate at which the NPV of an investment becomes zero. It helps in comparing the project's return with the cost of capital, and projects with an IRR higher than the cost of capital are considered acceptable.
- Payback Period: Payback period measures the time required for the investment to recoup its initial cost. Shorter payback periods are preferred, as they indicate faster returns on the investment.
- Discounted Payback Period: Similar to the payback period, but it considers discounted cash flows to account for the time value of money.
- Profitability Index (PI): PI compares the present value of cash inflows to the present value of cash outflows. A PI greater than 1 indicates a financially viable project.

Cost-Benefit Analysis of Automobile Investments

Cost-benefit analysis is a systematic evaluation of the costs incurred and benefits gained from an investment project. In the context of the automobile industry, cost-benefit analysis includes(Eldem, 2022; Kompalla et al., 2016):

- Investment Costs: Identifying and quantifying all costs associated with the project, including upfront investment, production costs, research and development expenses, and marketing costs.

- Benefits: Estimating the anticipated benefits, such as increased sales revenue, cost savings, improved market share, and enhanced brand value resulting from the investment.
- Intangible Benefits: Considering intangible benefits like improved brand image, customer loyalty, and market positioning, which may not have immediate financial impacts but can contribute to long-term success.
- Discounting: Discounting future cash flows to account for the time value of money and determine the net present value of the project.
- Sensitivity Analysis: Assessing the impact of changing key assumptions or variables on the project's financial outcomes to understand its robustness.

Risk Analysis and Mitigation in Automobile Investments

Automobile investments involve inherent risks, such as technological uncertainties, market volatility, regulatory changes, and competitive pressures. Risk analysis and mitigation involve:

- Identifying Risks: Identifying potential risks that could adversely affect the project's success, including external and internal factors.
- Risk Assessment: Evaluating the probability and potential impact of each identified risk on the investment.
- Risk Mitigation Strategies: Implementing risk mitigation strategies to minimize the impact of adverse events. This may include diversifying product portfolios, hedging against currency fluctuations, and establishing risk-sharing partnerships.
- Contingency Planning: Developing contingency plans to address unforeseen events and uncertainties that may arise during the investment lifecycle.

Evaluation of Long-Term Investments in the Automobile Industry

Long-term investments in the automobile industry involve significant capital outlays and have a far-reaching impact on the company's future.

- Technology and Innovation: Assessing the potential of new technologies and innovations to drive long-term competitive advantage and market leadership.
- Market Potential: Analyzing the market potential for the investment, considering factors like market size, growth prospects, and customer demand.
- Regulatory Environment: Understanding how changing regulatory norms and policies can influence the feasibility of long-term investments.

- Environmental Impact: Evaluating the sustainability and environmental impact of the investment to meet growing consumer and regulatory demands for eco-friendly solutions.
- Strategic Fit: Aligning the investment with the company's long-term strategic goals and vision.

Working Capital Management Practices of Leading Automobile Companies: TVS Motors- Case Study

TVS Motor Company, a prominent two-wheeler manufacturer in India, focuses on working capital management practices (Figure 1) as a case study in both domestic and international markets(Mohanty et al., 2023).

- **Efficient Inventory Management**: TVS Motor Company adopts efficient inventory management practices to optimize its working capital. The company carefully manages its raw material inventory to avoid excess holding costs and minimize stockouts. Additionally, they have streamlined their production processes to ensure the right level of work-in-progress inventory, reducing production cycle times.

Figure 1. Working capital management practices in TVS motors

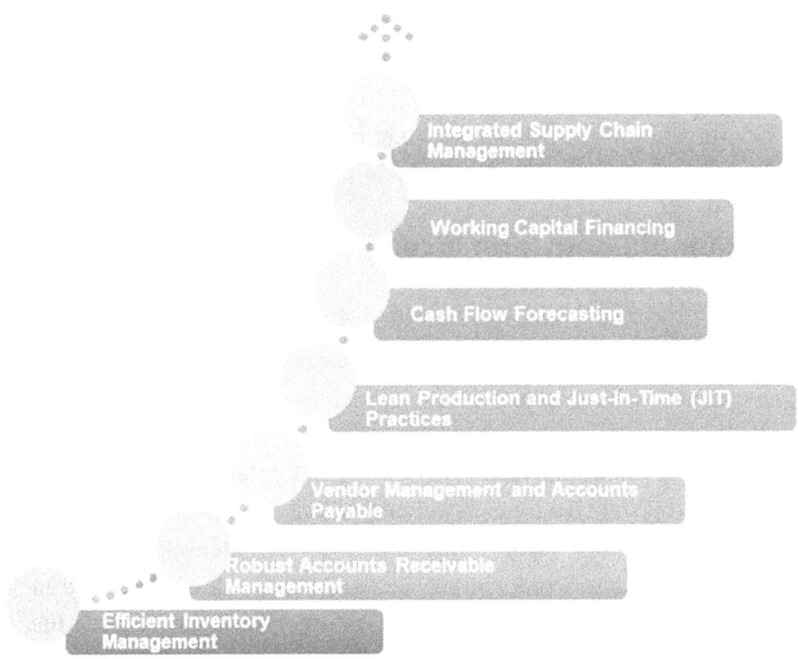

- **Robust Accounts Receivable Management**: TVS focuses on managing its accounts receivable efficiently. The company has well-defined credit policies for dealers and customers to ensure timely payment collections. By closely monitoring receivables and following up on overdue payments, TVS can minimize the impact of bad debts and improve its cash flow.
- **Vendor Management and Accounts Payable**: TVS Motor Company maintains strong relationships with its suppliers and negotiates favorable credit terms to manage its accounts payable effectively. Timely payments to suppliers are essential to maintain smooth operations and foster trust with business partners.
- **Lean Production and Just-in-Time (JIT) Practices**: TVS follows lean production principles and JIT practices, reducing excess inventory and the need for working capital tied up in stocks. This approach allows the company to respond quickly to market demands and minimize inventory holding costs.
- **Cash Flow Forecasting**: TVS employs cash flow forecasting to anticipate its working capital needs accurately. By forecasting cash flows, the company can plan its cash requirements more effectively, avoiding liquidity issues and ensuring financial stability.
- **Working Capital Financing**: To meet short-term working capital needs, TVS Motor Company may utilize various financing options, such as short-term loans or lines of credit. This approach helps bridge any temporary cash flow gaps and ensures uninterrupted operations.
- **Integrated Supply Chain Management**: TVS has implemented an integrated supply chain management system to enhance efficiency, reduce lead times, and manage working capital requirements effectively. This approach facilitates better coordination between suppliers, manufacturers, and distributors, resulting in cost savings and improved cash flow.
- **Continuous Improvement**: TVS Motor Company believes in continuous improvement and regularly reviews its working capital management practices. By identifying inefficiencies and implementing process enhancements, the company seeks to optimize its working capital and maintain a competitive edge in the industry.

TVS Motor Company, a leading Indian two-wheeler manufacturer, effectively manages its working capital through efficient inventory management, robust accounts receivable and payable practices, lean production, cash flow forecasting, and integrated supply chain management. This approach ensures sustainable growth in a competitive market, maintaining a strong financial position and a prominent role in the Indian and global automobile industry.

Working Capital Management Practices of Leading Automobile Companies: Honda Motor

As of my knowledge cutoff in September 2021, Honda Motor Co., Ltd. is a prominent Japanese multinational corporation and one of the leading automobile manufacturers globally. Let's explore the working capital management practices of Honda Motor Co. as a case study(Boopathi, 2023):

- **Efficient Inventory Management**: Honda adopts a well-organized inventory management system to optimize working capital. The company strategically manages its raw material inventory to minimize excess inventory costs and prevent production delays. Additionally, Honda's efficient inventory practices allow them to respond promptly to fluctuations in market demand.
- **Tight Accounts Receivable Management**: Honda focuses on efficient accounts receivable management to enhance working capital. The company implements credit policies that encourage timely payment collections from dealers and customers. By closely monitoring receivables and implementing strict credit terms, Honda minimizes the risk of bad debts and maintains a healthy cash flow.
- **Strong Supplier Relationships and Accounts Payable**: Honda maintains strong relationships with its suppliers and negotiates favorable credit terms to manage accounts payable efficiently. Timely payments to suppliers help strengthen business relationships and ensure a smooth supply chain, contributing to improved working capital management.
- **Lean Manufacturing and Just-in-Time (JIT) Practices**: Honda is known for its adoption of lean manufacturing principles and JIT practices. By implementing JIT manufacturing, Honda reduces excess inventory, streamlines production processes, and minimizes the working capital tied up in inventory. This approach allows the company to optimize production efficiency and respond to market demands effectively.
- **Cash Flow Forecasting**: Honda employs cash flow forecasting to predict working capital needs accurately. The company's meticulous forecasting process helps in planning cash requirements and ensuring adequate liquidity to support day-to-day operations and capital investment.
- **Working Capital Financing**: To address short-term working capital needs, Honda may use working capital financing options, such as short-term loans or revolving credit facilities. This enables the company to manage temporary cash flow fluctuations and maintain financial stability.
- **Supply Chain Integration**: Honda has implemented an integrated supply chain management system that fosters collaboration among suppliers,

manufacturers, and distributors. Streamlining the supply chain enhances efficiency, reduces lead times, and optimizes working capital requirements.

- **Continuous Improvement**: Honda is committed to continuous improvement in all aspects of its operations, including working capital management. The company regularly reviews its financial performance and working capital practices to identify areas for optimization and efficiency enhancement.

Honda Motor Co. maintains a strong financial position and operational efficiency in the competitive automobile industry through effective working capital management practices. Their focus on inventory optimization, accounts receivable and payable, lean manufacturing, and cash flow forecasting enables them to navigate market fluctuations and sustain growth. This information is based on available knowledge up to September 2021, and may include further developments or changes.

INVESTMENT DECISIONS IN THE AUTOMOBILE SECTOR: A COMPARATIVE STUDY

Investment Decisions in the Automobile Sector are illustrated in Figure 2. It is illustrated as given below(Jeong et al., 2009; Raman, 2021a).

Figure 2. Investment decisions in automobile sector

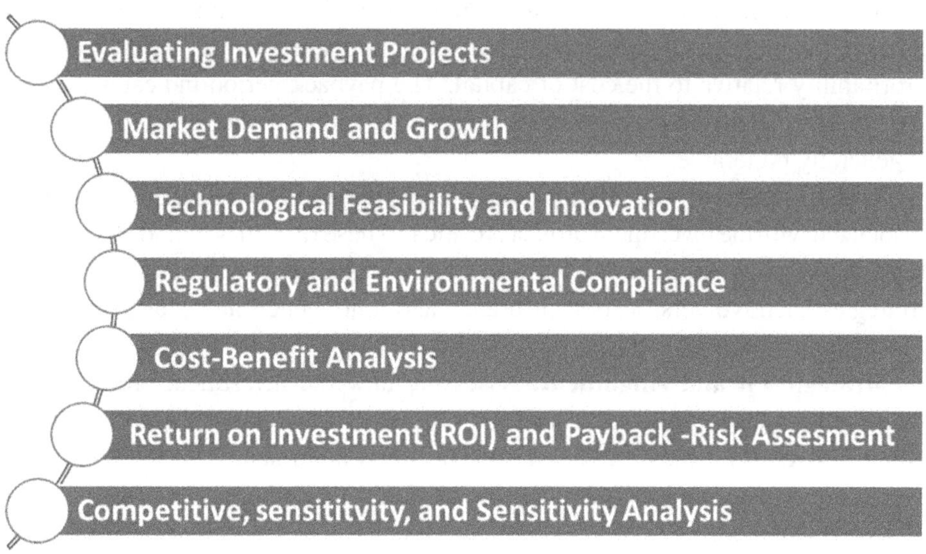

Evaluating Investment Projects in the Automobile Industry: Evaluating investment projects in the automobile industry is a complex process involving factors like feasibility and long-term success. This comparative study examines common investment evaluation criteria in the sector.

Market Demand and Growth Prospects: Analyzing the current and future market demand for the proposed automobile project is crucial. Factors such as customer preferences, demographic trends, and economic conditions should be considered. Evaluating the growth prospects of the market segment in which the project will operate helps determine the potential for market share expansion and revenue growth.

Technological Feasibility and Innovation: Assessing the technological feasibility of the investment project is essential to ensure that the proposed product or technology can be developed and produced with existing capabilities or within the projected timeframe. Evaluating the level of innovation and uniqueness of the project can provide a competitive advantage in the market.

Regulatory and Environmental Compliance: Understanding and complying with regulatory requirements, safety standards, and emission norms are critical for any automobile investment project. Considering the project's environmental impact and its alignment with sustainability goals is essential, especially with increasing consumer demand for eco-friendly vehicles.

Cost-Benefit Analysis: Conducting a comprehensive cost-benefit analysis helps compare the projected costs of the investment project against the expected benefits over its lifecycle. This analysis includes upfront investment costs, operating expenses, projected revenue, and potential cost savings or additional revenue generated.

Return on Investment (ROI) and Payback Period: Calculating the expected ROI of the investment project allows decision-makers to assess the project's profitability relative to the cost of capital. The payback period indicates the time required for the project to recover its initial investment. A shorter payback period is generally preferable.

Risk Assessment and Mitigation: Identifying and evaluating potential risks associated with the investment project is critical. These risks may include technology risks, market risks, regulatory risks, and economic risks. Implementing risk mitigation strategies, such as diversification, insurance, and contingency plans, can help manage potential uncertainties.

Strategic Fit and Alignment: Assessing how the investment project aligns with the company's long-term strategic objectives is vital to ensure consistency with the overall business direction. The project's alignment with the company's core competencies and its potential to complement existing product lines should also be considered.

Competitive Analysis: Conducting a competitive analysis helps understand the level of competition in the market segment targeted by the investment project.

Identifying potential competitive advantages and barriers to entry can provide insights into the project's market positioning.

Financial Modelling and Sensitivity Analysis: Developing detailed financial models to project the project's financial performance over time can aid in decision-making. Sensitivity analysis allows decision-makers to understand how changing key assumptions impact the project's financial outcomes, providing insights into its robustness.

Impact of Economic Factors on Automobile Working Capital and Investment

Economic factors significantly influence the working capital requirements and investment decisions of automobile companies. These factors can create both opportunities and challenges for the industry, impacting cash flow, profitability, and long-term growth prospects(Alexis et al., 2018).

- Economic Growth and Consumer Spending: During periods of economic growth and rising consumer spending, the demand for automobiles tends to increase. As a result, automobile companies may experience higher sales and production volumes, leading to an increased need for working capital to manage higher inventory levels, accounts receivable, and accounts payable.
- Interest Rates and Cost of Capital: Changes in interest rates can impact the cost of borrowing for automobile companies. Higher interest rates may lead to increased borrowing costs, affecting the availability of working capital financing. Companies may need to assess their investment projects' feasibility under different interest rate scenarios to optimize capital allocation.
- Inflation and Raw Material Costs: Inflationary pressures can raise the cost of raw materials, manufacturing, and other operational expenses. Rising costs can impact profit margins and working capital requirements, as companies need to manage higher inventory and production costs.
- Exchange Rates and Currency Fluctuations: Automobile companies that engage in international trade may be exposed to currency fluctuations. Changes in exchange rates can affect the cost of imported components and the revenue from exports, impacting working capital needs and investment decisions.
- Government Policies and Regulations: Changes in government policies and regulations, such as emission norms and safety standards, can influence the types of investments automobile companies make. Compliance with new regulations may require significant capital investments and impact working capital requirements.
- Consumer Credit Availability: The availability of consumer credit and financing options can influence automobile demand. If consumer credit

becomes less accessible, it may lead to a slowdown in vehicle sales, affecting working capital and investment planning.

- Business Cycle and Seasonality: Economic cycles and seasonal fluctuations can impact automobile demand. During economic downturns or off-peak seasons, automobile companies may experience reduced sales, leading to lower cash flows and increased working capital needs.
- Technological Advancements: Technological advancements in the automobile industry can create investment opportunities. Companies may need to invest in research and development to stay competitive and introduce new technologies, impacting both working capital and long-term investment decisions.
- Industry Competitiveness: A highly competitive automobile industry can influence pricing strategies and profit margins. Companies may need to carefully manage working capital to maintain competitive pricing while preserving profitability.
- Consumer Confidence and Sentiment: Consumer confidence and sentiment can influence purchasing decisions. Positive consumer sentiment may lead to increased vehicle demand, impacting working capital needs and investment in production capacity.

Automobile companies must implement robust financial planning, cash flow forecasting, and scenario analysis to adapt to economic fluctuations, maintain stability, and capitalize on growth opportunities in the dynamic automobile sector.

Macroeconomic Factors Influencing the Automobile Industry

- Economic Growth: The overall economic growth of a country or region has a significant impact on automobile demand. During periods of economic expansion, increased consumer spending and business investment can lead to higher vehicle sales. Conversely, economic downturns can result in reduced consumer confidence and lower automobile sales(Lokhande & Rana, 2016).
- Interest Rates: Fluctuations in interest rates can influence consumer borrowing costs for auto loans and affect purchasing decisions. Higher interest rates may discourage vehicle financing, leading to a slowdown in sales.
- Inflation: Inflationary pressures can impact the cost of raw materials, production, and operating expenses for automobile manufacturers. Companies may need to adjust pricing and manage working capital efficiently to cope with rising costs.

- Exchange Rates: For multinational automobile companies, changes in exchange rates can affect import and export costs. A strong domestic currency may make imports cheaper but hurt export competitiveness, and vice versa.
- Unemployment Rate: The level of unemployment in an economy can influence consumer spending on big-ticket items like automobiles. Higher unemployment rates may reduce vehicle demand as consumers become more cautious about making significant purchases.

Microeconomic Factors Affecting Working Capital Management

- Industry Competition: Intense competition in the automobile industry can lead to price pressure and impact profit margins. Companies may need to optimize working capital to maintain profitability while offering competitive prices.
- Supplier Relations: Strong relationships with suppliers can impact credit terms and inventory management. Efficient supply chain management can help in negotiating favorable payment terms and reduce working capital requirements.
- Customer Credit Policies: Automobile companies' credit policies for customers can influence accounts receivable management. Well-defined credit terms and timely payment collections are essential for working capital optimization.
- Inventory Management: Efficient inventory management practices can significantly impact working capital. Reducing excess inventory and adopting just-in-time (JIT) manufacturing can optimize working capital utilization.
- Sales and Marketing Strategies: Effective sales and marketing strategies can influence demand forecasting and inventory planning. Companies need to align sales forecasts with production schedules to avoid excess inventory buildup.

Economic Trends and Investment Decisions in the Automobile Sector

- Shift to Electric and Sustainable Vehicles: The global trend towards electric and sustainable vehicles is influencing investment decisions in the automobile industry. Companies are investing in electric vehicle technology, charging infrastructure, and sustainable manufacturing practices(Natarajan et al., 2006).

- Autonomous Driving Technology: The development of autonomous driving technology is driving investment in research and development. Automobile companies are investing in partnerships and acquisitions to stay at the forefront of this transformative technology.
- Shared Mobility and Mobility-as-a-Service (MaaS): The rise of shared mobility and MaaS platforms is impacting investment decisions. Companies are exploring opportunities in ride-sharing services, car-sharing platforms, and new mobility solutions.
- Digitalization and Connectivity: Investment in digitalization and connectivity features is essential for enhancing vehicle capabilities and providing advanced infotainment systems. Automobile companies are investing in integrating connected features into their products.
- Global Market Expansion: Economic trends, such as emerging markets and changing consumer preferences, influence companies' decisions to expand into new markets. Investment in market research and establishing a presence in new regions is essential for growth.

Macroeconomic and microeconomic factors significantly impact automobile sector working capital management and investment decisions. Automobile companies can optimize working capital, seize growth opportunities, and maintain a competitive edge by closely monitoring and adapting to changing economic trends.

FUTURE OUTLOOK AND RECOMMENDATIONS: PROSPECTS FOR THE AUTOMOBILE INDUSTRY

The automobile industry is undergoing significant transformation due to technological advancements, consumer preferences, and environmental regulations, shaping its future outlook(Mohanty et al., 2023).

- Electric and Autonomous Vehicles: The adoption of electric vehicles (EVs) and the development of autonomous driving technology will continue to accelerate. Governments worldwide are implementing stricter emissions regulations, pushing automakers to invest heavily in electric mobility. Additionally, advancements in autonomous driving technology are expected to revolutionize the transportation landscape, leading to safer and more efficient vehicles.
- Connectivity and Digitalization: Connectivity features in vehicles, such as advanced infotainment systems and vehicle-to-vehicle communication, will become more prevalent. Automobile companies will invest in enhancing

vehicle connectivity to cater to consumers' demand for seamless integration with digital devices and services.

- Shared Mobility and Mobility-as-a-Service (MaaS): The rise of shared mobility and MaaS platforms will impact the traditional automotive ownership model. Consumers are increasingly embracing ride-sharing and car-sharing services, which may lead to changes in consumer behavior and preferences.
- Sustainability and Environmental Concerns: Sustainability will remain a key focus for the automobile industry. Companies will invest in eco-friendly manufacturing processes, renewable energy adoption, and recyclable materials to reduce their carbon footprint. The demand for sustainable vehicles and eco-conscious practices will drive further innovation in the industry.
- Digital Sales and E-Commerce: The pandemic has accelerated the shift towards digital sales and e-commerce in the automotive sector. Online platforms for vehicle sales, virtual showrooms, and contactless transactions will gain prominence.
- Supply Chain Resilience: The global supply chain disruptions experienced during the pandemic highlighted the importance of supply chain resilience. Automobile companies will invest in building more robust and diversified supply chains to mitigate risks and ensure continuity.
- Urban Mobility Solutions: The growth of urbanization and the need for sustainable transportation in crowded cities will fuel the development of urban mobility solutions. Light electric vehicles, micro-mobility options, and urban logistics solutions will gain traction.
- Focus on Data and Cybersecurity: With increased connectivity, vehicle data security will become a critical concern. Automobile companies will invest in robust cybersecurity measures to safeguard customer data and protect vehicles from cyber threats.

Recommendations for the Automobile Industry

- Embrace Sustainability: Automobile companies should invest in sustainable practices, promote EV adoption, and focus on environmental responsibility. Sustainable initiatives will resonate with consumers and align with future regulatory requirements.
- Invest in Electric Mobility: Companies should invest in electric vehicle research, development, and charging infrastructure. EVs will play a significant role in shaping the future of transportation, and early adopters will gain a competitive advantage.

- Develop Mobility Solutions: Automobile manufacturers can explore opportunities in shared mobility and MaaS. Collaborating with mobility service providers or launching their own mobility platforms can diversify revenue streams and adapt to changing consumer preferences.
- Enhance Digitalization: Automobile companies must prioritize digitalization efforts, providing seamless online customer experiences, and adopting data analytics for market insights. Investments in digital sales channels and customer engagement platforms will be essential.
- Strengthen Supply Chains: The pandemic exposed vulnerabilities in supply chains. Companies should invest in building resilient supply chains with multiple sourcing options and robust risk management practices.
- Collaborate on Autonomous Technology: Collaboration and partnerships in autonomous driving technology can accelerate progress and reduce development costs. Companies should consider joining forces to advance autonomous capabilities.
- Focus on Customer Experience: Delivering exceptional customer experiences will be crucial. Companies should invest in personalized services, after-sales support, and user-friendly vehicle interfaces to build customer loyalty.
- Agility and Innovation: The future automobile industry will require agility and constant innovation. Companies should foster a culture of innovation, encourage experimentation, and be prepared to adapt to rapid changes in the market.

Improving Working Capital Management Practices

- Efficient Inventory Management: Adopt lean manufacturing principles and just-in-time (JIT) practices to minimize excess inventory and reduce carrying costs. Implement advanced forecasting techniques to optimize inventory levels based on demand patterns.
- Streamline Accounts Receivable: Implement strict credit policies and offer discounts for early payments to encourage timely collections from customers. Utilize automated billing and invoicing systems to expedite the receivables process.
- Optimize Accounts Payable: Negotiate favorable credit terms with suppliers and maintain strong supplier relationships. Take advantage of early payment discounts while managing payment schedules effectively.
- Cash Flow Forecasting: Develop robust cash flow forecasting models to anticipate working capital needs and identify potential cash flow gaps in

advance. Regularly update and revise the forecasts to reflect changing business conditions.

- Working Capital Financing: Explore various working capital financing options, such as short-term loans, lines of credit, or factoring arrangements, to address temporary cash flow requirements and bridge funding gaps.

Enhancing Investment Decision-Making in the Automobile Sector

- In-depth Market Research: Conduct comprehensive market research to understand consumer preferences, emerging trends, and future demands. Identify market gaps and opportunities for innovation and differentiation.
- Technological Assessment: Stay abreast of technological advancements and assess their potential impact on the industry. Invest in research and development to develop new technologies or collaborate with technology partners.
- Sustainability and ESG Considerations: Integrate environmental, social, and governance (ESG) considerations into investment decision-making. Focus on sustainable practices and products that align with consumer demands for eco-friendly options.
- Risk Analysis and Scenario Planning: Conduct thorough risk analysis and scenario planning for potential investment projects. Assess the financial, operational, and market risks associated with each project to make informed decisions.
- Partnerships and Collaborations: Explore strategic partnerships and collaborations with other companies or technology providers to share expertise, resources, and risks related to new investment projects.

Policy Implications and Recommendations for Industry Stakeholders

- Government Support for Electric Mobility: Governments should offer incentives, subsidies, and favorable policies to promote the adoption of electric vehicles. This support will accelerate investments in EV technology and charging infrastructure.
- R&D Grants and Tax Incentives: Governments can incentivize research and development in the automobile industry by offering grants and tax benefits to companies investing in innovative technologies.

- Regulatory Certainty: Policy frameworks should provide clarity and predictability to automobile companies regarding emissions standards, safety regulations, and other industry-specific requirements. This certainty will facilitate better investment planning.
- Infrastructure Development: Governments should invest in developing charging infrastructure for electric vehicles and smart mobility solutions to support the growth of the electric mobility ecosystem.
- Education and Skill Development: Encourage education and skill development programs to equip the workforce with the required expertise to adapt to new technologies and industry developments.
- Data Privacy and Security Regulations: Implement robust data privacy and cybersecurity regulations to safeguard customer data and protect against cyber threats in connected vehicles.
- Environmental Regulations and Incentives: Governments should establish strict environmental regulations and offer incentives for adopting sustainable practices and eco-friendly technologies in automobile manufacturing.

Implementing these recommendations and policies can improve automobile companies' working capital management, investment decisions, and drive sustainable growth in the evolving sector. Encouraging sustainability and innovation will help the industry transition into an environmentally friendly and technologically advanced future(Haralayya, 2021).

The various financial parameters have been optimized by various statistical and optimization techniques such as Taguchi(Boopathi, 2022c, 2022b, 2022d, 2022f; Boopathi et al., 2021, 2023; Boopathi, Haribalaji, et al., 2022; Boopathi, Thillaivanan, et al., 2022; Gunasekaran et al., 2022; Sampath & Myilsamy, 2021; Yupapin et al., 2023), RSM(Boopathi & Sivakumar, 2012, 2013; Dass james & Boopathi, 2016), TOPSIS, and VIKOR(Boopathi, 2021, 2022a; Jaganathan et al., 2012; Myilsamy & Sampath, 2021; Sampath et al., 2021; Saravanan et al., 2022). The Internet of Things and modern technologies have been applied to improve the overall profits of automobile industries(Boopathi, 2022e, 2022b; Gunasekaran et al., 2022; Samikannu et al., 2023; Sampath et al., 2023; Sampath & Myilsamy, 2021; Saravanan et al., 2022; Yupapin et al., 2023).

CONCLUSION

The automobile industry is undergoing a transformative phase driven by technological advancements, changing consumer preferences, and environmental concerns. Effective working capital management and informed investment decision-making are crucial for automobile companies to thrive in this dynamic and competitive landscape.

The automobile industry faces both challenges and opportunities in the future. To improve working capital management practices, companies should optimize inventory, streamline accounts receivable and payable, forecast cash flows, and explore working capital financing options. Enhancing investment decision-making requires in-depth market research, technological assessment, sustainability considerations, and strategic partnerships.

Policy implications and recommendations call for government support for electric mobility, R&D grants, regulatory certainty, infrastructure development, education, data privacy, and environmental regulations. By implementing these measures, the industry can drive sustainable growth, align with consumer demands, and build a resilient future in the evolving automobile sector. Embracing innovation and sustainability will be crucial for companies to remain competitive and meet the changing demands of the automotive market.

ACRONYMS

TVS - TVS Motor Company
EVs - Electric Vehicles
JIT - Just-in-Time
MaaS - Mobility-as-a-Service
ESG - Environmental, Social, and Governance
R&D - Research and Development

REFERENCES

Alexis, S. J., Kumar, P. S. S. R., Vinoth, K. R., Ragul, V. V., & Kumar, N. S. (2018). Improved Mechanical Properties of AA5083 Reinforced with Multiwall Carbon Nanotubes for Automobile Applications. *International Journal of Vehicle Structures \& Systems, 10*(4), 278–281.

Boopathi, S. (2021). Improving of Green Sand-Mould Quality using Taguchi Technique. *Journal of Engineering Research*. doi:10.36909/jer.14079

Boopathi, S. (2022a). An experimental investigation of Quench Polish Quench (QPQ) coating on AISI 4150 steel. *Engineering Research Express*, *4*(4), 45009. doi:10.1088/2631-8695/ac9ddd

Boopathi, S. (2022b). An Extensive Review on Sustainable Developments of Dry and Near-Dry Electrical Discharge Machining Processes. *Journal of Manufacturing Science and Engineering*, *144*(5), 50801. doi:10.1115/1.4052527

Boopathi, S. (2022c). An investigation on gas emission concentration and relative emission rate of the near-dry wire-cut electrical discharge machining process. *Environmental Science and Pollution Research International*, *29*(57), 86237–86246. doi:10.100711356-021-17658-1 PMID:34837614

Boopathi, S. (2022d). Cryogenically treated and untreated stainless steel grade 317 in sustainable wire electrical discharge machining process: A comparative study. *Environmental Science and Pollution Research International*, 1–10. doi:10.100711356-022-22843-x PMID:36057706

Boopathi, S. (2022e). Experimental investigation and multi-objective optimization of cryogenic Friction-stir-welding of AA2014 and AZ31B alloys using MOORA technique. *Materials Today. Communications*, *33*, 104937. doi:10.1016/j.mtcomm.2022.104937

Boopathi, S. (2022f). Performance Improvement of Eco-Friendly Near-Dry Wire-Cut Electrical Discharge Machining Process Using Coconut Oil-Mist Dielectric Fluid. *Journal of Advanced Manufacturing Systems*. doi:10.1142/S0219686723500178

Boopathi, S. (2023). An Investigation on Friction Stir Processing of Aluminum Alloy-Boron Carbide Surface Composite. In *Materials Horizons: From Nature to Nanomaterials* (pp. 249–257). Springer. doi:10.1007/978-981-19-7146-4_14

Boopathi, S., Haribalaji, V., Mageswari, M., & Asif, M. M. (2022). Influences of Boron Carbide Particles on the Wear Rate and Tensile Strength of Aa2014 Surface Composite Fabricated By Friction-Stir Processing. *Materiali in Tehnologije*, *56*(3), 263–270. doi:10.17222/mit.2022.409

Boopathi, S., Lewise, K. A. S., Subbiah, R., & Sivaraman, G. (2021). Near-dry wire-cut electrical discharge machining process using water-air-mist dielectric fluid: An experimental study. *Materials Today: Proceedings*, *49*(5), 1885–1890. doi:10.1016/j.matpr.2021.08.077

Boopathi, S., & Sivakumar, K. (2012). Experimental comparative study of near-dry wire-cut electrical discharge machining (WEDM). *European Journal of Scientific Research*, *75*(4), 472–481.

Boopathi, S., & Sivakumar, K. (2013). Experimental investigation and parameter optimization of near-dry wire-cut electrical discharge machining using multi-objective evolutionary algorithm. *International Journal of Advanced Manufacturing Technology*, *67*(9–12), 2639–2655. doi:10.100700170-012-4680-4

Boopathi, S., Thillaivanan, A., Azeem, M. A., Shanmugam, P., & Pramod, V. R. (2022). Experimental investigation on abrasive water jet machining of neem wood plastic composite. *Functional Composites and Structures*, *4*(2), 25001. doi:10.1088/2631-6331/ac6152

Boopathi, S., Venkatesan, G., & Anton Savio Lewise, K. (2023). Mechanical Properties Analysis of Kenaf–Grewia–Hair Fiber-Reinforced Composite. In *Lecture Notes in Mechanical Engineering* (pp. 101–110). Springer. doi:10.1007/978-981-16-9057-0_11

Brandenburg, M. (2016). Supply chain efficiency, value creation and the economic crisis—An empirical assessment of the European automotive industry 2002–2010. *International Journal of Production Economics*, *171*, 321–335. doi:10.1016/j.ijpe.2015.07.039

Dass J. A., & Boopathi, S. (2016). Experimental Study of Eco-friendly Wire-Cut Electrical Discharge Machining Processes. *International Journal of Innovative Research in Science, Engineering and Technology*, *5*(1), 666–675.

Demiraj, R., Dsouza, S., & Abiad, M. (2022). Working Capital Management Impact on Profitability: Pre-Pandemic and Pandemic Evidence from the European Automotive Industry. *Risks*, *10*(12), 236. doi:10.3390/risks10120236

Eldem, B. (2022). *Impact of COVID-19 pandemic on operational activities at FORD OTOSAN: A case study of automotive industry*. Instytut Organizacji Systemów Produkcyjnych.

Gunasekaran, K., Boopathi, S., & Sureshkumar, M. (2022). Analysis of a Cryogenically Cooled Near-Dry Wedm Process Using Different Dielectrics. *Materiali in Tehnologije*, *56*(2), 179–186. doi:10.17222/mit.2022.397

Haralayya, B. (2021). Consumer Buying Behaviour with Reference to Bajaj Auto Ltd. *IRE Journals*, *5*(1), 131–140.

Huang, C., Chan, F. T. S., & Chung, S. H. (2022). The impact of payment term extensions on the working capital management of an automotive supply chain. *International Journal of Production Research*, *60*(24), 7360–7383. doi:10.1080/00207543.2022.2065549

Jafari, F., & Prabhakar Rao, D. (2015). Study the Relation between Working Capital System and Profitability in Auto Manufacturing Industry in India. *Journal of Resources Development and Management*, *6*, 14–25.

Jaganathan, P., Naveen, T., & Sivasubramanian, R. (2012). Machining Parameters Optimization of WEDM Process Using Taguchi Method. *Ijest*, *2*(12), 1–4.

Jeong, W., Park, M., & Min, J. U. (2009). Triple-a supply chain management for automobile industry: A case study of Renault Samsung Motors. *Journal of International Logistics and Trade*, *7*(1), 57–70. doi:10.24006/jilt.2009.7.1.57

Kompalla, A., Kopia, J., & Tigu, P. G. (2016). An application of agile principles on business strategies within IT-based industries and automotive enterprises. *Zifp*, 1–17.

Lind, L., Monto, S., & Kärri, T. (2019). Mapping working capital models in the automotive industry. *International Journal of Integrated Supply Management*, *12*(4), 285–308. doi:10.1504/IJISM.2019.103170

Lind, L., Pirttilä, M., Viskari, S., Schupp, F., & Kärri, T. (2012). Working capital management in the automotive industry: Financial value chain analysis. *Journal of Purchasing and Supply Management*, *18*(2), 92–100. doi:10.1016/j.pursup.2012.04.003

Lokhande, M. A., & Rana, V. S. (2016). Marketing Strategies of Indian Automobile Companies: A Case Study of Maruti Suzuki India Limited. SSRN *Electronic Journal*. doi:10.2139/ssrn.2719399

Mohanty, A., Venkateswaran, N., Ranjit, P. S., Tripathi, M. A., & Boopathi, S. (2023). Innovative strategy for profitable automobile industries: Working capital management. In *Handbook of Research on Designing Sustainable Supply Chains to Achieve a Circular Economy* (pp. 412–428). IGI Global. doi:10.4018/978-1-6684-7664-2.ch020

Myilsamy, S., & Sampath, B. (2021). Experimental comparison of near-dry and cryogenically cooled near-dry machining in wire-cut electrical discharge machining processes. *Surface Topography : Metrology and Properties*, *9*(3), 35015. doi:10.1088/2051-672X/ac15e0

Natarajan, N., Vijayarangan, S., & Rajendran, I. (2006). Wear behaviour of A356/25SiCp aluminium matrix composites sliding against automobile friction material. *Wear*, *261*(7–8), 812–822. doi:10.1016/j.wear.2006.01.011

Pirttilä, M., Virolainen, V. M., Lind, L., & Kärri, T. (2020). Working capital management in the Russian automotive industry supply chain. *International Journal of Production Economics*, *221*, 107474. doi:10.1016/j.ijpe.2019.08.009

Pratap Singh, H., & Kumar, S. (2014). Working capital management: A literature review and research agenda. *Qualitative Research in Financial Markets*, *6*(2), 173–197. doi:10.1108/QRFM-04-2013-0010

Raman, U. (2021a). a Study on Productivity Growth of Automobile Industry in a Vuca World. *Elementary Education Online, 20*(5), 3472. https://ilkogretim-online.org/index.php?mno=66785

Raman, U. (2021b). a Study on Productivity Growth of Automobile Industry in a Vuca World. *Elementary Education Online*. https://ilkogretim-online.org/index.php?mno=66785

Rao, F. J. P. D. P. (2015). *Study the Relation between Working Capital System and Profitability in Auto Manufacturing Industry in India.*

Samikannu, R., Koshariya, A. K., Poornima, E., Ramesh, S., Kumar, A., & Boopathi, S. (2023). Sustainable Development in Modern Aquaponics Cultivation Systems Using IoT Technologies. In *Human Agro-Energy Optimization for Business and Industry* (pp. 105–127). IGI Global. doi:10.4018/978-1-6684-4118-3.ch006

Sampath, B., & Myilsamy, S. (2021). Experimental investigation of a cryogenically cooled oxygen-mist near-dry wire-cut electrical discharge machining process. *Strojniski Vestnik. Jixie Gongcheng Xuebao*, *67*(6), 322–330. doi:10.5545v-jme.2021.7161

Sampath, B., Naveenkumar, N., Sampathkumar, P., Silambarasan, P., Venkadesh, A., & Sakthivel, M. (2021). Experimental comparative study of banana fiber composite with glass fiber composite material using Taguchi method. *Materials Today: Proceedings*, *49*(5), 1475–1480. doi:10.1016/j.matpr.2021.07.232

Sampath, B., Sasikumar, C., & Myilsamy, S. (2023). Application of TOPSIS Optimization Technique in the Micro-Machining Process. In IGI:Trends, Paradigms, and Advances in Mechatronics Engineering (pp. 162–187). IGI Global.

Saravanan, M., Vasanth, M., Boopathi, S., Sureshkumar, M., & Haribalaji, V. (2022). Optimization of Quench Polish Quench (QPQ) Coating Process Using Taguchi Method. *Key Engineering Materials*, *935*, 83–91. doi:10.4028/p-z569vy

Vazquez, X. H., Sartal, A., & Lozano-Lozano, L. M. (2016). Watch the working capital of tier-two suppliers: A financial perspective of supply chain collaboration in the automotive industry. *Supply Chain Management*, *21*(3), 321–333. doi:10.1108/SCM-03-2015-0104

Viskari, S., Lind, L., Kärri, T., & Schupp, F. (2012). Using working capital management to improve profitability in the value chain of automotive industry. *International Journal of Services and Operations Management*, *13*(1), 42–64. doi:10.1504/IJSOM.2012.048275

Yupapin, P., Trabelsi, Y., Nattappan, A., & Boopathi, S. (2023). Performance Improvement of Wire-Cut Electrical Discharge Machining Process Using Cryogenically Treated Super-Conductive State of Monel-K500 Alloy. *Iranian Journal of Science and Technology. Transaction of Mechanical Engineering*, *47*(1), 267–283. doi:10.100740997-022-00513-0

Chapter 10
Enhancing Employee Resilience in the Face of Disruption:
A Case Study of E-Training at National Hydropower Corporation

Sunil Kumar
Lovely Professional University, India

A. Dushyanth Kumar
https://orcid.org/0000-0002-9483-9274
Mittal School of Business, India

ABSTRACT

This case study examines employees' resilience at the Chamera power plant in Himachal Pradesh, India, during the COVID-19 pandemic. It investigates the impact of e-Training initiatives as catalysts for organizational change. The study utilizes a focus group interview method with nine participants, including executives and non-executives who actively engaged in e-Training. Findings reveal that the implementation of e-Training programs resulted in attributes such as time management, goal focus, self-driven orientation, collaboration, capacity building, positive mindset, and improved self-efficacy. These attributes contributed to employee resilience. The study highlights the importance of e-Training interventions and technology adoption in fostering employee resilience and bridging gaps in understanding organizational resilience.

DOI: 10.4018/978-1-7998-9213-7.ch010

INTRODUCTION

Amidst the pandemic, organizations recognize the need to prepare their workforces through rigorous training to navigate changes and contribute to success (Subba Rao, 2014). Continuous learning enhances employee resilience, enabling them to face adversity with strength and adaptability. Training programs elevate flexibility, skills, and abilities, enabling excellence in volatile situations (Mitsakis, 2020). Motivated employees exhibit concentration, determination, and a sense of belongingness, which are vital for optimal performance (Atkinson, 1964; Campbell and Pritchard, 1976; Weiner, 1980). Ensuring employee motivation is crucial, and organizations should assess the effectiveness of their policies and culture in fostering resilience (Swanson Richard, 1994).

Employees' enthusiasm for acquiring new knowledge through training is essential for becoming experts in their roles (Scardamalia & Bereiter, 1992; Stolovitch & Keeps, 1992). Training programs provide opportunities for problem-solving, peer motivation, guidance, and teamwork (Sambrook, 2005). Digital technologies, especially virtual training, play a crucial role in updating technical knowledge and developing soft skills (Gegenfurtner et al., 2020; Thalhammer, 2014). Embracing electronic training not only saves time and money but also contributes to environmentally friendly practices (Agariya & Singh, 2012; Granda et al., 2015; Zaibnab et al., 2017). Implementing e-training programs aims to enhance employees' resilience and internal capabilities, facilitating organizational survival and success during crises (Granda et al., 2015).

Resilience, defined as the ability to bounce back from adversity and progress through teamwork and learning, is crucial for employees (Southwick et al., 2014). Employee resilience involves utilizing resources, adapting, and contributing to organizational growth, particularly during disruptive situations (Na¨swall et al., 2013; Nguyen et al., 2016). Technological adaptation during volatile times and increased resilience levels indicate a positive approach and attitude (Gillham et al., 2013; Cooper et al., 2013; Youssef & Luthans, 2007).

Investing in education and training enhances employees' performance levels, wages, and benefits, as well as firm productivity, according to Gattiker (1995). Resilience levels, adaptability to technology, understanding the firm's environment, and acquiring knowledge through training contribute to the stability of a firm (Festing and Eidems, 2011). Continuous training programs are crucial for developing employees' technical and soft skills, ensuring their capability development (Ameen & Baharom, 2019). Allocating budgets for training is essential to align training with organizational goals (Sudhakar & Basariya, 2017). Training programs enhance employees' skills, adaptability, and attitudes, enabling remarkable results in achieving organizational goals (Maheshwari & Vohra, 2018). Training also fosters a competitive spirit among employees, leading to improved performance (Owoyemi et al., 2011).

Proactive assessment of employees' training needs and evaluation of performance after training programs are necessary for building a strong and capable workforce (Padmasiri et al., 2018). Effective training programs generate higher employee commitment and overall performance (Owoyemi et al., 2011).

Traditional training methods are shifting towards digital platforms due to technological advancements and convenience, with platforms like Zoom, Google Meet, and Teams being widely used for e-training programs and conferences (The American Psychological Association, 2017). Employees can develop technical and non-technical skills through these platforms, as well as utilize social media for digital communication (Nguyen et al., 2016). The adoption of technology during adverse situations indicates employee resilience and their ability to navigate challenges (Sharma & Sharma, 2020). Resilient employees can assess their environment, adapt to disruptions, and leverage personal connections for support (Gligor et al., 2019). Resilient workforces recover faster from failures and challenges, demonstrating adaptability and responsiveness to changes in business markets (Shin et al., 2012).

Employee resilience levels can be measured by assessing their efficiency, perceived group efficiency, group dynamics, job skills learning, and communication within the group (Sharma & Sharma, 2020). Socio-economic and demographic factors such as salary, gender, age, and educational background influence employee resilience levels (Wang et al., 2014). Employee well-being plays a crucial role in fostering resilience at the individual, group, and organizational levels, motivating employees to navigate adverse situations (Williams & Shepherd, 2016). Employee engagement is key to resilience, with positive attitudes and engagement facilitating flexibility in work-life roles (Nguyen et al., 2016). Building employee resilience contributes to enhanced organizational resilience, allowing employees to thrive in disaster contexts (Teng-Calleja et al., 2020).

Resilience, as described by Masten (2001), is a common occurrence resulting from human adaptive processes. Developing resilience within workforces is valuable human capital that leads to positive attitudes, behavioral changes, and improved performance during turbulent situations. Workforces that navigate crises enhance their interactions, communication, and teamwork through guidance, agility, and resilience (Bardoel et al., 2014). Resilient employees from various disciplines demonstrate collaboration and information-sharing, emphasizing the need for management to establish policies that continuously enhance resilience (Madrigano et al., 2017). By providing training, organizational support, and flexible job arrangements, organizations can help employees increase their resilience levels and overall performance. Practicing flexibility in structural designs is also important for fostering resilience (Douglas, 2020).

Employees' resilience levels contribute to positive relations between firms and their workforce, as well as the development of responsive and adaptable processes and practices (Lim et al., 2020). To improve resilience, organizations should adopt evidence-based approaches, develop competencies, establish supportive structures, and implement effective leadership models (Madrigano et al., 2017). Resilience dimensions include navigating turbulent situations, adapting tactics and operations, and quickly assessing the environment (Gligor et al., 2019). Sub-dimensions of resilience encompass team learning orientation, flexibility, network ties, shared language, composition, task design, group norms, perceived efficacy of team members, and efficacy for collective team action (Sharma & Sharma, 2020). Organizational resilience involves creating employee agility and resilience to face challenges and seize opportunities (Seville, 2016). Employee and organizational resilience are crucial, and measures to enhance employee well-being are essential for motivation in adverse situations (Williams & Shepherd, 2016).

Themes of Employee Resilience

- Vision: The cognitive and behaviour based ideas for future. Based on various conscious motivational needs to determine the life goals through actions in the environmental context (Nair, 2003).
- Determination: The human positive attribute of persistent efforts, interest and adaption to change for long term goal attainment (Datu et. al., 2016)
- Interaction: Individual compatibility to the surrounding material and human aspects to perform task effectively, includes collaboration with others, positive attitude, learning, team spirit, negotiation and networking (Collin and Valleala, 2005; Edwards, 1991; Kristof-Brown et al., 2002; Nardi and Whittaker, 2002).
- Relationships: Knowing the rules and following the agreements between employee and employer, between employee and employee (Gennard and Judge, 2005). Relationship need motivation to solve problems (Armstrong, 2005). Relationship maintain trust among employees and involve communication (Bajaj et. al, 2013; George and Jones, 2008).
- Problems solving: Equip employees with skills to identify root causes through collective culture, organizational learning and supportive leadership (Mohaghegh & Furlan, 2020). Organization use the on the job training and job rotation as interventions to equip there employees in problem solving skills (Allwood and Lee, 2004).
- Organization: Organizational structure, ordering, controlling mechanisms and arrangements of human, processes and structures "Organizing involves enacting change in the environment and retaining the causal relationships" (Bantz, 1989); established in the interpretation of causes and effects in and out of the organization

- Self-confidence: Employees' awareness of their abilities (Goleman, 2015). "An individual feels *competent, confident, and capable* and believes that he can do it because of his/her strengths. *Experience, actual potential, achievements, and realistic expectations"* (Fadli et al., 2020).
- Adaptability: Continuous learning, acceptance to ideas, technology and new roles (Breu et al., 2002; Muduli, 2016). Identification of opportunities and anticipate the change quickly (Gligor et.al, 2019).
- Flexibility: To function and adjust effectively under stress and in changing operative situations (Breu et al., 2002; Sherehiy, 2008)
- Proactive: Proactive individuals ''select, create, and influence work situations that increase the likelihood of career success" (Seibert, Crant & Kraimer, 2001). Positively related to subjective career and job outcomes (Erdogan & Bauer, 2005; Seibert et al., 1999) Positive learning goal orientation throughout the career with energy.

In this regard, framed nine questions based on identified themes. Questions were asked to focus group on the following themes (see Table 1).

Table 1. Theme(s) based question for focus group interview

Theme(s)	Focus group interview question
Vision	Do you have goals in your life? Do you know how to achieve your goals? E-Training programs are helpful in this regard.
Determination	Do you have strong determination to achieve your goals? E-Training programs are helpful in this regard.
Interaction	Do you interact with people and enjoy the company of other people in current job?
Relationships	Do you maintain relationships with other people and share your thoughts during e-trainings?
Problems solving	Do you solve problems for yourself and others during e-training programs?
Organization	Do you schedule your plans and review them periodically? E-Training programs are helpful in this regard.
Self-confidence	Do you feel self-confident while facing challenges and achieving targets and e-training helps in this?
Flexibility and adaptability	Do you adjust to change and accommodate others with you during change and challenges? E-training programs are helpful in this regard.
Proactive	Do you feel the change is an opportunity and resolve the same with energy? And e-training programs are helpful in this regard.

METHODOLOGY

This case study employs a qualitative research approach to explore the development of employee resilience through e-training interventions at the Chamera Power Plant Stage-I, located in Himachal Pradesh, India. The research methodology utilizes the 'focus group interview' method to collect data from a diverse group of employees who participated in various e-training programs during 2020-21. The focus group consists of nine participants, including five executives and four non-executives (supervisors).

The training programs attended by the participants focused on updates related to machinery knowledge, functional and soft skills, leadership development, as well as yoga, health, and lifestyle. The details of these training programs, including the training duration, participants' attendance, and other relevant information, were collected from the plant's intranet.

To analyze the collected data, a content analysis approach was employed. The focus group interviews aimed to explore the development of employee resilience within the organizational context through the implementation of e-training interventions. Additionally, virtual yoga and health programs were conducted for the employees and their families as part of the resilience-building initiatives.

The focus group interviews took place in the plant's training hall, where the participants were briefed in both English and Hindi to ensure a better understanding of the topics discussed and the questions posed. Throughout the interviews, the participants shared their understandings, opinions, experiences, and views regarding the impact of e-training interventions on their resilience levels.

Table 2. Focus group respondents' profile

<table>
<tr><th>Respon-dent</th><th>Designation</th><th>Nature of job</th><th>Type of Training attended</th><th>Name of training program</th><th>The method used during the training</th><th>No. of training programs attended</th></tr>
<tr><td>1</td><td>Manager</td><td>Technical field</td><td>Functional</td><td rowspan="3">Concept of Commissioning of Hydropower Projects. Testing of Generators, Transformers, Reactors, Cables, Switchyard Equipment, and Transformer. Renovation & Modernization of Power Plants</td><td rowspan="3">Webinars/ Online workshops</td><td>5</td></tr>
<tr><td>2</td><td>Manager</td><td>-Do-</td><td>Functional</td><td>5</td></tr>
<tr><td>3</td><td>Manager</td><td>-Do-</td><td>Functional</td><td>4</td></tr>
<tr><td>4</td><td>Manager</td><td>Finance</td><td>Functional/ Behavioural</td><td>Corporate Governance, Domestic & International Finance. Yoga & Health</td><td rowspan="3">Webinars/ Online workshops</td><td>3</td></tr>
<tr><td>5</td><td>Dy. Manager</td><td>HR</td><td>Functional/ Behavioural</td><td>Breaking the Ceiling. Business Analytics. Yoga & Health.</td><td>3</td></tr>
<tr><td>6</td><td>Office Superintendent</td><td>IT&C</td><td>Functional/ Behavioural</td><td>Work-Life Balance & Positive Thinking. Yoga & Health.</td><td>5</td></tr>
<tr><td>7</td><td>Office Superintendent</td><td>HR</td><td>Functional/ Behavioural</td><td rowspan="2">Assessment of Competency. Work-Life Balance & Positive Thinking. Yoga & Health.</td><td rowspan="3">Webinars/ Online workshops</td><td>5</td></tr>
<tr><td>8</td><td>Office Superintendent</td><td>Electrical</td><td>Functional/ Behavioural</td><td>4</td></tr>
<tr><td>9</td><td>Office Superintendent</td><td>IT&C</td><td>Behavioural</td><td>Work-Life Balance & Positive Thinking. Yoga & Health.</td><td>4</td></tr>
</table>

Source: Compiled by the author(s)

Content Analysis

In the Table 3 theme based content analysis of employee resilience acquired through e-training is presented. In the theme 'vision' employees perceived short term goal management with planning, focus and time management. In the theme 'determination' the e-training helps employees to find solutions and self-improvement during pandemic. In the third theme 'interaction' the employee perceived team work, communication and interactivity during e-training programs.

Table 3. Themes based content analysis

Statement/question(s)	Theme(s)	Content analysis
Do you have goals in your life? Do you know how to achieve your goals? E-Training programs are helpful in this regard?	Vision	Planning, time management, focus, short term goal management
Do you have strong determination to achieve your goals? E-Training programs are helpful in this regard?	Determination	Motivated to concentrate on self, achievement oriented, helping to find solution.
Do you interact with people and enjoy the company of other people?	Interaction	Improved interaction and communication skills, and teamwork.
Do you maintain relationships with other people and share your thoughts? E-training programs are aiding for this?	Relationships	Openness, sharing, relationship barriers
Do you solve problems for yourself and others?	Problems solving	Mutual solution to problems, collaborative culture, and confined to own time and job
Do you schedule your plans and review them periodically?	Organization	Planning and reviewing day today work, work and life balance, hectic schedules
Do you feel self-confident while facing challenges and in achieving targets? E-Training programs are helpful in this regard?	Self-confidence	Supportive, skill development, energetic, self-trust, improved capacity to face challenges
Do you adjust to change and accommodate others with you during change and challenges? E-Training programs are helpful in this regard.	Adaptability & Flexibility	Positive attitude, collaboration, self-adjustment,
Do you feel the change is an opportunity and resolve the same with energy? E-Training programs are helpful in this regard.	Proactive	Self-efficacy, openness to experience, conscientiousness.

Source: Compiled by the author(s)

In the case of theme 'relationship' the employees perceived relationship barriers due to online platforms. But perceived improved sharing and openness during virtual trainings. The employees work on mutual solutions with flexibility during e-trainings. Under 'organization' theme of resilience during e-trainings employees were planning and reviewing their work on regular basis, but the schedules become more hectic due to increase in online activities. In the 'self-confidence theme of resilience employees perceived more energetic, support, and skill with improved capacity during e-trainings. For 'adaptability' theme of resilience during pandemic employees' self-adjustment with positive attitude and collaboration with others in training was perceived as crucial factor. Finally, in the 'proactive' aspect of resilience through e-training employees perceived higher conscientiousness and new experience in the work-life roles.

Findings

This case study investigates the impact of e-training interventions on employee resilience at the National Hydropower Corporation. The findings reveal several positive outcomes related to employee resilience, performance, and overall organizational effectiveness.

Firstly, the collaboration between the HR and IT departments played a crucial role in encouraging employee participation and ensuring the smooth implementation of e-training programs. The flexible and cost-effective nature of virtual training methods proved successful for the power plant, allowing employees to develop resilience levels to thrive in adverse situations.

The adoption of e-training methods enabled employees to view disruptions as opportunities for growth and development, enhancing their skills, knowledge, and abilities (Breu et al., 2002; Chonko & Jones, 2005). The utilization of flexible technologies and internet infrastructure supported the necessary changes within the organization.

Measurement of employee resilience levels was observed through various indicators, including group learning, content assimilation through online classes, improved communication and idea exchange among groups, team cohesion, target focus, and increased efficiency (Sharma & Sharma, 2020).

The study also revealed that employees experienced improvements in their vision for the future, work-life balance, and determination to achieve organizational targets. Attendance in virtual training programs revived their ambitions and motivation levels. Regular planning and review of their actions led to progress in target achievement. Employees demonstrated an openness to adopting the latest technology and showed flexibility in upgrading their skills. They actively sought solutions for machinery-related issues and worked towards building positive relationships with their peers, superiors, and subordinates, thereby improving teamwork. Additionally, employees reported increased self-confidence, upgraded knowledge and skills, and gained motivation through participation in a wide range of e-training programs. Instead of perceiving the pandemic as a threat, they viewed it as an opportunity to enhance their knowledge and soft skills.

These findings indicate that e-training interventions have significantly contributed to enhancing employee resilience at the National Hydropower Corporation. By embracing virtual training methods and focusing on developing employee skills and knowledge, the organization has fostered a proactive and resilient workforce capable of thriving in disruptive situations.

CONCLUSION

This study examines the development of employee resilience through e-Training to navigate technological changes and disruptive situations. Continuous learning is vital for employees to confront adversity with resilience, making training programs essential. The Power Plant case study demonstrates the benefits of digital technology in turning crises into opportunities. The findings highlight the positive impact of e-Training on attitudes, soft skills, and technical knowledge. Further research is needed, and adaptability to technology is crucial in VUCA times. Resilience is enhanced through job flexibility, skill development, communication, and coordination. Strengthening employee resilience improves performance, efficiency, and environmental awareness. The research is limited to a specific unit, and future studies can explore resilience in different sectors.

REFERENCES

Agariya, A. K., & Singh, D. (2012). e-Learning quality: Scale development and validation in Indian context. *Knowledge Management & E-Learning: An International Journal*, *4*(4), 500–517.

Allwood, J. M., & Lee, W. L. (2004). The impact of job rotation on problem-solving skills. *International Journal of Production Research*, *42*(5), 865–881. doi:10.1080/00207540310001631566

Ameen, A., & Baharom, M. N. (2019). An appraisal of the effect of training on employee performance in an organization: A theoretical discussion. *Asian Journal of Multidisciplinary Studies*, *7*(3), 27–31.

American Psychological Association. (n.d.). *Road to resilience*. APA. http://www.apa.org/helpcenter/road-resilience.aspx

Armstrong, M. (2005). *Armstrong's Handbook of Management and Leadership: Approaches to HRM and L&D*. Kogan Page Limited Publishing.

Atkinson, J. W. (1964). *An introduction to motivation*. American Book.

Bajaj, R., Sinha, S., & Tiwari, V. (2013). Crucial factors of human resource management for good employee relations: A case study. *International Journal of Mining, Metallurgy, and Mechanical Engineering*, *1*(2), 90–92.

Bantz, C. R. (1989). Organizing and the social psychology of organizing. *Communication Studies*, *40*(4), 231–240. doi:10.1080/10510978909368276

Bardoel, E. A., Pettit, T. M., De Cieri, H., & McMillan, L. (2014). Employee resilience: An emerging challenge for HRM. *Asia Pacific Journal of Human Resources*, *52*(3), 279–297. doi:10.1111/1744-7941.12033

Breu, K., Hemingway, C. J., Strathern, M., & Bridger, D. (2002). Workforce agility: The new employee strategy for the knowledge economy. *Journal of Information Technology*, *17*(1), 21–31. doi:10.1080/02683960110132070

Chonko, L. B., & Jones, E. (2005). The need for speed: Agility selling. *Journal of Personal Selling & Sales Management*, *25*(4), 371–382.

Collin, K., & Valleala, U. M. (2005). Interaction among employees: How does learning take place in the social communities of the workplace and how might such learning be supervised? *Journal of Education and Work*, *18*(4), 401–420. doi:10.1080/13639080500327873

Cooper, C. L., Flint-Taylor, J., & Pearn, M. (2013). *Building resilience for success: A resource for managers and organizations* (Vol. 8). Palgrave Macmillan. doi:10.1057/9781137367839

Datu, J. A. D., & Valdez, J. P. M. (2016). Psychological capital predicts academic engagement and well-being in Filipino high school students. *The Asia-Pacific Education Researcher*, *25*(3), 399–405. doi:10.100740299-015-0254-1

Douglas, S. (2020). Mitigating workplace adversity through employee resilience. *Strategic HR Review*, *19*(6), 279–283. doi:10.1108/SHR-06-2020-0063

Edwards, J. R. (1991). Person-job fit: A conceptual integration, literature review, and methodological critique. *Journal of Vocational Behavior*, *38*(3), 255–288.

Erdogan, B., & Bauer, T. N. (2005). Enhancing career benefits of employee proactive personality: The role of fit with jobs and organizations. *Personnel Psychology*, *58*(4), 859–891. doi:10.1111/j.1744-6570.2005.00772.x

Fadli, A., Hou, A., Juliansyah, R., & Tambunan, D. (2020). The effect of self-confidence moderation on the effect of emotional intelligence on employee work stress at PT. Orange Indonesia Mandiri Medan. Budapest International Research and Critics Institute (BIRCI-Journal): Humanities and Social Sciences, 3(4), 2851-2856.

Festing, M., & Eidems, J. (2011). A process perspective on transnational HRM systems—A dynamic capability-based analysis. *Human Resource Management Review*, *21*(3), 162–173. doi:10.1016/j.hrmr.2011.02.002

Gattiker, U. E. (1995). Firm and taxpayer returns from training of semiskilled employees. *Academy of Management Journal*, *38*(4), 1152–1173. doi:10.2307/256624

Gegenfurtner, A., Zitt, A., & Ebner, C. (2020). Evaluating webinar-based training: A mixed methods study of trainee reactions toward digital web conferencing. *International Journal of Training and Development*, *24*(1), 5–21. doi:10.1111/ijtd.12167

Gennard, J., & Judge, G. (2005). *Employee relations*. CIPD Publishing.

George, J. M., & Jones, G. R. (2008). *Understanding and Managing Organizational Behavior* (5th ed.). Pearson/Prentice Hall.

Gillham, J. E., Abenavoli, R. M., Brunwasser, S. M., Linkins, M., Reivich, K. J., & Seligman, M. E. (2013). Resilience education. In *The Oxford Handbook of Happiness* (pp. 609–630). Oxford University Press.

Gligor, D., Gligor, N., Holcomb, M., & Bozkurt, S. (2019). Distinguishing between the concepts of supply chain agility and resilience. *International Journal of Logistics Management*, *30*(2), 467–487. doi:10.1108/IJLM-10-2017-0259

Goleman, D. (2015). Emotional Intelligence (EQ). *Journal of K*, *6*, 71–77.

Granda, J. C., Nuño, P., García, D. F., & Suárez, F. J. (2015). Autonomic platform for synchronous e-Training in dispersed organizations. *Journal of Network and Systems Management*, *23*(1), 183–209. doi:10.100710922-013-9290-4

Kristof-Brown, A. L., Jansen, K. J., & Colbert, A. E. (2002). A policy-capturing study of the simultaneous effects of fit with jobs, groups, and organizations. *The Journal of Applied Psychology*, *87*(5), 985–993. doi:10.1037/0021-9010.87.5.985 PMID:12395823

Lim, D. H., Hur, H., Ho, Y., Yoo, S., & Yoon, S. W. (2020). Workforce resilience: Integrative review for human resource development. *Performance Improvement Quarterly*, *33*(1), 77–101. doi:10.1002/piq.21318

Madrigano, J., Chandra, A., Costigan, T., & Acosta, J. D. (2017). Beyond disaster preparedness: Building a resilience-oriented workforce for the future. *International Journal of Environmental Research and Public Health*, *14*(12), 1563. doi:10.3390/ijerph14121563 PMID:29236028

Maheshwari, S., & Vohra, V. (2018). Role of training and development practices in implementing change. *International Journal of Learning and Change*, *10*(2), 131–162. doi:10.1504/IJLC.2018.090911

Masten, A. S. (2001). Ordinary magic: Resilience processes in development. *The American Psychologist*, *56*(3), 227–238. doi:10.1037/0003-066X.56.3.227 PMID:11315249

Mitsakis, F. V. (2020). Human resource development (HRD) resilience: A new 'success element' of organizational resilience? *Human Resource Development International, 23*(3), 321–328. doi:10.1080/13678868.2019.1669385

Mohaghegh, M., & Furlan, A. (2020). Systematic problem-solving and its antecedents: A synthesis of the literature. *Management Research Review, 43*(9), 1033–1062. doi:10.1108/MRR-06-2019-0284

Muduli, A. (2016). Exploring the facilitators and mediators of workforce agility: An empirical study. *Management Research Review, 39*(12), 1567–1586. doi:10.1108/MRR-10-2015-0236

Nair, K. S. (2003). Life goals: The concept and its relevance to rehabilitation. *Clinical Rehabilitation, 17*(2), 192–202. doi:10.1191/0269215503cr599oa PMID:12625660

Nardi, B. A., & Whittaker, S. (2002). The place of face-to-face communication in distributed work. *Distributed Work, 83*(112), 10–7551.

Nguyen, Q., Kuntz, J. R., Näswall, K., & Malinen, S. (2016). Employee resilience and leadership styles: The moderating role of proactive personality and optimism. *New Zealand Journal of Psychology (Online), 45*(2), 13.

Owoyemi, O., Oyelere, M., Elegbede, T., & Gbajumo-Sheriff, M. (2011). Enhancing employees' commitment to the organization through training. *International Journal of Business and Management, 6*(7), 280–286.

Sambrook, S. (2005). Factors influencing the context and process of work-related learning: Synthesizing findings from two research projects. *Human Resource Development International, 8*(1), 101–119. doi:10.1080/1367886052000342591

Scardamalia, M., & Bereiter, C. (1992). An architecture for collaborative knowledge building. In *Computer-based Learning Environments and Problem Solving* (pp. 41–66). Springer. doi:10.1007/978-3-642-77228-3_3

Seibert, S. E., Crant, J. M., & Kraimer, M. L. (1999). Proactive personality and career success. *The Journal of Applied Psychology, 84*(3), 416–427. doi:10.1037/0021-9010.84.3.416 PMID:10380421

Seibert, S. E., Kraimer, M. L., & Liden, R. C. (2001). A social capital theory of career success. *Academy of Management Journal, 44*(2), 219–237. doi:10.2307/3069452

Seville, E. (2016). *Resilient organizations: How to survive, thrive and create opportunities through crisis and change*. Kogan Page Publishers.

Sharma, S., & Sharma, S. K. (2020). Probing the links between team resilience, competitive advantage, and organizational effectiveness: Evidence from the information technology industry. *Business Perspectives and Research*, *8*(2), 289–307. doi:10.1177/2278533719887458

Sherehiy, B. (2008). *Relationships between agility strategy, work organization, and workforce agility.* [Dissertation, University of Louisville].

Shin, J., Taylor, M. S., & Seo, M. G. (2012). Resources for change: The relationships of organizational inducements and psychological resilience to employees' attitudes and behaviors toward organizational change. *Academy of Management Journal*, *55*(3), 727–748. doi:10.5465/amj.2010.0325

Southwick, S. M., Bonanno, G. A., Masten, A. S., Panter-Brick, C., & Yehuda, R. (2014). Resilience definitions, theory, and challenges: Interdisciplinary perspectives. *European Journal of Psychotraumatology*, *5*(1), 25338. doi:10.3402/ejpt.v5.25338 PMID:25317257

Stolovitch, H. D., & Keeps, E. J. (Eds.). (1992). *Handbook of performance technology: A comprehensive guide for analyzing and solving performance problems in organizations*. Jossey-Bass.

Subba Rao, P. (2014). *Essentials of Human Resource Management and Industrial Relations*. Himalaya Publishing House.

Sudhakar, R., & Basariya, S. R. (2017). Perspectives and the factors influencing the effectiveness of training and development on employees' performance. *International Journal of Civil Engineering and Technology*, *8*(9), 135–141.

Swason Richard, A. (1994). *Analysis for improving performance: Tools for diagnosing organizations and documenting workplace expertise*. Ed. Berreti-Koehler.

Teng-Calleja, M., Hechanova, M. R. M., Sabile, P. R., & Villasanta, A. P. V. P. (2020). Building organization and employee resilience in disaster contexts. *International Journal of Workplace Health Management*, *13*(4), 393–411. doi:10.1108/IJWHM-09-2019-0122

Thalhammer, V. (2014). E-learning: An opportunity for older persons. In Learning Across Generations in Europe: Contemporary Issues in Older Adult Education (pp. 47-58). Brill.

Wang, J., Cooke, F. L., & Huang, W. (2014). How resilient is the (future) workforce in China? A study of the banking sector and implications for human resource development. *Asia Pacific Journal of Human Resources*, *52*(2), 132–154. doi:10.1111/1744-7941.12026

Weiner, B. (1980). The role of affect in rational (attributional) approaches to human motivation. *Educational Researcher*, *9*(7), 4–11. doi:10.3102/0013189X009007004

Williams, T. A., & Shepherd, D. A. (2016). Building resilience or providing sustenance: Different paths of emergent ventures in the aftermath of the Haiti earthquake. *Academy of Management Journal*, *59*(6), 2069–2102. doi:10.5465/amj.2015.0682

Youssef, C. M., & Luthans, F. (2007). Positive organizational behavior in the workplace: The impact of hope, optimism, and resilience. *Journal of Management*, *33*(5), 774–800. doi:10.1177/0149206307305562

Chapter 11
Governance in Post-COVID-19 China:
Challenges, Responses, and Opportunities

Mohamad Zreik
https://orcid.org/0000-0002-6812-6529
Sun Yat-sen University, China

ABSTRACT

In light of the COVID-19 pandemic, this chapter explores how Chinese leadership has changed since then. It provides an in-depth analysis of the profound societal and economic shifts that resulted from the pandemic and the novel responses that were necessary. Focusing on the importance of e-governance and AI technology, the chapter examines how the health crisis has affected Chinese politics, corporations, and health governance. New forms of governance that have emerged in reaction to the breakdown of established educational institutions are also explored. In addition, it investigates potential economic avenues for revival in the wake of the pandemic. Future directions for governance are discussed, with connections drawn to sustainability, entrepreneurship, and innovation. It is a great resource for learning more about how the world might change after COVID-19 due to new governance paradigms.

DOI: 10.4018/978-1-7998-9213-7.ch011

1. INTRODUCTION

The outbreak of the COVID-19 pandemic in Wuhan, China, which was notified by the World Health Organization (WHO) in March 2020, rapidly escalated into an unparalleled global health disaster (Zreik, 2023a). Rapid human-to-human transmission allowed the virus to quickly spread across China and eventually the world, posing significant threats to China's public health, economy, and general government (Li, 2021).

As the Chinese government rushed to stop the virus's spread, the country's system of government was tested. Lockdowns, testing campaigns, and contact-tracing systems were just some of the swift and decisive measures taken. Strict rules and a highly coordinated reaction characterized the Chinese government's response to the crisis, which was supported by extensive technological surveillance and data collection (Ke & Hsiao, 2022).

The economic consequences of the pandemic in China were swift and devastating. Due to the rapid spread of the virus, many factories and transportation hubs were closed, and many stores and restaurants went out of business. Particularly hard struck was the service sector, which includes companies like tourism and hospitality. Due to company shutdowns and reduced consumer spending, the unemployment rate skyrocketed (Wu et al., 2023).

However, the health crisis did cause some beneficial changes, most notably in the digital sector of the economy. The digital revolution of many industries has been accelerated by the soaring demand for online services including e-commerce, remote work platforms, online education, and digital health services (Sun, 2021). As a result of these changes, China's forms of governance have undergone significant modifications, most notably the increased use of cutting-edge technologies in public administration and service provision (Liu, James, & Man, 2022).

There were also major societal and economic repercussions from the pandemic, like as changes in consumer and lifestyle preferences, a heightened interest in public health, and a push toward greater digitalization and innovation (Ratten, 2020). These shifts presented new difficulties and opportunities for post-COVID-19 governance development. This chapter examines how COVID-19 affected Chinese governance models, the measures taken in response, and their long-term consequences.

The goal of this chapter is to provide a thorough examination of the ways in which Chinese government has evolved after COVID-19 pandemic. This examination covers a wide range of governmental fields, illuminating the difficulties caused by the health crisis, the complex solutions to it, and the new possibilities that have arisen as a result.

The political, corporate, and health governance paradigms in China, and how they were impacted and altered by the pandemic, are the primary emphasis of this chapter. The chapter analyzes the crisis's short- and long-term results, as well as the unconventional solutions put into place to deal with it. The goal of this chapter is to provide a nuanced comprehension of the complexity of handling a health crisis of this magnitude on a worldwide scale.

E-governance developments, which have been accelerated by the pandemic due to a growing reliance on communication technology and artificial intelligence, are also investigated in this chapter (Sharfuddin, 2020). This chapter aims to illuminate the potential impact of technological change on the future of Chinese government.

This chapter looks at the disruption of conventional pedagogical models and the subsequent development of novel approaches to educational leadership. The rapid growth of online education and the opportunities and threats it poses to educational leadership are discussed.

The economic effects of the pandemic and the ongoing recovery are also explored in this chapter. Economic growth after a pandemic is investigated, with a focus on how forms of economic governance might need to change to account for the new circumstances.

Finally, this chapter provides a roadmap for future crises by contributing to the development of efficient, malleable models of governance. It does this by linking the broader themes of sustainability, entrepreneurship, and innovation with lessons learned from China's experience and proposing pathways for future governance. It aspires to aid researchers, policymakers, economists, and anyone interested in governance in understanding the world after the COVID-19 pandemic has left its mark.

2. IMPACT OF THE PANDEMIC ON GOVERNANCE MODELS

2.1. Political Governance

2.1.1. Challenges Faced

China's political leadership was tested like never before by the COVID-19 outbreak. The Chinese government came under intense local and international scrutiny as the epicenter of the pandemic. One of the most pressing problems was stopping the spread of the virus. Public health measures, like as quarantines and travel restrictions, were necessary, but the government had to weigh the consequences for residents' everyday lives and rights (Wei et al., 2021). The sheer quantity of China's people and the vastness of its area made it extremely difficult to implement large-scale lockdowns.

The Chinese government also had the Herculean challenge of organizing a plethora of administrative agencies and resources in order to effectively address the situation. The intricacy of the health issue called for unprecedented collaboration across government agencies, sharing of data, and coordinated response from a single point of authority. Overcrowding in hospitals and a lack of medical professionals meant that the government had to find ways to ease the pressure on the healthcare system.

China was the target of criticism and geopolitical pressure from the outside world. The international narrative surrounding the government's early response to the outbreak, as well as allegations of information suppression, had to be managed. A major difficulty has been striking a balance between openness and protecting the country's reputation. In addition to coordinating internally, the government had to work with the World Health Organization (WHO), other countries, and worldwide supply networks to deal with the health issue (Torales et al., 2020).

Government leaders also had to keep the peace and public faith alive during the emergency. The public's compliance with health measures and the mitigation of panic needed effective communication despite the prevalence of fake news, anxiety, and uncertainty (Sinha, 2021). When responding to the pandemic, public opinion and social unity were critical factors.

2.1.2. Measures Taken

In light of the serious threats posed by the COVID-19 pandemic, the Chinese government adopted a number of strong actions to stop the spread of the virus and lessen its effects. Millions of people in multiple cities, including Wuhan, the virus's epicenter, were first placed under lockdown. The shutdown was extreme, but it helped stop the virus from spreading within and beyond China's borders. It gave the health care system and researchers more time to prepare for and cope with the virus (Anttiroiko, 2021).

The government's huge testing and contact-tracing program provided backing for the lockdown measures. In order to isolate affected persons and stop further infections, health officials, with the help of local community workers and volunteers, methodically tracked the infection chains. QR code-based health systems and contact tracing apps were heavily used to aid with these initiatives (Mbunge et al., 2022).

In addition, the government invested much in expanding access to healthcare. Rapid construction of new hospitals, widespread recruitment of medical staff from nearby provinces, and increased output of necessary medical equipment all served to fulfill the surging demand. Mask use and other preventative health measures were strictly enforced (Sun et al., 2021).

To prevent panic and keep the public informed, the Chinese government also conducted widespread information campaigns. Official information was provided through numerous media outlets, and press conferences and updates were held on a regular basis (Xu, Wu, & Cao, 2020). The government has boosted online surveillance and cracked down on rumors and fake news in an effort to counteract disinformation (Bernard et al., 2021).

From the outside, the Chinese government worked with WHO and other international groups to disseminate and discuss strategies for dealing with the pandemic. China supplied medical aid and shared its knowledge on handling the virus with other countries despite geopolitical sensitivities (Free & Hecimovic, 2021).

To prevent widespread unemployment and stabilize the economy, the government implemented fiscal stimulus, financial support for enterprises, and subsidies. These actions were critical in averting a further economic decline (Zreik, 2023a).

Collectively, these actions are indicative of the multifaceted strategy the Chinese government has adopted in response to the pandemic. The crisis has highlighted the need for a style of political government that is strong, adaptable, and technologically savvy enough to effectively respond to such unpredictable global events.

2.2. Corporate Governance

2.2.1. Business Disruptions

The corporate sector in China experienced unprecedented levels of disruption due to the COVID-19 outbreak. Companies of all stripes had to deal with the fallout of the unexpected halt in economic activity caused by the lockdown measures taken to contain the virus.

The impact on supply systems was particularly severe. Many companies experienced raw material shortages and production delays as a result of the shutdown of factories and the disruption of transportation networks (Butt, 2022). Being the "world's factory," China was hit especially hard because of the interruption to the global supply chain. In addition to harming domestic output, the shutdown of factories had a domino effect on worldwide markets, affecting everything from the auto industry to the electronics industry to the medicines industry (Zreik, 2023b).

The service industry was impacted just as severely. Consumer demand plummeted in the travel, tourism, hospitality, and brick-and-mortar retail sectors as a result of the travel bans and other social isolation policies (Tyagi & Pabalkar, 2021). There was a real danger of permanent closure for small and medium-sized businesses (SMEs), which are especially susceptible to extended periods of inactivity.

Additionally, companies encountered issues with human resources. Due to the potential threat to employee health, firms have to make immediate changes to safeguard staff. Companies' technological preparedness and capacity to manage a remote workforce were put to the test when many of them had to implement remote work arrangements overnight.

Another major difficulty for corporate governance was the unknown length and intensity of the pandemic. Planning, strategic decision making, and forecasting financial performance all grew increasingly challenging for businesses. As a result of these changes, companies have had to quickly rethink their approaches, adjust to the new standard, and fortify their systems to withstand shocks.

2.2.2. New Governance Strategies

Businesses in China have to immediately reevaluate their governance systems in reaction to the pandemic's effects on the economy. The need for these changes was obvious, but they also presented an opening for new ideas and ways of being in the world.

The new approaches to leadership emphasized digital transformation. As corporations were unable to rely on face-to-face contacts as much, they looked to digital alternatives to keep their businesses running (Reades & Crookston, 2021). With the advent of modern communication and collaboration technologies, working remotely became the norm. Demand for internet services increased across industries, including retail, media, and education (Hacker et al., 2020). Businesses who could swiftly adapt to digital channels and provide interesting digital content gained a competitive edge.

Corporate governance now also needs to ensure a reliable supply chain. Companies tried to stock up on essentials, diversify their supply bases, and set up local supply networks. The pandemic has hastened the shift toward digitalizing the supply chain, with businesses increasingly using tools like artificial intelligence (AI), blockchain, and the internet of things (IoT) to increase supply chain transparency and responsiveness (Free & Hecimovic, 2021).

Risk management and business continuity strategies also rose to prominence. Businesses took precautions to safeguard workers, maintain essential operations, and mitigate financial risks. They formed emergency response teams, instituted health and safety regulations, and rethought their financial policies to prevent insolvency.

In addition, businesses placed an emphasis on talking to and listening to their constituents. One of the most important responsibilities of management is communicating with and reassuring all relevant parties. Trust and confidence from stakeholders could only be preserved via open and honest discussion of actions taken, difficulties encountered, and future goals (De Villiers & Molinari, 2022).

Critically, the crisis highlighted the importance of incorporating social and environmental factors into corporate governance measures. Businesses were obligated to help the community respond to the pandemic by doing things like helping their employees and communities and donating to relief efforts. The pandemic highlighted the need for responsible business practices and greater emphasis on corporate social responsibility.

2.3. Health Governance

2.3.1. Public Health Crisis Management

China's health system experienced an unprecedented crisis as a result of the COVID-19 pandemic, which presented a significant challenge to health governance. The initial days of the outbreak were a tumultuous time for public health, as the virus swiftly spread, hospitals were overrun, and medical resources were stretched tight.

The Chinese government needed to take swift action to halt the spread of the virus and ensure the health care system could handle the rising number of cases (Sun et al., 2021). This was a difficult undertaking that required cooperation from numerous agencies, hospitals, and organizations. The health governance system had to function in emergency mode, making quick choices with incomplete and ever-changing data.

Strict containment measures were an integral part of the public health crisis management plan. Large-scale lockdowns, thorough testing, and exhaustive contact tracing were among the steps taken. Significant logistical coordination and the mobilization of a large number of resources and persons were necessary to carry out all of these tasks (Liu et al., 2022).

Managing the available resources in the healthcare system was also essential. Temporary hospitals were constructed, medical workers were relocated from other areas, and the manufacture of medical supplies was sped up to deal with the influx of patients. Allocating and managing resources effectively was essential for these actions to succeed.

One of the most important parts of crisis management was keeping the public informed. The government was responsible for disseminating information, facilitating training on safety precautions, and calming public anxiety (Kou, Chen, & Pan, 2021). To accomplish this, it had to strategically use several forms of media and technology for communication.

The reaction also featured significant innovation. China improved its response to crises by capitalizing on its technological advantages. Contact tracing, patient monitoring, and telemedicine services were only some of the uses for digital technologies.

2.3.2. Innovative Responses

China's health governance system utilized a number of novel techniques to effectively address the public health catastrophe brought on by the COVID-19 pandemic. The implementation of digital health technologies was one of the most revolutionary developments. Disease surveillance, contact tracing, and public health communication were all significantly aided by digital tools (Kamel Boulos & Geraghty, 2020). Example: health code applications helped keep people from getting out of control by keeping tabs on their health and where they went. The promise of Artificial Intelligence (AI) as a strong tool in public health situations was demonstrated by its use in anticipating disease transmission, automating tests, and even assisting in drug research (Kamak, 2023).

There was also a big growth in telemedicine. Online consultation platforms became an essential lifeline for non-COVID-19 patients as hospitals were overburdened and patients were forced to stay at home (Pappas & Frisch, 2022). This surge in telemedicine's popularity is indicative of where healthcare management is likely headed in the near future.

China used a novel approach to capacity growth by swiftly building temporary hospitals, dubbed 'Fangcang' hospitals, to isolate and treat COVID-19 patients with moderate symptoms (MacKenzie, 2020). This allowed for the most critical cases to be treated first in permanent hospitals, thus reducing the load on medical facilities.

Developmental advances in vaccines were also encouraged in China. Using inactivated viral, adenovirus vector, and protein subunit platforms, Chinese pharmaceutical and research institutions were among the first to create COVID-19 vaccines. In terms of China's ability to create vaccines, this was a huge step forward (Asundi, O'Leary, & Bhadelia, 2021).

The government also launched creative public-private partnerships to deal with the emergency. Businesses, nonprofits, and regular people pooled their resources, knowledge, and creativity to back the government's initiatives (Meijer & Webster, 2020).

3. THE ROLE OF E-GOVERNANCE AND AI

3.1. Trends and Developments

During China's crisis management of the COVID-19 pandemic, e-governance and AI played a pivotal role. Digital technologies provided an efficient means of continuing to perform governance duties, delivering public services, and managing the health problem as geographical separation became necessary (Ullah et al., 2021).

As a result, the momentum behind digitalization and the use of AI in government administration gained momentum.

There was a notable uptick in e-governance, the use of the internet for governing and providing public services. Online networks were used by governments of all levels to communicate data, roll out programs, and facilitate citizen participation. One prominent application of e-governance is the health code system, which tracked people's health and limited their freedom of movement. In addition, the government increased the scope of its internet offerings during the shutdown, allowing citizens to perform things like file taxes, register businesses, and access social security online (Milakovich, 2021).

The use of AI was also crucial in containing the situation. Disease surveillance, prediction modeling, diagnostics, and medication discovery all made substantial use of AI. To locate foci of infection and forecast the spread of the virus, for instance, artificial intelligence algorithms were applied to massive datasets. Artificial intelligence (AI)-driven research has benefited in the creation of therapies and vaccinations, while AI-powered diagnostic tools have increased testing speed and efficiency (Arora et al., 2021).

Smart cities, which use technology to improve municipal administration, emerged as a response to the crisis. Surveillance systems, traffic management, and healthcare platforms are just a few examples of ways AI has been put to use (Piccialli et al., 2021). These tools allowed for better situational awareness and management, more efficient use of resources, and higher quality public service.

Companies in the business world were quick to respond to the epidemic by embracing digital transformation through the use of cloud computing, artificial intelligence, and automation. Artificial intelligence was implemented in areas such as supply chain management, customer support, and remote work coordination, proving the importance of AI in strengthening the resilience of businesses.

3.2. Interplay Between Public Health Crisis and E-Governance

The COVID-19 public health emergency and the subsequent reactions highlighted the critical relationship between heath governance and e-government in China. The increased availability of digital health services and the use of digital tools for disease surveillance and control and public health communication are all examples of this trend.

One prime illustration of this interaction is the health code system. This system, accessible via mobile apps, used data analysis to determine an individual's health and risk factors. After reporting their medical history and whereabouts, citizens were given a color code (green, yellow, or red) that indicated their health status and their mobility restrictions (Wu et al., 2021). This instrument was essential in stemming the spread of the virus and giving authorities more control over the situation.

Another important use of e-governance in handling health crises is digital contact tracing. Authorities would be able to monitor the spread of an outbreak by following infected people as they go about their daily lives using mobile data analysis. To see the promise of digital solutions in public health situations, consider how much more effective this method was compared to conventional contact tracing.

The popularity of telemedicine sites also increased. As hospitals became overcrowded and patients were urged to recover at home, these platforms gave people a reliable means to communicate with doctors, get diagnoses, and even get prescriptions sent directly to their homes. This demonstrated the potential of e-governance to improve healthcare delivery and paved the way for the widespread use of digital health services in the future.

The government also made use of internet channels to spread word about the infection, precautions to take, and policy changes. This maintained openness and assisted in calming public nerves. The importance of e-governance in public health communication was also demonstrated by the use of social media platforms to counteract false information.

4. THE DISRUPTION AND REFORMATION OF EDUCATION SYSTEMS

4.1. Impact on Traditional Pedagogical Models

Traditional teaching practices in China were radically altered by the COVID-19 outbreak. Due to the countrywide closure of schools and the subsequent necessity for social isolation, traditional classroom instruction was abruptly halted. This affected millions of students throughout all educational levels, from kindergarten to college, creating enormous issues for educational administration (Oda Abunamous et al., 2022).

In-person instruction is at the center of most conventional pedagogical approaches, with the classroom serving as the primary location for instruction and student engagement. The adoption of distance education placed a strain on these structures. Unfortunately, many educators lacked the time or resources to properly prepare their course plans for online delivery. It was more challenging to engage students, evaluate their progress, and provide individualized guidance due to the lack of face-to-face contact.

The rise of online education has also shed light on and worsened existing disparities in the classroom. Unfortunately, not everyone has easy access to the internet and modern computing devices, two necessities for online education. This prompted worries about the digital divide and the potential for underprivileged students to fall farther behind their peers (Cheng et al., 2022).

Also, the unexpected change highlighted the shortcomings of more conventional approaches to encouraging independent and ongoing education. Students' increasing responsibility for their own education at home has called into question the use of teacher-led classes and standardized testing, highlighting the need for pedagogical innovation.

The results were similarly substantial in other areas of schooling. Internships and study abroad programs were cut, both of which provide students with valuable real-world experience. The cancellation of school days also disrupted vital services including the distribution of school lunches and the provision of counseling for students (Brahmankar, Bedarkar, & Mishra, 2022).

4.2. Emergence of Innovative Governance in Education

In China, new forms of educational governance emerged in reaction to the pandemic, with the goals of preserving the continuity of education and meeting the problems of the altered classroom setting.

The quick shift to online education was a crucial part of this breakthrough. Chinese students of all levels now have free and easy access to a comprehensive online learning platform developed by the government in tandem with academic institutions and technology firms (Ferri, Grifoni, & Guzzo, 2020). This exemplifies the potential of online learning environments to widen students' access to education by allowing them to study outside of class.

But it wasn't enough to just shift classroom activities online. To make online learning productive and interesting, new pedagogical approaches were required. Flipped classrooms, project-based learning, and gamified instruction were only some of the new approaches tried by educators. Tools for personalized learning, intelligent tutoring, and learning analytics were also developed, demonstrating an increase in the use of AI and big data in the classroom (Cui et al., 2023).

In addition, steps were done to deal with digital divide. The government made efforts to increase internet access, particularly in underserved and rural areas, and distributed electronic equipment to students in need. As an example of a more inclusive approach to educational governance, television and radio were used to reach students who lacked access to the internet (Tadesse & Muluye, 2020).

A new emphasis was placed on pupils' mental health and the development of their social and emotional skills. Schools have started using methods like online counseling services and well-being initiatives to help kids with their mental health.

The significance of developing psychological and behavioral flexibility in the face of stress was acknowledged.

Finally, the crisis prompted a reconsideration of education's ultimate purposes and guiding principles. There has been an increasing awareness that schools must do more than simply impart information if they are to prepare students for success in the twenty-first century workplace. Potentially, this will affect the direction of future educational reforms.

5. POST-PANDEMIC ECONOMY AND OPPORTUNITIES

5.1. Economic Impacts of COVID-19

The COVID-19 pandemic severely impacted the Chinese economy, leading to widespread disruptions. Demand and supply were both impacted by the halt in economic activity caused by the need for broad lockdowns, travel restrictions, and other containment measures (Zreik, Iqbal, & Rahman, 2022).

Lockdowns, labor shortages, and disruptions in the supply chain all had an impact on the day-to-day operations of enterprises. Production and efficiency fell especially low in the manufacturing, retail, and hospitality industries. Since they lack the resources of larger corporations and are more susceptible to shocks, small and medium-sized businesses (SMEs) took a disproportionately heavy impact (Xiao & Su, 2022).

Due to income losses and increased uncertainty, households cut back on their spending as a result of the pandemic, which reduced demand. A major contributor to China's economic growth in recent years, domestic consumption took a hit, especially in the travel, leisure, and hospitality industries.

International commerce and investment were also affected by the pandemic. China's export-driven sectors suffered as the global recession reduced demand for Chinese goods. The global economic uncertainties and disruptions in international travel and logistics have had an impact on foreign direct investment (Vo & Tran, 2021).

There were some positive effects on the economy. E-commerce, online entertainment, and healthcare all saw increased demand as a result of the pandemic. The recession has also hastened the shift to digital technologies and innovations, which may eventually boost productivity and competitiveness.

5.2. Economic Recovery and Potential Opportunities

China's economy has shown remarkable resilience and adaptability in the wake of the pandemic, with the country's government and the market both playing key roles in the recovery. However, the crisis has also provided fresh openings for economic growth, transformation, and innovation.

The healing process has been greatly aided by government policy. Tax cuts, low-interest loans, and direct subsidies are just some of the stimulus measures put in place to help firms and increase demand (Jomo & Chowdhury, 2020). In order to stimulate economic activity and create the groundwork for future growth, investment in infrastructure, especially digital infrastructure, was increased.

The economic crisis has also hastened the transition to digital methods of production. The new normal required enterprises across industries to adopt digital technology, e-commerce, and remote working strategies. This transition to digital has strengthened industries like technology, e-commerce, and logistics, opening up new avenues for economic growth and employment.

Opportunities have also appeared in the healthcare industry. The urgency of the situation has increased research and development in fields like digital health, telemedicine, and pharmaceuticals as a direct result of the pandemic. Consequently, there has been a rise in healthcare investment, which bodes well for economic expansion and the development of new jobs (Rafee et al., 2022).

The post-pandemic period has also placed an emphasis on green recovery. The crisis has increased the spotlight on the importance of sustainability by revealing the links between human health, the economy, and the environment. Investment in renewable energy, electric vehicles, and other green technology is anticipated to rise in light of the government's lofty carbon neutrality targets.

In addition, the pandemic has caused a reevaluation of global supply chains, which has opened up possibilities for regional growth. Greater investment and corporate expansion could occur in areas with strategic advantages as a result of the current push to diversify and strengthen supply chains.

5.3. Shifts in Economic Governance Models

China's government has made significant adjustments to its approach to economic administration as a result of the pandemic's economic consequences in order to better handle the crisis and stimulate recovery.

The emphasis on economic resilience and risk management has increased, marking a significant shift. The economy's weak spots, such as its reliance on a fragile supply chain and the fragility of small and medium-sized enterprises (SMEs), were exposed by the pandemic. The government has responded by instituting reforms to the supply chain, the resilience of businesses, and the management of financial risks (Free, C., & Hecimovic, 2021).

The importance of innovation in driving economic expansion has also grown. Economic resilience and competitiveness are key factors that the crisis highlighted the importance of digital technologies and innovation in driving. The government has been enacting a number of laws and initiatives aimed at fostering digital transformation, technical innovation, and the expansion of the digital economy (Zhang et al., 2022).

Fiscal policy's importance in dampening the effects of business cycles has grown. The government has employed fiscal instruments like tax cuts, increased spending, and direct help to firms and households in an effort to generate demand and support economic recovery, especially given the depth of the crisis (Wójcik & Ioannou, 2020). This proactive use of fiscal policy is indicative of progress toward a style of economic governance that is more adaptable to changing circumstances.

The importance of social security and growth that benefits all segments of society has also increased. As a result of the pandemic, there is now a greater emphasis on social fairness in economic policy. Efforts have been made to help the most vulnerable members of society, strengthen social safety nets, and provide employment opportunities.

In terms of economic governance, the idea of green development has emerged as a major player. Because of the pandemic, people are thinking more about the environment, health, and the economy as interconnected systems. The government is encouraging environmentally friendly businesses and technologies in an effort to reach carbon neutrality.

6. FUTURE DIRECTIONS FOR GOVERNANCE

6.1. Lessons Learned From the Pandemic

The COVID-19 pandemic has brought numerous difficulties for Chinese administration, but it has also taught important lessons that can be applied to future policies. To begin, the crisis has highlighted the significance of resilient governance structures. The ability to quickly adjust to and recover from setbacks is essential. Not only do health emergencies fall under this category, but so do recessions, natural disasters, and technological upheavals.

The pandemic has shown how important quick thinking and good judgment are. Controlling the virus and minimizing its effects required swift decision making based on available evidence. Because of this, a system of leadership that can rapidly collect, analyze, and respond to information was needed, while also being adaptable enough to change tactics as necessary.

Collaboration across disciplines has been highlighted as crucial. The economic, social, and educational systems are all affected by the pandemic as well as the health care system. Complex problems like these can only be solved by coordinating efforts across governmental agencies, highlighting the importance of taking a systemic, multidisciplinary approach.

The crisis has also shown how important digital technologies are to government administration. From remote education and e-commerce to disease surveillance and contact tracing, digital technologies have been crucial in crisis management and service continuity (Datta & Nwankpa, 2021). This demonstrates how e-governance and AI may improve governance in practice.

The pandemic has highlighted concerns about social equity. The crisis's disproportionate toll on certain demographics has highlighted the importance of equitable leadership that works to close the gap between socioeconomic groups and makes progress in the interest of all. Based on these findings, post-pandemic governance models can be rethought and reshaped to place greater emphasis on resilience, agility, integration, digitization, and inclusivity.

6.2. Potential Trends and Directions

Several possible trends and paths for governance in China in the post-pandemic age can be drawn from the lessons acquired during the pandemic. To begin, it's possible that themes of resilience and risk management will be explored further. In order to do so, it may be needed to improve the risk assessment and early warning capacities, as well as the resilience of essential institutions like healthcare, education, the economy, and infrastructure.

Second, emerging governance models are expected to emphasize flexibility and responsiveness. One way to achieve this goal is to use real-time data and predictive analytics to facilitate more adaptable and timely decision-making. Increased use of AI and other digital technologies in policymaking has the potential to promote governance that is both evidence-based and forward-looking.

Third, there may be a continuation of the movement toward unified, all-encompassing government. As a result, there may be a need for better communication and cooperation between various governmental agencies as they work together to solve difficult problems. It's possible that the idea of "whole-of-society" governance, in which the government, corporations, civil society, and individuals all work together, will grow in popularity (Li et al., 2022).

Fourth, e-governance is anticipated to take on a larger role in the future. There's room to increase the government's use of digital technologies in service delivery, citizen engagement, and resource management. In this respect, it will be important to cultivate digital infrastructure, data governance frameworks, and digital capabilities.

Finally, there may be a greater push for social justice and inclusive economic expansion. This may mean working to narrow income gaps, strengthen social safety nets, and advance policies that benefit all groups. It's possible that "leaving no one behind" will become a constitutional principle.

These possible developments mirror the shifting environment of authority following the pandemic. They pose both opportunities and problems for policymakers, necessitating a commitment to ongoing education, creative problem solving, and flexible approaches. The post-COVID-19 era of governance in China is expected to be exciting and marked by significant changes.

6.3. The Role of Sustainability, Entrepreneurship, and Innovation

After the pandemic, China's recovery and transformation will rely heavily on the leadership qualities of sustainability, entrepreneurship, and innovation. The pandemic highlighted the interconnectedness of health, economy, and environment, and this has led to sustainability becoming a primary concern in governance. China's goal of carbon neutrality is an example of how the country is prioritizing environmental protection as part of its development strategy (Liu et al., 2022). Policymaking, regulation, planning, and resource management could all benefit in the future from incorporating sustainable concepts. Green industry and technology promotion, sustainable city building, and encouraging a circular economy are all possibilities.

In the wake of the pandemic, entrepreneurship will once again fuel economic expansion and technological advancement. Businesses have been forced to adjust to the new normal and look for new opportunities as a result of the pandemic, which has both hampered and encouraged their entrepreneurial spirit (Floetgen et al., 2021). It's likely that the government will keep funding startups, creating a welcoming atmosphere for businesses, and encouraging the development of entrepreneurial skills. The formation of new businesses and the promotion of social cohesion are two other important aspects of inclusive economic expansion.

One of the most important aspects of governance in the future will be innovation. The importance of innovation in bolstering resilience and competitiveness has been highlighted by the pandemic's acceleration of digital transformation and technology innovation. To increase the efficacy and efficiency of government, it is possible that the government will continue to support technological advancements like artificial intelligence, big data, and blockchain. Encourage public-private collaborations in R&D and other forms of innovation-related funding are possible strategies here.

7. CONCLUSION

The COVID-19 pandemic has had far-reaching effects on China's governance structures, highlighting weaknesses and accelerating changes across a variety of fields. As a result of the crisis, the relevance of digital technology and the need for social fairness have been brought to the forefront, while resilience, agility, and integration in governance have been highlighted.

Despite its difficulties, the pandemic has also provided new openings for reforming government. Future directions for governance are being shaped by the lessons learnt from the crisis, with an emphasis on building resilience, making use of new technology, boosting integration, and encouraging inclusion.

Key topics in post-pandemic governance include sustainability, entrepreneurship, and innovation. Health, the economy, and the environment are all interconnected, and this realization is leading to a shift toward sustainability as a guiding principle in policy formulation and governance. Jobs are being created, and more people are becoming part of society as a result of economic revitalization and transformation. Innovation, especially digital and technology innovation, is improving the efficiency and effectiveness of governance by providing new approaches to addressing difficult problems.

Learning, adapting, and innovating will be necessary for the journey towards a post-COVID-19 governance model. As it travels this path, China is adding to the body of international knowledge on governance in the face of severe crises, providing lessons and insights that can be used by other nations and regions.

Even if we can't know what will happen, the pandemic taught us that proactive, adaptable, and forward-thinking leadership is essential. The future of governance, it seems, lies not in reestablishing the status quo but in creating a new normal—one that is robust, inclusive, and sustainable, and therefore able to deal with the complexity and uncertainties of the twenty-first century.

REFERENCES

Anttiroiko, A. V. (2021). Successful government responses to the pandemic: Contextualizing national and urban responses to the COVID-19 outbreak in east and west. [IJEPR]. *International Journal of E-Planning Research*, *10*(2), 1–17. doi:10.4018/IJEPR.20210401.oa1

Arora, G., Joshi, J., Mandal, R. S., Shrivastava, N., Virmani, R., & Sethi, T. (2021). Artificial intelligence in surveillance, diagnosis, drug discovery and vaccine development against COVID-19. *Pathogens (Basel, Switzerland), 10*(8), 1048. doi:10.3390/pathogens10081048 PMID:34451513

Asundi, A., O'Leary, C., & Bhadelia, N. (2021). Global COVID-19 vaccine inequity: The scope, the impact, and the challenges. *Cell Host & Microbe, 29*(7), 1036–1039. doi:10.1016/j.chom.2021.06.007 PMID:34265241

Bernard, R., Bowsher, G., Sullivan, R., & Gibson-Fall, F. (2021). Disinformation and epidemics: Anticipating the next phase of biowarfare. *Health Security, 19*(1), 3–12. doi:10.1089/hs.2020.0038 PMID:33090030

Brahmankar, Y., Bedarkar, M., & Mishra, M. (2022). An entrepreneurial way of engaging student entrepreneurs at business school during pandemic. *International Journal of Innovation Science, 14*(3/4), 428–444. doi:10.1108/IJIS-11-2020-0264

Butt, A. S. (2022). Understanding the implications of pandemic outbreaks on supply chains: An exploratory study of the effects caused by the COVID-19 across four South Asian countries and steps taken by firms to address the disruptions. *International Journal of Physical Distribution & Logistics Management, 52*(4), 370–392. doi:10.1108/IJPDLM-08-2020-0281

Cheng, H., Lyu, K., Li, J., & Shiu, H. (2022). Bridging the Digital Divide for Rural Older Adults by Family Intergenerational Learning: A Classroom Case in a Rural Primary School in China. *International Journal of Environmental Research and Public Health, 19*(1), 371. doi:10.3390/ijerph19010371 PMID:35010629

Cui, Y., Ma, Z., Wang, L., Yang, A., Liu, Q., Kong, S., & Wang, H. (2023). A survey on big data-enabled innovative online education systems during the COVID-19 pandemic. *Journal of Innovation & Knowledge, 8*(1), 100295. doi:10.1016/j.jik.2022.100295

Datta, P., & Nwankpa, J. K. (2021). Digital transformation and the COVID-19 crisis continuity planning. *Journal of Information Technology Teaching Cases, 11*(2), 81–89. doi:10.1177/2043886921994821

De Villiers, C., & Molinari, M. (2022). How to communicate and use accounting to ensure buy-in from stakeholders: Lessons for organizations from governments' COVID-19 strategies. *Accounting, Auditing & Accountability Journal, 35*(1), 20–34. doi:10.1108/AAAJ-08-2020-4791

Ferri, F., Grifoni, P., & Guzzo, T. (2020). Online learning and emergency remote teaching: Opportunities and challenges in emergency situations. *Societies (Basel, Switzerland)*, *10*(4), 86. doi:10.3390oc10040086

Floetgen, R. J., Strauss, J., Weking, J., Hein, A., Urmetzer, F., Böhm, M., & Krcmar, H. (2021). Introducing platform ecosystem resilience: Leveraging mobility platforms and their ecosystems for the new normal during COVID-19. *European Journal of Information Systems*, *30*(3), 304–321. doi:10.1080/0960085X.2021.1884009

Free, C., & Hecimovic, A. (2021). Global supply chains after COVID-19: The end of the road for neoliberal globalisation? *Accounting, Auditing & Accountability Journal*, *34*(1), 58–84. doi:10.1108/AAAJ-06-2020-4634

Hacker, J., vom Brocke, J., Handali, J., Otto, M., & Schneider, J. (2020). Virtually in this together–how web-conferencing systems enabled a new virtual togetherness during the COVID-19 crisis. *European Journal of Information Systems*, *29*(5), 563–584. doi:10.1080/0960085X.2020.1814680

Jomo, K. S., & Chowdhury, A. (2020). COVID-19 pandemic recession and recovery. *Development*, *63*(2-4), 226–237. doi:10.105741301-020-00262-0 PMID:33223764

Kamak, L. P. (2023). *Programming pedagogy in the age of accessible artificial intelligence* [Doctoral dissertation, Cornell University].

Kamel Boulos, M. N., & Geraghty, E. M. (2020). Geographical tracking and mapping of coronavirus disease COVID-19/severe acute respiratory syndrome coronavirus 2 (SARS-CoV-2) epidemic and associated events around the world: How 21st century GIS technologies are supporting the global fight against outbreaks and epidemics. *International Journal of Health Geographics*, *19*(1), 1–12. doi:10.118612942-020-00202-8 PMID:32160889

Ke, X., & Hsiao, C. (2022). Economic impact of the most drastic lockdown during COVID-19 pandemic—The experience of Hubei, China. *Journal of Applied Econometrics*, *37*(1), 187–209. doi:10.1002/jae.2871 PMID:34518735

Kou, Y., Chen, P., & Pan, J. X. (2021). The service experiences of public libraries during the COVID-19 emergency in Wuhan: Three case studies. *Journal of the Australian Library and Information Association*, *70*(3), 287–300. doi:10.1080/24750158.2021.1960251

Li, B., Qian, J., Xu, J., & Li, Y. (2022). Collaborative governance in emergencies: Community food supply in COVID-19 in Wuhan, China. *Urban Governance*, *2*(1), 188–196. doi:10.1016/j.ugj.2022.03.002

Li, M. (2021). Public health crises in comparison: China's epidemic response policies from SARS to COVID-19. *Global Public Health: An International Journal for Research, Policy and Practice*, *16*(8-9), 1223–1236. doi:10.1080/17441692.2021.1919735 PMID:33891518

Liu, H., Liang, Z., Zhang, S., & Liu, L. (2022). Sociodemographic and policy factors associated with the transmission of COVID-19: Analyzing longitudinal contact tracing data from a northern Chinese city. *Journal of Urban Health*, *99*(3), 582–593. doi:10.100711524-022-00639-1 PMID:35641716

Liu, W., James, T. S., & Man, C. (2022). Governance and public administration in China. *Policy Studies*, *43*(3), 387–402. doi:10.1080/01442872.2022.2054091

Liu, Z., Deng, Z., He, G., Wang, H., Zhang, X., Lin, J., Qi, Y., & Liang, X. (2022). Challenges and opportunities for carbon neutrality in China. *Nature Reviews. Earth & Environment*, *3*(2), 141–155. doi:10.103843017-021-00244-x

MacKenzie, D. (2020). Stopping the Next Pandemic: How Covid-19 Can Help Us Save Humanity. Hachette UK.

Mbunge, E., Ndumiso, N., Kavu, T. D., Dandajena, K., Batani, J., & Fashoto, S. G. (2022). Towards QR Code Health Systems Amid COVID-19: Lessons Learnt from Other QR Code Digital Technologies. In *The Science behind the COVID Pandemic and Healthcare Technology Solutions* (pp. 129–143). Springer International Publishing. doi:10.1007/978-3-031-10031-4_7

Meijer, A., & Webster, C. W. R. (2020). The COVID-19-crisis and the information polity: An overview of responses and discussions in twenty-one countries from six continents. *Information Polity*, *25*(3), 243–274. doi:10.3233/IP-200006

Milakovich, M. E. (2021). *Digital governance: Applying advanced technologies to improve public service*. Routledge. doi:10.4324/9781003215875

Oda Abunamous, M., Boudouaia, A., Jebril, M., Diafi, S., & Zreik, M. (2022). The decay of traditional education: A case study under covid-19. *Cogent Education*, *9*(1), 2082116. doi:10.1080/2331186X.2022.2082116

Pappas, H. P., & Frisch, P. H. (2022). *Leveraging Technology as a Response to the COVID Pandemic: Adapting Diverse Technologies, Workflow, and Processes to Optimize Integrated Clinical Management*. CRC Press.

Piccialli, F., Di Cola, V. S., Giampaolo, F., & Cuomo, S. (2021). The role of artificial intelligence in fighting the COVID-19 pandemic. *Information Systems Frontiers*, *23*(6), 1467–1497. doi:10.100710796-021-10131-x PMID:33935585

Rafee, B. M., Zaheed, S. M., Ali, R. M., Asan, S. J., Raheem, A. A., & Ahmed, R. S. (2022). A Moral Obligation of Health Care Service for Non-Covid Patients: A Reviews. *Journal of Positive School Psychology*, *6*(2), 6060–6069.

Ratten, V. (2020). Coronavirus (covid-19) and entrepreneurship: Changing life and work landscape. *Journal of Small Business and Entrepreneurship*, *32*(5), 503–516. doi:10.1080/08276331.2020.1790167

Reades, J., & Crookston, M. (2021). Face-To-Face and central place: COVID and the prospects for cities. *Built Environment*, *47*(3), 326–335. doi:10.2148/benv.47.3.326

Sharfuddin, S. (2020). The world after Covid-19. *The Round Table*, *109*(3), 247–257. doi:10.1080/00358533.2020.1760498

Sinha, D. (2021). *Pandemic, governance and communication: The curious case of COVID-19*. Taylor & Francis. doi:10.4324/9781003247388

Sun, S., Xie, Z., Yu, K., Jiang, B., Zheng, S., & Pan, X. (2021). COVID-19 and healthcare system in China: Challenges and progression for a sustainable future. *Globalization and Health*, *17*(1), 1–8. doi:10.118612992-021-00665-9 PMID:33478558

Sun, T. (2021). *Digital Banking Support to Small Businesses amid COVID-19: Evidence from China*. International Monetary Fund. doi:10.5089/9781513585192.065

Tadesse, S., & Muluye, W. (2020). The impact of COVID-19 pandemic on education system in developing countries: A review. *Open Journal of Social Sciences*, *8*(10), 159–170. doi:10.4236/jss.2020.810011

Torales, J., O'Higgins, M., Castaldelli-Maia, J. M., & Ventriglio, A. (2020). The outbreak of COVID-19 coronavirus and its impact on global mental health. *The International Journal of Social Psychiatry*, *66*(4), 317–320. doi:10.1177/0020764020915212 PMID:32233719

Tyagi, P., & Pabalkar, D. V. (2021). Impact of COVID-19 over purchasing behaviour of the consumers. *European Journal of Molecular and Clinical Medicine*, *8*(2), 561–571.

Ullah, A., Pinglu, C., Ullah, S., Abbas, H. S. M., & Khan, S. (2021). The role of e-governance in combating COVID-19 and promoting sustainable development: A comparative study of China and Pakistan. *Chinese Political Science Review*, *6*(1), 86–118. doi:10.100741111-020-00167-w

Vo, T. D., & Tran, M. D. (2021). The impact of covid-19 pandemic on the global trade. *International Journal of Social Science and Economics Invention*, *7*(1), 1–7. doi:10.23958/ijssei/vol07-i01/261

Wei, Y., Ye, Z., Cui, M., & Wei, X. (2021). COVID-19 prevention and control in China: Grid governance. *Journal of Public Health (Oxford, England)*, *43*(1), 76–81. doi:10.1093/pubmed/fdaa175 PMID:32978620

Wójcik, D., & Ioannou, S. (2020). COVID-19 and finance: Market developments so far and potential impacts on the financial sector and centres. *Tijdschrift voor Economische en Sociale Geografie*, *111*(3), 387–400. doi:10.1111/tesg.12434 PMID:32836484

Wu, J., Xie, X., Yang, L., Xu, X., Cai, Y., Wang, T., & Xie, X. (2021). Mobile health technology combats COVID-19 in China. *The Journal of Infection*, *82*(1), 159–198. doi:10.1016/j.jinf.2020.07.024 PMID:32730998

Wu, J., Zhan, X., Xu, H., & Ma, C. (2023). The economic impacts of COVID-19 and city lockdown: Early evidence from China. *Structural Change and Economic Dynamics*, *65*, 151–165. doi:10.1016/j.strueco.2023.02.018 PMID:36876039

Xiao, D., & Su, J. (2022). Macroeconomic lockdown effects of COVID-19 on small business in China: Empirical insights from SEM technique. *Environmental Science and Pollution Research International*, *29*(42), 63344–63356. doi:10.100711356-022-20071-x PMID:35451716

Xu, W., Wu, J., & Cao, L. (2020). COVID-19 pandemic in China: Context, experience and lessons. *Health Policy and Technology*, *9*(4), 639–648. doi:10.1016/j.hlpt.2020.08.006 PMID:32874851

Zhang, T., Shi, Z. Z., Shi, Y. R., & Chen, N. J. (2022). Enterprise digital transformation and production efficiency: Mechanism analysis and empirical research. *Ekonomska Istrazivanja*, *35*(1), 2781–2792. doi:10.1080/1331677X.2021.1980731

Zreik, M. (2023a). From Boom to Bust: A Study of China's Economy in the Wake of COVID-19 Outbreak in H1 2020. *BRICS Journal of Economics*, *4*(1), 147–171. doi:10.3897/brics-econ.4.e101050

Zreik, M. (2023b). Analytical study on Foreign Direct Investment Divestment Inflows and Outflows in Developing Economies: Evidence of China. *Chinese Economy*, 1–16. doi:10.1080/10971475.2023.2193118

Zreik, M., Iqbal, B. A., & Rahman, M. N. (2022). Outward FDI: Determinants and Flows in Emerging Economies: Evidence from China. *China and WTO Review*, *8*(2), 385–402. doi:10.14330/cwr.2022.8.2.07

Chapter 12
The Governance of Public Education Institutions in Portugal:
The General Council

Isabel Cristina Guerreiro Pimentel Maia
https://orcid.org/0000-0002-2051-2383
Faculdade de Economia, Universidade de Coimbra, Portugal

ABSTRACT

Governance models evolved dynamically, complex, global, and interactive. The aim of this study was to analyze non-superior public education institutions in Portugal, with the new model of governance, in which the school opened for society. The work of the multiple case study presented followed a qualitative methodology and the principles of the founded theory analyzing the elements of the General Council: their participation and shame. The authors consider four school groups, with different academic and socioeconomic profiles. The data collected in interviews, document analysis and unmarked observation were subject to content analysis. Obstacles to the execution of the GC's competences and the effective participation of its members highlight pressures exercised by the director in decision making, monopolizing the information provided to the GC, aggravating during the pandemic. The authors ended up with recommendations for the operation of the most effective and democratic GC.

DOI: 10.4018/978-1-7998-9213-7.ch012

INTRODUCTION

At the end of the last century, in a parallel way to the whole process of globalization, governance evolved significantly, as with interest in its study at the academic level.

The attention given to governance follows globalization, assimilating in the first phase the principles of new public management and, later, those of the new public governance that legitimizes the representation of external stakeholders in the strategic management bodies of public and complex institutions are the ones non Higher Public Education Institutions. This opening of non higher public education institutions with society integrates vertical and horizontal and multilevel network systems.

In our work, governance is considered global and interactive, translating itself in a complex set of institutional norms and processes at a given territorial level, reconciling interrelationships (of internal and external stakeholders), adapted to the challenges placed at its various levels and in Network, which enforces individual participation, operation and decision making of an organ.

If governance studies in Higher Public Education institutions have multiplied, the same does not happen in the non Higher Public Education Institutions, where few authors include the theme in some texts where they address this theme.

The objective of this work is to analyze how the governance model is being implemented in the non higher public education institutions instituted in Portugal - Drecreto-Lei nº75/2008, de 22 de abril. Given the appreciation that the law gives to the role of external stakeholders, in which for the first time they are included in the participation of the strategic management of non Higher Public Education Institutions, we intend to analyze how the various elements of the general council in decision -making of Non Higher Public Education Institutions.

This chapter is divided into five points beyond the introduction: the management of non-higher education from a multilevel perspective; The general council as a management body in the democratic model of the non Higher Public Education Institutions; Case study, analyzed results and final considerations.

The Management of Non-Higher Education in a Multilevel Perspective

Governance models in complex institutions such as non higher public education institutions are not implemented in the same way, with the same results, in the various countries, neither within the same country - at various levels of governance - nor at the various non -higher public education. institutions in Portugal. Cultural, economic and social contexts, the traditions of each country, each region and even each organization are different and seem to influence the existence of different implemented functional models (Barroso, 2018; Osborne, 2010).

The complexity of the education system has questioned and challenged the implementation of educational governance at its various levels - transnational, national, regional, local and organizational.

The design of the structural model of the law began to be the basis of our empirical design, having been complemented through the analysis resulting from the case study.

In recent decades, the complexity of the actually implemented governance models and the growing requirement of the various stakeholders of the non higher public education institutions have had identical procedural responses in the various countries of the European Union (as an example), made in decentralization proposals and the search for New Governance Instruments (Barroso, 2017; OECD, 2017). However, this type of response, depending on exogenous factors that constitute the identity of the non Higher Public Education Institutions, in some cases, ends up creating a cyclical effect of complexity, making it necessary to adjust instruments that allow effective participation of all stakeholders in medium and long term decision making.

In Portugal, the tension of this multilevel management has been shown between two poles: on the one hand, between the policies suggested by the supranational and international institutions and the convergence of national and local policies; On the other hand, between the state intervention and the new forms of participation of new stakeholders, representatives of society (see Figure 1 and 2).

At the transnational level we have the objective of strategic results management with the strong incentive to use benchmarking practices (comparison of results and control of these, for exemple, PISA). At national and lower levels, the process is decentralization – almost a denationalization, according to Justino & Batista (2013) – with the transfers of skills to the levels immediately below, where the management of procedures dictates the entire mechanism. At the regional and local level the transfer of skills. This state control of procedures is manifested, for exemple, in data collection through electronic platforms directly from schools (NHPEI) – see Figure 2)

Figure 1. Multilevel governance model
Source: Adapted from (Justino & Batista, 2013)

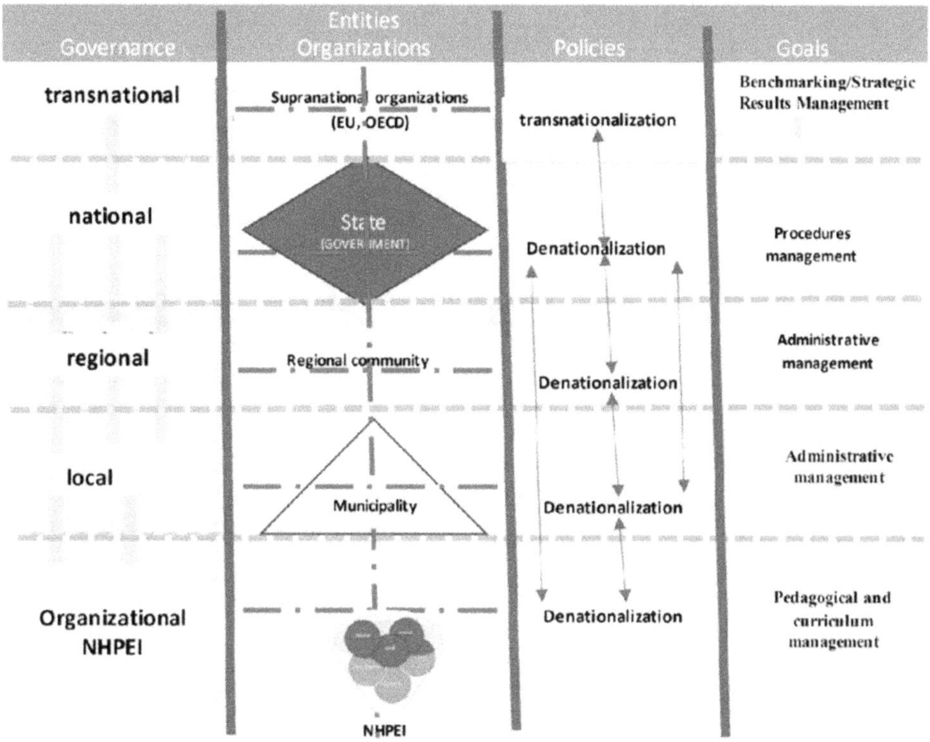

At the regional and local level the transfer of skills (Lei n.º 50/2018, de 16 de agosto, and Lei n.º 21/2019, de 30 de janeiro), It aims to simplify administrative management through the intercity communities - regional municipal groups - and municipalities. Currently, intercity communities generate school transport, and the offer of vocational education, and municipalities generate non -teaching human resources, cafeterias and school meals, physical resources and buildings and social support to the school community.

At the micro level, at the organizational level is the non higher public education institutions that is responsible for pedagogical management and part of curriculum management (25% of curriculum management, the remaining 75% managed by the central state). We consider that at this level a deconcentration is processed - transfer of competences - than decentralization, as the transfers of competences are accompanied by little autonomy and resources for the management and decision of these same attributions (see Figure 2).

Figure 2. Multilevel governance scheme
Source: adapted from (Justino & Batista, 2013)

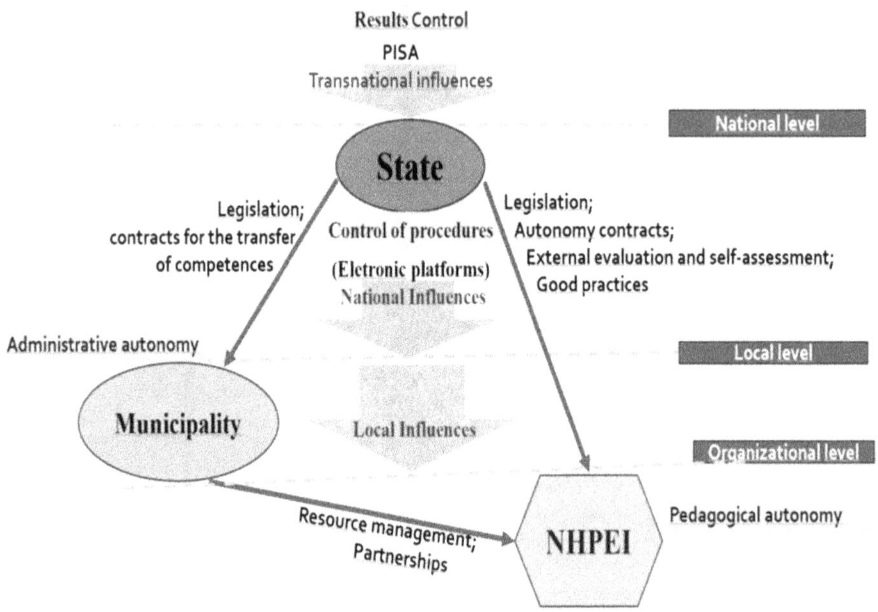

Our empirical analysis is dedicated to the micro level, at the level of the non Higher Public Education Institutions, and falls on the new governance body, the general council and its operating change before the Covid-19 pandemic with the new governance model and the Verification of possible changes in governance behavior during pandemic, with the distance from the school's physically stakeholders. The general council is the only collegial body in the current governance model in education in Portugal, which reflects the change of paradigm through the principles of the new public governance, legitimizing the new external stakeholders - representatives of society - in the decision making of the strategic direction of the institution.

2. THE GENERAL COUNCIL AS A MANAGEMENT BODY IN THE DEMOCRATIC MODEL OF THE NON-HIGHER PUBLIC EDUCATION INSTITUTIONS

The governance model, instituted it includes the two governance bodies: the general council and the Director. The general council is the high school, strategic management and is a single deliberative body, with democratic participation, now with new actors outside the non Higher Public Education Institutions: guardians of education, municipality and representatives of society (see Figure 3).

The executive body, the director, is now unipessoal, elected (with the possibility of being dismissed) by the general council (see Figure 3).

Figure 3. Composition general council/director
Source: Own elaboration

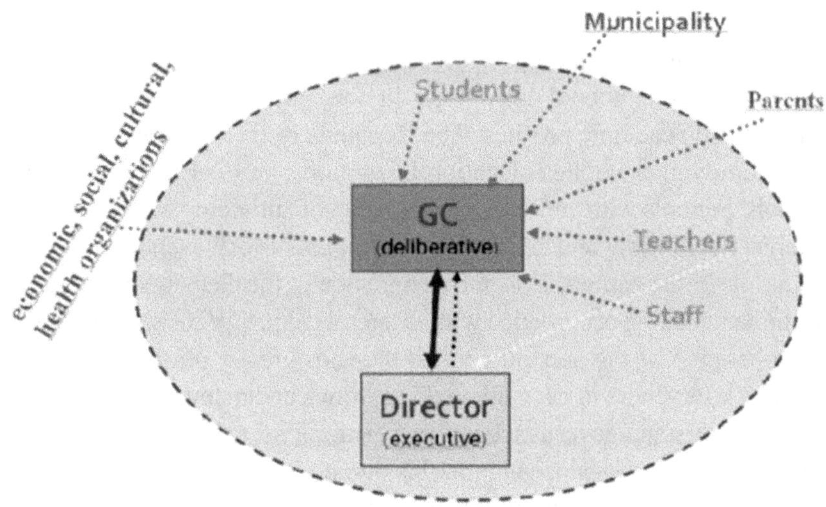

Source: Own elaboration

This democraticity with the entry of new stakeholders into the strategic management body induces a certain dynamic and complexity to the decision making of the institutions. The representation of society is ensured by the presence of actors from economic organizations, health and culture cooperated in the local community.

In this new dynamics of operation of the general council, participation and representation are two dimensions much linked to each other, as part of the study of public governance models (Kooiman, 2010). The participation of each representative element, whether it opts for an attitude/position of agent or steward[1] - implies an informal mechanism of interaction with the various actors of the general council (Bevir, 2010).

Case Study

From the perspective of realizing how the governance model has been implemented in the non higher public education institutions in Portugal, we decided to conduct an investigation through a case study, because only in this way can we know how effectively the model of Governance, that is, asking the various actors intervening in the process, what perceptions they have. However, we replicated data collection at the end of the Covid-19 pandemic, which we had made until 2019.

In this study, we followed a qualitative methodology by adopting the principles of Grounded Theory (Corbin & Strauss, 2008), with the empirical analysis of a case study of multiple units (Yin, 2015).

We considered four school groupings in the same county, with different socioeconomic and academic profiles. The four units of the case study include all types of the non -Higher Public Education Institutions: vertical school groupings; United schools; Schools with and without a contract of autonomy with the state and also of different teaching degrees and socioeconomic profile of the school community.

The legal rule of the composition and designation of the elements of the general council is implemented in accordance with Decreto-Lei n.º 75/2008, de 22 de abril. In fact, the operation of the general council depends greatly on the attitudes and behaviors of its interveners in decision making, so we understand that it is of great importance to understand governance in these institutions, to know the perceptions of each of them actors who participate In this organ.

The sample found for this work (in the phase before the COVI-19) was closed by theoretical saturation (Glaser & Strauss, 2006), justified by the type of qualitative investigation and meeting the principles of Grounded Theory. Saturation was reached when we realized that the inclusion of new respondents no longer added to the reflection based on the data regarding the dimensions considered, when the twenty -nine interviews conducted (Denzin & Lincoln, 2005).

We used different empirical materials - semi -structured interviews (to the elements of all groups represented in the general council, including the director of the institutions and the chairman of the general council), formal and non -formal documents of each non Higher Public Education Institutions, daily fieldwork and focus groups. The data collected were triangulated and subject to different analysis techniques, which allowed us to ensure their credibility and validity (Bevir, 2017; Bevir & Rhodes, 2007). This first data collection dedicated to academic work was performed before the Covid-19 pandemic in Portugal, and the questions were returned to their respondents, with the same criterion, in 2022, after the reopening of schools and in-person meetings of the general council.

The research issues we have made – *How is the new governance model in the non Higher Public Education institutions being implemented? And how do the various elements of the general council participate in the decision making of Non Higher Public Education Institutions?* – allow the understanding of the context and perspectives of the participants, only possible with the conduct of qualitative research. Data analysis was thus carried out based on content analysis according to the principles followed by Bardin (2016).

In 2022, already in a state of pandemic control in Portugal, with the reopening of schools and after the long period of the general council meetings, we returned the questions to the respondents of the previous investigation – having only been replaced by some respondents from the previous phase to Pandemic, by their peers in these organs, of the non higher public education institutions - and we ask them to contextualize the answers in the experience after the pandemic.

A category for coding of the material considered for content analysis was prepared, coding was carried out with the support of Maxqda 2018 software according to the codes book made, facilitating systematic work, more quickly, rigorously and allowing the comparison and systematic validation of the data considered (Seale, 2002).

The triangulation of the data and the careful definition of the categories, in the context of content analysis performed, allowed to identify the main dimensions of the theme under study and to understand how they relate, according to the model we arrived in the first phase of investigation (before pandemic).

On the other hand, the validation of coding became indispensable through inter judge coding reliability, in the same context and with the same book of codes, enabling the reduction of errors or bias (Muñoz-Leiva, Montoro Ríos, & Luque Martínez, 2006). We performed other tests such as the Cohen Kappa coefficient - with 622 coding compared by each jury, 89% were of agreement, resulting in a cohen kappa of 0.88, translating good reliability, according to the Cohen analysis scale (Cohen, 1960).

Results Analyzed

Regarding the general councils of the Study Units, and in compliance with the legal provisions, each agency is composed of twenty -one, representatives of the various stakeholder groups, ensuring that the number of teachers and staff does not exceed 50% of the total number of organ elements.

We considered in our sample twenty -nine respondents, each element of a group represented in the general council, in the four study units, to which we added the president of the body and the director (who is not part of the general council, but is invited Assiduous of all meetings of the agency and participates as if it were an element of the agency) of each non Higher Public Education Institutions.

The theoretical review of governance models in education allowed to immediately identify two important dimensions - representation and participation - that we analyzed in detail in our multiple case studies.

According to (Kooiman, 2010), the representation assumes two forms: the symbolic - when the representative represents something undefined or an absent group - and the descriptive - when the representative participates for himself, but in the name of someone. In this case, with the exception of representatives of the municipality and the local community (society), all have a descriptive representation. On the other hand, representatives of the general council are designated in three different ways: elected by peers - teachers, staff and students; nominated - elements of the municipality, or, co-opted by the body-representatives of the local community (Decreto-Lei n.º 75/2008, de 22 de abril).

The perception that each respondent has regarding his representation and the way he conditiones his participation in decision making, reflects the democraticity in the organ and guarantees him from different eyes, behaviors and interests in the general council (Lima, 2012).

Regarding the perception of their role, that is, who actually represent decision making, twenty five of the twenty -nine respondents (86%) assume that they represent themselves and do not consider that they represent their represented, nor the Its pairs of the body, having aggravated this percentage after the pandemic, verifying twenty seven of the twenty-nine respondents (93%): *"Pretend that I tell, my role is make -believe"* (community representative); *"With the pandemic each one spoke for themselves, nor the conviviality of the teacher room was at the time of coffee, and there is this removal of wanting to deal with serious subjects"* (teacher).

However, sixteen of the twenty-nine manifest that they follow the opinion of the director, regardless of his own opinion, having aggravated in the postpandy, manifested by twenty-one of the twenty-nine respondents: *"Who influences is the director, of rest goes everything with him"*(parents); *"Now, during the pandemic, you are still more noticeable than those who say what it is to do, and no one contradicts it, A is the director, now communication between people is much smaller, perhaps because of the habit we had in the pandemic to be isolated, Everyone would rather say yes and continue* "(chairman of the general council).

The twenty respondents of the twenty-nine followed the opinion and decision of the teachers represented (before the pandemic) and, in turn, the teachers did the same before the decision or any opinion of the director. If it was this before the pandemic, now they still manifest the same opinion more firmly.

Understandably, it is no wonder that twenty-four of the twenty-nine stated that the director's presence in the body was the great influence of the group's decision making as a whole and that now (after the pandemic) If this same perception: *"The director does not let anyone send, only he sends and decides. What he says is like*

King" (chairman of the general council); *"Nothing has improved with the distance in the meetings during the pandemic, quite the opposite and, even I think the director even has more power"* (teacher).

The concept of participation is studied here within the conceptual structure of governance in education in non -higher education. Participation is analyzed considering the representatives of a democratic and heterogeneous decision body, with a specific look, in relation to effective behaviors and attitudes, regarding the objectives to be achieved. From the moment each element assumes its place in the general council is not allowed to choose to participate or not, it only has the freedom to participate in a different way – "non –participation" is a way to participate (Pinto, 2000).

According to data collection, we analyzed the following categories in relation to participation: i) decision making; ii) democraticity; iii) regulation; iv) degrees of involvement; v) guidance; vi) expectations to enter the organ; vii) constraints; viii) confidence; ix) communication and x) information.

We share here, only the results of seven of these ten categories, the most noticed:

Decision making, regardless of each of the stakeholders representing their peers or themselves, as we have seen, is important to understand how the group's decision (organ) influences. Pateman (1992) analyzes three levels of participation: total, partial and pseudo -partition. The results on the representation had already shown that the teachers (twenty) induced decision making, including the strong opinion of the director, who themselves assumed to follow. Teachers control the decision, based on the opinion of the director, having a total (or almost total) participation in the decision making of the general council: *"Whatever, the teachers fully obey the director... All well controlled by the director"* (municipality); *"The decision is all concentrated in the principal and those who are evaluated by him inside the school, especially the teachers, nothing has changed for the better during the pandemic, but rather centralism is still in the principal and I think it is still much larger. During the pandemic and with the distance of teachers at school, the principal was alone to decide and command."* (teacher).

Despite this majority opinion of the respondents, twelve of the twenty -nine agreed with the presence of the director in all meetings of the general council and thirteen referred to the importance of being present to inform the entire body, considering that the director could be present only in Beginning of each meeting or being present in just a few meetings according to the agenda, this opinion remains in the same proportion. Finally, only four respondents did not agree with the director's presence at the general council meetings, which remains as well. The same analysis of perception is maintained after the pandemic, with the marked importance that one has to acquire greater freedom to express opinion, even before the presence of the director: *"There has to be the courage to say all this in the presence of the director and not to be thinking about what can hurt us directly or indirectly."* (staff).

Perhaps for all of this, eighteen of the twenty -nine respondents assumed to have the perception of getting in the general council having a pseudoParticipation, that is, their participation did not influence the decision making at the agency. In the postpandeia phase, this feeling was still reinforced and now, by twenty and one respondents: *"We are there to say yes... the director decides everything and then we approve to go well... He does the documents, he thinks the documents, it has to be everything as he wants "* (student); *"With the pandemic nothing changed in this respect, if it continues, as it was and the other colleagues who were there in the previous term also said, but it is even there, we do nothing, we change the decision at all. We are students and they are the parents or teachers, they send it."* (student). Part of the respondents (nine) understood that in part they were able to interfere in some way in partial points of the decision making, but recognized and (now) recognize that decision making is influenced by those who have a so -called total participation, although not being element of the general council, that is, the director.

The degrees of involvement, as a criterion of participation, are reflected in the attitudes and behaviors of the participants. According to Lima (1998), there can be a participation: active-with a great commitment of the participant-passive-translates an alienation or total disinterest, in a position of "extra"- or reserved-being an intermediate point of involvement and interest in the agency's meetings and actions.

Regarding the perception of an active participation, only one president of the general council and a director showed it: *"I give my opinion, yes... we always do together, me and the director... we have a Franco dialogue"* (chairman of the general council) . On the other hand, regarding a reserved participation, there were eight respondents, from the twenty -nine: *"I participate little, which they really ask me"* (teacher). Most (nineteen) were aware that their participation is substantially passive, now, in the postpandy, they have further and firmer further and more firmly: *"I prefer to be quiet and only participate if it is very necessary. Vote what the director wants and so is all right."* (teacher); *"As I said before the pandemic, it remains. And now the meetings and meetings for zoom, without being eyes, still allowed to be more sure that it is accepting what comes to the meeting and nothing more, it is not there that anything is decided... "* (teacher). The same type of response is maintained, in general, of all respondents, after the school closure period, with distance contacts, through digital platforms.

External stakeholders manifest this passivity (before and after pandemic) in about 83% of respondents, while internal stakeholders by about 53% (in the case of teachers, 50% respond that they are passive and the rest understands to be reserved, but none deemed active).

The guidance for participation, according to Pinto (2000) - based, in part, in Bajoit (1988) - and Lima (1998) can be: convergent - aligning personal objectives with those of the organ or organization -; divergent - to misalign personal objectives with those of the organ or organization, even if it is temporary, or a form of protest, or provocation for change (for good causes); apathic - the individual does only what is asked, nothing more - and finally abandonment - as a condition of rupture with the organ or the organization, or even with someone responsible.

Only ten of the twenty -six respondents to this question recognized having a convergent guidance (although they refer to the appearance given by unanimously the voting, given the reference to the influence of the director in these votes): *"There are no problems, a school knows... it's just unanimity."* (municipality). Sharing the rest for having a divergent participation (three), *"in normal affairs... yes, I am always against."* (non-teaching); apathetic (seven) *"I have to be there and let it pass"* (student); or abandonment (six) *"approve and that's it, no one wants to know and I don't either."* (parents). Nothing changed for the better, after the experience with the pandemic, on the contrary, the unanimity of the votes (according to the minutes) were, almost 100%. Not because they are all even in agreement, but for *"leaving as it is, that is, the director's opinion prevails. It is not the distance, in the computer score, that we will be discussing opinions to end everything agreeing with the director's proposal."* (teacher).

Expectations to the entry of the various elements of the general council in the agency, they were referred to as very positive and motivating by twenty -two of the twenty -nine respondents, and is even relevant to the acceptance of the place in the organ. Only seven did not express having had any expectations at the outset, when the initial invitation. From expectations, the most noticed subcategories were: effective participation in decision making (ten); the interest of the represented (nine); the recognition of legitimacy (five); the liberation of participation (four). However, after the experience of participation during at least a term in the general council, many consider it to have less expectations (or even none), once again, the perception of the school period remained during the school period during the school the pandemic.

The most referenced **constraints** were: the limits to freedom of participation; illusory participation, conflicts, disinterest of the represented, the lack of recognition of legitimacy, structural formalisms, and others, such as the lack of time, or the lack of information for the decision, or the lack of recognition of the general council .

Regarding **confidence** we identified two types: Trust and Reliance. We still considered Trust negative and positive (functioning the negative in certain cases, such as distrust) and internal reliance, in turn, positive and negative. Sixteen respondents, of the twenty-seven who corresponded to this question, assumed a negative Trust: *"This is a person with no possibility of trusting. Who does not inspire confidence to anyone... My trust in him is total distrust."* (chairman of the general council), in which nine of them do not trust the director as a person - who participates in virtually all the agency meetings and five expressed the same perception as to the president of the agency.

As for the positive Trust, the targets remain the same: the director with five respondents and six relatively to the chairman of the body and two teachers.

Regarding the reliance, at the general council level, of twenty-two respondents, thirteen refer it as negative and eleven of these thirteen respondents identify the director body: *"There is the director there, but it really says that there is no right to suspicion, but there is, if there is... "* (municipality).

However, still nine respondents, they refer to it as positive, with six respondents to reference the director before and after the pandemic experience.

As for **the information,** which we understand how the message conveyed between the issuer and the receiver, we considered two subcategories: the sought and the available.

The information sought is nonexistent to help decision making (triangula, to confirm this data, with document analysis, in this case the minutes). The justification presented by the respondents, in general, is the lack of time. They have no time availability to treat issues outside the meetings and, even at the meeting, the agenda is very overwhelmed. In addition to the lack of time, they claim the lack of their own staff for the general council, which would facilitate confirmation of the information provided by the director and facilitated the research of more information needed for a conscious decision making. During the closing of schools, during the pandemic, less information was sought, beyond the evolution of the disease and the measures to have in schools.

Regarding the information provided to the elements of the general council, the respondents claim to be all sent only by the director, according to the agenda that establishes him with the president of the body: *"We do not have the information we want, but to which the director wants... Everything comes prepared by the director.*" (local community). Fact that became bound during the pandemic.

The possibility of existence of an available information asymmetry is large, according to some respondents, because most of the agenda matters are documents presented by the director, for approval by the general council (see Figure 4 and 5).

Schematically we reached the next analysis model:

Figure 4. Governance analysis model in non higher education
Source: own elaboration

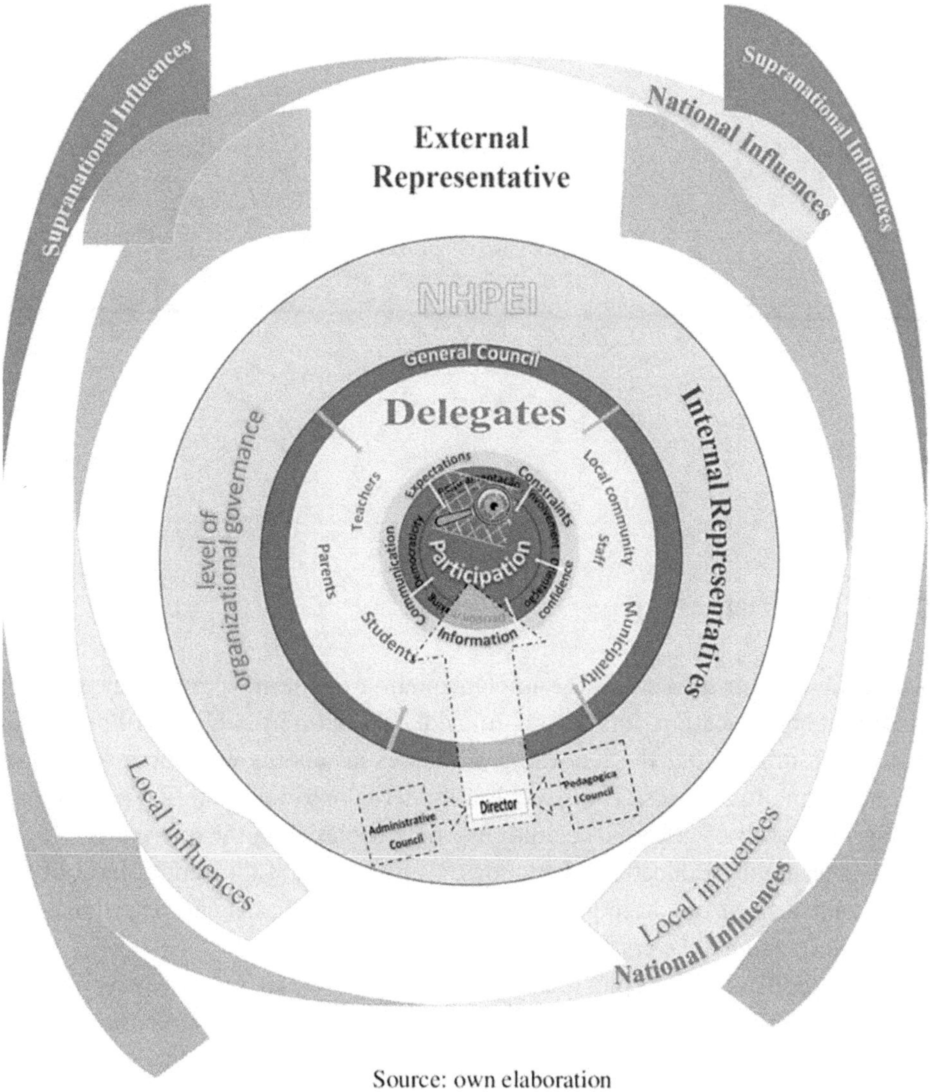

Source: own elaboration

Figure 5. Participation in the general council of NHPEI
Source: own elaboration

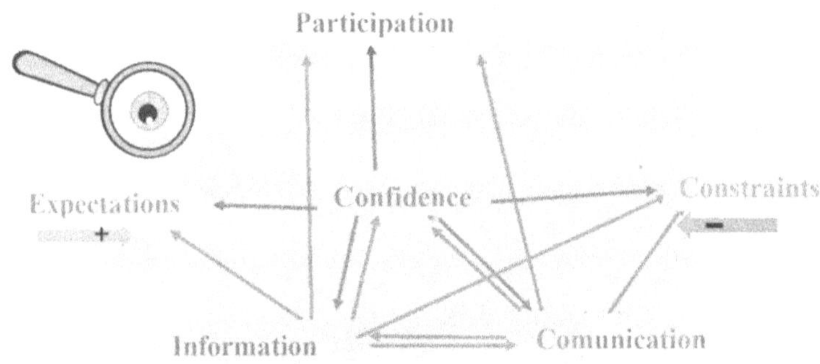

CONCLUSION

This analysis aimed to study the implementation of the new governance model in non-higher education, in Portugal immediately before the Covid-19 pandemic and was resumed, after the reopening of classes in schools with the resuming of general council meetings. The structural model is notoriously influenced among the various levels of governance, until its implementation at the micro level, ie the non Higher Public Education Institutions. Construction at the central level of the state is influenced by altering supranational level paradigms and determines the various infranational layers.

As a theoretical or conceptual basis we follow the governance perspectives that best filed our work (Bevir, 2017; Klijn, 2010; Kooiman, 1993, 2010; Osborne, 2010; Pierre & Peters, 2020; Rhodes, 1997) and adapted to the system of Portuguese education. The coexistence of a multilevel and network governance in education accumulates the coordination of stakeholders at various levels, much by the contribution of the evolution of globalization. However, despite supranational influences and the obligation to transpose norms and adapt international policies, dynamics have no heavy meaning and has been adaptable at national level (Kooiman, 2008).

The challenge of good governance in complex organizations (in non Higher Public Education Institutions) is to find a fluid and healthy communication relationship, with autonomy and freedom based on symmetrical and transparent information, so that the participation of the various actors in taking Decision can be active and convergent, in a climate of organizational trust.

Regarding the type of representation in the organ, each member (external or internal stakeholder) has the notion that it represents some group and not themselves. However, confronted with the question, only four did not answer that they represented themselves and their interests.

The effective role of participation in the general council was referred to only a small minority (teachers). The vast majority are aware that he has an illusory role, "extra" to have a quorum at the general council meeting, without any influence on decision making, and therefore, there is a conscious pseudoParticipation of a large number of Respondents, since they are largely limited to accepting the decisions of other elements without any action.

The heterogeneity of the various stakeholders in the general council would predict a diversity of involvement and consequently their participation. However, we were surprised that most of the elements assume to have a passive participation. The expectations to the entrance of the organ were lost and the embarrassment became real, as we found. The convergent guidance verified in the decision-making votes was apparent, since most expressed that they were influenced by the opinion of the director or teachers (who, in turn, follow the director's willingness), which explains That, on average, more than 80% of decisions are made unanimously - an elaborate unanimity.

In any case, the unexpected closure of schools and the rapid need for adaptation of the school community to the resource of teaching and governance of multimodal distance (digital, television, printed, etc…) showed the resilience of the system (Santos, 2021). The proposed digitization goals for a decade later, were accelerated in a few days allowing a surprising digitization of portuguese society and, in particular, the educational community. If on the one hand, it brought several stakeholders closer to schools for the rapid adaptation and solving of pedagogical problems, apparently distanced communication between them at the governance unit (the school), according to our fieldwork. Although not a direct goal of our empirical study, the school during the pandemic has discovered the socioeconomic inequalities of students and families: overcrowded houses for a learning environment, lack of computer resources and internet access, among many others.

Based on the work done, and after some discussion with experts and elements of the outbreaks, it is possible to advance with some good practices recommendations for the governance of the general council.

Some general principles:

- The general council is composed of a plural and heterogeneous set of actors (internal stakeholders and external to the organization), which participates, communicates with transparency and establishes a relationship of trust.
- The general council should not be dominated by any of the groups represented in it, nor by someone who holds a position of evaluator before any of the elements of the general council.
- Decision making of the general council should be based on a dynamic and democratic process, with the effective involvement of all elements.
- All elements of the general council must have conditions appropriate to the full exercise of their functions.

Recommendations:

i) The general council must, previously to co -optation, establish the selection and profile criteria of the members to coopt, in line with the structuring and strategic internal documents of Non Higher Public Education Institutions.
ii) The general council shall provide initial formation to all its members, which includes, in particular, technical literacy and content of the functions and objectives of the agency, in order to equitably level the necessary knowledge of the free and autonomous participation of each element in the Council general.
iii) The director must ensure the production and circulation of information in a timely, rigorous and transparent manner.
iv) The general council must deliberate on the means and instruments necessary for its operation and the exercise of its competences, and may have its own budget registered in the Management Account of Non Higher Public Education Institutions, Administrative Support and Consulting Service own.
v) Periodically (semiannual or quarterly), the director must present to the general council a report of compliance with objectives and the plan, as an instrument of monitoring, evaluation and work base for an executive improvement plan.
vi) The presence of the director at each general council meeting must be considered given the need of the agency to obtain information and its competence for the supervision it exercises.

The adoption of a qualitative approach based on Grounded Theory was thoughtful, despite the possible inevitable risks - even though it met all the recommended criteria for the least possible deviation - since we wanted to understand and describe a phenomenon in a complex context, with detail and Depth, in the middle of real ground, where the structural model of governance is implemented. The variety of discourses, techniques and practices added knowledge and through it we achieved different perspectives of the study of the same object, which allowed us new results in the development of an empirically grounded governance model based on the data collected and the observed context. The analysis earlier and after an unexpected phenomenon, such as pandemic, where schools have had to reinvent distance learning processes and tools, may allow you to provide some new elements to consider in a future strategic plan.

The fact that we chose a multiple case study with four non Higher Public Education institutions can be considered a limitation, but we understand to be an advantage because it allows directly and detailed to collect data from various actors in their usual context.

Possible generalization is analytical, that is, it can be replicated in the reinterpretation of existing studies or concrete cases or new cases, and also induce new questions or include those we put here in future investigations.

Interestingly, the studies conducted in the scope of higher education present conclusions very similar to those we arrived in this investigation. The director's figure is replaced by the rector, equally elected and deprived by the new strategic management body, the general council, as in non -higher education. This new deliberative body has opened universities and polytechnic to society through the admission of external stakeholders. The composition, in addition to the freedom of the number of elements of the agency, has another important difference regarding non -higher education: the obligation to elect a president who is an external stakeholder, representative of society (Lei n.º 62/2007, de 10 de setembro).

Among the works published on governance, specifically on the general council in Higher Education and whose empirical analysis is the most similar to the work done here (Oliveira, Peixoto, & Silva, 2014), presents considerations very similar to those we arrived for this study of case. Regarding the information provided for decision making in the general council, this is sent by the dean who has his own staff (such as the director) - a situation that is claimed at both levels of education because it does not happen in the face of the elements of the general council. Also in this study, the lack of time on the part of the elements of the general council is a justification for not seeking information. As well as the presence of the dean - just as that of the director - is noted as an influence on behavior, attitude and the participation of the elements of the general council and, specifically, on decision making - which eventually accompanies the Rector's opinion (or the director). As for the agenda of each meeting is compact, extensive and indicated tendentially by the rector (as with the director). The role of the rector at the meetings is that of a protagonist, no doubt the central figure, around which everything unfolds, like the director.

It would be recommended that, in the future, the governance model in education and its conceptual relations, as well as the recommendations we suggest here, be tested in the non higher public education institutions, adapting to different contexts and each school. The continuity of other work points, in time, that allows longitudinal analysis from these data and from this perspective to contribute to governance more adapted to new times, innovation, new technologies and digitization in education in a form sustainable.

If any lesson to Covid-19 may have left us to citizens and institutions that they have to know how to deal with more resilience to uncertainty that is real, may have even changed the way of thinking, attitudes and actions in this new normal life.

REFERENCES

Bajoit, G. (1988). Exit, voice, loyalty... and apathy. Les réactions individuelles au mécontentement. *Persée - Revue française de sociologie*(n.º 29-2), 325-345.

Bardin, L. (2016). *Análise de conteúdo*. Lisboa: Edições 70.

Barroso, J. (2017). Centralização, descentralização, autonomia e controlo. In *O Governo das Escolas. Democracia, controlo e performatividade* (pp. 23–40). Edições Húmus.

Barroso, J. (2018). A Transversalidade das Regulações em Educação: Modelo de Análise para o Estudo das Políticas Educativas em Portugal. *Educação & Sociedade, 39*(145), 1075-1097.

Bevir, M. (2010). *Democratic Governance*. Princeton University Press. doi:10.1515/9781400836857

Bevir, M. (2017). Mainstreaming Moments in Governance Theories: Some Observations. *Journal of Asian Review of Public Affairs and Policy, 2*(3), 23-54.

Bevir, M., & Rhodes, R. A. W. (2007). Decentred Theory, Change and Network Governance. In *Theories of Democratic Network Governance* (pp. 77–91). Palgrave Macmillan. doi:10.1057/9780230625006_5

Cohen, J. (1960). A Coefficient of Agreement for Nominal Scales. *Educational and Psychological Measurement, 20*(1), 37-46.

Corbin, J. M., & Strauss, A. L. (2008). Basics of Qualitative Research: Techniques and Procedures for Developing Grounded Theory. Los Angeles: Sage Publications.

Davis, J. H., Schoorman, F. D., & Donaldson, L. (1997). Toward a Stewardship Theory of Management. *The Academy of Management Review, 22*(1), 20-47.

Denzin, N. K., & Lincoln, Y. S. (2005). The SAGE Handbook of Qualitative Research (3.ª ed.). Londres: SAGE Publications.

Frey, B. S. (1997). *Not Just for the Money: An Economic Theory of Personal Motivation*. Edward Elgar Publishing.

Glaser, B. G., & Strauss, A. L. (2006). *The Discovery of Grounded Theory: Strategies for Qualitative Research*. Aldine Publishing.

Justino, D., & Batista, S. (2013). Redes de escolas e modos de regulação do sistema educativo. In Educação - Temas e Problemas, 12(13), 41-60.

Klijn, E. H. (2010). Trust in governance networks: looking for conditions for innovative solutions and outcomes. In S. P. Osborne (Ed.), *The New Public Governance?* (pp. 303–321). Routledge.

Kooiman, J. (1993). Social-Political Governance: Introduction. In J. Kooiman (Ed.), *Modern Governance: New Government–Society Interactions* (pp. 1–8). SAGE.

Kooiman, J. (2008). Exploring the Concept of Governability. *Journal of Comparative Policy Analysis, 10*(2), 171-190.

Kooiman, J. (2010). Governance and governability. In S. P. Osborne (Ed.), *The New Public Governance?* (pp. 72–86). Routledge.

Lima, L. C. (1998). A Escola como Organização e a Participação na Organização Escolar (2.ª ed.). Braga: Universidade do Minho.

Lima, L. C. (2012). Democratização da Escola, Participação Comunitária e Cidadania Critica. *Princípios Gerais da Administração Escolar, 1*, 148-157. http://www.acervodigital.unesp.br/handle/123456789/65259

Muñoz-Leiva, F., Montoro Ríos, F. J., & Luque Martínez, T. (2006). Assessment of Interjudge Reliability in the Open-Ended Questions Coding Process. *Quality & Quantity, 40*(4), 519-537.

OECD. (2017). Résultats du PISA 2015: Vol. II. *Politiques et Pratiques pour des Établissements Performants*. OECD.

Osborne, S. P. (2010). The (New) Public Governance: a suitable case for treatment? In S. P. Osborne (Ed.), *The New Public Governance?* (pp. 1–17). Routledge. doi:10.4324/9780203861684

Pateman, C. (1992). *Participação e teoria democrática*. Paz e Terra.

Pierre, J., & Peters, B. G. (2020). *Governance, Politics and the State*. Red Globe Press.

Pinto, C. A. (2000). Sociologia da Escola (4.ª ed.). Lisboa: MConselho Geralraw Hill.

Rhodes, R. A. W. (1997). *Understanding Governance: Policy Networks, Governance, Reflexivity and Accountability*. Open University Press.

Rodrigues, A. A. D. d. O. N. e. (2013). Uma análise comparativa entre a Teoria da Agência e a Stewardship. *Revista Fafibe On-Line, Ano VI*(6), 67-77.

Santos, M. E. B. (2021). *Efeitos da pandemia COVID-19 na educação: Desigualdades e medidas de equidade*. Conselho Nacional de Educação.

Seale, C. (2002). Quality Issues in Qualitative Inquiry. *Qualitative Social Work, 1*(1), 97-110.

Yin, R. K. (2015). Estudo de Caso: Planejamento e Métodos (5.ª ed.). Porto Alegre: Bookman.

ENDNOTE

1 According to the agency theory, within the organization, each individual (agent) should consider the goals of this one before their own goals while for Stewardship Theory, this each element (Steward) interacts and aligns individual goals with those of the organization itself. (Frey, 1997; Rodrigues, 2013). In the case of non Higher Public Education Institutions, groups represented in the General Council may choose to have their own interests to satisfy and defend - for example: students, teachers, staff and parents - or, given their collective importance of Non Higher Public Education Institutions for Society, the extent of greater interest - the public and social interest, such as education - common to the whole organization should prevail. (Davis, Schoorman, & Donaldson, 1997). It may always be an option for each representative in the General Council to behave as an agent or be steward. It can even coexist in the same organ different options of decision making that identifies within the two papers.

Compilation of References

Abdelhalim, K. (2010). Participatory Upgrading of Informal Areas: A Decision-makers' Guide for Action. Cairo: Participatory Development Programme in Urban Areas (PDP) in Egypt.

Åberg, A. C., Elf, M., Nordmark, S., Lyhagen, J., Lindberg, I., & Finch, T. (2018). 66 *The swedish version of the normalisation process theory measurement s-nomad: translation, adaptation, and pilot testing*. Biomed Central.

AbouKorin, S. A., Han, H., & Mahran, M. G. (2021). Role of urban planning characteristics in forming pandemic resilient cities – Case study of Covid-19 impacts on European cities within England, Germany and Italy. *Cities (London, England)*, *118*, 103324. doi:10.1016/j.cities.2021.103324 PMID:34539022

Acioly, C. (2021). Street-Led Citywide Slum Upgrading: Connecting the Informal and the Formal City Through Area-Based Planning and Infrastructure Improvement. In O. García-Villalba, Resilient Urban Regeneration in Informal Settlements in the Tropics: Upgrading Strategies in Asia and Latin America (pp. 11-35). Singapore: Springer Nature Singapore. doi:10.1007/978-981-13-7307-7_2

Aduhene, D. T., & Osei-Assibey, E. (2021). Socio-economic impact of COVID-19 on Ghana's economy: Challenges and prospects. *International Journal of Social Economics*, *48*(4), 543–556. doi:10.1108/IJSE-08-2020-0582

Agariya, A. K., & Singh, D. (2012). e-Learning quality: Scale development and validation in Indian context. *Knowledge Management & E-Learning: An International Journal*, *4*(4), 500–517.

Ahorsu, D. K., Lin, C.-Y., Imani, V., Saffari, M., Griffiths, M. D., & Pakpour, A. H. (2022). The Fear of COVID-19 Scale: Development and Initial Validation. *International Journal of Mental Health and Addiction*, *20*(3), 1537–1545. doi:10.100711469-020-00270-8 PMID:32226353

Akdeniz, G., Kavakci, M., Gozugok, M., Yalcinkaya, S., Kucukay, A., & Sahutogullari, B. (2020). A Survey of Attitudes, Anxiety Status, and Protective Behaviors of the University Students During the COVID-19 Outbreak in Turkey. *Frontiers in Psychiatry*, *11*(695), 1–9. doi:10.3389/fpsyt.2020.00695 PMID:32760303

Akour, A., Al-Tammemi, A. B., Barakat, M., Kanj, R., Fakhouri, H. N., Malkawi, A., & Musleh, G. (2020). The Impact of the COVID-19 Pandemic and Emergency Distance Teaching on the Psychological Status of University Teachers: A Cross-Sectional Study in Jordan. *The American Journal of Tropical Medicine and Hygiene, 103*(6), 2391–2399. doi:10.4269/ajtmh.20-0877 PMID:33124547

Akuffo-Addo. (2020). *Updates on how Measures taken against spread of the COVID-19*. Akuffo-Addo.

Al-Dairi, A. (2007). *Informal housing areas in Syria and linking them with the characteristics of families and population (In arabic)*. Damascus. http://cbssyr.sy/studies/st24.pdf

Alexis, S. J., Kumar, P. S. S. R., Vinoth, K. R., Ragul, V. V., & Kumar, N. S. (2018). Improved Mechanical Properties of AA5083 Reinforced with Multiwall Carbon Nanotubes for Automobile Applications. *International Journal of Vehicle Structures \& Systems, 10*(4), 278–281.

Alimohamadi, Y., Holakouie-Naieni, K., Sepandi, M., & Taghdir, M. (2020). Effect of social distancing on COVID-19 incidence and mortality in Iran since February 20 to May 13, 2020: An interrupted time series analysis. *Risk Management and Healthcare Policy*, *13*, 1695–1700. doi:10.2147/RMHP.S265079 PMID:33061703

Allam, Z., & Jones, S. (2020, September). Pandemic stricken cities on lockdown. Where are our planning and design professionals [now, then and into the future]. *Land Use Policy*, *97*, 104805. doi:10.1016/j.landusepol.2020.104805 PMID:32508374

Allwood, J. M., & Lee, W. L. (2004). The impact of job rotation on problem-solving skills. *International Journal of Production Research*, *42*(5), 865–881. doi:10.1080/0020754031000 1631566

Al-Ruwaili, A. K. (2017). *Real Estate Development and Investment Law (15) of 2008 AD and its amendments (In arabic)*. Damascus University.

Altena, E., Baglioni, C., Espie, C. A., Ellis, J., Gavriloff, D., Holzinger, B., Schlarb, A., Frase, L., Jernelöv, S., & Riemann, D. (2020). Dealing with sleep problems during home confinement due to the COVID-19 outbreak: Practical recommendations from a task force of the European CBT-I Academy. *Journal of Sleep Research*, *29*(4), 1–7. doi:10.1111/jsr.13052 PMID:32246787

Ameen, A., & Baharom, M. N. (2019). An appraisal of the effect of training on employee performance in an organization: A theoretical discussion. *Asian Journal of Multidisciplinary Studies*, *7*(3), 27–31.

American Psychological Association. (n.d.). *Road to resilience*. APA. http://www.apa.org/helpcenter/road-resilience.aspx

Ammar, N., Aly, N. M., Folayan, M. O., Khader, Y., Virtanen, J. I., Al-Batayneh, O. B., Mohebbi, S. Z., Attia, S., Howaldt, H.-P., Boettger, S., Maharani, D. A., Rahardjo, A., Khan, I., Madi, M., Rashwan, M., Pavlic, V., Cicmil, S., Choi, Y.-H., Joury, E., & El Tantawi, M. (2020). Behavior change due to COVID-19 among dental academics—The theory of planned behavior: Stresses, worries, training, and pandemic severity. *PLoS One*, *15*(9), e0239961. doi:10.1371/journal.pone.0239961 PMID:32991611

Anitha, C., R, K. C., Vivekanand, C. V., Lalitha, S. D., Boopathi, S., & R, R. (2023, February). Artificial Intelligence driven security model for Internet of Medical Things ({IoMT}). *IEEE Explore*. IEEE. doi:10.1109/ICIPTM57143.2023.10117713

Anner, M. (2020) *Abandoned? The Impact of Covid-19 on Workers and Businesses at the Bottom of Global Garment Supply Chains.*

Anttiroiko, A. V. (2021). Successful government responses to the pandemic: Contextualizing national and urban responses to the COVID-19 outbreak in east and west. [IJEPR]. *International Journal of E-Planning Research*, *10*(2), 1–17. doi:10.4018/IJEPR.20210401.oa1

Armstrong, M. (2005). *Armstrong's Handbook of Management and Leadership: Approaches to HRM and L&D*. Kogan Page Limited Publishing.

Arora, G., Joshi, J., Mandal, R. S., Shrivastava, N., Virmani, R., & Sethi, T. (2021). Artificial intelligence in surveillance, diagnosis, drug discovery and vaccine development against COVID-19. *Pathogens (Basel, Switzerland)*, *10*(8), 1048. doi:10.3390/pathogens10081048 PMID:34451513

Arslan, G., & Allen, K. A. (2022). Exploring the association between coronavirus stress, meaning in life, psychological flexibility, and subjective well-being. *Psychology Health and Medicine*, *27*(4), 803–814. doi:10.1080/13548506.2021.1876892 PMID:33487048

Asundi, A., O'Leary, C., & Bhadelia, N. (2021). Global COVID-19 vaccine inequity: The scope, the impact, and the challenges. *Cell Host & Microbe*, *29*(7), 1036–1039. doi:10.1016/j.chom.2021.06.007 PMID:34265241

Atkinson, J. W. (1964). *An introduction to motivation*. American Book.

Aziz, A., Islam, M. M., & Zakaria, M. (2020). COVID-19 exposes digital divide, social stigma, and information crisis in Bangladesh. *Media Asia*, *47*(3–4), 144–151. doi:10.1080/01296612.2020.1843219

Babu, B. S., Kamalakannan, J., Meenatchi, N., M, S. K. S., S, K., & Boopathi, S. (2023). Economic impacts and reliability evaluation of battery by adopting Electric Vehicle. *IEEE Explore*, 1–6. IEEE. doi:10.1109/ICPECTS56089.2022.10046786

Bajaj, R., Sinha, S., & Tiwari, V. (2013). Crucial factors of human resource management for good employee relations: A case study. *International Journal of Mining, Metallurgy, and Mechanical Engineering*, *1*(2), 90–92.

Bajoit, G. (1988). Exit, voice, loyalty... and apathy. Les réactions individuelles au mécontentement. *Persée - Revue française de sociologie*(n.° 29-2), 325-345.

Bakator, M., & Radosav, D. (2020). Analyzing the Digital Education Revolution. *International Conference on Information Technology and Development of Education-ITRO*. IEEE.

Bamfo, I., Sarfo, J. O., Ansah, E. W., & Amoah, S. K. (2020). The impact of health on economic development: Ghana's COVID-19 management so far. *European Journal of Economic Studies*, *9*(1), 3–10.

Band, R., Bradbury, K., Morton, K., May, C., Michie, S., Mair, F. S., Murray, E., McManus, R. J., Little, P., & Yardley, L. (2017). Intervention planning for a digital intervention for self-management of hypertension: A theory, evidence-and person-based approach. *Implementation Science : IS*, *12*(1), 1–13. doi:10.118613012-017-0553-4 PMID:28231840

Bantz, C. R. (1989). Organizing and the social psychology of organizing. *Communication Studies*, *40*(4), 231–240. doi:10.1080/10510978909368276

Bar, G. (2021). ADB Helps Bangladesh on Road to Recovery from COVID-19. *Asian Development Bank*.https://www.adb.org/results/adb-helps-bangladesh-road-recovery-covid-19

Bardin, L. (2016). *Análise de conteúdo*. Lisboa: Edições 70.

Bardoel, E. A., Pettit, T. M., De Cieri, H., & McMillan, L. (2014). Employee resilience: An emerging challenge for HRM. *Asia Pacific Journal of Human Resources*, *52*(3), 279–297. doi:10.1111/1744-7941.12033

Barnwal, A. (2020). *How can covid 19 steer city leadership sustainability?* Global Environment Facility. https://www.thegef.org/blog/how-covid-19-can-steer-city-leadership-sustainability

Barone, M. T. U., Ngongo, B., Harnik, S. B., de Oliveira, L. X., Végh, D., de Luca, P. V., Pedrosa, H. C., Giraudo, F., Cardona-Hernandez, R., Chaudhury, N., & Menna-Barreto, L. (2021). COVID-19 associated with diabetes and other noncommunicable diseases led to a global health crisis. *Diabetes Research and Clinical Practice*, *171*, 108587. doi:10.1016/j.diabres.2020.108587 PMID:33307134

Barroso, J. (2018). A Transversalidade das Regulações em Educação: Modelo de Análise para o Estudo das Políticas Educativas em Portugal. *Educação & Sociedade, 39*(145), 1075-1097.

Barroso, J. (2017). Centralização, descentralização, autonomia e controlo. In *O Governo das Escolas. Democracia, controlo e performatividade* (pp. 23–40). Edições Húmus.

Battiston, P., & Gamba, S. (2021). COVID-19: R0 is lower where outbreak is larger. *Health Policy (Amsterdam)*, *125*(2), 141–147. doi:10.1016/j.healthpol.2020.10.017 PMID:33309293

Behera, B. C. (2021). Challenges in handling COVID-19 waste and its management mechanism: A Review. *Environmental Nanotechnology, Monitoring \& Management, 15*, 100432.

Ben Salem, S., Mansour, N., & Haddad, M. (2020). Health Crisis (Covid-19) and the French Economy. *Journal of the International Academy for Case Studies*, *26*(5), 1–10.

Bereitschaft, B., & Scheller, D. (2020). How Might the COVID-19 Pandemic Affect 21st Century Urban Design, Planning, and Development? *Urban Science (Basel, Switzerland)*, *4*(4), 56–78. doi:10.3390/urbansci4040056

Berger, R., & Czakert, J. P. (2022). Stress Management and Resilience Building. In *Organisational Excellence and Resilience* (pp. 63–88). Springer., doi:10.1007/978-3-030-85120-0_2

Bernard, R., Bowsher, G., Sullivan, R., & Gibson-Fall, F. (2021). Disinformation and epidemics: Anticipating the next phase of biowarfare. *Health Security*, *19*(1), 3–12. doi:10.1089/hs.2020.0038 PMID:33090030

Bevir, M. (2017). Mainstreaming Moments in Governance Theories: Some Observations. *Journal of Asian Review of Public Affairs and Policy, 2*(3), 23-54.

Bevir, M. (2010). *Democratic Governance*. Princeton University Press. doi:10.1515/9781400836857

Bevir, M., & Rhodes, R. A. W. (2007). Decentred Theory, Change and Network Governance. In *Theories of Democratic Network Governance* (pp. 77–91). Palgrave Macmillan. doi:10.1057/9780230625006_5

BoG. (2020). *Summary of Economic and Financial Data*. Bank of Ghana, Accra. https://www.bog.gov.gh/wp-content/uploads/2020/08/Summary-of-Economic-and-Financial-Data-July-2020

BoG. (2022). *Summary of Economic and Financial Data. Bank of Ghana, Accra.* BoG. https://www.bog.gov.gh/wp-content/uploads/2022/08/Summary-of-Economic-and-Financial-Data-July-2022

Boopathi, S. (2021). Improving of Green Sand-Mould Quality using Taguchi Technique. *Journal of Engineering Research*. doi:10.36909/jer.14079

Boopathi, S., Arigela, S. H., Raman, R., Indhumathi, C., Kavitha, V., & Bhatt, B. C. (2023). Prominent Rule Control-based Internet of Things: Poultry Farm Management System. *IEEE Explore*, 1–6. IEEE. doi:10.1109/ICPECTS56089.2022.10047039

Boopathi, S., Khare, R., Jaya Christiyan, K. G., Muni, T. V., & Khare, S. (2023). Additive manufacturing developments in the medical engineering field. In Development, Properties, and Industrial Applications of 3D Printed Polymer Composites (pp. 86–106). IGI Global. doi:10.4018/978-1-6684-6009-2.ch006

Boopathi, S. (2022). Cryogenically treated and untreated stainless steel grade 317 in sustainable wire electrical discharge machining process: A comparative study. *Environmental Science and Pollution Research International*, 1–10. doi:10.100711356-022-22843-x PMID:36057706

Boopathi, S. (2022a). An experimental investigation of Quench Polish Quench (QPQ) coating on AISI 4150 steel. *Engineering Research Express*, *4*(4), 45009. doi:10.1088/2631-8695/ac9ddd

Boopathi, S. (2022b). An Extensive Review on Sustainable Developments of Dry and Near-Dry Electrical Discharge Machining Processes. *Journal of Manufacturing Science and Engineering*, *144*(5), 50801. doi:10.1115/1.4052527

Boopathi, S. (2022c). An investigation on gas emission concentration and relative emission rate of the near-dry wire-cut electrical discharge machining process. *Environmental Science and Pollution Research International*, *29*(57), 86237–86246. doi:10.100711356-021-17658-1 PMID:34837614

Boopathi, S. (2022e). Experimental investigation and multi-objective optimization of cryogenic Friction-stir-welding of AA2014 and AZ31B alloys using MOORA technique. *Materials Today. Communications*, *33*, 104937. doi:10.1016/j.mtcomm.2022.104937

Boopathi, S. (2022f). Performance Improvement of Eco-Friendly Near-Dry Wire-Cut Electrical Discharge Machining Process Using Coconut Oil-Mist Dielectric Fluid. *Journal of Advanced Manufacturing Systems*. doi:10.1142/S0219686723500178

Boopathi, S. (2023). An Investigation on Friction Stir Processing of Aluminum Alloy-Boron Carbide Surface Composite. In *Materials Horizons: From Nature to Nanomaterials* (pp. 249–257). Springer. doi:10.1007/978-981-19-7146-4_14

Boopathi, S., Balasubramani, V., & Sanjeev Kumar, R. (2023). Influences of various natural fibers on the mechanical and drilling characteristics of coir-fiber-based hybrid epoxy composites. *Engineering Research Express*, *5*(1), 15002. doi:10.1088/2631-8695/acb132

Boopathi, S., Haribalaji, V., Mageswari, M., & Asif, M. M. (2022). Influences of Boron Carbide Particles on the Wear Rate and Tensile Strength of Aa2014 Surface Composite Fabricated By Friction-Stir Processing. *Materiali in Tehnologije*, *56*(3), 263–270. doi:10.17222/mit.2022.409

Boopathi, S., Lewise, K. A. S., Subbiah, R., & Sivaraman, G. (2021). Near-dry wire-cut electrical discharge machining process using water-air-mist dielectric fluid: An experimental study. *Materials Today: Proceedings*, *49*(5), 1885–1890. doi:10.1016/j.matpr.2021.08.077

Boopathi, S., & Sivakumar, K. (2012). Experimental comparative study of near-dry wire-cut electrical discharge machining (WEDM). *European Journal of Scientific Research*, *75*(4), 472–481.

Boopathi, S., & Sivakumar, K. (2013). Experimental investigation and parameter optimization of near-dry wire-cut electrical discharge machining using multi-objective evolutionary algorithm. *International Journal of Advanced Manufacturing Technology*, *67*(9–12), 2639–2655. doi:10.100700170-012-4680-4

Boopathi, S., Thillaivanan, A., Azeem, M. A., Shanmugam, P., & Pramod, V. R. (2022). Experimental investigation on abrasive water jet machining of neem wood plastic composite. *Functional Composites and Structures*, *4*(2), 25001. doi:10.1088/2631-6331/ac6152

Boopathi, S., Venkatesan, G., & Anton Savio Lewise, K. (2023). Mechanical Properties Analysis of Kenaf–Grewia–Hair Fiber-Reinforced Composite. In *Lecture Notes in Mechanical Engineering* (pp. 101–110). Springer. doi:10.1007/978-981-16-9057-0_11

Botha, A., & Ford, M. (2008). "Digital Life Skills" for the young and mobile "Digital Citizens." *Policy*, 1–7. http://researchspace.csir.co.za/dspace/handle/10204/2513

Brahmankar, Y., Bedarkar, M., & Mishra, M. (2022). An entrepreneurial way of engaging student entrepreneurs at business school during pandemic. *International Journal of Innovation Science, 14*(3/4), 428–444. doi:10.1108/IJIS-11-2020-0264

Brandenburg, M. (2016). Supply chain efficiency, value creation and the economic crisis—An empirical assessment of the European automotive industry 2002–2010. *International Journal of Production Economics, 171*, 321–335. doi:10.1016/j.ijpe.2015.07.039

Breu, K., Hemingway, C. J., Strathern, M., & Bridger, D. (2002). Workforce agility: The new employee strategy for the knowledge economy. *Journal of Information Technology, 17*(1), 21–31. doi:10.1080/02683960110132070

Bridgewater Advisors. (2020). *Economic Impact of COVID-19: A summary of economic implications*. Bridgewater Advisors Limited.

Brooks, S. K., Webster, R. K., Smith, L. E., Woodland, L., Wessely, S., Greenberg, N., & Rubin, G. J. (2020). The Psychological Impact of Quarantine and How to Reduce it: Rapid Review of the Evidence. SSRN *Electronic Journal*, 1-20. doi:10.2139/ssrn.3532534

Brotherhood, L., Cavalcanti, T., Da Mata, D., & Santos, C. (2022). Slums and pandemics. *Journal of Development Economics, 157*, 102882. doi:10.1016/j.jdeveco.2022.102882 PMID:35463050

Brown, M. E. (Ed.). (1993). *Ethnic conflict and international security*. Princeton University Press.

Buchanan, R. (2011). Paradox, promise and public pedagogy: Implications of the federal government's digital education revolution. *The Australian Journal of Teacher Education, 36*(2), 67–78. doi:10.14221/ajte.2011v36n2.6

Butt, A. S. (2022). Understanding the implications of pandemic outbreaks on supply chains: An exploratory study of the effects caused by the COVID-19 across four South Asian countries and steps taken by firms to address the disruptions. *International Journal of Physical Distribution & Logistics Management, 52*(4), 370–392. doi:10.1108/IJPDLM-08-2020-0281

Buzan, B., Buzan, B. G., W'ver, O., Wæver, O., & Buzan, O. W. B. (2003). *Regions and powers: the structure of international security* (Vol. 91). Cambridge University Press. doi:10.1017/CBO9780511491252

Buzan, B., & Hansen, L. (2009). *The evolution of international security studies*. Cambridge University Press. doi:10.1017/CBO9780511817762

Byun, N., Choi, Y., & Choi, J. (2014). The Neighborhood Unit: Effective or Obsolete? *Journal of Asian Architecture and Building Engineering, 13*(3), 617–624. doi:10.3130/jaabe.13.617

C40 Cities Climate Leadership Group. (2020, July). *How to Build Back Better with a 15-Minute City*. C40 Knowledge Hub. https://www.c40knowledgehub.org/s/article/How-to-build-back-better-with-a-15-minute-city?language=en_US

Camerin, F., & Fabris, L. (2021). Towards the Post-Pandemic (Healthy) City: Barcelona's Poblenou Superblock Challenges and Opportunities. *Housing and Home*, *2*, 65–74. doi:10.2307/j.ctv1rnpj94.12

Cao, W., Fang, Z., Hou, G., Han, M., Xu, X., Dong, J., & Zheng, J. (2020). The psychological impact of the COVID-19 epidemic on college students in China. *Psychiatry Research*, *287*, 1–5. doi:10.1016/j.psychres.2020.112934 PMID:32229390

Capolongo, S., Buffoli, M., Brambilla, A., & Rebecchi, A. (2020). Healthy urban planning and design strategies to improve urban quality and attractiveness of places. TECHNE-Journal of technology for architecture and environment, 271-279. doi:10.13128/techne-7837

Capoor, M. R., & Bhowmik, K. T. (2017). Current perspectives on biomedical waste management: Rules, conventions and treatment technologies. *Indian Journal of Medical Microbiology*, *35*(2), 157–164. doi:10.4103/ijmm.IJMM_17_138 PMID:28681801

Center for Disease Control (CDC). (2018). Lesson 1: Introduction to epidemiology. CDC. [REMOVED HYPERLINK FIELD]

Cha, V. D. (2000). Globalization and the study of international security. *Journal of Peace Research*, *37*(3), 391–403. doi:10.1177/0022343300037003007

Cheng, H., Lyu, K., Li, J., & Shiu, H. (2022). Bridging the Digital Divide for Rural Older Adults by Family Intergenerational Learning: A Classroom Case in a Rural Primary School in China. *International Journal of Environmental Research and Public Health*, *19*(1), 371. doi:10.3390/ijerph19010371 PMID:35010629

Chonko, L. B., & Jones, E. (2005). The need for speed: Agility selling. *Journal of Personal Selling & Sales Management*, *25*(4), 371–382.

Cohen, J. (1960). A Coefficient of Agreement for Nominal Scales. *Educational and Psychological Measurement, 20*(1), 37-46.

Collin, K., & Valleala, U. M. (2005). Interaction among employees: How does learning take place in the social communities of the workplace and how might such learning be supervised? *Journal of Education and Work*, *18*(4), 401–420. doi:10.1080/13639080500327873

Cooper, C. L., Flint-Taylor, J., & Pearn, M. (2013). *Building resilience for success: A resource for managers and organizations* (Vol. 8). Palgrave Macmillan. doi:10.1057/9781137367839

Corbin, J. M., & Strauss, A. L. (2008). Basics of Qualitative Research: Techniques and Procedures for Developing Grounded Theory. Los Angeles: Sage Publications.

County Health Rankings. (2022). *2022 County Health Rankings National Findings Report*. County Health Rankings. https://www.countyhealthrankings.org/reports/2022-county-health-rankings-national-findings-report

Couture Ménard, M. E., & Pavot, D. (2016). INTRODUCTION: LES PANDÉMIES ET LE DROIT: VERS UNE PLUS GRANDE SOLIDARITÉ?. *Revue de droit de l'Université de Sherbrooke, 46*(2), 251-259.

Crompton, J. (2013). The health rationale for urban parks in the nineteenth century in the USA. [Retrieved from CGTN.]. *World Leisure Journal, 55*(4), 333–346. doi:10.1080/04419057.2013.836557

CSJ. (2022). *A 20-Year Review of Ghana's Public Debt: Trends*. Drivers and Implications.

Cui, Y., Ma, Z., Wang, L., Yang, A., Liu, Q., Kong, S., & Wang, H. (2023). A survey on big data-enabled innovative online education systems during the COVID-19 pandemic. *Journal of Innovation & Knowledge, 8*(1), 100295. doi:10.1016/j.jik.2022.100295

Dannreuther, R. (2014). *International security: The contemporary agenda*. John Wiley & Sons.

Das, A., Roy, S., Parvez, M., & Hasan, M. M. (2020, September). Decentralized activity centers in rural Bangladesh: A step towards effective emergency situation management in the post-pandemic cities. *Journal of Urban Management, 10*(3), 242-254. doi:10.1016/j.jum.2021.07.002

Dass J. A., & Boopathi, S. (2016). Experimental Study of Eco-friendly Wire-Cut Electrical Discharge Machining Processes. *International Journal of Innovative Research in Science, Engineering and Technology, 5*(1), 666–675.

Datta, P., Mohi, G., & Chander, J. (2018). Biomedical waste management in India: Critical appraisal. *Journal of Laboratory Physicians, 10*(01), 6–14. doi:10.4103/JLP.JLP_89_17 PMID:29403196

Datta, P., & Nwankpa, J. K. (2021). Digital transformation and the COVID-19 crisis continuity planning. *Journal of Information Technology Teaching Cases, 11*(2), 81–89. doi:10.1177/2043886921994821

Datu, J. A. D., & Valdez, J. P. M. (2016). Psychological capital predicts academic engagement and well-being in Filipino high school students. *The Asia-Pacific Education Researcher, 25*(3), 399–405. doi:10.100740299-015-0254-1

Davis, J. H., Schoorman, F. D., & Donaldson, L. (1997). Toward a Stewardship Theory of Management. *The Academy of Management Review, 22*(1), 20-47.

De Pooter, H. (2019). Aperçu de la coopération internationale en matière de surveillance et de riposte aux épidémies et aux pandémies. In Santé et droit international, Actes du colloque de Rennes I de la SFDI (pp. 225-245).

De Villiers, C., & Molinari, M. (2022). How to communicate and use accounting to ensure buy-in from stakeholders: Lessons for organizations from governments' COVID-19 strategies. *Accounting, Auditing & Accountability Journal, 35*(1), 20–34. doi:10.1108/AAAJ-08-2020-4791

Debus, M. E., & Unger, D. (2017). The interactive effects of dual-earner couples' job insecurity: Linking conservation of resources theory with crossover research. *Journal of Occupational and Organizational Psychology, 90*(2), 225–247. doi:10.1111/joop.12169

Del Rio, C., & Malani, P. N. (2020). COVID-19—New insights on a rapidly changing epidemic. *Journal of the American Medical Association*, *323*(14), 1339–1340. doi:10.1001/jama.2020.3072 PMID:32108857

Deloitte. (2020). *Economic impact of COVID-19 Pandemic on the economy of Ghana: summary of fiscal measures and Deloitte views*. Deloitte.

Demiraj, R., Dsouza, S., & Abiad, M. (2022). Working Capital Management Impact on Profitability: Pre-Pandemic and Pandemic Evidence from the European Automotive Industry. *Risks*, *10*(12), 236. doi:10.3390/risks10120236

Denzin, N. K., & Lincoln, Y. S. (2005). The SAGE Handbook of Qualitative Research (3.ª ed.). Londres: SAGE Publications.

Douglas, S. (2020). Mitigating workplace adversity through employee resilience. *Strategic HR Review*, *19*(6), 279–283. doi:10.1108/SHR-06-2020-0063

Dryhurst, S., Schneider, C. R., Kerr, J., Freeman, A. L. J., Recchia, G., van der Bles, A. M., Spiegelhalter, D., & van der Linden, S. (2020). Risk Perceptions of COVID-19 Around The World. *Journal of Risk Research*, *23*(7–8), 994–1006. doi:10.1080/13669877.2020.1758193

Dubey, D. (2020). Psychological Impact Of COVID-19. In S. Baker, R. R. Nadikattu, S. M. Mohammad, & S. Satish (Eds.), *COVID-19 Pandemic Update 2020* (pp. 165–175). Royal Book Publishing. doi:10.26524/royal.37.15

Eberhard, D. M., Simons, G. F., & Fennig, C. D. (Eds.). (2022). *Ethnologue: Languages of the World.* Twenty-fifth edition. Dallas, Texas: SIL International. http://www.ethnologue.com

Edwards, J. R. (1991). Person-job fit: A conceptual integration, literature review, and methodological critique. *Journal of Vocational Behavior*, *38*(3), 255–288.

El-Amin, A. (2022). The benefits and impact of COVID-19 lockdown on the environment. *Environmental Sciences and Ecology: Current Research (ESECR)*, *3*(1).

Eldem, B. (2022). *Impact of COVID-19 pandemic on operational activities at FORD OTOSAN: A case study of automotive industry*. Instytut Organizacji Systemów Produkcyjnych.

Elf, M., Nordmark, S., Lyhagen, J., Lindberg, I., Finch, T., & Åberg, A. C. (2018). The Swedish version of the Normalization Process Theory Measure S-NoMAD: Translation, adaptation, and pilot testing. *Implementation Science : IS*, *13*(1), 1–12. doi:10.118613012-018-0835-5 PMID:30509289

Erdogan, B., & Bauer, T. N. (2005). Enhancing career benefits of employee proactive personality: The role of fit with jobs and organizations. *Personnel Psychology*, *58*(4), 859–891. doi:10.1111/j.1744-6570.2005.00772.x

Fadli, A., Hou, A., Juliansyah, R., & Tambunan, D. (2020). The effect of self-confidence moderation on the effect of emotional intelligence on employee work stress at PT. Orange Indonesia Mandiri Medan. Budapest International Research and Critics Institute (BIRCI-Journal): Humanities and Social Sciences, 3(4), 2851-2856.

Farr, M., Banks, J., Edwards, H. B., Northstone, K., Bernard, E., Salisbury, C., & Horwood, J. (2018). Implementing online consultations in primary care: A mixed-method evaluation extending normalization process theory through service co-production. *BMJ Open*, *8*(3), e019966. doi:10.1136/bmjopen-2017-019966 PMID:29555817

Feldman, R. S. (2019). *Essentials of Understanding Psychology*. McGraw-Hill.

Ferri, F., Grifoni, P., & Guzzo, T. (2020). Online learning and emergency remote teaching: Opportunities and challenges in emergency situations. *Societies (Basel, Switzerland)*, *10*(4), 86. doi:10.3390oc10040086

Festing, M., & Eidems, J. (2011). A process perspective on transnational HRM systems—A dynamic capability-based analysis. *Human Resource Management Review*, *21*(3), 162–173. doi:10.1016/j.hrmr.2011.02.002

Fierke, K. M. (2015). *Critical approaches to international security*. John Wiley & Sons.

Finch, T., Girling, M., May, C., Mair, F., Murray, E., & Treweek, S. (2016). Can we measure implementation progress using Normalization Process Theory? Development and validation of the NoMAD survey tool. *48th Congress of the international Society of Paediatric oncology*. National Institutes of Health.

Finch, T. L., Girling, M., May, C. R., Mair, F. S., Murray, E., Treweek, S., McColl, E., Steen, I. N., Cook, C., Vernazza, C. R., Mackintosh, N., Sharma, S., Barbery, G., Steele, J., & Rapley, T. (2018). Improving the normalization of complex interventions: Part 2 - validation of the NoMAD instrument for assessing implementation work based on normalization process theory (NPT). *BMC Medical Research Methodology*, *18*(1), 135. doi:10.118612874-018-0591-x PMID:30442094

Floetgen, R. J., Strauss, J., Weking, J., Hein, A., Urmetzer, F., Böhm, M., & Krcmar, H. (2021). Introducing platform ecosystem resilience: Leveraging mobility platforms and their ecosystems for the new normal during COVID-19. *European Journal of Information Systems*, *30*(3), 304–321. doi:10.1080/0960085X.2021.1884009

Free, C., & Hecimovic, A. (2021). Global supply chains after COVID-19: The end of the road for neoliberal globalisation? *Accounting, Auditing & Accountability Journal*, *34*(1), 58–84. doi:10.1108/AAAJ-06-2020-4634

Frey, B. S. (1997). *Not Just for the Money: An Economic Theory of Personal Motivation*. Edward Elgar Publishing.

Friis, R., & Sellers, T. (2014). *Epidemiology for public health practice* (5th ed.). Jones & Bartlett Learning.

Gattiker, U. E. (1995). Firm and taxpayer returns from training of semiskilled employees. *Academy of Management Journal*, *38*(4), 1152–1173. doi:10.2307/256624

GCSC & RPC. (2020). *Regional Planning Project for the coastal region*. Damascus.

Gegenfurtner, A., Zitt, A., & Ebner, C. (2020). Evaluating webinar-based training: A mixed methods study of trainee reactions toward digital web conferencing. *International Journal of Training and Development*, *24*(1), 5–21. doi:10.1111/ijtd.12167

Gennard, J., & Judge, G. (2005). *Employee relations*. CIPD Publishing.

George, J. M., & Jones, G. R. (2008). *Understanding and Managing Organizational Behavior* (5th ed.). Pearson/Prentice Hall.

Ghana Statistical Service. (2020). Mobility Analysis to support the Government of Ghana in responding to the COVID-19 outbreak. *Stats Ghana*. https://statsghana.gov.gh/gsspublications.php?category=MTkwMDE4MjI2Ny4xMDg=/webstats/90r897632o (accessed August 2020).

Gillham, J. E., Abenavoli, R. M., Brunwasser, S. M., Linkins, M., Reivich, K. J., & Seligman, M. E. (2013). Resilience education. In *The Oxford Handbook of Happiness* (pp. 609–630). Oxford University Press.

Glaser, B. G., & Strauss, A. L. (2006). *The Discovery of Grounded Theory: Strategies for Qualitative Research*. Aldine Publishing.

Glasser, H., Chang, D. P. Y., & Hickman, D. C. (1991). An analysis of biomedical waste incineration. *Journal of the Air \& Waste Management Association, 41*(9), 1180–1188.

Gliem, J. A., & Gliem, R. R. (2003). *Calculating, interpreting, and reporting Cronbach's alpha reliability coefficient for Likert-type scales*. Midwest Research-to-Practice Conference in Adult, Continuing, and Community Education.

Gligor, D., Gligor, N., Holcomb, M., & Bozkurt, S. (2019). Distinguishing between the concepts of supply chain agility and resilience. *International Journal of Logistics Management*, *30*(2), 467–487. doi:10.1108/IJLM-10-2017-0259

Godinic, D., Obrenovic, B., & Khudaykulov, A. (2020). Effects of Economic Uncertainty on Mental Health in the COVID-19 Pandemic Context: Social Identity Disturbance, Job Uncertainty, and Psychological Well-Being Model. *International Journal of Innovation and Economic Development*, *6*(1), 61–74. doi:10.18775/ijied.1849-7551-7020.2015.61.2005

GoG. (2020). *Mid-Year Review of the Biudget Statement of Economic Policy of Government of Ghana and Supplementary Estimates for the Financial Year*. Ministry of Financial and Economic Planning.

GoG. (2021). *The Budget Statement and Economic Policy of the Government of Ghana for the Year 2022*. Ministry of Finance.

Gold, K. (2020). *COVID-19 puts urban density to the test*. THE GLOBE AND MAIL. https://www.theglobeandmail.com/real-estate/article-covid-19-puts-urban-density-to-the-test/

Goleman, D. (2015). Emotional Intelligence (EQ). *Journal of K*, *6*, 71–77.

González-Sanguino, C., Ausín, B., Castellanos, M. Á., Saiz, J., López-Gómez, A., Ugidos, C., & Muñoz, M. (2020). Mental health consequences during the initial stage of the 2020 Coronavirus pandemic (COVID-19) in Spain. *Brain, Behavior, and Immunity*, *87*, 172–176. doi:10.1016/j.bbi.2020.05.040 PMID:32405150

Gössling, S., Scott, D., & Hall, C. M. (2020). Pandemics, tourism and global change: A rapid assessment of COVID-19. *Journal of Sustainable Tourism*, 1–20.

Gowri, N. V., Dwivedi, J. N., Krishnaveni, K., Boopathi, S., Palaniappan, M., & Medikondu, N. R. (2023). Experimental investigation and multi-objective optimization of eco-friendly near-dry electrical discharge machining of shape memory alloy using Cu/SiC/Gr composite electrode. *Environmental Science and Pollution Research International*, 1–19. doi:10.100711356-023-26983-6 PMID:37126160

Granda, J. C., Nuño, P., García, D. F., & Suárez, F. J. (2015). Autonomic platform for synchronous e-Training in dispersed organizations. *Journal of Network and Systems Management*, *23*(1), 183–209. doi:10.100710922-013-9290-4

Grange, M. (2014). Ebola: Le droit international au soutien de la lutte contre une épidémie transfrontière. *Annuaire Français de Droit International*, *60*(1), 685–706. doi:10.3406/afdi.2014.4770

Grant, J. (2006). Planning the good community: New urbanism in theory and practice. London: Routledge (Taylor and Francis).

GSS. (2013). *2010 population and housing census: National analytical report*. Ghana Statistical Service.

GSS. (2019). *Ghana living standard survey (GLSS7). Main report*. Ghana Statistical Service Accra.

GSS. (2021). *2021 Population and Housing Census: Press Release on provisional results*. Ghana Statistical Service, Accra.

Gunasekaran, K., Boopathi, S., & Sureshkumar, M. (2022). Analysis of a Cryogenically Cooled Near-Dry Wedm Process Using Different Dielectrics. *Materiali in Tehnologije*, *56*(2), 179–186. doi:10.17222/mit.2022.397

Hacker, J., vom Brocke, J., Handali, J., Otto, M., & Schneider, J. (2020). Virtually in this together–how web-conferencing systems enabled a new virtual togetherness during the COVID-19 crisis. *European Journal of Information Systems*, *29*(5), 563–584. doi:10.1080/0960085X.2020.1814680

Halbesleben, J. R. B., Neveu, J.-P., Paustian-Underdahl, S. C., & Westman, M. (2014). Getting to the "COR": Understanding the Role of Resources in Conservation of Resources Theory. *Journal of Management*, *40*(5), 1334–1364. doi:10.1177/0149206314527130

Hamouche, S. (2020). COVID-19 and employees' mental health: Stressors, moderators and agenda for organizational actions. *Emerald Open Research*, *2*, 1–15. doi:10.35241/emeraldopenres.13550.1

Haque, A., & Pant, A. B. (2022). Mitigating COVID-19 in the face of emerging virus variants, breakthrough infections, and vaccine hesitancy. *Journal of Autoimmunity*, *127*, 102792. doi:10.1016/j.jaut.2021.102792 PMID:34995958

Haralayya, B. (2021). Consumer Buying Behaviour with Reference to Bajaj Auto Ltd. *IRE Journals*, *5*(1), 131–140.

Harper, C. A., Satchell, L., Fido, D., & Latzman, R. D. (2020). Functional fear predicts public health compliance in the COVID-19 pandemic. doi:10.31234/osf.io/jkfu3osf.io/jkfu3

Hasan, H. F. (2021). Legal and health response to COVID-19 in the Arab countries. *Risk Management and Healthcare Policy*, *14*, 1141–1154. doi:10.2147/RMHP.S297565 PMID:33758566

Hobfoll, S. E. (1989). Conservation of resources: A new attempt at conceptualizing stress. *The American Psychologist*, *44*(3), 513–524. doi:10.1037/0003-066X.44.3.513 PMID:2648906

Horesh, D., Lev-Ari, R. K., & Hasson-Ohayon, I. (2020). Risk factors for psychological distress during the COVID-19 pandemic in Israel: Loneliness, age, gender, and health status play an important role. *British Journal of Health Psychology*, *25*(4), 925–933. doi:10.1111/bjhp.12455 PMID:32656926

Howlett, M. (2019). Moving policy implementation theory forward: A multiple streams/critical juncture approach. *Public Policy and Administration*, *34*(4), 405–430. doi:10.1177/0952076718775791

Huang, Y., Sun, M., & Sui, Y. (2020). How digital contact tracing slowed Covid-19 in East Asia. *Harvard Business Review*. https:// hbr.org/2020/04/how-digital-contact-tracing-slowed-covid-19-in-east-asia

Huang, C., Chan, F. T. S., & Chung, S. H. (2022). The impact of payment term extensions on the working capital management of an automotive supply chain. *International Journal of Production Research*, *60*(24), 7360–7383. doi:10.1080/00207543.2022.2065549

Huang, J., Gates, A. J., Sinatra, R., & Barabási, A.-L. (2020). Historical comparison of gender inequality in scientific careers across countries and disciplines. *Proceedings of the National Academy of Sciences of the United States of America*, *117*(9), 4609–4616. doi:10.1073/pnas.1914221117 PMID:32071248

Huang, Y., & Zhao, N. (2020). Generalized anxiety disorder, depressive symptoms and sleep quality during COVID-19 outbreak in China: A web-based cross-sectional survey. *Psychiatry Research*, *288*, 1–6. doi:10.1016/j.psychres.2020.112954 PMID:32325383

Ilyas, S., Srivastava, R. R., & Kim, H. (2020). Disinfection technology and strategies for COVID-19 hospital and bio-medical waste management. *The Science of the Total Environment*, *749*, 141652. doi:10.1016/j.scitotenv.2020.141652 PMID:32822917

Imran, M. A., & Ahmed, I. (2020). Job Insecurity in Private Education Sector Considering COVID-19 Pandemic: Bangladesh Panorama. *American International Journal of Business and Management Studies*, *2*(2), 41–51. doi:10.46545/aijbms.v2i2.245

Izutsu, T., & Tsutsumi, A. (2010). Quality of Life of Urban Slum Residents. In V. Preedy & R. Watson (Eds.), *Handbook of Disease Burdens and Quality of Life Measures* (pp. 3383–3396). Springer. doi:10.1007/978-0-387-78665-0_195

Jacobsen, K. H. (2020). Will COVID-19 generate global preparedness? *Lancet, 395*(10229), 1013–1014. doi:10.1016/S0140-6736(20)30559-6 PMID:32199074

Jafari, F., & Prabhakar Rao, D. (2015). Study the Relation between Working Capital System and Profitability in Auto Manufacturing Industry in India. *Journal of Resources Development and Management, 6*, 14–25.

Jaganathan, P., Naveen, T., & Sivasubramanian, R. (2012). Machining Parameters Optimization of WEDM Process Using Taguchi Method. *Ijest, 2*(12), 1–4.

Jaiswal, A., & Arun, C. J. (2020). Unlocking the COVID-19 Lockdown: Work from Home and Its Impact on Employees.Research Square, 1-27. doi:10.21203/rs.3.rs-34556/v1

Janardhana, K., Anushkannan, N. K., Dinakaran, K. P., Puse, R. K., & Boopathi, S. (2023). *Experimental Investigation on Microhardness, Surface Roughness, and White Layer Thickness of Dry EDM*. Engineering Research Express. doi:10.1088/2631-8695/acce8f

Jasim, M. M. (2020). Poor, rural DU students still missing out on online classes. *The Business Standard.* https://www.tbsnews.net/bangladesh/education/poor-rural-du-students-still-missing-out-online-classes-102625

Jeevanantham, Y. A., A, S., V, V., J, S. I., Boopathi, S., & Kumar, D. P. (2023). Implementation of Internet-of Things (IoT) in Soil Irrigation System. *IEEE Explore*, 1–5. doi:10.1109/ICPECTS56089.2022.10047185

Jeong, W., Park, M., & Min, J. U. (2009). Triple-a supply chain management for automobile industry: A case study of Renault Samsung Motors. *Journal of International Logistics and Trade, 7*(1), 57–70. doi:10.24006/jilt.2009.7.1.57

Jin, D. (2020). Rethinking of the Development of Urban Planning Disciplines in Response to COVID-19 Epidemic. *Journal of Human Settlements in west China,* (5), 1-6. doi:10.13791/j.cnki.hsfwest.20200501

Jin, Y., Yang, H., Ji, W., Wu, W., Chen, S., Zhang, W., & Duan, G. (2020). Virology, epidemiology, pathogenesis, and control of COVID-19. *Viruses, 12*(4), 372. https://www.mdpi.com/1999-4915/12/4/372/htm. doi:10.3390/v12040372 PMID:32230900

Jomo, K. S., & Chowdhury, A. (2020). COVID-19 pandemic recession and recovery. *Development, 63*(2-4), 226–237. doi:10.105741301-020-00262-0 PMID:33223764

Jon, I. (2020). A manifesto for planning after the coronavirus: Towards planning of care. *Planning Theory, 19*(3), 329–345. doi:10.1177/1473095220931272

Justino, D., & Batista, S. (2013). Redes de escolas e modos de regulação do sistema educativo. In Educação - Temas e Problemas, 12(13), 41-60.

Kakderi, C., Oikonomaki, E., & Papadaki, I. (2021). Smart and Resilient Urban Futures for Sustainability in the Post COVID-19 Era: A Review of Policy Responses on Urban Mobility. *Sustainability (Basel)*, *13*(11), 6486. doi:10.3390u13116486

Kakodkar, P., Kaka, N., & Baig, M. N. (2020). A comprehensive literature review on the clinical presentation and management of the pandemic coronavirus disease 2019 (COVID-19). *Cureus*, *12*(4). doi:10.7759/cureus.7560 PMID:32269893

Kamak, L. P. (2023). *Programming pedagogy in the age of accessible artificial intelligence* [Doctoral dissertation, Cornell University].

Kamel Boulos, M. N., & Geraghty, E. M. (2020). Geographical tracking and mapping of coronavirus disease COVID-19/severe acute respiratory syndrome coronavirus 2 (SARS-CoV-2) epidemic and associated events around the world: How 21st century GIS technologies are supporting the global fight against outbreaks and epidemics. *International Journal of Health Geographics*, *19*(1), 1–12. doi:10.118612942-020-00202-8 PMID:32160889

Kamruzzaman, M. (2020). COVID-19: Bangladesh mulls suspending Friday prayers. *Anadolu Agency*. https://www.aa.com.tr/en/asia-pacific/covid-19-bangladesh-mulls-suspending-friday-prayers/1780251

Kandel, N., Chungong, S., Omaar, A., & Xing, J. (2020). Health security capacities in the context of COVID-19 outbreak: An analysis of International Health Regulations annual report data from 182 countries. *Lancet*, *395*(10229), 1047–1053. doi:10.1016/S0140-6736(20)30553-5 PMID:32199075

Kannan, E., Trabelsi, Y., Boopathi, S., & Alagesan, S. (2022). Influences of cryogenically treated work material on near-dry wire-cut electrical discharge machining process. *Surface Topography : Metrology and Properties*, *10*(1), 15027. doi:10.1088/2051-672X/ac53e1

Kennedy, A., Rogers, A., Chew-Graham, C., Blakeman, T., Bowen, R., Gardner, C., Lee, V., Morris, R., & Protheroe, J. (2014). Implementation of a self-management support approach (WISE) across a health system: A process evaluation explaining what did and did not work for organizations, clinicians and patients. *Implementation Science : IS*, *9*(1), 129. doi:10.118613012-014-0129-5 PMID:25331942

Kentikelenis, A., Gabor, D., Ortiz, I., Stubbs, T., McKee, M., & Stuckler, D. (2020). Softening the blow of the pandemic: Will International Monetary Fund and World Bank make things worse? *The Lancet. Global Health*, *8*(6), e758–e759. doi:10.1016/S2214-109X(20)30135-2 PMID:32278363

Ke, X., & Hsiao, C. (2022). Economic impact of the most drastic lockdown during COVID-19 pandemic—The experience of Hubei, China. *Journal of Applied Econometrics*, *37*(1), 187–209. doi:10.1002/jae.2871 PMID:34518735

Khatatbeh, M. (2020). Efficacy of Nationwide Curfew to Encounter Spread of COVID-19: A Case From Jordan. *Frontiers in Public Health*, *8*, 1–3. doi:10.3389/fpubh.2020.00394 PMID:32984234

Khavarian-Garmsir, A., & Sharifi, A. (2020, September 18). The COVID-19 pandemic: Impacts on cities and major lessons for urban planning, design, and management. *The Science of the Total Environment*. PMID:33370924

Kivunja, C. (2014). Teaching Students to Learn and to Work Well with 21st Century Skills: Unpacking the Career and Life Skills Domain of the New Learning Paradigm. *International Journal of Higher Education*, *4*(1), 1–11. doi:10.5430/ijhe.v4n1p1

Klijn, E. H. (2010). Trust in governance networks: looking for conditions for innovative solutions and outcomes. In S. P. Osborne (Ed.), *The New Public Governance?* (pp. 303–321). Routledge.

Kompalla, A., Kopia, J., & Tigu, P. G. (2016). An application of agile principles on business strategies within IT-based industries and automotive enterprises. *Zifp*, 1–17.

Kooiman, J. (2008). Exploring the Concept of Governability. *Journal of Comparative Policy Analysis, 10*(2), 171-190.

Kooiman, J. (1993). Social-Political Governance: Introduction. In J. Kooiman (Ed.), *Modern Governance: New Government–Society Interactions* (pp. 1–8). SAGE.

Kooiman, J. (2010). Governance and governability. In S. P. Osborne (Ed.), *The New Public Governance?* (pp. 72–86). Routledge.

Kou, Y., Chen, P., & Pan, J. X. (2021). The service experiences of public libraries during the COVID-19 emergency in Wuhan: Three case studies. *Journal of the Australian Library and Information Association*, *70*(3), 287–300. doi:10.1080/24750158.2021.1960251

Kristof-Brown, A. L., Jansen, K. J., & Colbert, A. E. (2002). A policy-capturing study of the simultaneous effects of fit with jobs, groups, and organizations. *The Journal of Applied Psychology*, *87*(5), 985–993. doi:10.1037/0021-9010.87.5.985 PMID:12395823

Kumara, V., Mohanaprakash, T. A., Fairooz, S., Jamal, K., Babu, T., & B., S. (2023). Experimental Study on a Reliable Smart Hydroponics System. In *Human Agro-Energy Optimization for Business and Industry* (pp. 27–45). IGI Global. doi:10.4018/978-1-6684-4118-3.ch002

La Barbera, M., & Lombardo, E. (2019). "The Long and Winding Road": A Comparative Policy Analysis of Multilevel Judicial Implementation of Work–Life Balance in Spain. *Journal of Comparative Policy Analysis*, *21*(1), 9–24. doi:10.1080/13876988.2017.1363949

Laborde, D., Martin, W., Swinnen, J., & Vos, R. (2020). COVID-19 risks to global food security. *Science*, *369*(6503), 500–502. doi:10.1126cience.abc4765 PMID:32732407

Laing, T. (2020, April). The economic impact of the Coronavirus 2019 (Covid-2019): Implications for the mining industry. *The Extractive Industries and Society*, *7*(2), 580–582. doi:10.1016/j.exis.2020.04.003 PMID:32300537

Lak, A., Shakouri Asl, S., & Maher, A. (2020). Resilient urban form to pandemics: Lessons from COVID-19. *Medical Journal of the Islamic Republic of Iran*, *71*. Advance online publication. doi:10.47176/mjiri.34.71 PMID:33306051

Li, B., Qian, J., Xu, J., & Li, Y. (2022). Collaborative governance in emergencies: Community food supply in COVID-19 in Wuhan, China. *Urban Governance*, *2*(1), 188–196. doi:10.1016/j.ugj.2022.03.002

Li, M. (2021). Public health crises in comparison: China's epidemic response policies from SARS to COVID-19. *Global Public Health: An International Journal for Research, Policy and Practice*, *16*(8-9), 1223–1236. doi:10.1080/17441692.2021.1919735 PMID:33891518

Lima, L. C. (1998). A Escola como Organização e a Participação na Organização Escolar (2.ª ed.). Braga: Universidade do Minho.

Lima, L. C. (2012). Democratização da Escola, Participação Comunitária e Cidadania Critica. *Princípios Gerais da Administração Escolar, 1*, 148-157. http://www.acervodigital.unesp.br/handle/123456789/65259

Lim, D. H., Hur, H., Ho, Y., Yoo, S., & Yoon, S. W. (2020). Workforce resilience: Integrative review for human resource development. *Performance Improvement Quarterly*, *33*(1), 77–101. doi:10.1002/piq.21318

Lind, L., Monto, S., & Kärri, T. (2019). Mapping working capital models in the automotive industry. *International Journal of Integrated Supply Management*, *12*(4), 285–308. doi:10.1504/IJISM.2019.103170

Lind, L., Pirttilä, M., Viskari, S., Schupp, F., & Kärri, T. (2012). Working capital management in the automotive industry: Financial value chain analysis. *Journal of Purchasing and Supply Management*, *18*(2), 92–100. doi:10.1016/j.pursup.2012.04.003

Lionis, C., Papadakaki, M., Saridaki, A., Dowrick, C., O'Donnell, C. A., Mair, F. S., van den Muijsenbergh, M., Burns, N., de Brún, T., O'Reilly de Brún, M., van Weel-Baumgarten, E., Spiegel, W., & MacFarlane, A. (2016). Engaging migrants and other stakeholders to improve communication in cross-cultural consultation in primary care: A theoretically informed participatory study. *BMJ Open*, *6*(7), e010822. doi:10.1136/bmjopen-2015-010822 PMID:27449890

Lipscy, P. Y. (2020). COVID-19 and the Politics of Crisis. *International Organization*, *74*(S1), E98–E127. doi:10.1017/S0020818320000375

Li, Q., Miao, Y., Zeng, X., Tarimo, C. S., Wu, C., & Wu, J. (2020). Prevalence and factors for anxiety during the coronavirus disease 2019 (COVID-19) epidemic among the teachers in China. *Journal of Affective Disorders*, *277*, 153–158. doi:10.1016/j.jad.2020.08.017 PMID:32828002

Liu, H., Liang, Z., Zhang, S., & Liu, L. (2022). Sociodemographic and policy factors associated with the transmission of COVID-19: Analyzing longitudinal contact tracing data from a northern Chinese city. *Journal of Urban Health*, *99*(3), 582–593. doi:10.100711524-022-00639-1 PMID:35641716

Liu, J., Zhou, J., Yao, J., Zhang, X., Li, L., Xu, X., & Yan, J. (2020). Impact of meteorological factors on the COVID-19 transmission: A multi-city study in China. *The Science of the Total Environment*, *726*, 138513. doi:10.1016/j.scitotenv.2020.138513 PMID:32304942

Liu, N., Zhang, F., Wei, C., Jia, Y., Shang, Z., Sun, L., Wu, L., Sun, Z., Zhou, Y., Wang, Y., & Liu, W. (2020). Prevalence and predictors of PTSS during COVID-19 outbreak in China hardest-hit areas: Gender differences matter. *Psychiatry Research*, *287*, 112921. doi:10.1016/j.psychres.2020.112921 PMID:32240896

Liu, W., James, T. S., & Man, C. (2022). Governance and public administration in China. *Policy Studies*, *43*(3), 387–402. doi:10.1080/01442872.2022.2054091

Liu, Z., Deng, Z., He, G., Wang, H., Zhang, X., Lin, J., Qi, Y., & Liang, X. (2022). Challenges and opportunities for carbon neutrality in China. *Nature Reviews. Earth & Environment*, *3*(2), 141–155. doi:10.103843017-021-00244-x

Loch, A. P., Finch, T., Fonsi, M., & Soárez, P. C. D. (2020). Cross-cultural adaptation of the NoMAD questionnaire to Brazilian Portuguese. *Revista da Associação Médica Brasileira*, *66*(10), 1383–1390. doi:10.1590/1806-9282.66.10.1383 PMID:33174931

Logemann, M., Aritz, J., Cardon, P., Swartz, S., Elhaddaoui, T., Getchell, K., Fleischmann, C., Helens-Hart, R., Li, X., Palmer-Silveira, J. C., Ruiz-Garrido, M., Springer, S., & Stapp, J. (2022). Standing strong amid a pandemic: How a global online team project stands up to the public health crisis. *British Journal of Educational Technology*, *53*(3), 577–592. doi:10.1111/bjet.13189 PMID:35600422

Lokhande, M. A., & Rana, V. S. (2016). Marketing Strategies of Indian Automobile Companies: A Case Study of Maruti Suzuki India Limited. SSRN *Electronic Journal*. doi:10.2139/ssrn.2719399

López, I., Ortega, J., & Pardo, M. (2020, April). Mobility infrastructures in cities and climate change: An analysis through the superblocks in Barcelona. *Atmosphere (Basel)*, *11*(4), 410. doi:10.3390/atmos11040410

Lucka, D. (2018). How to build a community. New Urbanism and its critics. *Urban Development Issues*, 17-28. doi:10.2478/udi-2018-0025

Lythgoe, M. P., & Middleton, P. (2020). Ongoing clinical trials for the management of the COVID-19 pandemic. *Trends in Pharmacological Sciences*, *41*(6), 363–382. doi:10.1016/j.tips.2020.03.006 PMID:32291112

MacKenzie, D. (2020). Stopping the Next Pandemic: How Covid-19 Can Help Us Save Humanity. Hachette UK.

Mackres, E. (2020). *Insights from Big Data on How COVID-19 Is Changing Society.* TheCityFix. https://thecityfix.com/blog/insights-big-data-covid-19-changing-society-eric-mackres/

Madrigano, J., Chandra, A., Costigan, T., & Acosta, J. D. (2017). Beyond disaster preparedness: Building a resilience-oriented workforce for the future. *International Journal of Environmental Research and Public Health*, *14*(12), 1563. doi:10.3390/ijerph14121563 PMID:29236028

Maheshwari, S., & Vohra, V. (2018). Role of training and development practices in implementing change. *International Journal of Learning and Change*, *10*(2), 131–162. doi:10.1504/IJLC.2018.090911

Mahmud, A., & Buckee, C. (2020). Bangladesh must enact widespread surveillance and social distancing measures. *The Daily Star*. https://www.thedailystar.net/opinion/news/bangladesh-must-enact-widespread-surveillance-and-social-distancing-measures-1886344

Mahmud, A., Dasgupta, A., Gupta, A. D., Hasan, M. K., & Kabir, K. R. (2021). Current status about COVID-19 impacts on online education system: A review in Bangladesh. SSRN *Electronic Journal*.https://doi.org/ doi:10.2139/ssrn.3785713

Mahmud, F. (2020). Coronavirus: In dense Bangladesh, social distancing a tough task. *Aljazeera*. https://www.aljazeera.com/news/2020/3/20/coronavirus-in-dense-bangladesh-social-distancing-a-tough-task

Malisch, J. L., Harris, B. N., Sherrer, S. M., Lewis, K. A., Shepherd, S. L., McCarthy, P. C., Spott, J. L., Karam, E. P., Moustaid-Moussa, N., Calarco, J. M. C., Ramalingam, L., Talley, A. E., Cañas-Carrell, J. E., Ardon-Dryer, K., Weiser, D. A., Bernal, X. E., & Deitloff, J. (2020). Opinion: In the wake of COVID-19, academia needs new solutions to ensure gender equity. *Proceedings of the National Academy of Sciences of the United States of America*, *117*(27), 15378–15381. doi:10.1073/pnas.2010636117 PMID:32554503

Maslow, A. H. (1943). A theory of human motivation. *Psychological Review*, *50*(4), 370–396. doi:10.1037/h0054346

Masten, A. S. (2001). Ordinary magic: Resilience processes in development. *The American Psychologist*, *56*(3), 227–238. doi:10.1037/0003-066X.56.3.227 PMID:11315249

Maurel, R. (2020). " L'(in) activité du Conseil de sécurité face au Covid-19: où est confinée la “communauté” internationale”?”, Dossier. *[Colloque virtuel] Droit et Coronavirus. Le droit face aux circonstances sanitaires exceptionnelles.* RDLF Revue des droits et libertés fondamentaux. Revue des droits et libertés fondamentaux.

Mavrot, C., Hadorn, S., & Sager, F. (2019). Mapping the mix: Linking instruments, settings and target groups in the study of policy mixes. *Research Policy*, *48*(10), 103614. doi:10.1016/j.respol.2018.06.012

May, C., & Finch, T. (2009). Implementing, embedding, and integrating practices: an outline of normalization process theory. *Sociology, 43*(3), 535-554. Doi.org/ 10.1177/0038038509103208

Mbunge, E., Ndumiso, N., Kavu, T. D., Dandajena, K., Batani, J., & Fashoto, S. G. (2022). Towards QR Code Health Systems Amid COVID-19: Lessons Learnt from Other QR Code Digital Technologies. In *The Science behind the COVID Pandemic and Healthcare Technology Solutions* (pp. 129–143). Springer International Publishing. doi:10.1007/978-3-031-10031-4_7

Megahed, N., & Ghoneim, E. (2020). Antivirus-built environment: Lessons learned from Covid-19 pandemic. *Sustainable Cities and Society*, *61*, 102350. doi:10.1016/j.scs.2020.102350 PMID:32834930

Mehaffy, M., Porta, S., & Romice, O. (2014). The “neighborhood unit” on trial: A case study in the impacts of urban morphology. *Journal of Urbanism*, *8*(2), 1–19.

Meijer, A., & Webster, C. W. R. (2020). The COVID-19-crisis and the information polity: An overview of responses and discussions in twenty-one countries from six continents. *Information Polity*, *25*(3), 243–274. doi:10.3233/IP-200006

Meng, Q., & Wang, G. (2018). A research on sources of university faculty occupational stress: A Chinese case study. *Psychology Research and Behavior Management*, *11*, 597–605. doi:10.2147/PRBM.S187295 PMID:30573995

Milakovich, M. E. (2021). *Digital governance: Applying advanced technologies to improve public service*. Routledge. doi:10.4324/9781003215875

Mirnezami, S. J., de Boer, C., & Bagheri, A. (2019). Groundwater governance and implementing the conservation policy: The case study of Rafsanjan Plain in Iran. *Environment, Development and Sustainability*, 1–28.

Mitsakis, F. V. (2020). Human resource development (HRD) resilience: A new 'success element' of organizational resilience? *Human Resource Development International*, *23*(3), 321–328. doi:10.1080/13678868.2019.1669385

Mohaghegh, M., & Furlan, A. (2020). Systematic problem-solving and its antecedents: A synthesis of the literature. *Management Research Review*, *43*(9), 1033–1062. doi:10.1108/MRR-06-2019-0284

Mohanty, A., Venkateswaran, N., Ranjit, P. S., Tripathi, M. A., & Boopathi, S. (2023). Innovative strategy for profitable automobile industries: Working capital management. In *Handbook of Research on Designing Sustainable Supply Chains to Achieve a Circular Economy* (pp. 412–428). IGI Global. doi:10.4018/978-1-6684-7664-2.ch020

Mondira, R. T. (2021). PohelaBoishakh celebrations go virtual for the second year in a row. *The Daily Star*. https://www.thedailystar.net/arts-entertainment/news/pohela-boishakh-celebrations-go-virtual-the-second-year-row-2077605

Moorhouse, B. L. (2020). Adaptations to a face-to-face initial teacher education course 'forced' online due to the COVID-19 pandemic. *Journal of Education for Teaching*, *46*(4), 609–611. doi:10.1080/02607476.2020.1755205

Moreno, C., Allam, Z., Chabaud, D., Gall, C., & Pratlong, F. (2021). Introducing the "15-Minute City": Sustainability, Resilience and Place Identity in Future Post-Pandemic Cities. *Smart Cities*, *4*(1), 93–111. doi:10.3390martcities4010006

Morin, C. M., Carrier, J., Bastien, C., & Godbout, R. (2020). Sleep and circadian rhythm in response to the COVID-19 pandemic. *Canadian Journal of Public Health*, *111*(5), 654–657. doi:10.1726941997-020-00382-7 PMID:32700231

Mosleh, S. M., Kasasbeha, M. A., Aljawarneh, Y. M., Alrimawi, I., & Saifan, A. R. (2022). The impact of online teaching on stress and burnout of academics during the transition to remote teaching from home. *BMC Medical Education*, *22*(1), 1–10. doi:10.118612909-022-03496-3 PMID:35725450

Mowbray, H. (2020). In Beijing, coronavirus 2019-nCoV has created a siege mentality. *BMJ (Clinical Research Ed.)*, *368*, m516. doi:10.1136/bmj.m516 PMID:32033967

Muduli, A. (2016). Exploring the facilitators and mediators of workforce agility: An empirical study. *Management Research Review*, *39*(12), 1567–1586. doi:10.1108/MRR-10-2015-0236

Muñoz-Leiva, F., Montoro Ríos, F. J., & Luque Martínez, T. (2006). Assessment of Interjudge Reliability in the Open-Ended Questions Coding Process. *Quality & Quantity, 40*(4), 519-537.

Murphy, I. (2011). Educational reform and the enacted curriculum in English - a narrative from the field of the digital education revolution. *Engineers Australia*, *46*(1), 62–72.

Muthmainnah, M., Al Yakin, A., Massyat, M., Lulaj, E., & Bayram, G. E. (2022a). Developing Students' Life Skills Through Edupreneurship in the Digital Era. In Contemporary Studies in Economic and Financial Analysis (Vol. 109A, pp. 169–190). Emerald Publishing Limited. doi:10.1108/S1569-37592022000109A011

Myilsamy, S., & Sampath, B. (2021). Experimental comparison of near-dry and cryogenically cooled near-dry machining in wire-cut electrical discharge machining processes. *Surface Topography : Metrology and Properties*, *9*(3), 35015. doi:10.1088/2051-672X/ac15e0

Nair, K. S. (2003). Life goals: The concept and its relevance to rehabilitation. *Clinical Rehabilitation*, *17*(2), 192–202. doi:10.1191/0269215503cr599oa PMID:12625660

Narayanan, L., Pandit, M., Basu, S., Karmakar, A., Bidhan, V., Kumar, H., & Brar, K. (2020). Impact of lockdown due to COVID-19 outbreak: lifestyle changes and public health concerns in India.Preprints,2020060129. https://www.preprints.org/manuscript/202006.0129/v1

Nardi, B. A., & Whittaker, S. (2002). The place of face-to-face communication in distributed work. *Distributed Work*, *83*(112), 10–7551.

Natarajan, N., Vijayarangan, S., & Rajendran, I. (2006). Wear behaviour of A356/25SiCp aluminium matrix composites sliding against automobile friction material. *Wear*, *261*(7–8), 812–822. doi:10.1016/j.wear.2006.01.011

Neazy, S. N. (2019). Rise of the educated unemployed. *Dhaka Tribune*. https://www.dhakatribune.com/opinion/op-ed/2019/06/28/rise-of-the-educated-unemployed

Nevile, A., Kay, A., & Carey, G. (2018). Value choices in a mixed economy of care: How politics shapes the implementation of complex social policies. *Social Policy and Administration*, *52*(7), 1290–1302. doi:10.1111pol.12391

Nguyen, Q., Kuntz, J. R., Näswall, K., & Malinen, S. (2016). Employee resilience and leadership styles: The moderating role of proactive personality and optimism. *New Zealand Journal of Psychology (Online)*, *45*(2), 13.

Nielsen, W., Miller, A., & Hoban, G. F. (2012). *The digital education revolution : New South Wales science teachers ' response to laptop ubiquity.*

Nielsen, W., Miller, K. A., & Hoban, G. (2015). Science Teachers' Response to the Digital Education Revolution. *Journal of Science Education and Technology*, *24*(4), 417–431. doi:10.100710956-014-9527-3

Nieuwenhuijsen, J. M. (2020). *Post-COVID-19 Cities: New Urban Models to Make Cities Healthier*. IS Global. https://www.isglobal.org/en/healthisglobal/-/custom-blog-portlet/post-covid-19-cities-new-urban-models-to-make-cities-healthier/4735173/0

Norouzi, N., & Movahedian, H. (2021). Right to Education in Mother Language: In the Light of Judicial and Legal Structures. In Handbook of Research on Novel Practices and Current Successes in Achieving the Sustainable Development Goals (pp. 223-241). IGI Global.

Norouzi, N. (2021). Post-COVID-19 and globalization of oil and natural gas trade: Challenges, opportunities, lessons, regulations, and strategies. *International Journal of Energy Research*, *45*(10), 14338–14356. doi:10.1002/er.6762 PMID:34219899

Norouzi, N., & Ataei, E. (2021a). Covid-19 Crisis and Environmental law: Opportunities and challenges. *Hasanuddin Law Review*, *7*(1), 46–60. doi:10.20956/halrev.v7i1.2772

Norouzi, N., & Ataei, E. (2021b). Environmental Protection Regulations in the Light of Public Law and Social Obligations. *Research Journal of Ecology and Environmental Sciences*, *1*(1), 1–16.

Norouzi, N., Khanmohammadi, H. U., & Ataei, E. (2021). The Law in the Face of the COVID-19 Pandemic: Early Lessons from Uruguay. *Hasanuddin Law Review*, *7*(2), 75–88. doi:10.20956/halrev.v7i2.2827

Oda Abunamous, M., Boudouaia, A., Jebril, M., Diafi, S., & Zreik, M. (2022). The decay of traditional education: A case study under covid-19. *Cogent Education*, *9*(1), 2082116. doi:10.1080/2331186X.2022.2082116

Odii, A., Odinakachukwu M. N., Aniakor,M. C.,Owelle, I. C., Aniagboso, M. C., &Uzuanwu,O. W. (n.d.). Effect of COVID-19 lockdown on poor urban households in Nigeria: Where do we go from here? *Ianna Journal of Interdisciplinary Studies, 2*(1).

OECD. (2017). Résultats du PISA 2015: Vol. II. *Politiques et Pratiques pour des Établissements Performants*. OECD.

Ofori-Atta. (2020). *Economic impact of COVID-19 pandemic on the economy of Ghana. Ministry of Finance statement to parliament on 30th March 2020.* Ministry of Finance.

Okech, E., & Nyadera, I. (2022). Urban green spaces in the wake of Covid-19 pandemic: Reflections from Nairobi, Kenya. *GeoJournal*, *87*(6), 4931–4945. doi:10.100710708-021-10540-0 PMID:34776594

Olszewska-Guizzo, A., Fogel, A., Benjumea, D., & Tahsin, N. (2022, may 3). Sustainable Solutions in Urban Health: Transdisciplinary Directions in Urban Planning for Global Public Health. In W. V. Leal Filho, Sustainable Policies and Practices in Energy, Environment and Health Research. World Sustainability Series. (pp. 223-243). Springer, Cham.

Onu, B., Surendran, S. S., & Price, T. (2014). Impact of inadequate urban planning on municipal solid waste management in the Niger Delta Region of Nigeria. *Journal of Sustainable Development*, *7*(6), 27–45. doi:10.5539/jsd.v7n6p27

Onyina, P. A. (2021). A Literature Review of the Consequences of a Lockdown Ghanaian Economy Dominated by the Informal Sector during the COVID-19 Pandemic Era. *Pentvars Business Journal*, *13*(1), 89–98.

Ooi, G., & Kai, H. (2007). Urbanization and Slum Formation. *Journal of Urban Health*, *84*(S1), 27–34. doi:10.100711524-007-9167-5 PMID:17387618

Oriewo, O. (2020). *THE EFFECT OF LAND USE PLANNING ONECONOMIC VULNARABILITY TO DISASTERMANAGEMENTINLOW INCOME NEIGHBOURHOODS OFELDORET URBAN AREA, KENYA*. MMUST.

Osborne, S. P. (2010). The (New) Public Governance: a suitable case for treatment? In S. P. Osborne (Ed.), *The New Public Governance?* (pp. 1–17). Routledge. doi:10.4324/9780203861684

Oum, S., Kates, J., & Wexlex, A. (2022). *Econiomic Impact of COVID-19 on PEPFAR Countries*. KKF Foundation.

Owoyemi, O., Oyelere, M., Elegbede, T., & Gbajumo-Sheriff, M. (2011). Enhancing employees' commitment to the organization through training. *International Journal of Business and Management*, *6*(7), 280–286.

Pappas, H. P., & Frisch, P. H. (2022). *Leveraging Technology as a Response to the COVID Pandemic: Adapting Diverse Technologies, Workflow, and Processes to Optimize Integrated Clinical Management*. CRC Press.

Park, Y. (2016). *8 Digital Life Skills All Children Need – and a Plan for Teaching Them*. In World Economic Forum.

Pasupathi, P., Sindhu, S., Ponnusha, B. S., & Ambika, A. (2011). Biomedical waste management for health care industry. *International Journal of Biological and Medical Research*, *2*(1), 472–486.

Pateman, C. (1992). *Participação e teoria democrática*. Paz e Terra.

Patricios, N. (2002). The neighborhood concept: A retrospective of physical design and social interaction. *Journal of Architectural and Planning Research*, 70–90.

Pelling, M. (2020). *Tomorrow's Cities and Covid-19: A discussion document*. Tomorrow's Cities is the UK Research and Innvovation (UKRI) & Global Challenges Research Fund (GCRF). https://www.tomorrowscities.org/tomorrows-cities-and-covid-19-discussion

Phillips, R. (2005). Challenging The Primacy Of Lectures: The Dissonance Between Theory And Practice In University Teaching. *Journal of University Teaching & Learning Practice*, *2*(1), 4–15. doi:10.53761/1.2.1.2

Piccialli, F., Di Cola, V. S., Giampaolo, F., & Cuomo, S. (2021). The role of artificial intelligence in fighting the COVID-19 pandemic. *Information Systems Frontiers*, *23*(6), 1467–1497. doi:10.100710796-021-10131-x PMID:33935585

Pierre, J., & Peters, B. G. (2020). *Governance, Politics and the State*. Red Globe Press.

Pinto, C. A. (2000). Sociologia da Escola (4.ª ed.). Lisboa: MConselho Geralraw Hill.

Pinto, F., & Akhavan, M. (2022). Scenarios for a Post-Pandemic City: Urban planning strategies and challenges of making "Milan 15-minutes city. *Transportation Research Procedia*, *60*, 370–377. doi:10.1016/j.trpro.2021.12.048

Pire, J., & Boivin, G. (2020). Pandemics Throughout History. *Frontiers in Microbiology*, *11*, 631736. doi:10.3389/fmicb.2020.631736 PMID:33584597

Pirttilä, M., Virolainen, V. M., Lind, L., & Kärri, T. (2020). Working capital management in the Russian automotive industry supply chain. *International Journal of Production Economics*, *221*, 107474. doi:10.1016/j.ijpe.2019.08.009

Polit, D. F., & Beck, C. T. (2012). Nursing research: generating and assessing evidence for nursing practice. 9th ed. Baltiomore: Wolters Kluwer Health/Lippincott Williams & Wilkins.

Polit, D. F., & Beck, C. T. (2006). The content validity index: Are you sure you know what's being reported? Critique and recommendations. *Research in Nursing & Health*, *29*(5), 489–497. doi:10.1002/nur.20147 PMID:16977646

Polit, D. F., & Beck, C. T. (2008). *Nursing research: Generating and assessing evidence for nursing practice*. Lippincott Williams & Wilkins.

Pooter, H. D. (2013). *Le droit international face aux pandémies: vers un système de sécurité sanitaire collective?* [Doctoral dissertation, University of Paris].

Pozoukidou, G., & Chatziyiannaki, Z. (2021). 15-Minute City: Decomposing the New Urban Planning Eutopia. *Sustainability (Basel)*, *13*(2), 928. doi:10.3390u13020928

Pratap Singh, H., & Kumar, S. (2014). Working capital management: A literature review and research agenda. *Qualitative Research in Financial Markets*, *6*(2), 173–197. doi:10.1108/QRFM-04-2013-0010

Qiu, J., Shen, B., Zhao, M., Wang, Z., Xie, B., & Xu, Y. (2020). A nationwide survey of psychological distress among Chinese people in the COVID-19 epidemic: Implications and policy recommendations. *General Psychiatry*, *33*(2), e100213. doi:10.1136/gpsych-2020-100213 PMID:32215365

Rafee, B. M., Zaheed, S. M., Ali, R. M., Asan, S. J., Raheem, A. A., & Ahmed, R. S. (2022). A Moral Obligation of Health Care Service for Non-Covid Patients: A Reviews. *Journal of Positive School Psychology*, *6*(2), 6060–6069.

Ragheb, A., & El-Ashmawy, R. (2021). Strategic actions of urban development to define the intervention policies of slums. *City. Territory and Architecture*, *8*(1), 1–18. doi:10.118640410-021-00139-w

Raman, U. (2021a). a Study on Productivity Growth of Automobile Industry in a Vuca World. *Elementary Education Online, 20*(5), 3472. https://ilkogretim-online.org/index.php?mno=66785

Raman, U. (2021b). a Study on Productivity Growth of Automobile Industry in a Vuca World. *Elementary Education Online*. https://ilkogretim-online.org/index.php?mno=66785

Rani, R., Kumar, R., Mishra, R., & Sharma, S. (2021). Digital health: A panacea in COVID-19 crisis. *Journal of Family Medicine and Primary Care, 10*(1), 62. doi:10.4103/jfmpc.jfmpc_1494_20 PMID:34017704

Rao, F. J. P. D. P. (2015). *Study the Relation between Working Capital System and Profitability in Auto Manufacturing Industry in India.*

Rapanta, C., Botturi, L., Goodyear, P., Guàrdia, L., & Koole, M. (2020). Online university teaching during and after the Covid-19 crisis: Refocusing teacher presence and learning activity. *PostdigitalScience and Education*, *2*(3), 923–945. doi:10.100742438-020-00155-y

Ratten, V. (2020). Coronavirus (covid-19) and entrepreneurship: Changing life and work landscape. *Journal of Small Business and Entrepreneurship*, *32*(5), 503–516. doi:10.1080/08276331.2020.1790167

Raza, W. A. (Ed.). (2021). *Corona Tale*. Anyaprokash.

Reades, J., & Crookston, M. (2021). Face-To-Face and central place: COVID and the prospects for cities. *Built Environment*, *47*(3), 326–335. doi:10.2148/benv.47.3.326

Reddy, M. A., Reddy, B. M., Mukund, C. S., Venneti, K., Preethi, D. M. D., & Boopathi, S. (2023). Social Health Protection During the COVID-Pandemic Using IoT. In *The COVID-19 Pandemic and the Digitalization of Diplomacy* (pp. 204–235). IGI Global. doi:10.4018/978-1-7998-8394-4.ch009

Reeve, J., Britten, N., Byng, R., Fleming, J., Heaton, J., & Krska, J. (2018). Identifying enablers and barriers to individually tailored prescribing: A survey of healthcare professionals in the UK. *BMC Family Practice*, *19*(1), 17. doi:10.118612875-017-0705-2 PMID:29334913

Rhodes, R. A. W. (1997). *Understanding Governance: Policy Networks, Governance, Reflexivity and Accountability*. Open University Press.

Riggioni, C., Comberiati, P., Giovannini, M., Agache, I., Akdis, M., Alves-Correia, M., & Beken, B. (2020). A compendium answering 150 questions on COVID-19 and SARS-CoV-2. *Allergy*, *75*(10), 10–1111. https://www.researchgate.net/profile/Rodrigo_Jimenez-Saiz2/publication/342165769_A_compendium_answering_150_questions_on_COVID-19_and_SARS-CoV-2/links/5f168b824585151299ad5a51/A-compendium-answering-150-questions-on-COVID-19-and-SARS-CoV-2.pdf. doi:10.1111/all.14449 PMID:32535955

Rodrigues, A. A. D. d. O. N. e. (2013). Uma análise comparativa entre a Teoria da Agência e a Stewardship. *Revista Fafibe On-Line, Ano VI*(6), 67-77.

Rostami, P., Ashcroft, D. M., & Tully, M. P. (2018). A formative evaluation of the implementation of a medication safety data collection tool in English healthcare settings: A qualitative interview study using normalization process theory. *PLoS One*, *13*(2), e0192224. doi:10.1371/journal.pone.0192224 PMID:29489842

RPC-Syria. (2011). *National framework for regional planning, draft copy (in arabic)*. RPC.

S., P. K., Sampath, B., R., S. K., Babu, B. H., & N., A. (2022). Hydroponics, Aeroponics, and Aquaponics Technologies in Modern Agricultural Cultivation. In *Trends, Paradigms, and Advances in Mechatronics Engineering* (pp. 223–241). IGI Global. doi:10.4018/978-1-6684-5887-7.ch012

Sachan, M., & Bhattacharya, A. (2012). Mining statistically significant substrings using the chi-square statistic. *Proceedings of the VLDB Endowment International Conference on Very Large Data Bases*, *5*(10), 1052–1063. doi:10.14778/2336664.2336677

Sagulkoo, P., Plaimas, K., & Suratanee, A., & Maes, M. (2022). Immunopathogenesis and immunogenetic variants in COVID-19. Current Pharmaceutical Design.

Sahal, B. C., R, D., A, A., Thrinath, B. V. S., Boopathi, S., * J. R., & Sudhakar, M. (2022). *IOT Based Smart Energy Meter For Smart Grid.*

Sajid, E. (2020). Police enforce social distancing through humiliation, harassment. *The Business Standard.* .https://www.tbsnews.net/coronavirus-chronicle/coronavirus-bangladesh/police-enforce-social-distancing-through-humiliation

Salgado-Delgado, R., Osorio, A. T., Saderi, N., & Escobar, C. (2011). Disruption of Circadian Rhythms: A Crucial Factor in the Etiology of Depression. *Depression Research and Treatment*, *2011*, 1–9. doi:10.1155/2011/839743 PMID:21845223

Sambrook, S. (2005). Factors influencing the context and process of work-related learning: Synthesizing findings from two research projects. *Human Resource Development International*, *8*(1), 101–119. doi:10.1080/1367886052000342591

Samikannu, R., Koshariya, A. K., Poornima, E., Ramesh, S., Kumar, A., & Boopathi, S. (2023). Sustainable Development in Modern Aquaponics Cultivation Systems Using IoT Technologies. In *Human Agro-Energy Optimization for Business and Industry* (pp. 105–127). IGI Global. doi:10.4018/978-1-6684-4118-3.ch006

Sampath, B. C. S., & Myilsamy, S. (2022). Application of TOPSIS Optimization Technique in the Micro-Machining Process. In Trends, Paradigms, and Advances in Mechatronics Engineering (pp. 162–187). IGI Global. doi:10.4018/978-1-6684-5887-7.ch009

Sampath, B., Sasikumar, C., & Myilsamy, S. (2023). Application of TOPSIS Optimization Technique in the Micro-Machining Process. In IGI:Trends, Paradigms, and Advances in Mechatronics Engineering (pp. 162–187). IGI Global.

Sampath, B., & Myilsamy, S. (2021). Experimental investigation of a cryogenically cooled oxygen-mist near-dry wire-cut electrical discharge machining process. *Strojniski Vestnik. Jixie Gongcheng Xuebao*, *67*(6), 322–330. doi:10.5545v-jme.2021.7161

Sampath, B., Naveenkumar, N., Sampathkumar, P., Silambarasan, P., Venkadesh, A., & Sakthivel, M. (2021). Experimental comparative study of banana fiber composite with glass fiber composite material using Taguchi method. *Materials Today: Proceedings*, *49*(5), 1475–1480. doi:10.1016/j.matpr.2021.07.232

Santos, M. E. B. (2021). *Efeitos da pandemia COVID-19 na educação: Desigualdades e medidas de equidade*. Conselho Nacional de Educação.

Saravanan, M., Vasanth, M., Boopathi, S., Sureshkumar, M., & Haribalaji, V. (2022). Optimization of Quench Polish Quench (QPQ) Coating Process Using Taguchi Method. *Key Engineering Materials*, *935*, 83–91. doi:10.4028/p-z569vy

Satici, B., Gocet-Tekin, E., Deniz, M. E., & Satici, S. A. (2020). Adaptation of the Fear of COVID-19 Scale: Its association with psychological distress and life satisfaction in Turkey. *International Journal of Mental Health and Addiction*, 1–9. doi:10.100711469-020-00294-0 PMID:32395095

Saunders, M., Lewis, P., & Thornhill, A. (2012). *Research Methods for Business Students* (6th ed.). Pearson Education.

Scardamalia, M., & Bereiter, C. (1992). An architecture for collaborative knowledge building. In *Computer-based Learning Environments and Problem Solving* (pp. 41–66). Springer. doi:10.1007/978-3-642-77228-3_3

Scott, M. (2020). Covid-19, Place-making and Health. *Planning Theory & Practice*, *21*(3), 343–348. doi:10.1080/14649357.2020.1781445

Seale, C. (2002). Quality Issues in Qualitative Inquiry. *Qualitative Social Work, 1*(1), 97-110.

Seibert, S. E., Crant, J. M., & Kraimer, M. L. (1999). Proactive personality and career success. *The Journal of Applied Psychology*, *84*(3), 416–427. doi:10.1037/0021-9010.84.3.416 PMID:10380421

Seibert, S. E., Kraimer, M. L., & Liden, R. C. (2001). A social capital theory of career success. *Academy of Management Journal*, *44*(2), 219–237. doi:10.2307/3069452

Selvaraj, S., Prasadh, S., Fuloria, S., Subramaniyan, V., Sekar, M., Ahmed, A. M., Bouallegue, B., Hari Kumar, D., Sharma, V. K., Maziz, M. N. H., Sathasivam, K. V., Meenakshi, D. U., & Fuloria, N. K. (2022). COVID-19 Biomedical Plastics Wastes—Challenges and Strategies for Curbing the Environmental Disaster. *Sustainability (Basel)*, *14*(11), 6466. doi:10.3390u14116466

Senthil, T. S. R. Ohmsakthi vel, Puviyarasan, M., Babu, S. R., Surakasi, R., & Sampath, B. (2023). Industrial Robot-Integrated Fused Deposition Modelling for the 3D Printing Process. In Development, Properties, and Industrial Applications of 3D Printed Polymer Composites (pp. 188–210). IGI Global. doi:10.4018/978-1-6684-6009-2.ch011

Seville, E. (2016). *Resilient organizations: How to survive, thrive and create opportunities through crisis and change*. Kogan Page Publishers.

Shang, Y., Li, H., & Zhang, R. (2021). Effects of Pandemic Outbreak on Economies: Evidence From Business History Context. *Frontiers in Public Health*, *9*, 632043. doi:10.3389/fpubh.2021.632043 PMID:33777885

Sharfuddin, S. (2020). The world after Covid-19. *The Round Table*, *109*(3), 247–257. doi:10.1080/00358533.2020.1760498

Sharma, S., & Sharma, S. K. (2020). Probing the links between team resilience, competitive advantage, and organizational effectiveness: Evidence from the information technology industry. *Business Perspectives and Research*, *8*(2), 289–307. doi:10.1177/2278533719887458

Sherehiy, B. (2008). *Relationships between agility strategy, work organization, and workforce agility.* [Dissertation, University of Louisville].

Shigemura, J., Ursano, R. J., Morganstein, J. C., Kurosawa, M., & Benedek, D. M. (2020). Public responses to the novel 2019 coronavirus (2019-nCoV) in Japan: Mental health consequences and target populations. *Psychiatry and Clinical Neurosciences*, *74*(4), 281–282. doi:10.1111/pcn.12988 PMID:32034840

Shin, J., Taylor, M. S., & Seo, M. G. (2012). Resources for change: The relationships of organizational inducements and psychological resilience to employees' attitudes and behaviors toward organizational change. *Academy of Management Journal*, *55*(3), 727–748. doi:10.5465/amj.2010.0325

Shovon, F. R. (2020). DU to start online classes in July. *Dhaka Tribune*. https://archive.dhakatribune.com/bangladesh/2020/06/26/du-to-start-online-classes-from-the-first-week-of-july

Siche, R. (2020). What is the impact of COVID-19 disease on agriculture? *Scientia Agropecuaria*, *11*(1), 3–6. doi:10.17268ci.agropecu.2020.01.00

Singh, M., & Guo, W. (2010). The digital education revolution and languages: Insights from Sassen on transforming a Chinese academic into a trans-national researcher. *Global Student Mobility in the Asia Pacific: Mobility, Migration, Security and Wellbeing of International Students*, 117–140.

Singh, S., Ramesh Kumar, R., & Tiwari, M. K. (2021). Impact of COVID-19 on logistics systems and disruptions in food supply chain. *International Journal of Production Research*, *59*(7), 1993–2008. doi:10.1080/00207543.2020.1792000

Sinha, D. (2021). *Pandemic, governance and communication: The curious case of COVID-19.* Taylor & Francis. doi:10.4324/9781003247388

Song, X., Cao, M., Zhai, K., Gao, X., Wu, M., & Yang, T. (2021). The Effects of Spatial Planning, Well-Being, and Behavioural Changes During and After the COVID-19 Pandemic. *Frontiers in Sustainable Cities*, *3*, 686706. doi:10.3389/frsc.2021.686706

Southwick, S. M., Bonanno, G. A., Masten, A. S., Panter-Brick, C., & Yehuda, R. (2014). Resilience definitions, theory, and challenges: Interdisciplinary perspectives. *European Journal of Psychotraumatology*, *5*(1), 25338. doi:10.3402/ejpt.v5.25338 PMID:25317257

Spoorthy, M. S., Pratapa, S. K., & Mahant, S. (2020). Mental health problems faced by healthcare workers due to the COVID-19 pandemic–A review. *Asian Journal of Psychiatry*, *51*, 102119. doi:10.1016/j.ajp.2020.102119 PMID:32339895

Stolovitch, H. D., & Keeps, E. J. (Eds.). (1992). *Handbook of performance technology: A comprehensive guide for analyzing and solving performance problems in organizations*. Jossey-Bass.

Subba Rao, P. (2014). *Essentials of Human Resource Management and Industrial Relations*. Himalaya Publishing House.

Subha, S., Inbamalar, T. M., R, K. C., Suresh, L. R., Boopathi, S., & Alaskar, K. (2023, February). A Remote Health Care Monitoring system using internet of medical things ({IoMT}). *IEEE Explore*. IEEE. doi:10.1109/ICIPTM57143.2023.10118103

Sudhakar, R., & Basariya, S. R. (2017). Perspectives and the factors influencing the effectiveness of training and development on employees' performance. *International Journal of Civil Engineering and Technology*, *8*(9), 135–141.

Sun, P., Lu, X., Xu, C., Sun, W., & Pan, B. (2020). Understanding of COVID-19-19 based on current evidence. *Journal of Medical Virology*, *92*(6), 548–551. doi:10.1002/jmv.25722 PMID:32096567

Sun, S., Xie, Z., Yu, K., Jiang, B., Zheng, S., & Pan, X. (2021). COVID-19 and healthcare system in China: Challenges and progression for a sustainable future. *Globalization and Health*, *17*(1), 1–8. doi:10.118612992-021-00665-9 PMID:33478558

Sun, T. (2021). *Digital Banking Support to Small Businesses amid COVID-19: Evidence from China*. International Monetary Fund. doi:10.5089/9781513585192.065

Surveillances, V. (2020). The epidemiological characteristics of an outbreak of 2019 novel coronavirus diseases (COVID-19)—China, 2020. *China CDC Weekly*, *2*(8), 113–122. doi:10.46234/ccdcw2020.032 PMID:34594836

Swason Richard, A. (1994). *Analysis for improving performance: Tools for diagnosing organizations and documenting workplace expertise*. Ed. Berreti-Koehler.

Syrian Law Journal. (2018). The New Urban Renewal Law in Syria. *Syrian Law Journal*. https://www.syria.law/index.php/new-urban-renewal-law-syria/

Szymanski, F. M., Smuniewski, C., & Platek, A. E. (2020). Will the COVID-19 pandemic change national security and healthcare in the spectrum of cardiovascular disease? *Current Problems in Cardiology*, *45*(9), 100645. doi:10.1016/j.cpcardiol.2020.100645 PMID:32646545

Tadesse, S., & Muluye, W. (2020). The impact of COVID-19 pandemic on education system in developing countries: A review. *Open Journal of Social Sciences*, *8*(10), 159–170. doi:10.4236/jss.2020.810011

Talidong, K. J. B., & Toquero, C. M. D. (2020). Philippine teachers' practices to deal with anxiety amid COVID-19. *Journal of Loss and Trauma*, *25*(6-7), 573–579. doi:10.1080/15325024.2020.1759225

Taşan-Kok, T. (2020, july 16). *How to be Truly Open: Rethinking Public Spaces in the Post-Covid City*. Urbanet. https://www.urbanet.info/truly-open-rethinking-public-spaces-post-covid-city/

Teller, J. (2021). Urban density and Covid-19: Towards an adaptive approach. *Buildings & Cities*, *2*(1), 150–165. doi:10.5334/bc.89

Teng-Calleja, M., Hechanova, M. R. M., Sabile, P. R., & Villasanta, A. P. V. P. (2020). Building organization and employee resilience in disaster contexts. *International Journal of Workplace Health Management*, *13*(4), 393–411. doi:10.1108/IJWHM-09-2019-0122

Thalhammer, V. (2014). E-learning: An opportunity for older persons. In Learning Across Generations in Europe: Contemporary Issues in Older Adult Education (pp. 47-58). Brill.

The Daily Star. (2020). Online classes: Increasing the education divide. *The Daily Star.* https://www.thedailystar.net/opinion/news/online-classes-increasing-the-education-divide-1931409

Thelen, K. (2010). Varieties of capitalism and business history. *Business History Review*, *84*, 646–648. doi:10.2307/27917300 6

Torales, J., O'Higgins, M., Castaldelli-Maia, J. M., & Ventriglio, A. (2020). The outbreak of COVID-19 coronavirus and its impact on global mental health. *The International Journal of Social Psychiatry*, *66*(4), 317–320. doi:10.1177/0020764020915212 PMID:32233719

Trojovský, P., Dhasarathan, V., & Boopathi, S. (2023). Experimental investigations on cryogenic friction-stir welding of similar ZE42 magnesium alloys. *Alexandria Engineering Journal*, *66*(1), 1–14. doi:10.1016/j.aej.2022.12.007

Tyagi, P., & Pabalkar, D. V. (2021). Impact of COVID-19 over purchasing behaviour of the consumers. *European Journal of Molecular and Clinical Medicine*, *8*(2), 561–571.

Uddin, M., Mustafa, F., Rizvi, T. A., Loney, T., Suwaidi, H. A., Al-Marzouqi, A. H. H., & Nowotny, N. (2020). SARS-CoV-2/COVID-19: Viral genomics, epidemiology, vaccines, and therapeutic interventions. *Viruses*, *12*(5), 526. doi:10.3390/v12050526 PMID:32397688

Ullah, A., Pinglu, C., Ullah, S., Abbas, H. S. M., & Khan, S. (2021). The role of e-governance in combating COVID-19 and promoting sustainable development: A comparative study of China and Pakistan. *Chinese Political Science Review*, *6*(1), 86–118. doi:10.100741111-020-00167-w

UNESCO. (2020). *Urban Solutions: Learning from cities responses to COVID-19.* Online meeting report, Paris. m Rivista Siti. https://en.unesco.org/urban-solutions-Learning-from-cities-responses-to-COVID19

UN-Habitat. (2010). *Sustainable urban development and agenda 2030: UN habitat's programme framework: Participatory slum upgrading programme transforming the lives of one billion slum dwellers.* Nairobi: UN-Habitat. https://www.mypsup.org/library_files/downloads/SDGs%20and%20PSUP.pdf

UN-Habitat. (2019). *City-wide public space strategies a compendium of inspiring practices.* Nairobi: UNON Publishing Services Section. https://unhabitat.org/city-wide-public-space-strategies-a-compendium-of-inspiring-practices

UN-Habitat. (2020). *spatial planning guidelines during covid-19.* Kenya: UN Habitat. https://unhabitat.org/sites/default/files/2020/11/covid19_spatialplanning_eng1.pdf

UN-Habitat. (February 2022). *Analysis of Syrian Urban Law, Legal Thematic Paper.* Egypt: UN-HABITAT Regional Office for Arab States.

United Nations. (2020). *A UN framework for the immediate socio-economic response to COVID-19.* UN. https://www.un.org/sites/un2.un.org/files/un_framework_report_on_covid-19.pdf

Upadhya, C., & Rao, D. (2022). Dispossession without displacement: Producing property through slum redevelopment in Bengaluru, India. *Environment and Planning A. Economy and Space, 1*(17). doi:10.1177/0308518X221073988

Usman, B. A., Malik, N. A., & Alausa, K. M. (2015). Factors determining the choice of residential location in Ilorin, Nigeria. *Zaria Geographer, 22*(1), 109–122.

van den Berg, R. (2020, april 10). *Will covid 19 affect urban planning?* TheCityFix. https://thecityfix.com/blog/will-covid-19-affect-urban-planning-rogier-van-den-berg/

Vanitha, S. K. R., & Boopathi, S. (2023). Artificial Intelligence Techniques in Water Purification and Utilization. In *Human Agro-Energy Optimization for Business and Industry* (pp. 202–218). IGI Global., doi:10.4018/978-1-6684-4118-3.ch010

Vazquez, X. H., Sartal, A., & Lozano-Lozano, L. M. (2016). Watch the working capital of tier-two suppliers: A financial perspective of supply chain collaboration in the automotive industry. *Supply Chain Management, 21*(3), 321–333. doi:10.1108/SCM-03-2015-0104

Vennila, T., Karuna, M. S., Srivastava, B. K., Venugopal, J., Surakasi, R., & B., S. (2023). New Strategies in Treatment and Enzymatic Processes. In *Human Agro-Energy Optimization for Business and Industry* (pp. 219–240). IGI Global. doi:10.4018/978-1-6684-4118-3.ch011

Vis, C., Ruwaard, J., Finck, T., Rapley, T., Beurs, D. D., Stel, H. V., & Smit, J. (2019). *Towards an objective assessment of implementation processes for innovations in healthcare: a psychometric evaluation of the NoMAD questionnaire among mental healthcare professionals.* NIH.

Viskari, S., Lind, L., Kärri, T., & Schupp, F. (2012). Using working capital management to improve profitability in the value chain of automotive industry. *International Journal of Services and Operations Management, 13*(1), 42–64. doi:10.1504/IJSOM.2012.048275

Vo, T. D., & Tran, M. D. (2021). The impact of covid-19 pandemic on the global trade. *International Journal of Social Science and Economics Invention*, *7*(1), 1–7. doi:10.23958/ijssei/vol07-i01/261

Wang, C., Pan, R., Wan, X., Tan, Y., Xu, L., McIntyre, R. S., Choo, F. N., Tran, B., Ho, R., Sharma, V. K., & Ho, C. (2020). A longitudinal study on the mental health of general population during the COVID-19 epidemic in China. *Brain, Behavior, and Immunity*, *87*, 40–48. doi:10.1016/j.bbi.2020.04.028 PMID:32298802

Wang, C., Xu, H., & Lin, A. (2022). Informal settlements in the context of COVID-19: Pandemic restrictions and the building of community resilience. *Indoor and Built Environment*, *0*(0), 1–9. doi:10.1177/1420326X221097821

Wang, J., Cooke, F. L., & Huang, W. (2014). How resilient is the (future) workforce in China? A study of the banking sector and implications for human resource development. *Asia Pacific Journal of Human Resources*, *52*(2), 132–154. doi:10.1111/1744-7941.12026

Watermeyer, R., Crick, T., Knight, C., & Goodall, J. (2021). COVID-19 and digital disruption in UK universities: Afflictions and affordances of emergency online migration. *Higher Education*, *81*(3), 623–641. doi:10.100710734-020-00561-y PMID:32836334

Weiner, B. (1980). The role of affect in rational (attributional) approaches to human motivation. *Educational Researcher*, *9*(7), 4–11. doi:10.3102/0013189X009007004

Wei, Y., Ye, Z., Cui, M., & Wei, X. (2021). COVID-19 prevention and control in China: Grid governance. *Journal of Public Health (Oxford, England)*, *43*(1), 76–81. doi:10.1093/pubmed/fdaa175 PMID:32978620

Willberg, E., Fink, C., & Toivonen, T. (2023). The 15-minute city for all? – Measuring individual and temporal variations in walking accessibility. *Journal of Transport Geography*, *103521*, 103521. doi:10.1016/j.jtrangeo.2022.103521

Williams, T. A., & Shepherd, D. A. (2016). Building resilience or providing sustenance: Different paths of emergent ventures in the aftermath of the Haiti earthquake. *Academy of Management Journal*, *59*(6), 2069–2102. doi:10.5465/amj.2015.0682

Wisner, B., Adams, J., & World Health Organization. (2002). *Environmental health in emergencies and disasters: a practical guide.* World Health Organization. https://apps.who.int/iris/handle/10665/42561

Wójcik, D., & Ioannou, S. (2020). COVID-19 and finance: Market developments so far and potential impacts on the financial sector and centres. *Tijdschrift voor Economische en Sociale Geografie*, *111*(3), 387–400. doi:10.1111/tesg.12434 PMID:32836484

Wolever, R. Q., Finn, M. T., & Shields, D. (2022). The relative contributions of live and recorded online mindfulness training programs to lower stress in the workplace: Longitudinal observational study. *Journal of Medical Internet Research*, *24*(1), e31935. doi:10.2196/31935 PMID:35060911

World Food Programme. (2020). *Global Report on Food Crises.* United Nations World Food Programme (WFP).https://www.wfp.org/publications/2020-global-report-food-crises

World Health Organization (WHO). (2020a). *WHO Coronavirus Disease (COVID-19) Dashboard – China.* WHO. https://COVID-1919.who.int/region/wpro/country/cn

World Health Organization (WHO). (2020b). *WHO Coronavirus Disease (COVID-19) Dashboard – International.* WHO. https://COVID-1919.who.int

World Health Organization. (2020). *Advice for the Public: Coronavirus disease (COVID-19).* World Health Organization. https://www.who.int/emergencies/diseases/novel-coronavirus-2019/advice-for-public

Worldometer. (2022). *COVID-19 Coronavirus Pandemic Reported Cases and Deaths by Country or Territory.* WorldoMeter. www.worldometer.info [accessed on 24 Aug 2022, 7.53 am]

Wu, G., Yang, P., Xie, Y., Woodruff, H. C., Rao, X., Guiot, J., & Li, J. (2020). Development of a clinical decision support system for severity risk prediction and triage of COVID-19 patients at hospital admission: An international multicenter study. *The European Respiratory Journal*, 2001104. doi:10.1183/13993003.01104-2020

Wu, J., Xie, X., Yang, L., Xu, X., Cai, Y., Wang, T., & Xie, X. (2021). Mobile health technology combats COVID-19 in China. *The Journal of Infection*, *82*(1), 159–198. doi:10.1016/j.jinf.2020.07.024 PMID:32730998

Wu, J., Zhan, X., Xu, H., & Ma, C. (2023). The economic impacts of COVID-19 and city lockdown: Early evidence from China. *Structural Change and Economic Dynamics*, *65*, 151–165. doi:10.1016/j.strueco.2023.02.018 PMID:36876039

Xiao, D., & Su, J. (2022). Macroeconomic lockdown effects of COVID-19 on small business in China: Empirical insights from SEM technique. *Environmental Science and Pollution Research International*, *29*(42), 63344–63356. doi:10.100711356-022-20071-x PMID:35451716

Xu, C., Dong, Y., Yu, X., Wang, H., Tsamlag, L., Zhang, S., & Wang, Y. (2020). Estimation of reproduction numbers of COVID-19 in typical countries and epidemic trends under different prevention and control scenarios. *Frontiers of Medicine*, *14*(5), 1–10. doi:10.100711684-020-0787-4 PMID:32468343

Xu, W., Wu, J., & Cao, L. (2020). COVID-19 pandemic in China: Context, experience and lessons. *Health Policy and Technology*, *9*(4), 639–648. doi:10.1016/j.hlpt.2020.08.006 PMID:32874851

Yin, R. K. (2015). Estudo de Caso: Planejamento e Métodos (5.ª ed.). Porto Alegre: Bookman.

Youssef, C. M., & Luthans, F. (2007). Positive organizational behavior in the workplace: The impact of hope, optimism, and resilience. *Journal of Management*, *33*(5), 774–800. doi:10.1177/0149206307305562

Yupapin, P., Trabelsi, Y., Nattappan, A., & Boopathi, S. (2023). Performance Improvement of Wire-Cut Electrical Discharge Machining Process Using Cryogenically Treated Super-Conductive State of Monel-K500 Alloy. *Iranian Journal of Science and Technology. Transaction of Mechanical Engineering*, *47*(1), 267–283. doi:10.100740997-022-00513-0

Zarif, M. M. (2021). Dhaka's online food business. *The Daily Star.* https://www.thedailystar.net/supplements/30th-anniversary-supplements/golden-jubilee-beginnings/news/dhakas-online-food-business-2046349?amp

Zhai, P., Ding, Y., Wu, X., Long, J., Zhong, Y., & Li, Y. (2020). The epidemiology, diagnosis, and treatment of COVID-19. *International Journal of Antimicrobial Agents*, *55*(5), 105955. doi:10.1016/j.ijantimicag.2020.105955 PMID:32234468

Zhang, H., & Shaw, R. (2020). Identifying research trends and gaps in the context of COVID-19. *International Journal of Environmental Research and Public Health*, *17*(10), 3370. doi:10.3390/ijerph17103370 PMID:32408679

Zhang, S., Wang, Z., Chang, R., Wang, H., Xu, C., Yu, X., & Cai, Y. (2020). COVID-19 containment: China provides important lessons for a global response. *Frontiers of Medicine*, *14*(2), 1–5. doi:10.100711684-020-0766-9 PMID:32212059

Zhang, T., Shi, Z. Z., Shi, Y. R., & Chen, N. J. (2022). Enterprise digital transformation and production efficiency: Mechanism analysis and empirical research. *Ekonomska Istrazivanja*, *35*(1), 2781–2792. doi:10.1080/1331677X.2021.1980731

Zina, A., & Ahlem, S. (2021). Perception of E-learning during the health crisis of COVID-19: Case of algerian university teachers. *Journal of Information Technology Management*, *13*(2), 154–172. doi:10.22059/jitm.2021.80360

Zreik, M. (2023a). From Boom to Bust: A Study of China's Economy in the Wake of COVID-19 Outbreak in H1 2020. *BRICS Journal of Economics*, *4*(1), 147–171. doi:10.3897/brics-econ.4.e101050

Zreik, M. (2023b). Analytical study on Foreign Direct Investment Divestment Inflows and Outflows in Developing Economies: Evidence of China. *Chinese Economy*, 1–16. doi:10.1080/10971475.2023.2193118

Zreik, M., Iqbal, B. A., & Rahman, M. N. (2022). Outward FDI: Determinants and Flows in Emerging Economies: Evidence from China. *China and WTO Review*, *8*(2), 385–402. doi:10.14330/cwr.2022.8.2.07

About the Contributors

***

Sumanta Bhattacharya is a Research Scholar and Policy Analyst, Department of Textile Technology, MAKAUT and NALSAR, Howrah.

Sampath Boopathi completed his undergraduate in Mechanical Engineering and postgraduate in the field of Computer-Aided Design. He completed his Ph.D. from Anna University and his field of research includes Manufacturing and optimization. He published 60 more research articles in Internationally Peer-reviewed journals, one Patent grant, and three published patents.He has 16 more years of academic and research experiences in the various Engineering Colleges in Tamilnadu, India.()

V. Chandra Shekhar Rao works at the Department of Computer Science and Engineering, Kakatiya Institute of Technology and Science, Warangal, Telangana.

M. Durairaj is a faculty member in the Department of English at Panimalar Engineering College, located in Chennai, Tamil Nadu, India, with the address 600123.

Abeni El-Amin, Ph.D., Ed.D., D.PC., MPsy - I/O, LSSMBB, CCHW, has over two decades of experience and education in Business and Nonprofit Administration as an educator and practitioner. Further, as a higher education professor, she has designed and developed curriculum and training programs in business administration, educational leadership, health sciences/public health, legal studies/criminal justice, nonprofit administration, political science, and psychology. She has taught at several institutions of higher education including, Clark Atlanta University, Savannah State University, Mercer University, Saint Augustine's University, Shaw University, Wake Technical Community College, North Carolina State University, University of Dubuque, Ivy Tech Community College, Indiana University, Bellevue University, Grand Canyon University, University of the Cumberlands, Christian Brothers University, and Fort Hays State University, Robbins College of Business and Entrepreneurship/Shenyang Normal University (SNU) College of International Business, Shenyang, Liaoning Province, China and SIAS International University, Zhengzhou, Henan, China. Dr. El-Amin received her Ph.D. from Northcentral University in Business Administration, Organizational Leadership. Her doctoral dissertation was, Applying Lean Six Sigma Methodology as a Nonprofit Organizational Development Tool. She also received her Ed.D. from the University of the Cumberlands in Educational Leadership: Administration and Supervision and Ph.D. from Union Institute and University in Public Policy and Social Change (2023), Dissertation: Words and Deeds: Achieving a Workplace Culture Without Bias. She also received her Ph.D. from the Colorado Theological Seminary in Clinical Pastoral Counseling (Ph.D./D.PC.). Dr. El-Amin graduated from the Executive Masters of Nonprofit Administration (EMNA) at The University of Notre Dame's Mendoza School of Business, Grand Canyon University with a Masters in Industrial and Organizational Psychology and received an Executive Graduate Certificate in Nonprofit Administration from Duke University. Dr. El-Amin also received her Executive Graduate Certification as a Lean Six Sigma Master Black Belt (LSSMBB) from Florida Atlantic University. Dr. El-Amin has managed large corporate and government budgets; managed staff and developed sustainable programs. She is a globally recognized thought leader on diversity, equity, inclusion, and belonging (DEIB). She helps organizations develop cultures of belongingness through collaborative, innovative, and thought-provoking trainings. Dr. El-Amin is an author, international university lecturer, trainer, and speaker. Dr. El-Amin is the editor of Implementing Diversity, Equity, Inclusion, and Belonging Management in Organizational Change Initiatives and Implementing Diversity, Equity, Inclusion, and Belonging in Educational Management Practices - IGI Global. Dr. El-Amin is co-founder of Project Ricochet, Inc., a youth empowerment organization, which recently received a COVID health promotion grant (KY-OHE) for over $1 million, owner of Carbon Core Fitness, and co-founder of Titan and Mogul, Inc., a global consultancy that provides Lean Six Sigma and HR consultancy focusing on DEIB to improve organizational culture. She is also the author of, In Search of Servant Leadership and Determined to Serve: The Ricochet Effect and Titan Financial Legacy: The Ricochet Effect. Dr. El-Amin has led nonprofit organizations as the Director of Adult Education for UMCM Suncoast (Learning Empowered) in Largo, Florida. In service, the department received the 2019 U.S. Citizenship and Immigration Services (USCIS) Grant of $234,000. To promote team effectiveness, her management focus was on developing assessment tools utilizing appreciative inquiry methodology via training & development (T&D). She also served as a Graduate Fellow for the Neighborhood Initiatives Program, Housing and Urban Development (HUD) at Clark Atlanta University and in part managed a $3,000,000 grant. She researched welfare-to-work (TANF) issues in the 30314-zip code of Atlanta, Georgia to sponsor policy. She developed the Antioch Urban Ministries/Northyards Collaborative Employment Initiative (NCEI) to facilitate Life Skills Training, computer training modules, developed a resource guide, led community forums, managed the Global Positioning System (GPS) integration, and established a career placement database. She was the Tobacco Prevention Strategic Initiatives Coordinator for Community Wellness Partners in South Bend, Indiana, where she provided management of the policy strategy designed by Smoke Free St Joe. As the Tobacco Prevention Strategic Initiatives Coordinator, she directed the execution of the City of South Bend's tobacco prevention and control initiative and policy priorities based on research, evaluation metrics, and budget to pass the Article 13 Ordinance. She is also an American Lung Association (ALA) Tobacco Cessation Facilitator. She drove a $4,000,000 grant initiative for infant mortality with the Indiana State Department of Health. Additionally, she served The City of Dubuque, Iowa as the Executive Director/Chief Diversity Officer for the Multi-Cultural Family Center. Here she supported and partnered with Diversity, Equity, & Inclusion (DE&I) Councils, and other stakeholders across Dubuque, Iowa. Dr. El-Amin is a member of the Junior League of South Bend (Training and Resource, Past Chair). She is a member of Delta Sigma Theta Sorority, Incorporated and the Yoga Alliance. She is also a member of the American Society of Quality (ASQ), American College of Sports Management (ACSM), and the Society of Human Resource Managers (SHRM). She is an American Red Cross Instructor trainer and was an AmeriCorps Member for Disaster and Humanitarian Relief. She is a Kentucky Colonel, which is the highest service honor bestowed by the Commonwealth of Kentucky.

A. Gaurav works with the Department of Electronics and Communication Engineering, Sreenidhi Institute of Science and Technology, Hyderabad.

Maya Hassan has a PhD in Architectural Engineering (CQU China)Lecturer at Tishreen University.

V.S. Karpagavalli is an Assistant Professor and Head in the Department of Garment Designing at PSGR Krishnammal College for Women, Coimbatore. With expertise in the field of textiles and Fashion, she is dedicated to passion for teaching and research. She holds a M.Phil degree in the field of Costume Design and Fashion and currently pursuing (Ph.D) in the field of Textiles and Apparel Design. She received recognition and honours during her academic journey. With more than 10 years of teaching experience, V.S. Karpagavalli has taught a variety of courses in the field of Costume Design and Fashion. She is committed to fostering an engaging and inclusive learning environment, incorporating innovative teaching methods. She has contributed to the field with 20 publications, including journal articles, conference papers, and book chapters. She has presented her work at various national and international conferences.

A Dushyanth Kumar is a Research Scholar in Dept. of HRM, Mittal School of Business, Lovely Professional University, Jalandhar, India.

Mohammad Khasro Miah is a Professor of Human Resource Management, teaching at the School of Business and Economics, North South University, Dhaka, Bangladesh. He has taught different Human Resource Management courses in MBA and EMBA programs. Dr. Khasro earned Ph.D. and a Post-doctoral degree from Nagoya University, Japan, in 2004 and 2006, respectively, and a Post-doctoral degree from Northeastern University, USA, in 2010 under the Fulbright Awards. Before that, he received MBA in International Human Resource Management from Shiga University, Japan, in 2001. He has published more than 50 papers and presented more than 30 papers at international conferences in the US, Canada, Europe, the UK, China, Japan, and Australia.

M. Mohammed Asif works at the Department of Mechanical Engineering, Vignan's Lara Institute of Technology & Science Guntur.

Hamida Mosharraf Moniea is a lecturer at the Department of Management, School of Business & Economics in North South University. She holds a Master of Business Administration from New Jersey City University, USA and obtained a Bachelor of Arts in Business Management with Honours from the University of Worcester in the UK. Her research interest is in Entrepreneurship, Management, Human Resource Management, Marketing and International Marketing.

Muhammad Fayyaz Nazir is a Ph.D. student in the Department of Public Governance and Management, Faculty of Economics and Business Administration, Gent University, Belgium. Research interests include understanding public policy and implementation. The author has administrative and research experience. The author got a scholarship for a Ph.D. from the Higher Education Commission of Pakistan.

Nima Norouzi is an expert on the environmental and energy law and is currently working on the Covid-19 impacts on the legal systems.

Carlos M. Osegueda is a New Jersey-based independent researcher and consultant with experience in both the public and private sector. He has consulted and lead projects for different international organizations, such as Refelx, S.I and the Municipality of Mixco in Guatemala, and for DE Communications in the United

States. He received a B.A. in Philosophy from St. Peter's University and an MBA with a specialization in Marketing from New Jersey City University. During his spare time, Carlos' academic research interests include consumer behavior, leadership theory, and pop culture trends.

Lakshmana Phanendra Magulur works in the Department of Electronics and Communication Engineering, Sreenidhi Institute of Science and Technology, Hyderabad, Telangana.

P.V Pramila is a faculty member in the Department of Electronics and Communication Engineering at Sri Sairam College of Engineering, situated in Anekal, Bengaluru, India.

Shahzadah Fahed Qureshi did his Ph.D. from Wuhan University, China, and currently serving at Bahauddin Zakariya University, Multan, Pakistan. He served as a senior teacher and coordinator in the Public Administration program at the university. In this capacity, he supervised dozens of health sector managers in Pakistan. His research interests include public sector reforms and policy implementation in developing countries.

Parimal Roy studied in Anthropology, and later he obtained papers on MBA, Project management, and Criminology (paper is better than a certificate) to enhance his knowledge. He is currently working in a state own institution in the filed of Training & Development. Decolonizing, Marginal community, subaltern voice, Project management - all are interest arena in academic world. His written book is Extra-marital love in folk songs. Co-author of Captive minded intellectual; Quantitative Ethnography in Indigenous Research Methodology; and so many book chapters and journals.

Murugan S. is a faculty member in the Department of Education at B.P.S. Women University, located in Khanpur Kalan, Sonipat, with the address 131305

Ushasukhanya S. works in the Department of Networking and Communications, SRM Institute of Science and Technology, Kattankulathur, Tamil Nadu.

Tasnim Tarannum is a lecturer of Management in School of Business and Economics at North South University. She has been teaching Human Resource Management and Organizational Management in BBA. She has completed MSc. In Human Resource Management and Organisation from University of Nottingham, UK. Before that, she completed her BBA from BRAC University.

B. Uma Maheswari is a faculty member in the Department of Computer Science and Engineering at St. Joseph's College of Engineering, located in Chennai, Tamil Nadu, India.

Ellen Wayenberg is Professor at the Department of Public Governance and Management at Ghent University, Belgium. She specializes in public policy and administration with specific interest for policy analysis and evaluation, local government and multi-level governance. Ellen has published in highly-ranked journals such as Local Government Studies, Policy and Society, Policy Design and Practice, Public Administration Review, Public Policy and Administration and she has co-edited various international books (including 'The future of local self-government: European trends in autonomy, innovations and central-local relations' (2021)). She is a co-founder and a co-chair of the EGPA Study Group IV on Regional and Local Governance and a member of the European Association for Public Administration Accreditation (EAPAA) –committee.

Mohamad Zreik, a Postdoctoral Fellow at Sun Yat-sen University, is a recognized scholar in International Relations, specializing in China's Arab-region foreign policy. His recent work in soft power diplomacy compares China's methods in the Middle East and East Asia. His extensive knowledge spans Middle Eastern Studies, China-Arab relations, East Asian and Asian Affairs, Eurasian geopolitics, and Political Economy, providing him a unique viewpoint in his field. Dr. Zreik is a proud recipient of a PhD from Central China Normal University (Wuhan). He's written numerous acclaimed papers, many focusing on China's Belt and Road Initiative and its Arab-region impact. His groundbreaking research has established him as a leading expert in his field. Presently, he furthers his research on China's soft power diplomacy tactics at Sun Yat-sen University. His significant contributions make him a crucial figure in understanding contemporary international relations.

Index

V

W

www.ingramcontent.com/pod-product-compliance
Lightning Source LLC
LaVergne TN
LVHW080642011026
849160LV00014B/1295
* 9 7 8 1 7 9 9 8 9 2 1 4 4 *